D1475365

LEONARD BACON

Leonard Bacon in 1874

LEONARD BACON

NEW ENGLAND REFORMER AND
ANTISLAVERY MODERATE

Hugh Davis

LOUISIANA STATE UNIVERSITY PRESS
Baton Rouge

Copyright © 1998 by Louisiana State University Press

All rights reserved

Manufactured in the United States of America

First printing

07 06 05 04 03 02 01 00 99 98   5 4 3 2 1

Designer: Amanda McDonald Scallon

Typefaces: Bembo, Copperplate 32bc

Typesetter: Wilsted & Taylor Publishing Services

Library of Congress Cataloging-in-Publication Data

Davis, Hugh, 1941–
    Leonard Bacon : New England reformer and antislavery moderate /
Hugh Davis.
        p. cm.
    Includes bibliographical references and index.
    ISBN 0-8071-2287-4 (cloth : alk. paper)
        1. Bacon, Leonard, 1802–1881.   2. Congregational churches—United
States—Clergy—Biography.   I. Title.
BX7260.B15D38   1998
285.8′092—dc21
    [B]   98-24710
                                                                           CIP

The paper in this book meets the guidelines for permanence and durability of the Committee on Production Guidelines for Book Longevity of the Council on Library Resources. ∞

For my mentors,
Richard W. Smith
and
Merton L. Dillon

CONTENTS

In the eulogy he delivered at the memorial service for Leonard Bacon in early 1882, George L. Walker lauded Bacon for having been "the example of a minister who was a national power."[1] Flattering though this characterization was, Bacon himself might not have been entirely comfortable with it. He had, after all, derived enormous satisfaction from his pastorate at the prestigious Center Church in New Haven, Connecticut, where he had served for forty-one years, and he always had considered his congregation his primary responsibility. But he also had actively sought to connect his church and community to the larger world of organized benevolence, religious and reform journalism, social activism, and scholarship. Convinced that he was obligated to educate the American people on a broad range of social, political, and theological issues, he had edited and contributed to numerous newspapers and journals and written several books. Moreover, he had played an important role in various benevolent, reform, and scholarly organizations as well as in the Congregational Church. In these capacities he had influenced the thinking of large numbers of northern Protestants from the 1820s until the 1880s. Walker clearly had the advantage of perspective.

The son of New England Congregational missionaries to the Native Americans on the Michigan frontier who subsequently attempted to establish a Christian commonwealth in the Western Reserve area of Ohio, Bacon endeavored to extend evangelical religion and New England ideas and institutions to the rest of the nation and even overseas. At a time when the United States was experiencing rapid social and economic change, he warned against the evils of urbanization, immigration, irreligion, and materialism. To him and millions of other Americans who were influenced by the evangelical revivals of the Second Great Awakening, dire forces seemed to threaten from all sides. Evangelism, with its emphasis on the dangers to the soul and society posed by the rising tide of immorality and disorder, pointed in some measure toward a conservative social philosophy. Bacon lent a powerful voice and pen to the temperance, anti-Catholic, and colonization movements, and to the American Home Missionary Society, the American Tract Society, and other benevolent organizations, whose objectives included the restoration of order, morality, and racial and religious homogeneity in American society.

1. *Advance*, February 5, 1882.

Yet the message of immediate repentance, human ability, and the moral duty to transform the world, which Bacon and many other evangelicals preached and acted upon, also reflected the age's growing optimism that people could improve themselves and their society. Bacon embraced a social Christianity, the idea of progress, and the concepts of free will and self-improvement. As a spokesman for the progressive wing of the Congregational Church, he vigorously defended the innovations in evangelical theology developed by Nathaniel Taylor, Horace Bushnell, and Theodore Munger. In addition, for forty years he wrote and spoke forcefully against slavery, first as a leading antislavery colonizationist and later as an outspoken free-soil advocate who helped to mobilize northern public opinion against the Slave Power and its allies. His antislavery views, like his championing of fundamental rights for African Americans after the Civil War and his support for the temperance, public education, and social gospel causes, among others, were grounded in part in his vision of an open, progressive, and equitable society. Indeed, throughout his life he took up the theme of liberty, whether in his call for an end to slavery, his espousal of voluntary churches and a decentralized church polity, his attacks on the papacy and the extreme nativists, his advocacy of free agency in theology, his condemnation of both socialism and social Darwinism, his devotion to a voluntary abstinence from alcoholic beverages, or in his preference for states' rights over what he termed "centralized despotism."

Bacon and others of his time who sought to adapt, in a gradual, selective, and cautious manner, to the changing realities in American life exerted a powerful influence on their society. They spoke to, and shaped the thinking of, what Bacon characterized as "the great central mass," who consciously stood apart from both the radicals and the conservatives. Bacon was by no means a radical. He not only lacked their sense of urgency and moral outrage but also recoiled from their dogmatism and believed that their extreme views exacerbated tensions in American society and alienated those whose support was necessary for the achievement of desirable objectives. Nor did he generally stand with the conservatives, for he often could not brook their unyielding opposition to what he considered beneficial, and even necessary, change. Rather, Bacon's childhood experiences, his education, the varying demands and interests that he contended with as pastor of a church, and his social milieu in New Haven, the Congregational Church, and the "benevolent empire" led him, with few exceptions, to occupy a middle ground between the radicals and the conservatives. A combative and tenacious controversialist, he engaged in prolonged and bitter debates with, among others, the abolitionists as well as slaveholders and their northern allies on the slavery question, the prohibitionists on the liquor issue, the conservative Calvinists on theological matters, and both the Radical Republicans and the Democrats on Reconstruction policy. Yet he more often stood forth as a pragmatist and a conciliator who emphasized the need to accommodate and balance conflicting forces and ideas, to tolerate a diversity of viewpoints, and to focus upon the essential principles that he believed the warring parties in fact shared. Thus, at various times he labored diligently to reconcile northerners and southerners, blacks and whites, capital and labor, antislavery colonizationists and immediatists, the principles of autonomy and of centralization within the Congregational Church, evangelicalism and scholarship, eastern and western as well as conservative and progressive Congregationalists, Radical and conservative Republicans, and Congregationalists and other Protestants.

This biography examines Bacon's private life, especially his relationship with his family of origin and his wives and children, and studies his character and personality. It also explores his life within the larger social context to explain why he took the positions he did on a broad range of issues, what his role was in numerous reform and benevolent causes and the Congregational Church, and how he interacted with his clerical and reform associates. An investigation of Bacon's life enriches our knowledge of the nineteenth-century Protestant ministry and the evangelical mentality as well as our understanding of the efforts of Americans in Bacon's generation to address the moral and social issues of their time.

A C K N O W L E D G M E N T S

I would not have been able to write this book without the generous assistance of many helpful individuals and institutions. I am especially indebted to the staff of the Yale University Archives, who gave me every consideration a researcher could hope for. Numerous other institutions also ably assisted my research: the American Antiquarian Society, Andover Newton Theological Seminary, the Boston Public Library, the Congregational Library, the Connecticut Historical Society, Harvard University, the Library of Congress, the Massachusetts Historical Society, the New England Genealogical Society, the New Haven Colony Historical Society, and Syracuse University.

I have benefited greatly from the opportunity to draw on the knowledge and insights of fellow scholars who read all or part of the manuscript. I am particularly grateful to Merton L. Dillon, John R. McKivigan, Frederick J. Blue, and Randall M. Miller, whose invaluable criticism, encouragement, and advice served to improve this study.

Sabbatical leaves granted by Southern Connecticut State University enabled me to begin and complete this book. Connecticut State University research grants also facilitated my research, and the university's Faculty Development Fund paid for the typing of the manuscript. I deeply appreciate this generous institutional support. Rosemary Yanosik skillfully typed the various drafts. The editorial staff of Louisiana State University Press was very helpful and supportive throughout the process of revising and editing the manuscript.

Finally, my children—Andrew, Mark, Jenny, and Kate—deserve special thanks. Their love and emotional support are very important to me. My principal debt is to my wife, Jean, whose encouragement, understanding, love, sage advice, and endless patience have served to sustain me throughout this endeavor.

LEONARD BACON

I

THE EARLY YEARS

T HE first ten years of Leonard Bacon's life were spent on the Michigan and Ohio frontiers, far removed from the New England society that he would later celebrate. Yet he was very much a product of New England. His father's family had emigrated from England to Dedham, Massachusetts, in 1663, and his family were longtime residents of Connecticut. Moreover, his parents, David and Alice Parks Bacon, devoted the first twelve years of their married life to extending New England religion and society to both Native Americans and white settlers in the West.[1]

Both of Leonard's parents came from humble origins. His mother was orphaned at an early age and raised by grandparents, while his father's parents often experienced hard times and moved from town to town. Consequently, both David and Alice received little more than a common school education. After experiencing disappointment in a variety of business ventures, David was converted during a religious revival in the mid-1790s. Inspired by Jonathan Edwards' *Life of David Brainerd,* he then studied theology with the Reverend Levi Hart of Preston, Connecticut, where he met and married Alice Parks in 1800.[2] David's and Alice's dedication to the advancement of evangelical Christianity formed the very core of their

---

1. Theodore Bacon, *Delia Bacon: A Biographical Sketch* (Boston, 1888), 3–4; Theodore Dwight Bacon, *Leonard Bacon: A Statesman in the Church,* ed. Benjamin W. Bacon (New Haven, 1931), 3–4; Leonard Bacon, "David Bacon," *Congregational Quarterly,* XVIII (January, April, July, and October, 1876), 2–3, 9.

2. Thomas W. Baldwin, *Bacon Genealogy: Michael Bacon of Dedham, 1640, and His Descendants* (Cambridge, Mass., 1915), 235–36; Bacon, "David Bacon," 3–5, 8–9; *Proceedings in Commemoration of the Fiftieth Anniversary of the Settlement of Tallmadge; With the Historical Discourse of Hon. E. N. Sill, and Rev. L. Bacon. . . .* (Akron, 1857), 47.

lives together. Indeed, soon after they met he asked her to join him in "attempting to Christianize Pagans" on the western frontier.[3]

When David Bacon was hired by the Missionary Society of Connecticut in 1800 to work among the Indians in the Western Reserve area of the Ohio Territory, he became a pioneer in the incipient missionary movement. A product of the developing Second Great Awakening, it represented both an idealistic and a hegemonic effort to create a global community modeled upon New England society. The assumption that the fundamental principles and virtues of Puritan New England remained guideposts to civilization and progress underlay the missionary cause. With growing numbers of Connecticut residents migrating to central and western New York and the northeastern part of the Ohio Territory, the Missionary Society of Connecticut, organized in 1797, was determined to carry the Gospel into the wilderness and, thereby, to Christianize the West. It dispatched Bacon to the Western Reserve, but on an exploratory trip he went, instead, to the Michigan frontier. Ultimately, he persuaded the society to establish a mission there. As the first person in Connecticut to be ordained specifically to serve as a missionary to the heathen, David, accompanied by his new bride and her younger brother, walked to Buffalo and then took a boat to Detroit in early 1801.[4]

While in Detroit Bacon encountered numerous difficulties, including a very meager salary, the need to learn the Ojibway language, and the Indians' reluctance to change their way of life. Moreover, David's refusal to baptize children who had not had a religious experience angered a number of settlers. He was even judgmental toward his brother, Leonard, a physician in Hartford to whom David was deeply in debt, because Leonard had refused to turn to God. In the midst of these difficulties, a son, the first of seven children, was born on February 19, 1802. He was named Leonard after his recalcitrant uncle. But this event provided little immediate cause for celebration, for Alice nearly died in childbirth and was confined to bed for two months.[5]

Soon after Alice recovered, the Bacons established a mission on Mackinac Island,

3. Alice Parks to Zebulon Ely, March 1, 1800, David Bacon to Alice Parks, April, June 19, 1800, Alice Parks to David Bacon, May 20, 1800, in Bacon Family Papers, Yale University, New Haven, Conn.

4. David to Dr. Leonard Bacon, August 7, 1800, in Bacon Family Papers; John A. Andrew III, *Rebuilding the Christian Commonwealth: New England Congregationalists and Foreign Missions, 1800–1830* (Lexington, Ky., 1976), 1–2, 150–53; Bacon, "David Bacon," 6; Gaius Glenn Atkins and Frederick L. Fagley, *History of American Congregationalism* (Boston, 1942), 140–41; Joseph W. Phillips, *Jedidiah Morse and New England Congregationalism* (New Brunswick, N.J., 1983), 201; *Connecticut Evangelical Magazine,* I (November, 1800), 197–98.

5. Bacon, "David Bacon," 260–66; *Connecticut Evangelical Magazine,* I (November, 1800), 234–35, 237–38; David to Dr. Leonard Bacon, June 26, 1803, Alice to Dr. Leonard Bacon, July 1, 1802, in Bacon Family Papers.

a remote trading post and military station. During the next two years, David continued to experience setbacks. The Indians of the area generally resisted his attempts to "civilize" them and the French Canadian Catholics were hostile toward him—a matter his son would later emphasize in his accounts of David's life. Above all, David remained in dire financial straits. The Bacons' anxiety about their son in this inhospitable environment compounded their problems. As Alice remarked to her brother-in-law, "I am anxious about his life, his health and hope that I am in some measure anxious about his immortal part."[6]

Although David and Alice were dedicated to the missionary cause, they became increasingly disenchanted with the objects of their work and by their lack of success. When the missionary society, angered by Bacon's overdrafts on its account, requested that he go to New Connecticut (*i.e.*, the Western Reserve) to collect information on Native Americans in the area, he eventually acknowledged that it was best to leave what he termed "Sodom." David Bacon now faced another of the many crises in his life; the society's trustees were prepared to dismiss him from service because of the overdrafts. Leaving his wife, son, and infant daughter in Hudson, Ohio, David, still recovering from a serious illness (which was diagnosed at the time as malaria), walked to Connecticut in late 1804 to plead his case before the trustees. They ultimately found the drafts to be proper and agreed to hire him as a missionary in the Western Reserve, but he soon resigned his commission with the society, in part because he could scarcely support his family on the meager salary.[7] An even more important factor underlying his resignation, however, was his conviction that more could be done for the cause of Christianity and morality in the Western Reserve by establishing a "well-organized and Christianized township, with all the best arrangements of New England civilization," than by years of "desultory effort" as an itinerant preacher. As a visionary and a committed Calvinist who viewed New Connecticut as a western extension of the Puritan migration begun in the early seventeenth century, Bacon hoped to transform the Ohio wilderness into a model New England community where men and women would live by a rigorous moral code.[8]

Despite his brother's efforts to dissuade him from engaging in such a risky

6. Alice to Dr. Leonard Bacon, July 1, 1802, February 11, 1803, David to Dr. Leonard Bacon, July 2, 1802, June 1, 1804, in Bacon Family Papers; Bacon, "David Bacon," 394–405.

7. Alice to Dr. Leonard Bacon, February 11, 1803, David to Dr. Leonard Bacon, June 1, 1804, Leonard to David Bacon, September 10, 1804, David to Alice Bacon, December 29, 1804, in Bacon Family Papers; Theodore Dwight Bacon, *Leonard Bacon*, 20–23; Bacon, "David Bacon," 410–14, 562–65.

8. *Proceedings in Commemoration of the Fiftieth Anniversary of the Settlement of Tallmadge*, 50; Leonard Bacon, unpublished MSS, 1877, in Bacon Family Papers; Harlan Hatcher, *The Western Reserve: The Story of New Connecticut in Ohio* (Cleveland, 1949), 174–75.

scheme, in 1806 David signed a contract with Colonel Benjamin Tallmadge and Ephraim Starr of Connecticut, which gave him title to twenty square miles of land south of Hudson. He was responsible for selling the proprietors' land to residents of Connecticut and the Western Reserve. David envisioned the town of Tallmadge, which he established in 1807, as a model community, with a meetinghouse, a church, an academy, and a college, with him serving as both minister and proprietor.[9]

For nearly a year after moving to the township, the Bacons, who now had four children, lived in a small log cabin located several miles from their nearest neighbors. Leonard remembered his father's many prolonged absences between 1807 and 1812, when David was in Connecticut seeking to attract settlers to Tallmadge. His most vivid memories concerned the utter isolation of the place and his mother's fear when left alone with her small children. It was therefore a relief to have twelve families in the community by 1809, when David and Alice also established a church in their house. In addition, a school was started, which Leonard attended with a handful of other children, including Elizur Wright, Jr., later one of Bacon's principal antagonists on the slavery issue, whose family emigrated to Tallmadge in 1810. By that year, David's experiment seemed to be progressing well. With thirty families, a physician, a merchant, mills, a distillery, and twenty-five church members, he commented, "I think I never saw a better township of land than this."[10]

Much later in life Leonard tended to idealize his Tallmadge experience. He wrote of "the saintly and self-sacrificing father, the gentle yet heroic mother, the log cabin, from whose window we sometimes saw the wild deer bounding through the forest glades." Although Bacon's memory was selective, many aspects of the Tallmadge experience must have been enjoyable for a young boy. He took pleasure in wandering through the forest with his sister Susan, his only playmate during the first eight years of his life. He also enjoyed reading the Bible, *Pilgrim's Progress,* pieces from the *Connecticut Evangelical Magazine,* and various tracts. Above all, he distinctly remembered that his parents "took no small pains to impress religious truth on my mind." Consequently, he believed that he had been more inclined to "habits of reflexion" than most children of his age.[11]

Bacon's parents were orthodox Christians who believed that people were inherently sinful, yet they shared with Timothy Dwight and Lyman Beecher the conviction that good works were essential for a Christian life and that individuals were moral agents accountable to God for their actions. Bacon would hold to these beliefs

9. Williston Walker, *Ten New England Leaders* (New York, 1901), 24; Vivian C. Hopkins, *Prodigal Puritan: A Life of Delia Bacon* (Cambridge, Mass., 1959), 7; Bacon, "David Bacon," 566–67.

10. Bacon, "David Bacon," 566–69, 573; D. A. Upson to Bacon, October 24, 1879, in Bacon Family Papers; Theodore Dwight Bacon, *Leonard Bacon,* 25–26.

11. *Leonard Bacon: Pastor of the First Church in New Haven* (New Haven, 1882), 32; "Notes, 1818–1822," entry for September, 1822, in Bacon Family Papers.

throughout his life; indeed, they would be a driving force behind his many benevolent and reform endeavors. His parents were vigilant about their children's spiritual state, counseling them not to neglect the Bible and other "good books." They also insisted upon adherence to moral values and conduct and instilled a strong sense of devotion to a just God.[12]

Notwithstanding Bacon's pleasant memories of his childhood, the reality for David and Alice was very difficult. Because of the economic problems associated with the embargo, residents of Connecticut could not easily sell their farms and migrate, and those who came to Tallmadge had difficulty paying their taxes and making payments to Bacon. His inability to fulfill his contract with the proprietors threatened David with financial ruin. For Alice, David's yearlong trip to Connecticut in 1810–11 to negotiate with Colonel Tallmadge and to persuade people to migrate to the township compounded their problems. She confided to her husband that, with five children to care for and bleak prospects for the family, she was "almost worn down with fatigue and am frequently on the point of giving up." Nevertheless, she deeply sympathized with David's plight, stating that "you have almost worn out yourself in the arduous employment."[13]

Ever the optimist, David hoped until the very end to pay off his creditors and to "promote the spiritual and everlasting good of the thousands who are to inhabit the town of Tallmadge." Yet Colonel Tallmadge ultimately reneged on a deal to take farms in Connecticut in exchange for his lands in Tallmadge. This turn of events, David acknowledged, "broke my heart." He confessed that all he had realized from five years of arduous labor was "poverty, the alienation of old friends, the depression that follows a fatal defeat, and the dishonor that waits on one who cannot pay his debts." Consequently, in May, 1812, he abandoned his godly experiment and returned to Connecticut with his wife and five children.[14]

When David and Alice arrived in Connecticut they were destitute. During the next few years, David was forced to move from one temporary job to another, preaching and teaching on an interim basis. Finally, in 1815 he moved the family to his brother's home in Hartford. Soon thereafter, however, he left the family for extended periods of time in attempts to earn money. Not surprisingly, their frequent separations, their desperate financial situation, and their dependence on David's brother for room and board created tension between David and Alice.[15]

12. See David to Alice Bacon, September 16, 1811, in Bacon Family Papers.

13. Bacon, "David Bacon," 569–70, 573–74 (quotation), Alice to David Bacon, August 12, May 29, November 17, 1811, in Bacon Family Papers.

14. David to Alice Bacon, July 12, 19, November 6, 1811, Leonard to Colonel Benjamin Tallmadge, January 8, 1812, unpublished MSS, 256–57, in Bacon Family Papers; *Proceedings in Commemoration of the Fiftieth Anniversary of the Settlement of Tallmadge,* 59.

15. Bacon, "David Bacon," 586–87; unpublished MSS, 257–59, Alice to David Bacon, December 27, 1816, in Bacon Family Papers.

In the midst of this uncertainty and transience, young Leonard found a measure of stability in his life. David welcomed his brother's invitation in 1812 to have the ten-year-old boy live with his family, for this would allow his son to receive the classical education that David had never gotten. Soon after he arrived in Hartford, Leonard entered the Hartford Grammar School, a classical school that had been founded in 1664. In the early nineteenth century it averaged thirty students, and until 1817 it was free of charge. The school provided a rigorous training. Each student was required to "read English without hesitation, write a good copy-hand, and have some knowledge of arithmetic." Most of the classes were taught in Latin or Greek by recent graduates of Yale, and many of the students would later attend Yale.[16]

Leonard was an eager student. He had looked forward to attending the school, and he shared his father's conviction that a classical education was necessary to become a man of note. One of Leonard's classmates later remembered him as an "able, earnest, fearless, sarcastic, social, and warm-hearted" boy. He was not the most outstanding student at the school, but at a young age he displayed a penchant for literary effort. His father's visionary dreams and idealistic crusades may help to explain why *Don Quixote* and Timothy Dwight's *Conquest of Canaan* made a deep impression on him. Beyond this, Bacon later wrote that Dwight, Joel Barlow, and John Trumbull, known as the "Hartford Wits," one of the earliest literary circles in America, "were among the greatest [poets] then on the stage; indeed I hardly suspected that there were any others—unless I excepted myself; for even then I used to write what I thought poetry, which . . . was considered by my uncle and friends as rather extraordinary for a boy of my age."[17]

Hartford was a small city with a slow pace of life, but it was a center of government in Connecticut and had an active commercial and cultural life. Having spent his first ten years in a frontier setting, Bacon felt rather awkward and unpolished in an urban milieu. He acknowledged in 1822 that his best friend at school, who had grown up in Hartford, was more knowledgeable than he was, and therefore was able to introduce him to many "temptations."[18]

Looking back on his Hartford years from the perspective of a theological student, Bacon tended to set up his uncle and his parents as foils in something of a morality play. He believed that the religious impressions of his years in Tallmadge soon lost their influence in Hartford, and he held his uncle partly responsible for

16. Gurden W. Russell, *"Up Neck" in 1825* (Hartford, 1890), 79; Henry Barnard (ed.), "Hartford Grammar School," *American Journal of Education*, XXVIII (1878), 187, 196, 199–200, 205; *Discourses and Addresses at the Ordination of the Rev. Theodore Dwight Woolsey, LL.D., to the Ministers of the Gospel, and His Inauguration as President of Yale College, October 21, 1846* (New Haven, 1846), 37.

17. "Notes, 1818–1822," entry for September 1, 1822, in Bacon Family Papers.

18. *Ibid.*

this. He acknowledged that his father's brother was "a man of excellent character," but he was also mildly critical of his uncle for having "to a great extent neglected the duty of personal religious advice and instruction." It was, he concluded, only his parents' early influence that prevented him from becoming a "castaway" and explained why he was distinguished among his peers for the "sobriety and correctness of my conduct." Although he watched the progress of a religious revival in 1814 with "lively interest" and wished to join those classmates who were hopeful of regeneration, he did not have a religious experience during his years in Hartford.[19]

Whatever stability Leonard enjoyed while living at his uncle's house, especially after the rest of the family joined him there in 1815, was shattered by his father's death in 1817 at the age of forty-five. The death had an enormous impact on Leonard, then only fifteen years old. In a journal he began at that time, he recorded the gathering of the family at his father's bed and his mother leaning over to have David bless their infant son, Francis. Leonard slept on the floor next to his father's bed for several days, and shortly after his father's death he remarked poignantly, "And thou art gone from and shall never more behold thy face yet I hope to meet thee at length in that blessed world."[20]

Leonard's parents profoundly influenced his beliefs and actions as an adult. Through his involvement in the colonization, antislavery, temperance, and other reform and religious benevolence causes, he sought to emulate his father's efforts to create a moral and just world. Moreover, he acted upon his father's deathbed plea that he enter the ministry, a profession which Leonard identified with above all else in a multifaceted career. And though in his early twenties he chose not to accept a missionary post in the West, he was a lifelong supporter of the home and foreign missionary movements and actively sought to implement his father's dream of establishing colleges in the West. His father's request that he take care of his mother and six younger siblings also became a lifelong responsibility and, at times, a painful burden. Moreover, at least in his early adulthood this responsibility certainly enhanced his naturally serious demeanor.

Throughout his life Leonard remained very proud of his father's Tallmadge experiment, often returning to the town to commemorate its founding and at all times vigorously defending his father's reputation. But unlike his youngest sister, Delia, whose sympathy for her father's extravagant dreams may well have been partly responsible for her eccentric efforts to prove that Sir Francis Bacon actually wrote the plays generally attributed to William Shakespeare,[21] Leonard, nine years her

19. *Ibid.*

20. Alice Bacon to Clarissa Wright, January 2, 1818, journal entry for August 31, 1817, in Bacon Family Papers. In the quotation, elision of the pronouns "me" and "I" (*i.e.,* "from *me* and *I* shall") reflects the original.

21. Hopkins, *Prodigal Puritan,* vii, 8, *et passim.*

elder, had observed the disastrous effects of his father's failed dreams and the criticism that so pained him. Thus, he perhaps drew from his observation the lesson that one must not stray too far from mainstream public opinion or engage in risky ventures. Although Leonard was involved in a number of controversial, and in some cases unpopular, causes during his lengthy public career, he frequently searched for a middle ground on theological, political, and reform issues. In doing so, he sought to avoid what he considered extreme and untenable positions. Likewise, he was offered numerous prestigious positions outside of the ministry—several of which offered little long-term security—but chose to remain pastor of the same church for more than forty years.

Leonard also inherited from both parents a tenaciousness in the face of adversity and a sensitive pride that at times were manifested in an arrogant disdain for, and a prickly sarcasm toward, those who differed with him. Behind this self-righteousness and arrogance lurked, as it had to a greater degree with his father, both a sense of insecurity and the conviction that he was a self-made man.

Finally, Bacon's devotion to family, in the form of assisting his widowed mother and his siblings throughout their lives as well as providing everything he could for his own fourteen children, stemmed from both his positive and negative childhood experiences. Although his parents were strict and authoritative, they also nurtured their children with affection. Leonard knew that his mother and father cared deeply about him and wished the best for him. At the same time, his separations from his family, especially from his father, during his childhood intensified his attachment to them. Within a few months of his father's death, his enrollment at Yale and his mother's decision to move, for economic reasons, to western New York with most of her children sorely tested the family ties he so cherished.

2

A YALE EXPERIENCE

AVID Bacon had "most ardently wished" that his son attend Yale; and, according to Alice, this was something Leonard had "long sighed for and which you almost despaired of ever obtaining." Managing to meet Yale's rather stringent entrance requirements, he was admitted to the sophomore class in 1817, even though he was only fifteen years old. He later acknowledged that Yale officials had been "strangely kind in their estimation" of him, for he believed himself to be insufficiently prepared and the age requirement had been "somewhat relaxed."[1]

Because his mother was destitute and his uncle had to support his own family, Leonard could contribute nothing to his education. Thus, without scholarship assistance he could not have attended Yale. Much of his financial aid came from the Connecticut auxiliary of the American Education Society, founded in 1814 to provide a college education for "indigent young men of piety and promising talents" who had declared their intention of studying for the ministry. In accepting this aid Bacon indicated a determination to pursue a career to which, his mother pointedly reminded him, he had been "dedicated from . . . birth."[2]

The education society paid approximately one-half of his annual college expenses, but declining revenues and the desire to encourage students to rely on themselves by working or by seeking assistance from friends led it to begin in 1819 to require each beneficiary to sign a note for half of what he received. For Bacon and

1. Alice to Leonard Bacon, November 1, 1818, in Bacon Family Papers; Brooks Mather Kelley, *Yale: A History* (New Haven, 1974), 156; *Leonard Bacon: Pastor of the First Church in New Haven*, 77.

2. David F. Allmendinger, Jr., *Paupers and Scholars: The Transformation of Student Life in Nineteenth-Century New England* (New York, 1975), 60; Clifford S. Griffin, *Their Brothers' Keepers: Moral Stewardship in the United States, 1800–1865* (New Brunswick, N.J., 1960), 64–65; Alice to Leonard Bacon, November 22, 1819, Bacon to Samuel W. Collins, October 27, 1821, in Bacon Family Papers.

many other poor students this meant maintaining a marginal subsistence and paying off their debts over many years. Although Bacon appreciated the assistance he received, he admitted that being dependent upon the charity of others created "a thousand little privations and vexations and discouragements." Nevertheless, he added resolutely, "he who counts the cost before he begins and enters upon the undertaking with the right spirit will never repent of it."[3]

Leonard entered Yale at the moment the old order in Connecticut and at the college collapsed. In 1817 the Toleration party, drawing support largely from dissenting religious groups, triumphed in state elections, and in the following year it passed a new state constitution that disestablished the Congregational Church and ended public subsidies to Yale. At the same time, the death of President Timothy Dwight of Yale removed from the scene one of the most forceful defenders of the standing order.[4]

With a new president, a small physical plant, only six faculty members (including the president) and six tutors, meager library holdings, and serious financial problems, Yale was a struggling institution in 1817. Yet it was also a truly national institution that attracted growing numbers of young men from the South and the West. In addition, Jeremiah Day made numerous improvements at every level of the college during his tenure as president and worked closely with the faculty, especially Benjamin Silliman and James Kingsley, who had taught at Yale as long as he had.[5]

Day, like Dwight, believed that Yale was responsible for imposing rigorous discipline and fostering moral character and intellect among the students. Bacon and the seventy other students in his class attended the same required program of study and religious exercises, and for the most part they passively accepted the strict regimentation. During Leonard's years at Yale, the curriculum was almost entirely fixed. Much like students at other colleges, Leonard focused prior to the senior year on Greek, Latin, and mathematics. A few courses were offered in history, geography, science, English grammar, and rhetoric, but American and English literature were largely ignored. Day taught moral philosophy to seniors, who also took courses in ethics, composition, and belle lettres.[6]

The senior disputations with Day were the freest period of discussion in Leonard's years at Yale. These disputes enabled him to sharpen his debating skills and compelled him to take a stand, probably for the first time, on a number of issues that would later be of considerable interest to him. For example, in predicting that the

3. Allmendinger, *Paupers and Scholars,* 28–41, 71; "Connecticut Education Society," *Christian Spectator,* III (September, 1821), 495; Bacon to Samuel W. Collins, October 27, 1821, in Bacon Family Papers.

4. See Rollin G. Osterweis, *Three Centuries of New Haven, 1638–1938* (New Haven, 1953), 211–13.

5. Kelley, *Yale,* 140–52; Ralph Henry Gabriel, *Religion and Learning at Yale: The Church of Christ in the College and University, 1757–1957* (New Haven, 1958), 101–102.

6. Gabriel, *Religion and Learning at Yale,* 83–84, 109–10; John Mitchell, *Reminiscences of Scenes and Characters in College* (New Haven, 1847), 46–49.

"degenerate and corrupt" papacy would soon be destroyed, he foreshadowed his later involvement in the crusade against Catholicism. Moreover, in arguing that England, New England, and other northern areas in the Western world demonstrated more reason, love of liberty, industry, and artistic and scientific achievement than areas farther south, he sounded a theme that would be heard throughout his lifelong celebration of the Anglo-American (and especially New England) historical experience as well as in his developing antisouthern sentiment as the slavery controversy escalated.[7]

Bacon also debated a number of other issues that would later divide Americans. He was, for instance, critical of the federal government's Indian policy, terming it "a blot on our national character." Yet he exhibited, much as his parents had, a deep-seated cultural bias regarding Native Americans, praising efforts "to civilize them, and thus to render them useful members of Society." Likewise, he accepted the prevailing gender stereotypes. Notwithstanding his mother's example of caring for most of the family's needs during his childhood, Leonard maintained that women were created "to be in short an 'help meet' for men," and the sexes "were made to move in different spheres of action" and had "different faculties of a different nature."[8]

While at Yale Bacon devoted much of his time and energy to various benevolent, literary, and fraternal organizations on campus. In all, these activities illustrate important characteristics of his personality, beliefs, and interests at a formative stage of his life. Leonard had long hoped to have a religious experience. With considerable encouragement from his mother, he publicly professed religion in 1819 and pledged to follow his father's path as a minister, praying that "his mantle may rest upon me." A year earlier he had joined the Moral Society of Yale, founded in 1797 by defenders of orthodox Christianity who were convinced that morality was essential for salvation and "equally necessary to the usefulness and respectability of all human institutions."[9] His membership in this organization underscores the serious and sanctimonious side of Bacon's personality. Leonard regularly participated in debates on such matters as infant baptism, sectarianism, missionary efforts, and disinterested benevolence, and he served on the organization's executive committee. As a defender of the old order in Connecticut, he was deeply concerned that Amer-

---

7. Bacon, "Oration on the present condition and prospects of Italy," "On the comparative influence of Moral and Physical causes in the formation of character," Yale College Disputes, in Bacon Family Papers.

8. Bacon, "On the prospects of the North American Indian," Yale Dispute at Commencement, September 1820, "Are the abilities of the Sexes equal?" Yale College Disputes, 1820, in Bacon Family Papers.

9. Alice to Leonard Bacon, November 28, 1817, April 20, 1818, Leonard to Alice Bacon, March 4, 1819, in Bacon Family Papers; "Constitution of the Moral Society of Yale College. To Which Is Prefixed the Names of Those by Whom It Was Framed," Yale University, New Haven, Conn.

ica had "degenerated from the morality of our fathers" and their "unbending puritanism." The nation, he stated in his valedictory oration before the society in 1820, must "arrest the progress of luxury." Indeed, a few years later he regretted that he and other pious students had not "thoroughly and distinctly" separated themselves from their irreligious classmates.[10]

Yet throughout much of his life Leonard was optimistic about the future of the country and its institutions. He was particularly impressed by the benevolent exertions of American Christians, and saw his generation entering a new era in history. In calling upon Christians to live active lives, not simply to "set down and moralize on the events of life," he echoed the sentiments of Lyman Beecher, Timothy Dwight, and other pioneers in the world of organized benevolence. "The voice of Conscience and of God," he maintained, "bids us be up and doing." He further signaled his attachment to religious benevolence in an 1820 oration delivered before the Yale College Bible Society. Writing at the time of the revolutionary upheavals in Europe, he stated, with obvious hyperbole, that long after these events had faded into obscurity, the formation of Bible societies and other benevolent organizations would shed "a glory brighter and more lasting than that of any former age."[11]

During his undergraduate years, Bacon was perhaps most attracted to literary endeavors. What he wrote as a student was generally unpolished and of limited promise. But it betokened a lifelong penchant for writing on a wide variety of subjects, as the editor of, and contributor to, numerous magazines and newspapers and as the author of several books. In his valedictory speech before the Moral Society—an oration that contained the germ of an idea that Ralph Waldo Emerson later crystallized in "The American Scholar"—he presented a plea for the development of a national literature. Compared with the nation's literary character, he told the society, "the greatness of its power, the richness of its commerce, the bravery of its citizens, the firmness and durability of its government are nothing." Thus, members of the Moral Society must "effect a revolution" by working "to inspire the pride of literary patriotism."[12]

10. Peter Dobkin Hall, *The Organization of American Culture, 1700–1900: Private Institutions, Elites, and the Origins of American Nationality* (New York, 1982), 173; Bacon, "Valedictory Oration on the prospects of Our Country," June 29, 1820, in Bacon Family Papers; Bacon to Theodore Dwight Woolsey, July 27, 1823, in Woolsey Family Papers, Yale University, New Haven, Conn.

11. Bacon, "Valedictory Oration on the prospects of Our Country," June 29, 1820, Bacon to Alexander C. Twining, July 7, 1821, Bacon, "An Oration delivered before the Bible Society," April 17, 1820, in Bacon Family Papers. On the Yale College Bible Society and similar college organizations, see James McLachlan, "*The Choice of Hercules*: American Student Societies in the Early Nineteenth Century," in *The University in Society*, ed. Lawrence Stone, vol. II, *Europe, Scotland, and the United States from the Sixteenth to the Twentieth Century* (Princeton, 1974), 487–88, 493.

12. Bacon, "Valedictory Oration on the prospects of Our Country," June 29, 1820, in Bacon Family Papers; also Theodore Dwight Bacon, *Leonard Bacon*, 41.

Leonard's interest in literature was shared by many young Americans in the early nineteenth century. While at Yale he devoted significant time and energy to, and played a prominent role in, the Society of Brothers in Unity, one of many literary societies that flourished in the nation's colleges during the heady days following the War of 1812. These societies permitted students essentially to train themselves to develop, write, and defend their ideas outside of the often-rigid curriculum. Also, because college libraries of the time frequently were inadequate, members of the literary societies established rather substantial libraries that were used for the preparation of essays and orations. Finally, the growing size of classes, and the consequent impersonal relations at Yale and other colleges, enhanced the popularity of these student societies. At Yale, Brothers in Unity, founded in 1768 "to promote the intellectual improvement, the gentlemanly character, and the mutual good will of its several members," competed aggressively for new members with Linonian, which was dominated by southern students. Not only did the Brothers and Linonian enroll large numbers of students, create and teach their own curricula, and develop their own codes of conduct,[13] but they also formed an important component of the social life of the college. Several of Bacon's closest friends throughout his life—including Theodore Dwight Woolsey, Alexander C. Twining, Solomon Stoddard, and Edward Beecher—were fellow members of the Brothers.[14]

Among the many issues debated by the Brothers at their meetings were ones relating to African Americans, African colonization, and slavery—all of which would later be of enormous interest to Bacon. The question of whether it would be "politic in the United States to colonize free blacks" generated heated debate in 1818. Those who voted in the negative presented "many forcible arguments," which, according to the society's secretary, "appeared irresistible," including the assertion that the scheme was impractical and expensive and would involve the nation in European conflicts. The supporters of colonization, who ultimately prevailed, declared that it would constitute "a great deed of benevolence" and probably end the slave trade. This may well have been Leonard's initial exposure to debate on the merits of the American Colonization Society, founded a mere two years earlier, and it certainly served to focus his attention on the issue. Although no record exists of how he voted on this matter, from the early 1820s until the mid-1830s he would

13. "Constitution of the Brothers in Unity, 1831," p. 1, Yale University; Society of Brothers in Unity, *Constitution and Laws of the Society of Brothers in Unity* (New Haven, 1861), 3; Thomas S. Harding, *College Literary Societies: Their Contribution to Higher Education in the United States, 1815–1876* (New York, 1971), 30, 32–33, 46–49, 57–58, 67, 81–82; McLachlan, "*The Choice of Hercules:* American Student Societies in the Early Nineteenth Century," 459, 462–65, 472.

14. Entries for January 21, August 26, 1818, January 6, April 21, July 21, 1819, January 5, 1820, in "Records of the Society of Brothers in Unity," Book IV, July 10, 1816–March 12, 1828, Yale University, New Haven, Conn.

frequently reiterate the arguments presented by the affirmative side in the debate. Later in 1818 the society decided that differences in complexion between blacks and whites were based upon civilization, not natural causes, and that southern blacks should be repatriated to Africa. Only a few years later Bacon would emerge as a leading proponent of what George M. Fredrickson has termed "environmental racism"—that is, the belief that because white prejudice, not inherited traits, was responsible for the degraded state of American free blacks, colonization would enable them to be elevated.[15]

At the same time that Congress was engaged in the bitter Missouri debates, the Brothers also debated the issue of slavery in the territories. As a member of the committee that decided the issues to be discussed, Leonard was an interested and concerned participant. In 1819 a majority of the society's members decided that Congress should prohibit slavery in the territories. The Missouri debates were discussed with "considerable zeal" by the Brothers, pitting northern against southern students. Ultimately, the society rejected the argument that it was expedient to divide the Union, concluding that the interests of both sections must be taken into account.[16] Bacon probably voted with the majority on these issues, for while he opposed slavery and its extension into the West throughout the antebellum era, until the 1840s he generally sought to accommodate southern concerns about emancipation.

Not all of Bacon's activities associated with the Brothers in Unity focused on such serious matters. He also engaged in light-hearted satirical writing that poked fun at himself, his classmates, the college, and life in general. In his junior year he, Woolsey, and Twining decided to write a series of papers called the *Talebearer,* which ran for thirty issues during 1819 and were read by an officer at Brothers in Unity meetings. The *Talebearer* contained character sketches, literary criticism, didactic essays, and mock-heroic verses—some of them of rather high literary quality. The editors generally wrote with tongue in cheek in an attempt to enliven the rather dull meetings of the club.[17]

The editors were also determined to expose the pretensions of their classmates. Because many of the Brothers were anxious to draw attention to themselves, one editor asserted, "a great deal of folly must necessarily be displayed. This I shall attempt to hold up to ridicule." Bacon seemed especially inclined to employ sarcasm and to relish controversy, at one point brusquely urging Twining to increase the

15. *Ibid.,* entries for October 28, November 12, 1818; George M. Fredrickson, *The Black Image in the White Mind: The Debate on Afro-American Character and Destiny, 1817–1914* (New York, 1971), 12–15.

16. Entries for June 9, 1819, March 8, April 12, 1820, in "Records of the Society of Brothers in Unity," Book IV, July 10, 1816–March 12, 1828; Mitchell, *Reminiscences of Scenes and Characters in College,* 110.

17. *Talebearer,* February 10, 1819, Yale University, New Haven, Conn.

severity of his indictment of the members, even though this would meet with "the most violent opposition." The editors' satire could be heavy-handed. In one piece, for example, they ridiculed a member they called Benjamin Inkhorn, who considered himself brilliant and read "fanciful novels." They derisively termed Inkhorn's poetry "high sounding nonsense" and "gilded bombast," and they reported that a Mr. Simcoe used Inkhorn's windy speech to light his pipe.[18]

Bacon acknowledged that many of his poems and essays were "so caustic and personal that for me to transcribe them would be to incur the wrath of some of the respectable members of the society." Indeed, even some of his friends mildly chastised him for his sarcasm. As expected, and perhaps welcomed, the *Talebearer* was the target of "an extemporaneous effusion" of wrath from several members of the Brothers.[19]

Yet in some ways Leonard was his own harshest critic. Although his self-deprecating statements were intended in part to be humorous, they also reveal his awareness that he did not perform up to his capabilities or to the expectations of others. He attributed his lesser role in the *Talebearer* to the fact that he was "too indolent to write any thing like a regular lucubation [*sic*]." Thus, he considered his writings to be "like the prophecies of the Sibyl written on scattered leaves—without order or arrangement—without connection and always liable to be dissipated and lost." He was especially critical of his lack of consistency and resoluteness. "In whatever I undertake," he confessed, "I am enthusiastic for a while—but often as soon as the novelty of the thing is gone I lose all my ardour."[20]

Bacon's decision, at the age of seventeen, to write for an audience and to expose himself to criticism required a rather strong sense of self. He engaged in self-criticism, but even at an early age he at times shielded himself behind a tough exterior and acted as though he was nearly impervious to criticism. "I have ever professed and felt," he wrote Twining in 1819, "a total disregard of the opinions which others may express concerning my character and writings." Thus, he announced to Twining, with much bravado, that he was little affected by "those riotous proceedings" at the Brothers meetings in response to the *Talebearer*'s barbs.[21] This stubborn determination to stand his ground and to view his enemies as motivated by base designs would fortify him in his many battles with both abolitionists and conservatives on the slavery issue as well as with theological conservatives and others.

Yet a more accommodating and vulnerable side coexisted with his combative-

18. *Ibid.;* Bacon to Alexander C. Twining, August 10, 1819, in Bacon Family Papers; *Talebearer,* February 24, June 16, 1819.

19. *Talebearer,* December 8, March 31, 1819.

20. *Ibid.,* December 22, 1819.

21. Bacon to Alexander C. Twining, August 10, 1819, in Bacon Family Papers.

ness. Part of him clearly desired to be accepted by his peers. In 1819, for example, he informed Twining that he hoped the freshman class would support him for president of Brothers in Unity. Moreover, in the last few issues of the *Talebearer* he and Woolsey acknowledged that the members' general acceptance of the paper was a source of "much pleasure and affection."[22] As an adult he would in fact be known as something of a conciliator who searched for common ground that all parties in a dispute could occupy, and he frequently positioned himself as a moderate, avoiding what he considered to be extreme positions.

This complex mix of self-doubt and self-assurance, bravado and vulnerability, is common among teenagers who are searching for an identity and seeking to prove themselves to their peers. Yet for Bacon this adolescent struggle was exacerbated by the very difficult and often painful family situation that confronted him during his college years. His father's death two months before Leonard enrolled at Yale was part of the heavy emotional burden he bore. David's death was a recurring theme in Leonard's poetry, orations, and correspondence during these years. In 1822 he informed a boyhood friend that, just prior to entering Yale, "the world was to me a wide and dreary blank—my father, the best of fathers, was sinking into the grave. . . . The world looked dark and desolate to me." Similarly, in a poem dating from early 1818 he bemoaned the tragic fate of his family:

> And can my own weak arm sustain
> My weary aching head
> Or can my feeble hands supply
> My little ones with bread?
> In what remote secluded spot
> Can I search out a home
> Where I can drink my bitter cup
> Unpitied and alone?
> I had a friend who knew to feel
> And share my every woe.
> But he has bid a long farewell
> And death has laid him low.
>
> . . . .
>
> What woes can be compar'd with mine
> What anguish so severe?
> I sink beneath the oppressive weight
> penny and care.[23]

22. Bacon to Alexander C. Twining, August 10, 1819, in Bacon Family Papers; *Talebearer,* December 22, 1819.

23. Bacon to Samuel W. Collins, August 19, 1822, Bacon, "On being told that I must not rely upon my friends but depend wholly upon myself," February 23, 1818, in Bacon Family Papers.

By 1819, Leonard acknowledged that the passage of time had begun to heal some of the painful memories by "painting all the scenes of life in the loveliest colours." His mother attempted to help him through these difficult times, yet soon after he entered Yale, his family's situation grew more desperate. His Uncle Leonard's financial problems and his mother's inability to find sufficient sewing work in Hartford forced her to move to the western New York community of East Bloomfield in the fall of 1819. She took with her all of Leonard's brothers and sisters except Delia, then seven years old, who was placed in the home of the Honorable Thomas Williams, chief justice of the Connecticut Supreme Court. These developments produced enormous anguish, pressure, and guilt for Leonard. His mother and his sister Susan, then only fourteen, produced silk bonnets in their home in an effort to make ends meet, and when Susan's health deteriorated because of overwork, her younger sisters, Julia and Alice, took up braiding straw. Leonard's mother informed him that she could not afford to send her children to school and was too busy to teach them at home. Ultimately, abject poverty forced her to send Julia and Alice to live with other families.[24]

In her misery, Alice Bacon made it quite clear that Leonard was the privileged child in the family. She underscored the point by sending him a decidedly mixed message: how pleased she was that he was at Yale, even "though it should deprive me of your society and the aid which you might otherwise afford me." She also placed heavy pressure on Leonard to do well in college and to commit himself to the ministry. "I hope that you realize," she wrote in 1818, "that very much is depending on the manner in which you improve your present advantage for becoming a useful man."[25]

Leonard sought to act as something of a father figure for his younger brothers and sisters. But he felt guilty for not being able to assist his family or even to visit them during his last two years in college because of the distance and a lack of money. Bacon informed his mother that when he thought of her situation, "my heart shrinks within me," and he lamented his "entire inability to do anything for your assistance." He sought to assuage his sense of guilt by assuring his mother that God would protect her and that he hoped to "do something" for her when he graduated.[26] Nevertheless, the situation surely was difficult for a teenager to cope with.

Notwithstanding the emotional burden that he carried with him, Leonard generally enjoyed his years at Yale. His uncle informed Alice that her son had "many

24. Bacon, "Anticipation and Memory," in Junior Yale Disputes, 1819, Alice to Leonard Bacon, November 28, 1817, April 20, 1818, Alice to Dr. Leonard Bacon, February 22, June 2, 1819, Alice to Leonard Bacon, November 22, 1819, July 28, August 28, 1820, in Bacon Family Papers.

25. Alice to Leonard Bacon, November 1, 1818, February 23, 1819, in Bacon Family Papers.

26. Leonard to Alice Bacon, March 4, December 21, August 21, 1819, in Bacon Family Papers.

worthy friends who seem to take great interest in him." His closest friends at Yale were Twining, Woolsey, Chester Isham, John Brockway, and Solomon Stoddard, who lived in neighboring rooms. In their senior year they formed the Hexahedron, a secret organization with no official standing that served as something of a literary society and social club. They met in one another's rooms, where they read English poetry while eating sweet potatoes and drinking ale. The members swore a constitutional duty to correspond regularly with each other, devote a portion of their lives to literary pursuits, promote the interests of Yale, inform each other when they fell in love, and "support and increase the civil, religious, and literary institutions of our country."[27]

Bacon did not rigorously apply himself to his studies during his three years at Yale. This may well have been the result of a number of things: his self-proclaimed indolence, his sociability, his interest in literary pursuits, and the impact of his family's circumstances. His lack of devotion to his studies was particularly apparent in his senior year. As he confessed to Twining a few months after graduating, it "seems to me during the whole of my senior year I did nothing."[28] Indeed, Woolsey and other friends were convinced that he had not lived up to his promise, and at times lectured him on his superficial study habits. When it seemed obvious that he would not have a major role in the commencement exercises, he put up a brave front for his mother: "Although some feel anxious on this subject I am perfectly indifferent, for I have no fear of losing my last year's appointment nor do I desire to gain a higher one." Yet he in fact did well enough in his studies to be granted a small part in the graduation ritual, and his friends, if not Bacon, were pleased that his scholarship was "in some measure rewarded."[29]

Leonard was uncertain what he wished to do following his graduation. He enjoyed writing and believed that he was quite proficient at it. After having pieces accepted by the *Guardian,* a literary magazine published in New York, he informed his mother: "I am proud enough to think that I can write as well as some of his [the editor's] correspondents." But he never seriously considered making a living solely from writing.[30]

Bacon had long considered becoming a missionary. Citing his father's wishes, and believing that he was "born a missionary," during his junior year he determined to go either to the West or overseas. Yet his mother, citing Leonard's obligations to

27. Leonard to Alice Bacon, February 28, 1820, Dr. Leonard to Alice Bacon, February 28, 1820, Bacon to Alexander C. Twining, July 7, 1821, in Bacon Family Papers; *Leonard Bacon: Pastor of the First Church in New Haven,* 226–27; Gabriel, *Religion and Learning at Yale,* 90.

28. Bacon to Alexander C. Twining, July 7, 1821, in Bacon Family Papers.

29. Woolsey to Alexander C. Twining, May 17, 1820, in Woolsey Family Papers; Leonard to Alice Bacon, April 26, 1820, in Bacon Family Papers.

30. Leonard to Alice Bacon, April 26, 1820, in Bacon Family Papers.

his siblings and herself, discouraged him from accepting an overseas post. His family's precarious financial situation led Bacon seriously to contemplate teaching school for a year or two after graduation in order to save money for seminary studies and his family as well as to make himself "more eminently useful in after life."[31]

Bacon's failure to obtain a teaching job underlay his decision to attend theological seminary. The traditional pattern of studying with a minister for a few months was not a viable option; he considered it "exceedingly defective." Before making his decision, Leonard consulted with Lyman Beecher and other Connecticut religious leaders as well as his mother. He considered studying under the professors at Yale, which had not yet established a seminary. There he could combine his studies with teaching school, and thereby assist his family. But he concluded that "the advantages are doubtless greater at Andover" than at Yale or Princeton, because Andover had high standards of scholarship, lower costs, and a larger faculty that "go deep into the study of Biblical criticism, and Theology, and all those branches which are calculated to make a thorough scholar and a sound divine."[32]

Bacon was required to submit to the Andover faculty "satisfactory testimonials" that he professed "good natural and acquired talents," had "honorably completed a course of liberal education," sustained "a fair moral character," and was "in full communion with some Church of Christ." The faculty also examined him in the "learned languages" and asked him why he wished to pursue theological studies. Finally, he was required to declare that he believed the Scriptures were "a perfect rule of faith and practice." In the end, he was accepted for admission. When he left Hartford in October, 1820, with Chester Isham, a childhood and college friend, he proudly informed his mother that they had set out "pilgrim-like with our packs on our backs" to walk the one hundred miles to Boston. Though homesick and with virtually no money, he looked forward with enthusiasm to a thorough training for the ministry.[33]

31. Leonard to Alice Bacon, December 21, 1819, February 28, 1820, Alice to Leonard Bacon, November 22, 1819, in Bacon Family Papers.

32. Leonard to Alice Bacon, February 28, October 16, 1820, Alice to Leonard Bacon, July 28, 1820, in Bacon Family Papers; Theodore Dwight Bacon, *Leonard Bacon*, 42–43. On theological education at Yale prior to the founding of Yale Theological Seminary in 1822, see John Terrill Wayland, "The Theological Department in Yale College, 1822–1858" (Ph.D. dissertation, Yale University, 1933), 52–62. For the defects in the practice of studying with a parish minister, see William Warren Sweet, "The Rise of Theological Schools in America," *Church History*, VI (1937), 260–73.

33. *Laws of the Theological Institution of Andover* (Andover, Mass., 1817), 3–4; Leonard to Alice Bacon, December 16, 1820, in Bacon Family Papers.

3

THEOLOGY AND BENEVOLENCE
AT ANDOVER

BACON'S acceptance to Andover Theological Seminary was quite an accomplishment. In an era when seminaries were the leading educational institutions in America and furnished the prototype of professional education, Andover was the nation's premier seminary. The first three-year professional school of theology in the United States, it had an extensive library and a distinguished faculty, and its graduates were among the leading clergymen, college professors, missionaries, and officers of benevolent societies of the time.[1]

Andover was the product of a tenuous compromise between two warring factions within New England Congregationalism: the Hopkinsians and the Old Calvinists. Samuel Hopkins and other Hopkinsians were strict Calvinists, who emphasized the total depravity of individuals, God's sovereignty, and the need to submit to divine punishment for the glory of God.[2] While Timothy Dwight, Jedidiah Morse, and other Old Calvinists agreed with the Hopkinsians on a number of basic doctrines, as more moderate Calvinists they feared that the Hopkinsians' speculations and dogmatism would alienate many members of the church.[3]

Weary of a half century of conflict, these groups, after years of negotiation,

1. See J. Earl Thompson, Jr., "Abolitionism and Theological Education at Andover," *New England Quarterly,* XLVII (1974), 239–40; Donald M. Scott, *From Office to Profession: The New England Ministry, 1750–1850* (Philadelphia, 1978), 63–64; *Catalogue of the Professors and Students of the Theological Seminary, Andover, Massachusetts, February, 1822* (Andover, 1822).

2. For treatments of the Hopkinsians, see Daniel Day Williams, *The Andover Liberals: A Study in American Theology* (New York, 1941), 3–4; Rev. Leonard Woods, *History of the Andover Theological Seminary* (Boston, 1885), 31–38; Oliver Wendell Elsbree, "Samuel Hopkins and His Doctrine of Benevolence," *New England Quarterly,* VIII (1935), 534–50.

3. See Phillips, *Jedidiah Morse and New England Congregationalism,* 137–40; Bacon, *A Commemorative Discourse, on the Completion of Fifty Years from the Founding of the Theological Seminary at Andover* (Andover, 1858), 14–17; Marie Caskey, *Chariot of Fire: Religion and the Beecher Family* (New Haven, 1978), 37–42.

created a united front and founded Andover in 1808. All Andover professors were required to sign a creed that contained elements of both groups' essential beliefs. Although the seminary consciously sought to avoid the extremes, attempts to restate doctrines for an age of revivalism and Christian expansion perpetuated theological conflict between the orthodox factions. Andover was ever watchful against heretical opinions. But in reality the rules for avoiding heresy were ill-defined and the theological system that was presented to Bacon and other students was vague and controversial.[4] Tensions within the Andover system go far to explain why Bacon, while later standing close to Taylor, and then Bushnell, in their struggles with the conservative Calvinists, at times leaned toward a middle position in these theological battles.

Andover's academic requirements were structured and demanding. The first year was largely devoted to the study of sacred literature, the second to Christian theology, and the third to sacred rhetoric and ecclesiastical history, which included pastoral theology. This sequence was established so that students would learn the Westminster doctrines before becoming aware of the historical diversity of Christian thought. Students were examined yearly by the trustees and faculty. The daily regimen was equally demanding, consisting of classes and exercise interspersed with religious exercises that all students were required to "constantly, punctually, and seriously attend." The schedule was so predictable that Bacon informed Twining, "The only changes we have here are the changes of the moon and the wind and the weather." The social life of the seminary—especially the chapel services, Wednesday evening conferences, and yearly fasts—served to reinforce the prevailing orthodoxy. Andover's isolation from urban areas and colleges minimized the distractions from the seminary's code of piety and intensive study. It is no wonder that Moses Stuart, professor of sacred literature at Andover during Bacon's years as a student there, described Andover as a "sacred West Point."[5]

Yet for all its regimentation and its adherence to a strict Calvinism, Andover was open-minded in its methods of instruction. Bacon was encouraged to think systematically about philosophy and psychology as well as biblical and pastoral studies, and there was no reward for cautious reiteration of approved views. Moses Stuart embodied this central contradiction in Andover theology: he adhered to the Ando-

---

4. Steven E. Berk, *Calvinism Versus Democracy: Timothy Dwight and the Origins of American Evangelical Orthodoxy* (Hamden, Conn., 1974), 178–81; Bruce Kuklick, *Churchmen and Philosophers: From Jonathan Edwards to John Dewey* (New Haven, 1985), 85; Lewis Perry, *Childhood, Marriage, and Reform: Henry Clarke Wright, 1797–1870* (Chicago, 1980), 108–11.

5. John E. Todd, ed., *John Todd: The Story of His Life* (New York, 1876), 102, 109; *Laws of the Theological Institution of Andover,* 5–6; Bacon to Alexander C. Twining, January 12, 1821, November 6, 1822, in Bacon Family Papers; Henry K. Rowe, *History of Andover Theological Seminary* (Newton, Mass., 1933), 433; Williams, *The Andover Liberals,* 14.

ver creed that the Bible contained the word of God, but he also stretched the creed as far as possible to make room for investigation, discussion, and biblical criticism. Recognized as America's most competent philologist and grammarian, Stuart posited a "grammatico-historical interpretation" of the Bible, developed by German scholars, which argued that exegesis of the Scriptures required that they be understood in their original sense. As an evangelical Calvinist, however, Stuart's orientation was dogmatic, not scientific, for he was convinced that God's revelations in nature could not contradict His revelations in Scripture.[6]

Among the Andover faculty, Stuart had the greatest impact on Bacon's theological views and intellectual tendencies. Stuart was a stimulating teacher who instilled in his students an enthusiasm for learning, and his weekly conferences were eagerly awaited by Bacon and his classmates. Bacon was particularly impressed by Stuart's knowledge of languages and his willingness to permit an "open field of free investigation" in which students could object to his arguments. Bacon's veneration of the Bible was not shaken by his studies with Stuart. Indeed, though never a Hopkinsian, Bacon praised Stuart for making "Hopkinsianism scholarly and learned without making it irreverent toward the Scriptures on the one hand, or timidly deferential to human authority on the other."[7] Stuart's methods not only underlay Bacon's later questioning of certain orthodox doctrines but also influenced his devotion to historical study, his emphasis on marshaling original documents to buttress and inform the historical narrative, and his attempts to reconcile evangelism and scholarship.

Leonard Woods, a professor of Christian theology, was the other leading light at Andover. As the students' religious counselor, he invited them to discuss their doubts and fears about their own piety and difficulties. Of equal influence was his argument that the evangelical enterprise was more important than any doctrinal system. Given his limited concern about logical difficulties in his system of theology, especially on issues such as free agency and redemption, it is not surprising that Andover produced ministers such as Bacon, who tended to be energetic defenders and promoters rather than precise theological thinkers.[8]

6. Jerry Wayne Brown, *The Rise of Biblical Criticism in America, 1800–1870* (Middletown, Conn., 1969), 48–49, 51–54, 58, 98–102, 169–78; Berk, *Calvinism Versus Democracy,* 182–83; Kuklick, *Churchmen and Philosophers,* 90–91; Woods, *History of the Andover Theological Seminary,* 173–78.

7. Perry, *Childhood, Marriage, and Reform,* 114–15; Roland Bainton, *Yale and the Ministry: A History of Education for the Christian Ministry at Yale from the Founding in 1701* (New York, 1957), 91–92; Bacon, "Moses Stuart," *New Englander,* X (February, 1852), 50; Bacon to Theodore Dwight Woolsey, December 22, 1820, April 9, 1822, in Woolsey Family Papers; Leonard to Alice Bacon, December 16, 1820, sermon of January 11, 1852, in Bacon Family Papers.

8. See Williams, *The Andover Liberals,* 12–13, 17; Perry, *Childhood, Marriage, and Reform,* 123–26; Andover Lecture Notes, April 1822, in Bacon Family Papers; Bacon to Theodore Dwight Woolsey, April 9, 1822, in Woolsey Family Papers.

In the classroom Woods's style differed markedly from Stuart's. While Stuart was a far more stimulating teacher, Woods's courtly manner, cautious use of language, and earnestness deeply influenced Bacon. Woods presented written lectures and, like Stuart, he gave his students the right to interrupt to ask questions and discuss issues. But with Woods there was always the condition attached that no questions or discussion should be pursued in "a disputatious manner, or for the purpose of carrying a particular point."[9]

Bacon had little but praise for Stuart and Woods as teachers. But he was not entirely satisfied with his experience at Andover. He was concerned that at Andover writing style was neglected for "severer studies" and that the seminary lacked a deep sense of piety. Citing the overcrowded conditions and his belief that Yale's Chauncey Goodrich was "four times better" than Andover professors Ebenezer Porter and James Murdoch, during his second year at Andover, Bacon considered transferring to the recently established Yale Theological Seminary. He hoped to study under Nathaniel Taylor, whose sermons he had heard at Center Church while an undergraduate. Thus, he urged Woolsey, then a student at Princeton Theological Seminary, to join him at Yale in order to launch the seminary as "the rallying point—the strong fortress of orthodoxy." But Woolsey believed that Andover was much better managed than Yale, and Bacon, concluding that transferring would be too expensive and that he was too established at Andover, chose to remain there.[10]

Bacon's misgivings about Andover were only a minor factor in bringing on the bouts of melancholy he experienced during his years at the seminary. As a devout evangelical Calvinist, he considered himself a sinner who must seek God's forgiveness in order to be redeemed. He often noted in his diary that he was "heavy in heart," and he could be unsparing in his self-assessment. "I find myself sensual, proud, worldly, light-minded, vain, mean," he recorded in 1824, "one thing today and another tomorrow, but ever loathsome to God and even to myself."[11]

Bacon's despondent moods also stemmed from his family's tragedies and difficulties. He occasionally referred to "a melancholy time" when he thought of his father, but the poverty that he endured throughout his years at Andover was more pervasive and prolonged than his grief. As he informed a childhood friend in 1822, "I am still dependent, I am in debt, in perplexity, completely destitute of money,

9. Frank Hugh Foster, *The Life of Edwards Amasa Park (S.T.D., LL.D.): Abbott Professor, Andover Theological Seminary* (New York, 1936), 57–58; Woods, *History of the Andover Theological Seminary,* 160–61.

10. Bacon to Theodore Dwight Woolsey, December 22, 1820, December 21, 1821, September 16, 1822, Woolsey to Alexander C. Twining, April 24, 1822, in Woolsey Family Papers; Leonard to Alice Bacon, January 26, April 22, 1822, in Bacon Family Papers.

11. See Leonard to Alice Bacon, May 8, 1822, diary entries for July 30, August 31, September 12, 1824, in Bacon Family Papers.

and utterly ignorant how I am to be supported through the remaining year of my residence here." He was painfully aware that people knew he was poor. In a poem titled "My Window Curtains," he took pride in his Yankee heritage but exhibited a keen sensitivity concerning his tattered belongings:

> My window curtains are not made of silk,
> Nor yet of gorgeous calico
>
> . . . .
>
> No, they're made
> Of paper—hangings, not those splendid ones
> From France imported, and all pictured out
> With Grecian ruins and French gallantry
> But genuine Yankee stuff.[12]

Leonard's financial problems were exacerbated by his family's desperate situation. His mother's plight was so extreme that at one point he promised to leave Andover "without hesitation" if she wished him to do so. He continued to feel guilty for pursuing an education "when I might be doing something for you in your multiple difficulties and embarrassments." His mother surely intensified his feelings of guilt by delivering the double message of not wishing to stand in the way of his pursuit of a career while informing him that "if as a widowed destitute mother I have any claims upon you for aid I know it is in your heart to afford it to the utmost of your power."[13]

Bacon's painful separation from his family was made yet more difficult by the death of his youngest brother, Francis, who was killed by a runaway coach in 1822. Leonard was devastated by this tragic event. Although he worked through his "bitterness of grief" by visiting his mother's home several months later and by spending hours at his brother's grave, his inability to attend Susan's wedding in the summer of 1822 underscored his abject poverty and the distance that separated him from his family.[14]

Bacon devoted considerable attention to his siblings, particularly Delia, who lived in Hartford. He visited her as often as he could and counseled her on spiritual matters during a revival in 1821. From his vacation talks with Lyman Beecher, he learned that "serious" times during a revival provided a release for repressed enthusiasm. Leonard attempted to keep this in mind while walking and talking with Delia

---

12. Diary entry for October 5, 1824, Bacon to Samuel W. Collins, August 13, 1822, in Bacon Family Papers; "My Window Curtains," ibid.

13. Leonard to Alice Bacon, July 30, 1822, July 28, 1824, Alice to Leonard Bacon, July 28, 1824, in Bacon Family Papers.

14. Leonard to Susan Bacon Hodges, August 13, 1822, Bacon to Samuel W. Collins, August 13, 1822, Bacon to Alexander C. Twining, November 26, 1822, Alice to Leonard Bacon, June 22, 1822, in Bacon Family Papers.

during his visits to Hartford. When Delia soon returned to her prior state as the revival wound down, he was troubled by the fact that she did not seem to care. But he was far more shocked when she was caught stealing by the Williams family and was sent to her impoverished mother.[15]

Although these tribulations weighed heavily on Leonard, his experience with poverty and tragedy seems to have steeled his determination to overcome obstacles in his path. He subscribed to the widely held notion that adversity strengthens one's character. Affliction, he wrote a boyhood friend named Samuel Collins, "gives to the mind, in many instances, a seriousness and firmness of which it was before in a greater or lesser degree destitute." Even as his father had lain dying in 1817, he added, "I resolved with a kind of despairing enthusiasm, that I would climb that eminence" by becoming a minister.[16]

For all his seriousness and periodic melancholy, Bacon tended to be rather optimistic about his future, especially when he compared his situation with that of a few years earlier or with that of some of his fellow students. He wrote his friend that "in my loftiest wishes, in my wildest dreams, I did not once imagine that in so short a time I should climb so high." He even became adept at resisting the descent into the depths of despair. "I am learning to sit and look at the whirl and uproar of this great world till my head grows giddy and my heart is sick," he wrote Twining, "and then I say to myself, psha! I am growing melancholy and nervous . . . and who knows how soon I may become a hopeless helpless hypochondriac; and then my teeth feel as if I could bite in two a tenpenny nail."[17]

His determination "to do something and to be something" motivated Bacon to "study harder than I ever have before."[18] He also threw himself into the task of developing practical skills and learning the responsibilities required of the clergy. An important part of this training was learning how to write sermons. He found this skill, taught by Porter and Murdoch, difficult to master. "I find," he wrote Collins in 1822, "there is a great deal of 'head-work' to be done before a man is able to write a good or decent sermon" that would "produce the highest possible effect."[19] Indeed, during his long career as a minister he would frequently complain about the arduousness of this task.

During his third year at Andover, Bacon gained practical experience in the art

15. Leonard to Alice Bacon, July 30, 1821, Delia Williams to Alice Bacon, March 8, 1821, Alice to Leonard Bacon, April 16, 1822, in Bacon Family Papers.

16. Dr. Leonard Bacon to Bacon, August 27, 1824, Bacon to Samuel W. Collins, August 13, 1822, in Bacon Family Papers.

17. Bacon to Samuel W. Collins, August 13, 1822, Leonard to Alice Bacon, December 16, 1820, Bacon to Alexander C. Twining, December 16, 1823, in Bacon Family Papers.

18. Leonard to Alice Bacon, January 26, 1822, Bacon Family Papers; Bacon to Theodore Dwight Woolsey, December 25, 1820, in Woolsey Family Papers.

19. Bacon to Samuel W. Collins, December 20, 1822, in Bacon Family Papers.

of writing and delivering sermons by preaching frequently in Andover Chapel. In his sermons he developed a number of themes that were central to the evangelical message. For example, he argued that a friend of the world was an enemy of God, for God's word and people's feelings and opinions necessarily clashed. Moreover, while he praised America's prosperity, social progress, enterprise, and industry, he declared that society was filled with "error and immorality and shameless vice." Thus, he implored Andover students to rouse Christians to greater efforts to convert the world.[20]

Bacon had an opportunity to take the evangelical message beyond the Andover campus in 1823, when he and several other students were sent to Boston to assist ministers in their revival labors. His work, he informed his mother, was "particularly arduous and responsible" because the church where he was sent had no settled minister. Consequently, except for preaching on Sundays, he had to perform all the ministerial functions, including attending meetings and visiting the homes of likely converts. He gained confidence as a result of this experience as well as a month-long stint in a Salem church. "I found I could get along with those things more easily and more to my own satisfaction," he noted, "than my fears had led me to anticipate."[21]

While at Andover Bacon's interests extended far beyond his academic training. Among other things, he remained quite interested in literary pursuits. In his correspondence with the college friends who had formed the Hexahedron club, he often discussed his preferences in literature, which included John Milton, William Shakespeare, Lord Byron, and Sir Walter Scott. He also continued to write poetry for his own enjoyment and for public consumption. A few of his poems were accepted by the Connecticut *Mirror,* a newspaper published in Hartford, and the Boston *Recorder,* a religious newspaper, and he wrote verses for "albums," which were then in fashion among young women. By the early 1820s, however, his infatuation with poetry apparently was waning, in part because he had come to realize that it probably was not his forte.[22]

Yet Bacon by no means ceased to write as an avocation. While he never doubted that he would enter the ministry, he presciently predicted to Woolsey that "I think I shall hereafter become a writer for the public" on matters relating to theology,

20. Sermons of February 19, December 21, 1823, March 24, May 23, 1824, February 13, 1825, Seminary Sermons, 1822–1824, in Bacon Family Papers; Barbara M. Cross (ed.), *The Autobiography of Lyman Beecher* (Cambridge, Mass., 1961), I, 411–12.

21. Leonard to Alice Bacon, February 25, 1823, July 8, 1824, in Bacon Family Papers; Bacon to Theodore Dwight Woolsey, March 5, 1823, in Woolsey Family Papers.

22. Bacon to Theodore Dwight Woolsey, December 21, 1821, March 5, 1823, December 25, 1820, in Woolsey Family Papers; Solomon Stoddard to Bacon, August 18, 1821, Bacon to Alexander C. Twining, June 10, 1824, in Bacon Family Papers; Theodore Dwight Bacon, *Leonard Bacon,* 51–52, 54.

moral philosophy, "or in some department of literature." Some of his numerous extracurricular activities at Andover related directly to his interest in literature. He was extremely active outside the classroom, at one time serving on eight committees. His fellow students, he informed Woolsey, learned of his talent for "making a fuss," and therefore appointed him to every committee that required this talent.[23]

Bacon was a member of the standing committee, and then club president, of the Bartlett Atheneum, founded in 1818 "to improve its members in polite literature and general information." In 1823 he also helped to found the Porter Rhetorical Society, which was established by students "desirous of improvement in sacred eloquence for the purpose of rendering our lives more useful to the world." At its meetings members presented orations, compositions, and poems and debated a broad range of contemporary issues. In his declamations before the society Bacon strongly supported social reform and an aggressive Protestantism. For example, he urged that a strong leader, with the support of "real Christians," improve the school systems, and he especially blamed the Catholic Church for the wars in South America.[24]

Bacon also shared the romantic temperament of many of his generation in a time of economic growth, rising nationalism, and westward expansion at home and mounting challenges to the old order abroad. He and other students, for example, held meetings at Andover in which they made "a great number of flaming and spirit-stirring speeches" and collected money on behalf of Greek independence from the Turks. In an oration titled "In Defense of the Romantic," he also celebrated "great men," such as Caesar, Hannibal, and Christ, who he believed strived for eminence in spite of discouragement and whose imagination transcended reason. As an ambitious young man, he looked toward the day when he would play an important role in converting the world to Christianity. He espoused a muscular Christianity that required knowledgeable men willing to take decisive action. "Heresy," he wrote Twining, "is to be vanquished, the church is to be enlarged, the world is to be reformed, and Beechers not Fishers are to be instruments."[25]

---

23. Bacon to Theodore Dwight Woolsey, September 11, 1822, March 5, 1823, in Woolsey Family Papers.

24. "Records of the Review Association and of the Bartlett Atheneum of the Theological Seminary," 1–2, 27–29, 38, Andover Newton Theological Seminary, Newton Center, Mass.; "Constitution and Records of the Porter Rhetorical Society of the Theological Seminary," 3–4, Andover Newton Theological Seminary, Newton Center, Mass. Declamation on "The *importance* and the *means* of improving common school education," March 18, 1823, "Oration on the importance of Peace Societies," n.d., in Bacon Family Papers.

25. Bacon to Alexander C. Twining, December 16, 1823, "Onward—must be the motto of the man who aspires to distinction of what kind," December 7, 1820, "In defense of the romantic," July 3, 1821, Bacon to Alexander C. Twining, July 7, 1821, in Bacon Family Papers. For a discussion of the evangelical moralists' emphasis on action, not introspection, see Richard Rabinowitz, *The Spiritual Self in Everyday*

This chiliastic message was echoed by many American evangelicals. One of the central tenets of their evangelical system, especially among Congregationalists and Presbyterians, was Samuel Hopkins' contention that one enhanced the glory of God by engaging in disinterested benevolence to uplift the downtrodden and advance the Kingdom of God. At Andover, Woods, Stuart, and Porter served as powerful models for Bacon and his fellow students by playing prominent roles in the founding and operations of the American Education Society, the American Bible Society, the American Board of Commissioners for Foreign Missions, the American Home Missionary Society, and other organizations within the emerging "benevolent empire." During the 1820s and 1830s, these benevolent societies attracted the support of thousands of evangelical Protestants and raised large amounts of money to finance their far-flung operations. From these organizations' inception, numerous Andover graduates became secretaries, agents, and editors in the various benevolent societies. Although Porter warned Andover students against replacing vital religion with the Bible society and other benevolent causes, he emphasized that "the great objects of Christian benevolence, at this day, seem destined . . . to promote the interests of the church."[26]

While a seminary student, Bacon lent his voice and pen to the cause of benevolence. Hoping to earn money, to appeal to a broader evangelical audience, and to advance the cause of religious benevolence, he sent a few of his Andover orations to the *Christian Spectator,* an evangelical magazine published in New Haven. In one of his articles, which he signed "Benevolus," he reminded his readers that "the cause of active beneficence is the cause of God; and those who directly engage in it have so far the honor and happiness of being conformed to the highest standard of moral excellence." The operations of the Bible, missionary, and other benevolent societies as well as the revivals of religion, he added, underscored the fact that "the jubilee of the church is not far distant."[27]

During his vacations in 1821 and 1823, Bacon furthered the cause of disinterested benevolence by working for the Boston Society for the Moral and Religious Instruction of the Poor. This organization, like similar societies founded in New York and other cities in an era of heavy immigration, rapid urbanization, and indus-

Life: The Transformation of Personal Religious Experience in Nineteenth-Century New England (Boston, 1989), 107–108.

26. See Woods, *History of the Andover Theological Seminary,* 199–201; Elizabeth Twadell, "The American Tract Society, 1814–1860," *Church History,* XV (1946), 117–19; Ebenezer Porter, *Signs of the Times. A Sermon Preached in the Chapel of the Theological Seminary, Andover, on the Public Fast, April 3, 1823* (Andover, 1823), 6–7.

27. Leonard Bacon, "Motives to Active Benevolence," *Quarterly Christian Spectator,* IV (December, 1822), 617–18, 620–21; Vol. 13 of dissertations, presented December 11, 1821, in "Records of the Society of Inquiry Respecting Missions," Andover Newton Theological Seminary, Newton Center, Mass.

trialization, sought to redeem the poor and eradicate vice. These objects were pursued by preaching to sailors, unskilled laborers, and other groups in the Sabbath schools, almshouses, and churches, and by lobbying for the regulation of tippling shops. While these evangelical moralists held the "vast accumulated wealth" partly responsible for the city's vices and realized that employment was vital for individual self-control, they were primarily intent upon imposing social control and order on the "vicious portion" of the community.[28]

While working for the society, Bacon held several meetings a week and visited the poor in their homes. In visiting the Asylum of Female Orphans and the city jail, he informed his mother, he hoped to save the poor from "infamy and wretchedness." Nevertheless, he found the work difficult and exhausting and wondered how much of a difference it would make in people's lives. Indeed, at the time he seemed less motivated to do good than to earn money to live on, confiding to Collins that he chose to work for the society "especially because I am to receive *twenty dollars* for my services."[29]

Following his stint with the society, Bacon presented a report to its managers, which he then read to his professors. In it he chose to emphasize the value of his visits to homes, Sabbath schools, sailors' hospitals, jails, and the Penitent Female Refuge, his conversations with the poor, and his distribution of religious tracts and Bibles. He deleted any reference to the hostility that had greeted his efforts and exulted in finding "some gems of heaven beneath the rubbish of poverty and wretchedness."[30]

Much of Bacon's involvement in benevolent causes took place on campus. He devoted particular energy to the Society of Inquiry Respecting Missions, which had been established by students in 1811 "to devise and prosecute measures for the extension of Christianity, and in subserviency to this, to acquire and disseminate a knowledge of the literature, morals, and religion of different countries, and of the causes which operate on the moral improvement of mankind." From the foreign missionary movement's inception, the American Board of Commissioners for For-

28. Leonard to Alice Bacon, October 3, 1821, February 27, 1823, in Bacon Family Papers; Seventh Annual Report, pp. 1–3, "Records of the Boston Society for the Moral and Religious Instruction of the Poor," in William Jenks Papers, New England Historic Genealogical Society, Boston, Mass. For a treatment of a similar society in New York City, see Raymond A. Mohl, "Humanitarianism in the Preindustrial City: The New York Society for the Prevention of Pauperism, 1817–1823," *Journal of American History*, LVIII (1970), 576–99.

29. Leonard to Alice Bacon, October 3, 1821, Bacon to Alexander C. Twining, October 9, 1821, Bacon to Samuel W. Collins, October 27, 1821, in Bacon Family Papers.

30. Leonard to Alice Bacon, May 27, 1823, in Bacon Family Papers; Reports of December 27, 1821 and 1823, "Records of the Boston Society for the Moral and Religious Instruction of the Poor," in William Jenks Papers.

eign Missions was closely connected with Andover. This society had been founded in 1810 to serve as a vehicle for preserving orthodoxy at home and joining the clergy and the public in a religious crusade of global proportions. With the founding of the Society of Inquiry, a secret society whose officers carefully screened prospective initiates to make certain that only committed evangelicals were admitted, Andover became the focal point of interest in foreign missions. The society represented an early effort to institutionalize the energies unleashed by the Second Great Awakening, and during the first ten years after the commissioners' board was created all but one of its missionaries were Andover graduates.[31]

Bacon quite naturally was attracted to the Society of Inquiry. Not only had his parents been missionaries, but as a boy in Hartford he had listened to a native Hawaiian plead for assistance from missionaries, and his father had introduced him to the speaker as one consecrated to the work of Christ. Moreover, while a student at Yale he had witnessed the departure to Hawaii of the first group of missionaries sent there by American evangelicals. During his years at Andover, he played a prominent role in the Society of Inquiry, serving on several committees and as vice president. One of the committees he headed was responsible for collecting and publishing missionary hymns for use in monthly concerts as well as missionary and Bible association meetings. His *Hymns and Sacred Songs, for the Monthly Concert,* to which he contributed three of his own hymns, was one of the earliest attempts to give voice to the fervor for missions that was then sweeping the evangelical ranks. Shortly after the book's first publication in 1823, the American Board of Commissioners for Foreign Missions printed a thousand additional copies; years later Frederic M. Bird, an expert on hymnology, termed it "a landmark in the history of American hymnology, and perhaps of missions, too."[32]

By far the most important of Bacon's activities within the Society of Inquiry related to free blacks, slavery, and colonization. These efforts signaled the beginning of what would be the most significant reform and benevolent endeavors of his life. He would be a leading northern antislavery colonizationist prior to the mid-1830s

---

31. "Constitution of the Society of Inquiry Respecting Missions," 3, in "Records of the Society of Inquiry Respecting Missions"; William R. Hutchison, *Errand to the World: American Protestant Thought and Foreign Missions* (Chicago, 1987), 7–9, 43–46; Clifton Jackson Phillips, *Protestant America and the Pagan World: The First Half-Century of the American Board of Commissioners for Foreign Missions, 1810–1860* (Cambridge, Mass., 1968), 3–11.

32. Leonard Woolsey Bacon, "The Services of Leonard Bacon to African Colonization" *Liberia,* I (November, 1899), 1; Minutes of July 2, September 4, 1822, April 9, 16, 1823, in "Records of the Society of Inquiry Respecting Missions"; Bacon to Theodore Dwight Woolsey, March 5, 1823, in Woolsey Family Papers; Leonard to Alice Bacon, September 21, 1823, Rufus Anderson to Bacon, March 12, 1823, in Bacon Family Papers; *Independent,* May 5, 1881; Henry Wilder Foote, *Three Centuries of American Hymnody* (Cambridge, Mass., 1940), 214.

and a powerful voice for the moderate antislavery position during the 1840s and 1850s. Throughout these decades, as well as during the Reconstruction era, he also would write widely on race relations in the United States.

Following an appeal to the Society of Inquiry by a member from Kentucky, who urged cooperation between northern and southern Christians for the elevation of African Americans, Bacon was appointed to a committee of four charged with inquiring "whether this society ought, at present, to make any exertion in *favour of the black population of our country*" and recommending the means for achieving the objective. The committee's report, which Bacon wrote and presented to the Colonization Committee (consisting of twenty of the most zealous members of the Society of Inquiry), reflected widely held racial assumptions of white Americans. For nearly all whites, the belief that blacks were a degraded group who threatened the stability of society and could not hope to improve their condition in America was, as Winthrop Jordan notes, "a given, a timeless verity applicable to all societies in all ages." This pervasive racial prejudice served to perpetuate a system of draconian laws and segregation in both the North and the South.[33]

Bacon's contact with poor blacks in Boston while working for the Society for the Moral and Religious Instruction of the Poor, as well as his awareness of the mounting alarm among whites concerning free blacks, helped to shape his negative image of that group. Yet his observation of the conditions that confronted free blacks also elicited his sympathy for their plight. Moreover, he was influenced by an 1820 editorial by Jeremiah Evarts, secretary of the commissioners' board, in the evangelical magazine *Panoplist and Missionary Herald,* which chastised Christians for doing nothing to elevate African Americans.[34]

In his report to the Society of Inquiry, Bacon articulated themes that he would reiterate during the next several years. He drew largely from the recent report of the Boston Prison Discipline Society, which pointed to the disproportionate number

33. Minutes of February 18, 1823, in "Records of the Society of Inquiry Respecting Missions"; Winthrop D. Jordan, *White over Black: American Attitudes Toward the Negro, 1550–1812* (Chapel Hill, 1968), 569; J. Earl Thompson, Jr., "Lyman Beecher's Long Road to Conservative Abolitionism," *Church History,* XLII (1973), 94–95. On many colonizationists' concern about order and virtue in society, see David M. Streifford, "The American Colonization Society: An Application of Republican Ideology to Early Antebellum Reform," *Journal of Southern History,* XLV (1979), 201–220. The racial caste system in the North is discussed in Leonard P. Curry, *The Free Black in Urban America, 1800–1850: The Shadow of the Dream* (Chicago, 1981), 81–85; Leon Litwack, *North of Slavery: The Negro in the Free States, 1790–1860* (Chicago, 1961), 153–75.

34. Report of December 17, 1821, "Records of the Boston Society for the Moral and Religious Instruction of the Poor," in William Jenks Papers; Curry, *The Free Black in Urban America,* 82; Jeremiah Evarts, "On the Condition of the Blacks in This Country," *Panoplist and Missionary Herald,* XVI (June, 1820), 241; Bacon to Ralph R. Gurley, February 28, 1823, in "Records of the Society of Inquiry Respecting Missions."

of northern blacks in prisons and poorhouses; thus, he concluded that African Americans, especially in the northern cities, were "wandering like outcasts and foreigners" and filling the jails and asylums while largely being absent from the schools and churches. Although Bacon was not certain precisely how to apportion blame for the plight of African Americans, he conceded that white prejudice was largely responsible for the fact that blacks constituted a separate caste in America. Equally important, he, like Ralph R. Gurley, secretary of the American Colonization Society, acknowledged that "peculiar circumstances or powers of the individuals" permitted some blacks to acquire respectability and piety in this country. In the final analysis, however, he believed that African Americans were "degraded without any proper means of improvement, or any incentive to exertion."[35]

Bacon held slavery largely responsible for the degradation of African Americans. His antislavery sentiments derived from several sources. Both Stuart and Woods were critical of slavery. Moreover, in the late 1810s Rufus King, John Kenrick, George Bourne, and other antislavery spokesmen argued that the temporary acceptance of slavery in 1787 must not be allowed to subvert the principles of the Declaration of Independence or the preamble to the Constitution. Bacon was also influenced by Jonathan Edwards the Younger's sermon on slavery and the slave trade, the British Parliament's debate on slavery, and the Presbyterian Church's condemnation of the system in 1818.[36]

In addition, the Missouri debates did much to reawaken the somewhat dormant concern of New Englanders about slavery. Bacon acknowledged that a series of essays by Jeremiah Evarts during and immediately after the debates was especially influential in shaping his views; these articles, in fact, were the inspiration for the Society of Inquiry to consider the subject. Evarts' pieces are illustrative not only of the rising antislavery sentiment of the time but also of the lack of a definite objective among the antislavery forces. Evarts was impressed with the magnitude of the evil but had no remedy or clear solution. He condemned the internal slave trade, opposed any slavery in the new territories, claimed that slaveholders sinned in consenting to the iniquities of past generations, and warned that the system's cruelty

35. Report of February 18, 1823, pp. 1–3, Vol. 16 of Dissertations, Bacon to Ralph R. Gurley, February 28, 1823, in "Records of the Society of Inquiry Respecting Missions." Bacon reiterated these sentiments on many occasions in the early and middle 1820s. See Leonard Bacon, "The Reports of the American Society for Colonizing the Free People of Colour of the United States, 1818, 19, 20, 21, 22, 23," *Christian Spectator*, V (September, 1823), 485–94, and (October, 1823), 540–51; Leonard Bacon, *A Plea for Africa; Delivered in New-Haven, July 4th, 1825* (New Haven, 1825), 12–13.

36. See Thompson, "Abolitionism and Theological Education at Andover," 251, 253n; David Brion Davis, *The Problem of Slavery in the Age of Revolution, 1770–1823* (Ithaca, 1975), 332–33; Bacon, *Slavery Discussed in Occasional Essays, From 1833 to 1846* (New York, 1846), iii; Leonard Woolsey Bacon, "The Services of Leonard Bacon to African Colonization," I, 2–3.

eventually would provoke slaves to violent revenge. He also urged northerners to speak out boldly on the slavery issue and maintained that the Missouri Compromise effectively sanctioned slavery.[37]

Notwithstanding his sharp criticism of slavery, Evarts was unwilling to call for decisive action. Because he feared that any attempt to achieve immediate emancipation would produce a massacre in the South, he warned northerners to proceed with "prudence and caution," though the fundamental principle of freedom should never be abandoned. In the final analysis, Evarts' articles, which concluded with a vague endorsement of gradual emancipation, were little more than a call to righteous indignation and serious thought.[38]

Bacon's report clearly reflected Evarts' influence. The institution, he asserted, was "an immense moral and political evil" that impoverished the South, fostered the atrocities of the slave trade, and kept millions of slaves in ignorance. Writing in the wake of the Denmark Vesey slave plot in Charleston, South Carolina, he also warned of a second St. Domingo in which vengeful slaves would destroy the South but, in so doing, would unite white Americans in a concerted effort to exterminate blacks. If the slavery issue were debated and attempts were made to stem the expansion of the system, he stated, the institution might be abolished, or at least its evils would be alleviated.[39]

Yet Bacon presaged a lifelong commitment to moderation on the slavery issue by urging a cautious approach to the question. His caution stemmed in part from his fear, which was shared by many antislavery Americans in the wake of the Missouri debates, that the slavery issue might rend the fabric of the nation. "The excitement required," he warned, "is not a momentary, feverish, half-delirious excitement like that produced by the agitation of the Missouri question—it must be something more calm and permanent." Pointing to the "indignant invective" that surrounded the slavery issue in both sections, he called for an antislavery effort that would "unite the patriotic and benevolent in all parts of the country."[40]

Bacon's reluctance to urge decisive action against slavery was also a product of his Andover training. His professors supported social improvement, not radical challenges to the social order. Stuart, for example, called upon Christians to work to usher in the millennium, but he also warned that "anything in word or action which tends to excite civil discord and foment seditious spirit is hostile to the pre-

37. *Christian Union,* December 9, 1874; Jeremiah Evarts, "The Missouri Question," *Panoplist and Missionary Herald,* XVI (February, 1820), 62–72; Evarts, "On the Condition of the Blacks in This Country," 241–42, 481–83, 493–94.

38. Evarts, "The Missouri Question," 59; Evarts, "On the Condition of the Blacks in This Country," 241–42, 485–89, 492.

39. Volume 16 of dissertations, 3–11, in "Records of the Society of Inquiry Respecting Missions."

40. *Ibid.,* 11–15.

cepts and the spirit of Christ[ian] religion." Thus, the message that Bacon received from his professors, as well as such influential benevolent activists as Lyman Beecher and Jedidiah Morse, was that there were limits to reform and that the end did not justify every means, even when dealing with a sinful institution such as slavery.[41]

Bacon concluded that any attempt to effect a speedy end of slavery, or even to reform the system by instructing the mass of slaves, quite possibly would result in a race war. While he, much like Evarts, was practically paralyzed by the vastness of the task, he also urged a "great effort" against the system.[42] In writing this report, as well as on numerous other occasions during subsequent decades, he struggled to find an acceptable balance between pragmatism and principle on the race and slavery issues. He frequently expressed his abhorrence of slavery and his desire that it be eradicated as soon as possible, but then retreated in the face of "practical" considerations that he thought were more urgent, at least for the foreseeable future, than the achievement of what he believed was just and right.

In fact, his options for solving the problem were severely limited. Given his unwillingness either to abandon an ill-defined gradualist approach or to espouse fundamental rights for African Americans, the logical choice for Bacon was colonization. Not only were his professors early proponents of repatriation but Samuel J. Mills, a founder of the Society of Inquiry, had become a martyr to the cause and an inspiration for Andover students when he died off the coast of Africa in 1818 while serving as an agent for the American Colonization Society. Moreover, as the only organization in the 1820s capable of uniting conservative antislavery groups and evangelical activists, the society attracted the support of nearly all the major religious denominations. For many Americans the ACS represented a conscientious alternative to acquiescing in the existence of slavery and a relatively painless means of dealing with a complex moral and social problem. As a multi-interest organization it promised benefits for its diverse constituencies: eventual emancipation, without altering the basic structure of American society, for those who disliked slavery and feared civil war and insurrection; the repatriation of degraded free blacks for those who wished to uplift them as well as to protect the classical republican virtues of order, morality, and harmony; the launching of a holy enterprise for those who hoped to extend Christianity and civilization to Africa; and ridding southern society of a "troublesome presence" for those southerners who hoped to strengthen slavery.[43]

41. Stuart, quoted in Perry, *Childhood, Marriage, and Reform*, 139.

42. Volume 16 of dissertations, 16–17, in "Records of the Society of Inquiry Respecting Missions."

43. Robert Cholerton Senior, "New England Congregationalists and the Anti-Slavery Movement, 1830–1860" (Ph.D. dissertation, Yale University, 1954), 27, 44–45; Solomon Peck to Bacon, n.d., in Bacon Family Papers; Thompson, "Abolitionism and Theological Education at Andover," 250, 260; *Memoirs of American Missionaries, Formerly Connected with the Society of Inquiry Respecting Missions, In the*

Bacon's endorsement of the ACS reflected many dimensions of the society's varied agenda. The movement, he declared, would benefit the South by gradually ridding it of an institution that damaged its economy and threatened it with insurrection. At the same time, the North would no longer have to contend with "ignorant, disorderly, wretched" free blacks. While he conceded that repatriation was a "less magnificent object" than abolition, he hoped that the colonization of free blacks would encourage masters to free their slaves for shipment to Africa; in this way the system eventually would be "utterly abolished." Like Ralph R. Gurley and many other New England colonizationists, Bacon chose to emphasize the benevolent and missionary dimensions of the American Colonization Society's message. In espousing the concept of "environmental racism," he insisted that colonization would give African Americans "all the privileges of humanity in the land for which the God of nature designed them." In the spirit of Samuel J. Mills, he also viewed colonization as the means of civilizing and Christianizing Africa, with "the shadows of heathenism fleeing away" as fifty million Africans were converted. It was no wonder, he exclaimed, "that faith should be staggered, and benevolence overwhelmed at the prospect of a consummation so magnificent."[44]

While he prepared his report for the Society of Inquiry, Bacon maintained a regular correspondence with Gurley. The board of managers of the ACS was so impressed by Bacon's correspondence that it called a special meeting for June in Washington, where it hoped to devise means of broadening the base of the ACS and bringing added revenue into its nearly empty treasury. The board clearly coveted the support of the Andover students, for the school was the principal recruiting center for the foreign missionary movement.[45]

Bacon and Solomon Peck were chosen by the Society of Inquiry to attend the Washington meeting. En route to Washington they spent a week in Philadelphia conferring with E. B. Caldwell and Francis Scott Key, both prominent leaders in the cause, as well as leaders of the Presbyterian and Episcopal churches. The managers of the society warmly welcomed him and Peck and listened to their suggestions "with

---

Andover Theological Seminary (Boston, 1833), 29; Philip J. Staudenraus, *The African Colonization Movement, 1816–1865* (New York, 1961), 18–19. Historians have emphasized various aspects of the diverse colonization message. See, for example, Lawrence J. Friedman, "Purifying the White Man's Country: The American Colonization Society Reconsidered, 1816–1840," *Societas,* VI (1976), 1–24; Staudenraus, *The African Colonization Movement,* vii–viii, 15, 18–19, 22, 28–29; Streifford, "The American Colonization Society," 201–20.

44. Volume 16 of dissertations, 26–32, in "Records of the Society of Inquiry Respecting Missions." For Gurley's emphasis on the benevolent dimension of colonization, see Staudenraus, *The African Colonization Movement,* 117–18.

45. Ralph R. Gurley to Bacon, April 21, May 5, 1823, in "Records of the Society of Inquiry Respecting Missions"; Solomon Peck to Bacon, May 13, 1823, in Bacon Family Papers.

a far greater degree of respect and deference than we had any reason to anticipate." Noting that it was "greatly indebted" to Bacon for his recommendations, the board appointed him assistant to the Reverend Chester Wright of Vermont as the society's temporary agent for New England.[46]

The board acted on a number of Bacon's recommendations, including the establishment of a periodical, the appointment of traveling agents, and the coordination of a network of auxiliaries. Although the managers wished to believe that the ACS's fundamental problem was financial, not administrative, they also accepted his suggestion that the society be remodeled as a self-sustaining benevolent organization. The society indeed was in financial straits, but there was no consensus on a specific plan of action. The debate centered on whether it should lobby for federal aid or continue to rely on individual donations and create a system of agents and auxiliaries. Although only twenty-one years old and new to the cause as an activist, Bacon now stood forth, with Gurley, as a leading spokesman for the latter approach. He bluntly traced the society's problems to the managers' "want of that energy and business-like regularity of operations." Yet despite the board's encouragement and praise for Bacon, it cited financial problems in tabling his motion to charter at least four emigrant ships in 1823 and rejecting his proposal to create a special school where future colonists could learn how to build a colony and teach Christianity to Africans.[47]

Bacon's concerns about the viability of the American Colonization Society were further aroused by a conversation with David Hale, a leader of the Massachusetts Society for the Suppression of the Slave Trade, soon after Bacon returned to Andover. While he did not place much stock in Hale's complaint that the ACS relied excessively on the "empty influence" of Henry Clay, Andrew Jackson, and other southerners, he was very disturbed by Hale's assertion that the ACS had owed the Massachusetts group two thousand dollars for over two years. Thus, he informed Gurley that the debt must be paid immediately if the society hoped to raise money in New England.[48]

Nevertheless, Bacon remained steadfast in his support for the cause, urging professors at Yale to establish a state colonization society and touring New England

46. Leonard to Alice Bacon, May 27, June 30, 1823, in Bacon Family Papers; report by Peck and Bacon, June 23, 1823, in "Records of the Society of Inquiry Respecting Missions"; *Sixth Annual Report of the American Society for Colonizing the Free People of Colour of the United States* (Washington, D.C., 1823), 29–30.

47. Bacon to Ralph R. Gurley, July 12, 1823, Ralph R. Gurley to Peck and Bacon, June 6, 1823, Ralph R. Gurley to Bacon, July 12, 1823, in "Records of the Society of Inquiry Respecting Missions"; *Sixth Annual Report of the American Society for Colonizing the Free People of Colour of the United States,* 29–30; Staudenraus, *The African Colonization Movement,* 77–78.

48. Bacon to Ralph R. Gurley, July 12, 22, 1823, Bacon to John Tappan, September 2, 1824, in "Records of the Society of Inquiry Respecting Missions."

with Chester Wright in July, 1823. Because many New Englanders suspected that colonization would serve to strengthen the slave system and believed that the repatriation scheme was unrealistic, however, these efforts succeeded in raising little money, and no new auxiliaries were established. At the same time, though Bacon's studies forced him to decline Gurley's offer to serve as the society's agent for all of the northern states, his report to the Society of Inquiry was published. In articles that appeared in the *Christian Spectator* he also emphatically denied that the ACS was a missionary society or a society for suppressing the slave trade, for the improvement of blacks, or for the abolition of slavery. Rather, he considered it a society for establishing a colony in Africa, which represented the only effective means of elevating African Americans.[49]

During his senior year at Andover, Bacon therefore had moved quickly into the inner circle of the colonization movement. But as graduation approached he had to think seriously about embarking on a career. One option was to accept the American Colonization Society's offer to live in Washington, where he would serve as an agent and assist in managing the periodical soon to be established. He was tempted by this offer, believing that he had "that turn of mind, those habits of thought, those intellectual dispositions which qualify a man (so far as they go) for that particular kind of usefulness."[50]

Bacon ultimately rejected this offer, in part because he wished to be settled as a minister. Indeed, he was considered at this time for Nathaniel Taylor's old position at Center Church in New Haven. But Leonard Woods had other ideas. Arguing that Bacon was young and could avoid going further into debt by preaching occasionally, he urged Leonard to remain at Andover to prepare for a professorship or a similar literary position. Bacon believed that "a literary life appears more pleasant in prospect than any other," but he feared that Woods and others had "mistaken the character of my mind." He also had previously considered the possibility of taking a small parish in Connecticut or of becoming a missionary in the West. Confused and undecided, he turned to Joel Hawes, Woods, his uncle, and his mother for advice. Ultimately, he decided to remain at Andover for another year in the capacity of a resident licentiate. This plan, he wrote Woolsey, was "a very respectable one."[51]

Bacon was offered this position because of his sterling academic record and the

---

49. Bacon to Ralph R. Gurley, July 12, 1823, Ralph R. Gurley to Bacon, July 28, September 5, October 8, November 12, 1823, April 18, 1824, in "Records of the Society of Inquiry Respecting Missions"; Ralph R. Gurley to Bacon, January 9, 1824, in Bacon Family Papers; Bacon, "The Reports of the American Society for Colonizing the Free People of Colour of the United States," 485–94, 540–51.

50. Leonard to Alice Bacon, June 30, 1823, in Bacon Family Papers.

51. Leonard to Alice Bacon, April 22, 1822, June 30, July 22, September 21, 1823, Dr. Leonard Bacon to Bacon, January 16, July 15, 1823, in Bacon Family Papers; Bacon to Theodore Dwight Woolsey, July 29, 1823, in Woolsey Family Papers.

respect his professors had for him. Indeed, he was chosen to present the valedictory address at his commencement exercises. In his speech he delivered a paean to Christian benevolence, lauding it as action motivated by "all that is kind and generous in humanity." As he and his classmates were about to engage in "a high and arduous career," he was confident that they could enlarge the Kingdom of God.[52]

As a licentiate funded by the Abbott Foundation, Bacon developed a course of study and instructed classes in the Department of Rhetoric, assisted Porter, and preached occasionally on campus. For these duties he received room, board, library privileges, and tuition. In addition, he preached for several weeks at churches in Salem and other communities in the area. In all, he believed that his work was beneficial in that it allowed him to pay off some of his debts and to serve "a brief apprenticeship."[53]

While serving as a licentiate, Bacon received an offer to become pastor of a new church in Boston. Once more he agonized over the decision, consulting with both family and friends. While he preferred Boston to all other cities, he decided to postpone any commitment to the church until the end of 1824, and then only if no better opportunity arose. His stated reasons reveal much about what he wished for—and disliked—in a pastorate and what he felt qualified to do. He informed his mother that the Boston church's expectation that he go door to door "beating up for recruiting, to come to my meeting for the Sabbath," was work "for which of all labors I am least qualified." He also feared that the Boston position would provide little opportunity for using his talent for writing and speaking, which his professors, especially Porter, praised so highly. He confided to Woolsey that if he accepted the position, "I can never become a writer or a scholar. I must be little more than a mere haranguer and populum; for you know that a city minister has no leisure and of course no opportunity for improvement." Given his penchant for scholarly activity, it is not surprising that he was even willing to consider an offer to be editor of a religious or literary magazine upon completing his licentiate.[54]

Another offer by the American Colonization Society further complicated the situation for Bacon. This time it requested that he come to Washington to serve as general agent, secretary, and editor of the *African Repository and Colonial Journal*

---

52. *Catalogue of the Professors and Students of the Theological Seminary, Andover, Massachusetts, December, 1823* (Andover, 1823); Valedictory Address, 1823, in Bacon Family Papers.

53. Bacon to Theodore Dwight Woolsey, January 5, 1824, in Woolsey Family Papers; Leonard to Alice Bacon, November 15, 1823, Bacon to Alexander C. Twining, December 16, 1823, in Bacon Family Papers.

54. Bacon to Dr. Leonard Bacon, January 26, February 4, 1824, Joel Hawes to Bacon, February 4, 1824, Solomon Peck to Bacon, May 7, 1824, Alice to Leonard Bacon, January 24, 1824, Leonard to Alice Bacon, March 7, 1824, in Bacon Family Papers; Bacon to Theodore Dwight Woolsey, January 5, 1824, in Woolsey Family Papers.

while Gurley traveled to Africa. Gurley wrote that "no one can superintend this, better than yourself," and Bacon informed his mother that in many respects the position would "suit my disposition and feelings better than any other in the world." But once again he declined. In doing so, he made clear that his highest priorities were the church and his family and that his mother did not want him to live outside the Northeast.[55]

This clarity regarding his priorities, however, did not dispel the uncertainty about his future. If anything, as 1824 passed he became increasingly anxious. He had preached in a number of churches in the Boston area, but only one offered him a position. Moreover, he fretted about having no prospect of marrying. As each of his friends married, he complained to Collins, "I bid him Godspeed, and my own prospects of embarkation grow fainter and darker." He feared that he would become

> A stern and vinegar looking bachelor,
> Dyspeptic, disappointed, crabbed, cross,
> Scorned by the scornful, pitied by the kind.

This, he admitted to Collins, made him "one of the bluest and melancholic single gentlemen of your acquaintance." Indeed, his Uncle Leonard worried that Bacon's tendency to "indulge in . . . gloomy forebodings" would ruin his health and thereby deprive him of an honorable and useful place in the world.[56]

An offer to remain at Andover for another year as an assistant teacher in the rhetoric department only exacerbated the problem for Bacon. It would, he wrote in his diary, provide an opportunity to improve his preaching and critical faculties, to be in contact with "the first men that the country affords," and to write for the public. Yet he feared that another year at Andover would further delay his entrance into a career and worried that a professorship would provide an inadequate salary and would not suit his talents. He agreed with Woolsey's advice that the "retired" life of a professor devoted to "silent and inoperative study" was not for him. "I must be active," he wrote Woolsey, with considerable bravado, "I must keep moving; I must have immediate influence; every stroke that I strike must tell; or I am at a stand."[57]

Even Bacon's decision to travel to Hartford in September, 1824, to be ordained as an evangelist by the North Congregational Association of Hartford County did not signal a definite career choice. While he had long thought of following in his

55. Ralph R. Gurley to Bacon, June 24, 1824, in "Records of the Society of Inquiry Respecting Missions"; Leonard to Alice Bacon, July 8, 1824, in Bacon Family Papers.

56. Bacon to Samuel W. Collins, August 17, 1824, Dr. Leonard Bacon to Bacon, August 27, 1824, in Bacon Family Papers.

57. Diary entries for September 12, 13, 15, 1824, in Bacon Family Papers; Bacon to Theodore Dwight Woolsey, December 29, 1824, in Woolsey Family Papers.

father's footsteps, he in fact was unwilling to accept a missionary post unless he was no longer deeply in debt—a situation that was unlikely to develop in the near future. What ultimately may have clarified his career choices was the advice offered by Professor Porter, who told him that "preaching preaching preaching is the business" for him. He accepted Porter's advice, writing Woolsey, "There is no employment in the world that seems to me at this moment more pleasant than preaching the gospel to an intelligent and affectionate people."[58]

Indeed, the day after his ordination as an evangelist Bacon was invited to preach at Center Church in New Haven. Moses Stuart, who had been pastor of the church prior to becoming a professor at Andover, strongly recommended him for the post. Bacon preached two Sundays there, then traveled to western New York to visit his family. The congregation was generally impressed by his performance but was in no hurry to extend a call. Both Stuart and Nathaniel Taylor had left the church to accept professorships of theology, and during the two years since Taylor's departure a number of men who either were or would soon become eminent clergymen—including Edward Beecher, Albert Barnes, Samuel H. Cox, and Carlos Wilcox—had been invited to preach at Center Church.[59]

Wishing to make certain that they chose the right man, the members asked Bacon to preach a total of seven Sundays, instead of the four that he was originally scheduled to preach. Bacon himself had some doubts. Given the close scrutiny, he was anxious. More important, there clearly was some opposition from those who thought his preaching was "not enough 'in the revival style.'" Woolsey, who was then in New Haven, also reported that some members considered Bacon too young and independent, while others desired a settled minister. Yet Woolsey believed that Bacon's detractors were reasonable men, and Stuart assured him that support within the Ecclesiastical Society of Center Church was "much greater" than when he was settled there.[60]

Although the church ultimately called Bacon to be its pastor, Stuart's assessment of the congregation's mood was excessively optimistic; the Ecclesiastical Society held two meetings before it issued the call, with twenty dissenting votes out of eighty-eight cast, and offered him a salary of one thousand dollars. Bacon was con-

58. Leonard to Alice Bacon, September 30, 1824, in Bacon Family Papers; Bacon to Theodore Dwight Woolsey, July 20, December 29, 1824, in Woolsey Family Papers.

59. Diary entry for October 5, 1824, in Bacon Family Papers; *Leonard Bacon: Pastor of the First Church in New Haven,* 76–77, 190; Leonard Woolsey Bacon, *A Discourse Delivered in the Memorial Presbyterian Church, Detroit; Michigan; On the Occasion of the Unveiling of a Tablet, in Memory of the Late Leonard Bacon, D.D., December 24, 1882* (n.p., 1882).

60. Theodore Dwight Bacon, *Leonard Bacon,* 62–63; Leonard to Alice Bacon, December 28, 1824, diary entries for November 9, 30, December 30, 1824, in Bacon Family Papers; Theodore Dwight Woolsey to Bacon, December 19, 1824, in Woolsey Family Papers.

vinced that he must accept the offer. "We are to be on the lookout," he confided in his diary, "and when Providence gives us a fair opportunity to do something, do it; if it promises a magnificent result, do it." Whatever fears he had of getting along with the prominent men of Center Church, he wrote Woolsey, came not so much from a sense of inadequacy as from his "constitutional and habitual lightness of speech and demeanor," for which some of his friends had long chided him. In the final analysis, he believed that the church and New Haven would open the "door of usefulness," with Yale serving as an inspiration for study and the city as a pivotal point between New England and New York City. It would be his "duty," he asserted, "as I shall have the opportunity, to lead on matters cautiously but steadily to a consummation so desirable." Thus, even before he accepted the call, he had far broader horizons in mind than simply serving as pastor of Center Church. Having made his decision, he pronounced himself "as happy, as lighthearted, as buoyant with life and hope, as I was in my childhood."[61] He now embarked on what would prove to be a lifetime relationship with Center Church as well as a notable career in reform, religious benevolence, journalism, and literature.

61. *Leonard Bacon: Pastor of the First Church in New Haven,* 13–14, 16–17; Theodore Dwight Bacon, *Leonard Bacon,* 64–65; Bacon to Theodore Dwight Woolsey, December 29, 1824, in Woolsey Family Papers; diary entries for January 1, 15, 1825, in Bacon Family Papers.

4

CENTER CHURCH AND THE COLONIZATION MOVEMENT

ON the eve of his installation as pastor of Center Church, Bacon was subjected to a grueling examination of his theological views. In a confrontation that foreshadowed the bitter debates among Connecticut Congregationalists in the 1830s, the council, moderated by President Jeremiah Day of Yale, pitted supporters and detractors of Nathaniel Taylor's modification of orthodox Calvinist doctrines against each other. Although the examination left Bacon exhausted, "partly by excitement and partly by effort," he managed to answer the council's questions to the satisfaction of both parties. He also had to contend with church politics in selecting a person to deliver the ordination sermon. Because some members of Center Church were still angry at Moses Stuart for leaving the church fifteen years earlier to teach at Andover, Bacon played it safe by selecting Joel Hawes, his boyhood pastor in Hartford. All turned out well. Taylor's charge brought many in the audience to tears, and Hawes's sermon, which urged Bacon to deliver sermons that were "*warm* and weighty," was considered a "masterpiece" by Bacon.[1]

As Bacon listened to Hawes's friendly admonitions, he could not help but be impressed by the sight of those assembled for his ordination. Though the congregation included a number of farmers, artisans, and small shopkeepers, many of the political, business, intellectual, and professional elite of the city and the state also attended services here. Among the church's 550 members were Noah Webster, the noted lexicographer; James Hillhouse, a United States senator and perhaps the most prominent man in New Haven; the family of Eli Whitney, the renowned inventor

1. Bacon to Benjamin B. Wisner, March 11, 1825, diary entry for March 9, 1825, Bacon to Alexander C. Twining, January 7, 1825, in Bacon Family Papers; *Leonard Bacon: Pastor of the First Church in New Haven,* 20–21; Joel Hawes, *To Commend Truth to the Conscience the Object of a Faithful Minister. A Sermon Delivered March 9th, 1825, at the Installation of the Rev. Leonard Bacon, as Pastor of the First Congregational Church and Society in New Haven* (New Haven, 1825), 19.

and businessman who had died only two months earlier; Dennis Kimberly, Seth Staples, and Samuel J. Hitchcock, leaders of the Connecticut bar; Jonathan Knight, a noted surgeon; Henry Trowbridge, founder of the city's leading mercantile firm; Samuel F. B. Morse, later the inventor of the telegraph; most of the Yale professors; and many other prominent citizens. Not only did these men exercise significant influence over the economy, government, and social structure of New Haven and the state, but they also dominated the affairs of Center Church, one of the two or three most prestigious churches in New England. Less than a decade earlier Bacon had been penniless and with little hope for the future; he now found himself in a position of prominence and influence. Given his sudden ascension within the social order, it is perhaps not surprising that he felt intimidated and uncertain as he entered upon this daunting task. As he stated in his inaugural sermon to the congregation, "To be a minister here, where my efforts ought to have an immediate and a mighty bearing on the triumph of the gospel through our land and through the world—O it is a fearful thing."[2]

Center Church, officially known as First Church, stood in the center of the public green and was an imposing symbol of power, wealth, and status in a community that combined the attributes of a village with those of an educational, governmental, and commercial center. With the exception of several hundred African Americans, most of New Haven's approximately eight thousand inhabitants were of British stock. In many ways the social structure as well as the laws regarding amusements and observation of the Sabbath had changed little since the seventeenth century. Yet at the same time, New Haven was a dynamic and prosperous small city. It was by far the most populous community in Connecticut and, with Hartford, was the joint capital of the state. It was also a transportation center and the largest seaport on the Connecticut coast. Commercial establishments extended far along the waterfront, and mercantile houses, shipbuilding yards, Whitney's gun factory, and numerous carriage shops dotted the city's landscape, forming the basis for sustained commercial, financial, and industrial development in future decades.[3]

Despite Bacon's anxieties about how he would be received by his congregation, the people welcomed him warmly. A few months later they extended the same

2. See Oscar Edward Maurer, *A Puritan Church and Its Relation to Community, State, and Nation: Addresses Delivered in Preparation for the Three Hundredth Anniversary of the Settlement of New Haven* (New Haven, 1938), 107–108; *Leonard Bacon: Pastor of the First Church in New Haven*, 8, 59, 78–79, 190–91. For the occupations of some of the members of Center Church during the early years of Bacon's ministry, see *Patten's New Haven Directory, For the Years 1841–2. Number 2* (New Haven, 1841), 20, 38, 40–41, 52, 55, 58, 63, 77–78, 92, 96, 101.

3. Robert Austin Warner, *New Haven Negroes: A Social History* (New York, 1969), 1–2, 3–4, 11–12; Osterweis, *Three Centuries of New Haven*, 206–207, 237–38, 243–46, 251; Jarvis Means Morse, *A Neglected Period of Connecticut's History, 1818–1850* (New Haven, 1933), 11–12.

greeting to Lucy Johnson, a young woman he had met in Boston. They married in July, 1825, in Johnstown, New York. Leonard and Lucy, the sister-in-law of Benjamin B. Wisner, Bacon's friend who was pastor of Old South Church in Boston, had had a rather tumultuous courtship, in which she had rejected him and then been engaged to another man. But soon thereafter she accepted Bacon's proposal while he was in Boston to preach the funeral sermon for Chester Isham, perhaps his closest friend during the past ten years. At this time he and Lucy, with Isham's death clearly in mind, agreed to be "helpers to each other, in a world of sorrow—in a world of death."[4]

With his marriage and his movement into a career, Bacon fully entered into adulthood and achieved a degree of stability in his life. Yet he remained deeply in debt, even though immediately after his installation he sent to his debtors half of the five-hundred-dollar salary he received for the first six months. He and Lucy rented a small house, in which three children were born during the next few years—Rebecca Taylor in 1826, Benjamin Wisner in 1827, and Leonard Woolsey in 1830. Lucy, a loving and devoted mother who reveled in her children, was in charge of the daily child-rearing regimen. Whenever Leonard was away from home, she sent him detailed accounts of their daily routines; and on those rare occasions when she visited her sister Sarah in Boston without her children, she expressed both guilt and sorrow about the separation. A pious evangelical, she worried about the state of the children's souls, and she joined Leonard in the conviction that they must inculcate discipline and morality in their children. Her growing family required constant attention, which placed numerous demands on her. A younger sister, Leonard's mother, and one or more of his siblings periodically lived with them and assisted with household chores, and at times the Bacons were able to hire a servant, too. Thus their small house was often filled to capacity. Lucy was constantly forced to economize. More than a decade after they married, she still complained about the tight budget she adhered to and chided her husband for considering buying a home.[5]

Much as he would do during the next few decades, Bacon devoted enormous energy and concern—and some of what little money he had—to assisting his mother and siblings. His brother David was the major problem. He was so disobe-

4. Leonard to Alice Bacon, August 31, December 28, 1824, Bacon to Alexander C. Twining, January 7, 1825, Elizabeth to Lucy Johnson, October 26, 1824, Bacon to Alexander C. Twining, June 18, 1824, Diane Isham to Lucy Johnson, October 26, 1824, diary entry for May 6, 1825, in Bacon Family Papers; Leonard Bacon, "Memoir of the Late Rev. Chester Isham," *Christian Spectator,* VII (December, 1825), 613–17; Theodore Dwight Bacon, *Leonard Bacon,* 66–68.

5. Leonard to Alice Bacon, March 22, August 27, 1825, January 14, 1830, Lucy to Leonard Bacon, August 27, 1827, February 19, 21, 1838, Lucy Bacon to Phebe Johnson, November 21, 1828, Lucy Bacon to Sarah Wisner, May 10, 1831, July 12, 1832, April 21, 25, 1835, in Bacon Family Papers.

dient toward his mother that she sent him to live with Leonard and Lucy. Unfortunately, David proved to be as much of a problem for them, which eventually led Bacon to send him to live with a family in Fairfield. At the same time, Leonard had to deal with his mother's sense of hopelessness. In her troubled state she even accused Leonard of not wanting her to live with them in New Haven. And her problems only worsened. In 1827 she went to live with her daughters, but their desperate financial situation ultimately forced her to move in with Leonard and Lucy in 1828, at a time when Lucy's sister Elizabeth also lived with them.[6]

Caring for his own children as well as his siblings and mother necessarily distracted Bacon from his busy schedule as a minister. His many pastoral responsibilities included visiting the ill, becoming acquainted with every member of the congregation, counseling those who appeared to be awakened, and presenting Tuesday evening lectures. But because he believed that all other functions were to be subordinated to preaching the Gospel, he devoted a great deal of time to the preparation of sermons. Each Sunday he presented two sermons, which, in accordance with standard practice, contained an exegesis of biblical passages, a presentation of doctrine, and, with increasing emphasis, the application of that doctrine to daily life.[7]

Evangelical commentators of the time tended to underscore the useful and immediate results of preaching—that is, generating revivals and saving souls. This increasingly was viewed as the real test of effective preaching. The style and content of Bacon's preaching certainly were influenced by Leonard Woods and other professors at Andover. He acknowledged, however, that during the early years of his ministry he was most influenced by Nathaniel Taylor, his neighbor and friend who often attended services at Center Church. His contact with Taylor, he noted many years later, was "constant and intimate," and "my familiar intercourse with him taught me to think and taught me to preach."[8]

Although Bacon never fully agreed with Taylor on doctrinal matters, he largely concurred with the central tenets of the New Haven theology developed by Taylor,

6. Leonard to Alice Bacon, March 22, August 27, 1825, November 27, 1827, Alice to Leonard Bacon, May 28, September 4, 1825, January 11, April 5, 1826, July 14, 29, December 26, 1828, February 24, 1830, Julia and Alice to Leonard and David Bacon, August 10, 1828, Alice (sister) to Leonard Bacon, September 8, 1828, Delia Williams to Alice Bacon, April 29, 1829, Mrs. L. Spenser to Lucy Bacon, June 11, 1828, Lucy Bacon to Phebe Johnson, November 21, 1828, in Bacon Family Papers; Hopkins, *Prodigal Puritan*, 34–36.

7. Leonard Bacon, "Review of the Remains of the Rev. Carlos Wilcox," *Quarterly Christian Spectator*, 3rd series, I (March, 1829), 64–65. For treatment of the structure and emphasis of most evangelical sermons, see Sidney E. Mead, "The Rise of the Evangelical Conception of the Ministry in America, 1607–1850," in *The Ministry in Historical Perspective*, ed. H. Richard Niebuhr and Daniel D. Williams (New York, 1956), 229, 246.

8. *Leonard Bacon: Pastor of the First Church in New Haven*, 125; also Leonard to Lucy Bacon, September 10, 1832, in Bacon Family Papers.

his colleagues at Yale Theological Seminary, and Lyman Beecher. He, like Taylor, was an orthodox Calvinist who believed that all people were totally deficient in their obedience to God, which rendered them incapable of repenting and submitting to God "without the interference of a Divine Agency." Yet he and the New Haven theologians had little use for the rigidity of the strict Hopkinsians and other conservative Calvinists.[9]

Bacon applauded Taylor's attempt to render Calvinism more acceptable and relevant to nineteenth-century Americans in order to advance the evangelical revivals and stem the inroads of the Methodists, Episcopalians, and Unitarians.[10] He was an earnest defender of the Congregational form of church government as well as Calvinism. Nevertheless, he generally urged cooperation among evangelicals in all of the denominations. "Many of the distinctions which separate communities of Christians," he told his congregation in 1827, "are differences of comparatively slight importance affecting neither the substance nor the glory of the gospel."[11]

Above all, Bacon agreed with Taylor's contention that human sinfulness, the result of Adam's fall, must not be inconsistent with free agency. He especially rejected the Hopkinsians' assertion that God was the author of sin and that human guilt resulted from the inevitable physical effect of Adam's first transgression. He spoke frequently and forcefully on behalf of what Taylor termed in 1828 "certainty with power to the contrary." Any theories that supported the idea of physical depravity, he insisted, were "unnecessary," and no sinner had an excuse for rejecting the offer of salvation.[12]

Bacon, like Taylor, based his theological views on the conclusions of common sense and reason, arguing that the Bible must be tested by the rules of internal consistency and conformity to experience. He and other New Divinity clergymen were convinced that the success of religious revivals and the coming of the millennium must be accomplished by free moral agents who responded to rational entreaties to turn to a benevolent God. He frequently exhorted his congregation to prepare for a religious revival, asserting that a sense of expectation could help to bring about the desired result. Referring to "this unbelieving generation," he warned members

9. See, for example, sermons of March 11, April 10, September 18, 1825, September 9, 1827, in Bacon Family Papers.

10. For treatment of Taylor's theology, see, for example, Sidney Earl Mead, *Nathaniel William Taylor, 1786–1858: A Connecticut Liberal* (Hamden, Conn., 1967), 97–100, 125–26; Vincent Harding, *A Certain Magnificence: Lyman Beecher and the Transformation of American Protestantism, 1775–1863* (Brooklyn, 1991), 122–23; H. Shelton Smith, *Changing Conceptions of Original Sin* (New York, 1955), 87–103.

11. Bacon, "Review of the Economy of Methodism," *Quarterly Christian Spectator,* 3rd series, I (September, 1829), 509–513; sermon of April 13, 1827, in Bacon Family Papers.

12. Sermons of March 12, 1826, May 13, September 9, 1827, also September 18, 25, October 27, 1826, in Bacon Family Papers.

of his church that the Kingdom of God could not be achieved without revivals or revival measures. Yet perhaps because of his Andover training as well as the difficulty he experienced in stimulating a revival in his own church during the first few years of his ministry, Bacon, like Horace Bushnell two decades later, was more skeptical of the value of revivals than many evangelical preachers of the time. He was, quite naturally, somewhat defensive on this matter, assuring his congregation that "I speak not against revivals of religion, but against the idea that religion is for nothing but revivals."[13]

Nevertheless, despite his essential agreement with the theological views of his predecessor at Center Church, during the first few years of his ministry Bacon experienced serious difficulties. In the process, he disappointed many people, including himself, and came close to being dismissed by the congregation. This was a sobering and painful experience for an intelligent, articulate, brash young man.

Even prior to his probationary preaching in late 1824, Bacon had some sense of the problems that awaited him, confiding to his mother that the congregation "has shown very abundantly that they are hard to please." He worked hard to gain the people's favor by consciously seeking to develop "more faith, more zeal, more love, more devotion." But the rumblings of discontent soon began to swell to a crescendo. Several factors underlay the dissatisfaction of his parishioners. He was a young man, even by the standards of the time, when he accepted the call to an old and prestigious church. Moreover, he, like most seminary graduates, had little training in how to contend with the often complex and jarring demands and forces in the church, and no adequate pastoral guidebooks were available to provide practical advice on these and other matters. He was not alone in finding himself at odds with elements of his congregation. By the early nineteenth century, there was a noticeable decline of permanency among settled pastors throughout New England. As the result of internal disputes over doctrine or church membership, plus the attraction of posts in the growing number of benevolent societies and the developing job consciousness among ministers, the average tenure among Connecticut clergymen had dropped from thirty years in 1775 to below ten years after 1815. This trend toward impermanency also occurred at a time when ministers ceased to be deferred to as public officers in the community.[14]

Center Church was divided on matters of doctrine. A number of the elderly members of the church in the mid-1820s who had supported James Dana, the "Old

13. Prospectus of *Christian Spectator,* December, 1828; sermons of February 7, 1830, February 12, 19, 26, August 20, 1826, March 18, December 9, 1827, December 4, 1825, speech of January, 1827, in Bacon Family Papers.

14. Leonard to Alice Bacon, September 30, 1824, diary entry for May 18, 1825, in Bacon Family Papers. For analyses of important changes in the ministry during the early nineteenth century, see Scott, *From Office to Profession,* 3–7, 125, *et passim;* Andrew, *Rebuilding the Christian Commonwealth,* 36, 46, 53.

Light" minister, prior to his dismissal nearly twenty years earlier, probably looked askance at Bacon's weekly prayer meetings and his emphasis on free moral agency. However, Bacon appears to have disappointed far more members who were staunch supporters of religious revivals. Both of his most recent predecessors, Moses Stuart and Nathaniel Taylor, had presided over important revivals that added many new members to the church. In addition, both men had enjoyed considerable stature in the religious community, even beyond the boundaries of New England. Consequently, whatever he accomplished might well have been compared unfavorably with the careers of these men. The congregation certainly had high expectations for Bacon. One parishioner wrote anonymously in 1826 that he hoped Bacon would "preach as our *father Moses* did. His preaching made sinners afraid." Another member warned him that "you ought to feel that every echo of your voice in Dr. Taylor's Church cries out against you." That the congregation was "proudly grieved" by the loss of Stuart and Taylor to Andover and Yale seminaries in 1810 and 1822, respectively, only exacerbated the situation.[15]

Shortly after Bacon assumed his post, there were some stirrings of religious excitement in the church. With Taylor's assistance, he sought to nurture the awakening. But in the end, the revival did not materialize. Although Bacon justifiably reminded his parishioners that there had been much apathy in the church since the previous revival had ended in 1821, the fact remains that he was unable to generate a revival.[16]

Bacon was a facile writer, a learned man, and an eloquent speaker who, at times, was able to deliver a stirring sermon. But he soon realized that he "never had any such power in the pulpit" as had Stuart and Taylor "in their best days." Rather short and slight in stature, he did not have the commanding physical presence of Taylor. More important, his sermons tended to consist largely of serious, scholarly exegeses of scripture and were presented in a somewhat stiff and formal manner, with little intensity or verve. To some, he seemed both arrogant and dull. As one parishioner stated in 1826, "Oh *Rev. Sir* . . . do not cover up the truth by learning, we all know you are a scholar, but do preach in a plain, pointed manner." Others in the church were even more blunt in their criticism. W. Shedd, a former classmate of Bacon at Yale, for example, complained that his sermons seemed "too meager in thought" and "too pretty, too figurative, to have far too little of the simplicity of Gospel truth." Such harsh judgment must have been difficult for Bacon to accept; and the

15. Leonard Bacon, "Remembrance of Forty Years in the Parish," in *Four Commemorative Discourses: Delivered on His Sixty-third Birth-day, February 19, 1865; On the Fortieth Anniversary of His Installation, March 12, 1865; And on His Retirement from Pastoral Duties* (New Haven, 1866), 22; anonymous to Bacon, May 15, 1826, W. Shedd to Bacon, September 30, 1826, sermon of April 1828, in Bacon Family Papers.

16. Diary entries for May 18, 25, June 9, 23, 1825, sermon of December 4, 1825, in Bacon Family Papers; Bacon, *Four Commemorative Discourses,* 22–23.

situation was made worse by the warning from Senator Hillhouse and other influential members of the church that his sermons simply were not up to the standards of his predecessors.[17]

Bacon expected to be dismissed by the church and forced to look elsewhere for employment. Indeed, in 1828 he was one of two finalists for the editorship of *Spirit of the Pilgrims,* an evangelical magazine recently founded in Boston. At the last moment Lyman Beecher was chosen for the post, but Bacon clearly had not discouraged consideration of his name. In that year he admitted to his congregation that the constant "despondency brooding on the mind" and the "almost utter hopelessness of doing any good" had rendered him less diligent in his labors than he ought to have been. But he also candidly told his people that he was deeply hurt that "I have had in this great and intelligent and celebrated church none or next to none who were willing to hold up a pastor's hand or to exhort their brethren provoking them to love or good works." Given his sense of inadequacy and the discouraging circumstances, he confessed, "my spirit died within me and I have often been ready to abandon the work and flee to some retirement where I might be at rest."[18]

In the end, Bacon weathered the storm. This probably was in part the result of pure luck. Years later he noted that those who were most critical of him had little influence in the church, while "those whose unfavorable judgment, had it been freely uttered, would have been fatal to me, were very kind." The latter group included Hillhouse, who ultimately became one of his warmest supporters. Indeed, Giles Mansfield, a loyal ally, assured Bacon in 1828 that the strength of the opposition had been exaggerated. Yet Bacon survived this crisis in large part because his labors helped to generate a revival in 1828, during which forty-eight young people were converted. This did not immediately silence his critics, but during that year both he and Lucy noticed a discernible increase in the congregation's warmth toward him.[19]

Bacon's persevering in the face of adversity was due to his inner strength and patience. After the crisis had passed, he sought to be philosophical about it, choosing to emphasize the lesson that "it is good for a man to taste the bitterness of trial and to feel his weakness." Only then, he reasoned, could he become fully conscious of his imperfections and failures. For their part, the congregation seems to have heeded his request that "all old things be put out of the way and buried out of our

17. Sermon of April 1828, anonymous to Bacon, May 15, 1826, W. Shedd to Bacon, September 30, 1826, in Bacon Family Papers; Bacon, *Four Commemorative Discourses,* 23.

18. Benjamin B. Wisner to Bacon, March 28, 1828, sermon of April 1828, in Bacon Family Papers.

19. Bacon, *Four Commemorative Discourses,* 23; Giles Mansfield to Bacon, March 3, 1828, Lucy to Leonard Bacon, July 5, 1828, Leonard to Lucy Bacon, July 7, 1828, Lucy Bacon to Phebe Johnson, November 21, 1828, Lucy Bacon to Sarah Wisner, April 1829, in Bacon Family Papers; Bacon to Ralph R. Gurley, March 18, 1831, in American Colonization Society Papers, Library of Congress.

sight and out of our memory." There would be difficulties and disappointments in the years ahead, and he would never be an electrifying preacher. But his humbling experience seems to have led to an improvement in the quality of his sermons and to have made him acutely conscious of the need to appear more amiable and more committed to his people. In fact, many of his parishioners came to love and respect him and to appreciate his regular visits with each family in the church and his decision to make his home accessible to them.[20]

Bacon never again felt that his pastorate was in jeopardy. During his forty-one-year tenure at Center Church, he would speak out forcefully on such controversial matters as the Fugitive Slave Act, Republican party policies, and prohibition, which offended some members of his congregation. But these were the exceptions, not the rule. The burdens of the ministry, including managing his church and dealing with varying, and even competing, interests and demands among his parishioners, tended to push him toward resolving issues in dispute rather than rousing controversy.

The congregation appears to have felt warmly toward Lucy from the time she arrived in New Haven. She was a sociable person who was at ease welcoming church members into her home and organizing activities in the church. Her busy schedule included attendance at church meetings and Sunday services and an active role in the Sunday school program. Yet she was much more than a dutiful minister's wife. An intelligent and perceptive woman, she closely observed developments in Center Church and other parishes in Connecticut and reassured her husband that other ministers were experiencing similar problems. As a staunch defender of the New Haven theology and a close friend of Nathaniel Taylor and his wife, she deeply resented the conservatives' attacks on him, and once told her husband that a friend probably had become "a dreadful conservative" after frequently conversing with Leonard Woods. A devoted evangelical, she viewed revivals rather pragmatically, informing her sister Sarah that Taylor, Lyman Beecher, and other revival preachers should be judged above all by their ability to convert sinners. To that end, in the 1820s she periodically urged her brother-in-law, Benjamin Wisner, to come to New Haven to assist her husband and other ministers in the city in launching a revival. Indeed, she often advised Leonard to devote more time to preparing sermons and converting sinners than writing books and articles.[21]

Although a few of his parishioners would later complain that his many jour-

20. Sermons of 1828, March 14, 1830, in Bacon Family Papers; Bacon, *A Sermon to the First Church and Society in New Haven, 10th March, 1850, on Completing the Twenty-fifth Year of the Author's Service in the Pastoral Office* (New Haven, 1850), 15, 17–19.

21. Lucy Bacon to Sarah Wisner, August 8, 1825, April 1829, February 28, August 7, 1837, Lucy to Leonard Bacon, August 26, 1827, July 5, 1828, February 21, December 9, 1838, Lucy Bacon to Phebe Johnson, November 21, 1828, in Bacon Family Papers.

nalistic commitments and other activities distracted him from his pastoral duties, many of them took pride in his growing influence and notoriety in a variety of endeavors that extended far beyond the parish. He was determined to "stand here on the battlements of Zion," and believed that he could serve both his people and the evangelical cause by writing and speaking on a broad range of issues before the American people. As he noted in his inaugural sermon in 1825, "You would not wish to have a minister who should be unknown and whose influence should be unfelt beyond the limits of this congregation."[22]

Bacon's extraparish responsibilities developed shortly after he came to Center Church. He was, for example, one of a committee that edited the *Christian Spectator* from 1826 until its demise in 1838. The magazine, published monthly until 1828, when it became a quarterly, circulated mostly within Connecticut. Although the *Christian Spectator* was directed toward the "respectable classes" and applauded good taste and decorous behavior, it also attacked the luxury and decadence of the social elite. It sought above all to disseminate the evangelical message to an abstract and generalized evangelical community. Bacon wrote dozens of articles for the magazine on literary, ethical, and reform subjects, including most of those relating to slavery and colonization that appeared in its columns, while Stuart, Taylor, Chauncey Goodrich, and other contributors tended to concentrate on theological matters.[23]

Bacon's editorship of, and contributions to, the *Christian Spectator* placed heavy demands on his busy life, but he found it an important forum for expressing his views on social and religious issues. Like many other clergymen of the time, he became deeply involved in the expanding benevolent empire. During the 1820s and 1830s, a growing number of the most talented and zealous young pastors left the parish ministry for positions as secretaries, editors, and agents for the benevolent societies, which they viewed as more promising endeavors. Bacon's rejection of several offers of positions in benevolent organizations was atypical. He essentially chose to have it both ways: remaining at Center Church, where, especially after 1828, he thoroughly enjoyed his work, while actively participating in, and writing and speaking on behalf of, the missionary, tract, temperance, colonization, and other causes. In doing so he sought to maintain clerical influence in the world of religious benevolence at a time when the benevolent societies were, in some degree, usurping the local minister's leadership and impinging on his daily work in the parish. Requests for contributions to these causes indeed became so numerous that

22. W. Shedd to Bacon, September 30, 1826, in Bacon Family Papers; *Leonard Bacon: Pastor of the First Church in New Haven,* 58.

23. Scott, *From Office to Profession,* 49–50, 65–67; Prospectus of *Christian Spectator,* December, 1828; Frank Luther Mott, *A History of American Magazines, 1741–1850* (5 vols.; New York, 1930), II, 310; *Religious Intelligencer,* September 7, 1833.

the Connecticut General Association and other ministerial bodies established annual calendars for the competing movements.[24]

In articles that appeared in the *National Preacher,* which published sermons by clergymen from all the Protestant denominations, and the *Christian Spectator,* as well as in sermons he presented at Center Church, Bacon actively sought to foster disinterested benevolence among evangelical Christians. As an evangelical moralist he expected the converted to imitate the moral character of Christ by systematically doing good for others. By creating a host of benevolent societies, he wrote in a *National Preacher* article, "the church is arming all her sons for self-defence and for conquest."[25]

Bacon, like other evangelicals, posited a continual struggle against the temptations of the world. He warned his congregation that luxury, vice, and profligacy had taken root in the large cities and were spreading to New Haven, and even to the villages of Connecticut. That progress, he asserted in a Fast Day sermon in 1827, "must be resisted, must be staid, or we are ruined." He was especially concerned that rapid urbanization and the emerging market economy fostered selfishness, pride, the love of novelty, and social disorder. Yet he was by no means a hidebound conservative who instinctively opposed social and economic change. He celebrated the American reform efforts and recognized that much good flowed from challenges to the privileges and "curious antiquities" of the old order. In addition, notwithstanding his concern that excessive materialism prevented the work of regeneration, he tempered his criticism of capitalist values as well as wealth and the wealthy. Perhaps because the most influential members of his church were wealthy merchants, bankers, and lawyers, he chose to emphasize that the accumulation of riches required hard work and patience and that it was incumbent upon these men to contribute their wealth to good causes.[26]

Bacon worked actively to advance the cause of religious benevolence on several fronts. He strongly endorsed the American Education Society's objective of providing an adequate supply of pious and well-supported ministers, but he opposed the society's shift from grants to loans for students because he believed it meant that young men like himself would enter the ministry with an onerous debt load. Indeed, he struggled for several years to pay his debts to the society, and only suc-

24. Andrew, *Rebuilding the Christian Commonwealth,* 139; Scott, *From Office to Profession,* 68–69; sermon of November 10, 1833, in Bacon Family Papers.

25. Leonard Bacon, "Duties of Young Christians," *National Preacher,* III (June, 1828), 1; Leonard Bacon, "The Example of Christ," *National Preacher,* III (June, 1828), 9–14; sermon of December 13, 1829, in Bacon Family Papers; Scott, *From Office to Profession,* 47–48, 84–87.

26. See sermons of October 23, 1825, April 13, 22, July 3, 1827, September 28, 1828, November 8, 1829, in Bacon Family Papers.

ceeded in his effort with the generous assistance of his parishioners in the early 1830s.[27]

Bacon also devoted his energies to the American Sunday School Union. He was a founder, vice president, and pastoral overseer of the New Haven County auxiliary of the Connecticut Sabbath School Union, and he met weekly with Sabbath school teachers in Center Church to develop lessons for the students. Because Sabbath schools developed in children the habit of reading the Bible and a regard for the Sabbath, he told his parishioners, there was not an institution in America "which promises greater or more immediate results for the glory of God and the happiness of man." He also attended the founding meeting of the American Tract Society in 1825 and became a director of the society in 1837.[28]

As an outgrowth of his emphasis on the transcendent importance of a personal religious experience in the pursuit of interdenominational benevolence and the evangelization of the world, Bacon was an outspoken proponent of both home and foreign missions. Between 1825 and 1829, he served as secretary of the Domestic Missionary Society of Connecticut, and was one of its directors from 1832 to 1869. He especially sought to strengthen the many struggling Congregational churches in the state in order to combat vice and immorality and to resist the efforts of the Episcopalians, Methodists, and other partisans "to demolish all the churches that were planted by the Pilgrims."[29]

Bacon viewed the foreign missionary movement as a means of creating a global community modeled upon New England society. For him and other supporters of the American Board of Commissioners for Foreign Missions, religious principles and republican virtues remained guideposts to civilization and progress. The success of the missionary efforts, he believed, would check the divisive spirit of the time, return the Bible to its rightful place in a Christian commonwealth, and disseminate the Gospel throughout the world. His advocacy of foreign missions was also driven in part by a deep-seated cultural bias: he was convinced that non-Christians were

27. Leonard Bacon, "Brief View of the American Education Society," *Christian Spectator,* new series, I (February, 1827), 92–98; Bacon to Benjamin B. Wisner, November 16, 1829, sermon of July 7, 1833, in Bacon Family Papers; Theodore Dwight Bacon, *Leonard Bacon,* 90; New Haven *Chronicle,* May 22, 1827.

28. *Religious Intelligencer,* June 3, 1826, May 14, 1831; New Haven *Chronicle,* August 4, 1827; *Proceedings of the General Association of Connecticut, June 1830* (Hartford, 1830), 17; Leonard Bacon, "Review of the Life of Summerfield," *Quarterly Christian Spectator,* 3rd series, II (March, 1830), 126–27.

29. Sidney Earl Mead, "Denominationalism: The Shape of Protestantism in America," *Church History,* XXIII (1954), 301; Richard D. Shiels, "The Second Great Awakening in Connecticut: Critique of the Traditional Interpretation," *Church History,* XLIX (1980), 406–11; *Proceedings of the General Association of Connecticut, June 1825* (Hartford, 1825), 7; *Proceedings of the General Association of Connecticut, June 1829* (Hartford, 1829), 5; sermons of April 16, 1826, February 4, 1827, in Bacon Family Papers.

"polluted, selfish, sensual, and self-brutalized" people and prisoners of the "darkness and moral degradation of heathenism."[30]

Bacon also helped to launch the temperance movement in New Haven and Connecticut. The convergence of popular discontent with heavy drinking, a coherent temperance ideology, and a committed leadership led to the founding of the American Society for the Promotion of Temperance in 1826. In some respects the temperance movement was a conservative crusade that sought to force a volatile society to conform to a conservative Protestant image of order, purity, and stability.[31] But above all, a concern for personal holiness, the drive to active benevolence, and the belief that the power of evangelical religion could solve social problems motivated the movement's activists. The cause drew heavily on evangelicalism for both its language and its ideology, preaching that each person must refrain from evil and seek salvation. Evangelical clergymen such as Bacon came to consider intemperance the most heinous example of sin as self-gratification, with its course moving from initial desire to final ruin and the enslavement of the soul. In an era of transition to a competitive, urban, industrial, commercial society, the clergy, in concert with manufacturers, master craftsmen, merchants, physicians, and other upwardly mobile groups in communities experiencing rapid social and economic change, tended to embrace the cause. If material and moral progress were to be achieved, they reasoned, intemperance, which destroyed self-control and produced crime, indolence, and pauperism, must be checked.[32]

Social drinking was a deeply ingrained habit in the 1820s. Many of Bacon's parishioners drank liquor and wine, which were served at a public dinner following his ordination, and numerous establishments in the city sold alcoholic beverages. Bacon first spoke against intemperance in an 1827 sermon in which he branded it "universally the besetting and prevailing sin of the nation," filling the jails and almshouses and ruining families. He, like many other temperance advocates, expressed little sympathy for the alcoholic, terming him "a living nuisance to society." While he urged total abstinence from ardent spirits—not necessarily all alcoholic

30. Sermons of December 23, 1827, September 21, 1828, Bacon to Dr. Leonard Bacon, March 23, 1829, in Bacon Family Papers; Leonard Bacon, "Review of Works on Greece," *Quarterly Christian Spectator*, 3rd series, I (March, 1829), 179–82.

31. Franklin S. Bradley, *Recollections of Dr. Leonard Bacon* (n.p., n.d.), 4. For the social control theory as it relates to the temperance movement, see Norman H. Clark, *Deliver Us from Evil: An Interpretation of American Prohibition* (New York, 1976), 28–31; Joseph R. Gusfield, *Symbolic Crusade: Status Politics and the American Temperance Movement* (Urbana, 1963); Scott, *From Office to Profession*, 39–41.

32. For treatments of the ideology and constituency of the temperance movement, see, for example, Ian R. Tyrrell, *Sobering Up: From Temperance to Prohibition in Antebellum America, 1800–1860* (Westport, Conn., 1979), 54–57, 60–61, 63–64, 67, 69–74, 125–29, 174–75; W. J. Rorabaugh, *The Alcoholic Republic: An American Tradition* (New York, 1979), 189–208; Paul E. Johnson, *A Shopkeepers' Millennium: Society and Revivals in Rochester, New York, 1815–1837* (New York, 1978), 38–52.

beverages—he frequently warned (in spite of opposition from some members of his congregation) that moderate drinking would lead inexorably to excess.[33]

Bacon's contact with Benjamin B. Wisner, Leonard Woods, and Lyman Beecher—all founders of the American Temperance Society—was instrumental in drawing him into the cause. Moreover, the Connecticut General Association had passed resolutions against intemperance since 1820, though many local churches were slow to condemn moderate drinking. At times, Bacon spoke as a social conservative who viewed the temperance crusade as a means of reimposing order and morality on an unruly lower class. In a *Christian Spectator* article he decried the decline of morality and the absence of enforcement of laws against drunkenness under the new state constitution. He estimated that two-thirds of all paupers were drunks and that this was the major cause of crime among the working class. Yet he also spoke in the name of material and moral improvement, bemoaning the fact that intemperance threatened America's "wealth, harmony, happiness, and hopes" and was injurious to public health and morals. Speaking before the Young Men's Society for the Promotion of Temperance in New Haven in 1829, he urged its members to stand in the vanguard of a movement that would increase productivity and enhance national prosperity and progress.[34]

Bacon was an outspoken critic of the practice of licensing liquor dealers, believing that if drinking was in fact an evil, licensing merely sanctioned the vice and drew revenue from the corruption of the people. Moreover, he was convinced that "no legislation can effectively remove the evil." Only public opinion, which he considered "the supreme power" in a democratic society, not the power of the law, could effectively reform morals and manners.[35]

Although Bacon considered the temperance movement a cause all Christians must support, his benevolent endeavors during the early years of his ministry focused primarily on race, slavery, and colonization. Convinced that slavery was a sinful institution that threatened to destroy the nation and that white Christians were obligated to uplift blacks, he continued to speak out forcefully against the slave system and to urge the elevation of blacks in America as well as Africa. Yet he also

33. Sermon of March 4, 1827, in Bacon Family Papers. Bacon attacked moderate drinking in "Discourses on Intemperance," *Christian Spectator,* n.s., XII (December, 1827), 645–46; "Reports of Temperance Societies," *Christian Spectator,* n.s., II (May, 1828), 245–54; *Total Abstinence from Ardent Spirits; An Address Delivered, By Request of the Young Men's Temperance Society of New Haven, in the North Church, June 24, 1829* (New Haven, 1829), 8, 16.

34. *Leonard Bacon: Pastor of the First Church in New Haven,* 91–92, 174; *Contributions to the Ecclesiastical History of Connecticut. . . .* (New Haven, 1861), 214; Bacon, "Discourses on Intemperance," 587, 589, 653; Bacon, *Total Abstinence from Ardent Spirits,* 2–3, 17.

35. Bacon, "Reports of Temperance Societies," 256; sermons of April 17, November 26, 1829, July 4, 1830, in Bacon Family Papers.

remained certain that both the abolition of slavery and the improvement of blacks could best be achieved by repatriating African Americans to Africa.

It is not surprising that Bacon remained thoroughly committed to the colonization movement. Benjamin Silliman, Jeremiah Day, David Daggett, and other prominent New Haveners, as well as his friend and mentor Joel Hawes, had been associated with the American Colonization Society since its inception. Moreover, during the 1820s the cause increasingly appealed to the New England clergy as a missionary and humanitarian enterprise, promising emancipation and black improvement at home and a holy enterprise and civilization for Africa. Beginning in 1825, the Connecticut General Association endorsed colonization, and in 1827 it supported Bacon's recommendation that the churches collect funds for the cause on or near July 4 each year.[36]

In 1827 Bacon, in concert with Gideon Tomlinson, governor of Connecticut; Silliman; Thomas H. Gallaudet, principal of the American Asylum in Hartford; John T. Peters, a state supreme court justice; and other members of the state's social and political elite, founded the Connecticut Colonization Society.[37] In the society's early years Bacon served as its secretary, and then for many years as one of its managers. During the late 1820s, he also served the cause by frequently offering advice to Ralph R. Gurley on American Colonization Society matters, recruiting agents for the organization, raising funds throughout Connecticut, and, with Gallaudet, helping to organize the Massachusetts Colonization Society in 1830.[38]

Because of widespread suspicion that the ACS was largely under southern control, the colonization movement never had a fervent following in New England. Whatever gains the society made in the region were primarily the result of efforts by Bacon, whom J. Earl Thompson, Jr., has termed "the most persuasive proponent of colonization in New England" by the late 1820s.[39] Despite the slow progress of

36. John F. Fulton and Elizabeth H. Thomas, *Benjamin Silliman, 1779–1864: Pathfinder in American Science* (New York, 1947), 258; Staudenraus, *The African Colonization Movement*, 72, 86; *Proceedings of the General Association of Connecticut, June 1825*, 7; *Proceedings of the General Association of Connecticut, June, 1827* (Hartford, 1827), 6; *African Repository and Colonial Journal*, III (June, 1827), 122; *An Address to the Public by the Managers of the Colonization Society of Connecticut* (New Haven, 1828), 31.

37. *Eleventh Annual Report of the American Society for Colonizing the Free People of Colour of the United States* (Washington, D.C., 1828), 98; *African Repository and Colonial Journal*, III (April, 1827), 63, 92; *An Address to the Public by the Managers of the Colonization Society of Connecticut*, 12–14; *Fourth Annual Report of the Managers of the Colonization Society of the State of Connecticut* (New Haven, 1831), 2.

38. Ralph R. Gurley to Bacon, March 8, 17, June 22, 1825, June 10, 1828; Bacon to Ralph R. Gurley, March 15, 1827, September 13, 1828, in American Colonization Society Papers; Thomas H. Gallaudet to Bacon, July 8, 1830, in Thomas Hopkins Gallaudet Papers, Library of Congress.

39. Ralph R. Gurley to Thomas H. Gallaudet, August 15, 1829, in Thomas Hopkins Gallaudet Papers; American Colonization Society, *A Few Facts Respecting the American Colonization Society, and the Colony at Liberia* (Washington, D.C., 1830), 3–4; Thompson, "Lyman Beecher's Long Road to Conservative Abolitionism," 91.

the cause, Bacon frequently assured colonizationists that the prejudices in Connect-icut against the movement were weakening and pledged his continued commitment to its objectives. He acknowledged, however, that, owing to financial constraints, logistics, and other factors, the ACS would be unable to repatriate all African Americans to Africa in the foreseeable future. Thus, he concluded that, in the meantime, it was incumbent upon benevolent Christians to engage in efforts for black improvement in the United States. It was necessary, he wrote, "to investigate their condition, learn their necessities, instruct them in their duty, show them the value of property, stand ready to protect them, whenever and by whomsoever, their rights are infringed."[40]

Shortly after he came to Center Church, Bacon acted upon his desire to assist free blacks. In July, 1825, he and a few other young men—including Theodore Dwight Woolsey, Edward Beecher, and Alexander Twining, all friends from his Yale days—met in Bacon's study to establish the African Improvement Society. This "little club," as Bacon termed it, initially had no constitution or bylaws and kept its identity secret for a time in order to avoid antagonizing the people of New Haven. It met weekly in Bacon's study to "consult and plan for the elevation of the African race."[41]

The African Improvement Society was one of several efforts by benevolent whites in New York City, Philadelphia, and other northern cities in the mid- and late 1820s. These activists sought to provide a basic education for free blacks, to instill such conventional virtues as piety, frugality, and the work ethic, and to main-tain order in the developing urban centers.[42] Bacon's group declared its desire "to improve the intellectual, moral, and religious condition" of the eight hundred Afri-can Americans in New Haven, who constituted approximately one-ninth of the city's population. New Haven, like most other northern cities, represented a threat-ening environment for blacks. Although its economy was expanding, black people were given few opportunities to make a decent living. Most white merchants and mechanics refused to hire African Americans, and the influx of Irish immigrants meant that they, and not native-born black laborers, would be hired for unskilled

40. Bacon, "Reports of the Colonization Society," *Christian Spectator,* n.s., II (July, 1828), 358, 368–69; "Review on African Colonization," *Quarterly Christian Spectator,* 3rd series, II (September, 1830), 459–61, 481–82; Bacon to Ralph R. Gurley, June 4, 1828, July 6, 1830, in American Colonization Society Papers.

41. *Christian Union,* January 6, 1875; Leonard Woolsey Bacon, *Anti-Slavery Before Garrison: An Ad-dress Before the Connecticut Society of the Order of the Founders and Patriots of America, New Haven, September 19, 1902* (New Haven, 1903), 26–27; diary entry for June 22, 1825, in Bacon Family Papers.

42. See, for example, Elliott Cresson to Ralph R. Gurley, August 23, 1828, in American Coloniza-tion Society Papers; Carter G. Woodson, *The Education of the Negro Prior to 1861* (New York, 1915), 128–29; Gary B. Nash, *Forging Freedom: The Formation of Philadelphia's Black Community, 1720–1840* (Cam-bridge, Mass., 1988), 202–11; Carleton Mabee, *Black Education in New York State: From Colonial to Modern Times* (Syracuse, 1979), 18–19, 21, 36–37, 44.

work on canal construction. Consequently, nearly all blacks worked in low-paying menial jobs. Racial segregation was nearly universal in the city. Under the 1818 state constitution, which denied the vote to blacks, they were recognized as a separate social caste. In their daily lives African Americans were assigned to separate sections of churches, placed in separate schools, excluded from the better eating places, public lectures, and some transportation facilities, and forced to live in segregated sections of the city. Poverty, hard physical labor, and a poor diet combined to render the death rate among New Haven blacks twice that for whites.[43]

Although Bacon confided to Theodore Woolsey in 1826 that the African Improvement Society was "making no very great progress," it did achieve some success during the year that Bacon was actively involved in its affairs. For example, it hired Simeon Jocelyn, a white minister, to be pastor of the United African Congregational Church and established a library, a savings bank, a Sabbath school, a temperance society, and a day and evening school for both children and adults. In an 1827 address the society declared that blacks had as much right to live and work in New Haven as did whites. The denial of this basic right, the society stated, would "trample on the first principle of all religion and virtue." These benevolent activists shared the conviction that blacks were largely incapable of extricating themselves from poverty, vice, and ignorance without white assistance. But the organization, which enjoyed the support of prominent blacks and whites alike, sought to go beyond the prevailing racist explanations for the plight of blacks and maintained that they deserved "enlightened and philanthropic commiseration" rather than "censure and neglect."[44]

Bacon continued to support the African Improvement Society's activities after he ended his official connection with the organization in 1826. But he was convinced that such efforts must ultimately be directed primarily toward preparing African Americans to be "worthy and intelligent messengers of knowledge and salvation" to Africa. He and nearly all colonizationists believed that the mass of blacks were so degraded that they could not truly be elevated in America. As he stated in his 1828 report for the Connecticut Colonization Society, "It is to be taken for granted that *in present circumstances any effort to produce a general and thorough amelioration in the character and condition of the free people of colour must be to a great extent fruitless.*"[45]

43. *Freedom's Journal,* August 10, 1827; Warner, *New Haven Negroes,* v, 10–11, 17–23, 27–32. The condition of northern free blacks is discussed in Curry, *The Free Black in Urban America,* 16–34, 47–80; Litwack, *North of Slavery,* 153–75; Nash, *Forging Freedom,* 212–34.

44. New Haven *Chronicle,* May 22, April 21, 1827; *Third Annual Report of the African Improvement Society of New Haven* (New Haven, 1829), 3–6, 8–11, 13–15; *Religious Intelligencer,* April 28, 1827; *Freedom's Journal,* April 27, 1827.

45. *An Address to the Public by the Managers of the Colonization Society of Connecticut,* 5. For similar

This theme of black degradation was an important factor motivating Bacon and other colonizationists to embrace repatriation as a means of purifying American society and protecting the civil and religious liberties and republican virtues of whites. "We wish to have every corner of our communities searched," he wrote in reference to blacks in 1828, "and all their pollutions washed away." In seeking to rid society of blacks rather than to end racial prejudice in America, Bacon essentially conceded that racism was the product of immutable popular attitudes that precluded the amelioration of conditions and character. Deeply concerned about order and morality in society, keenly aware of the pervasive and deep-seated hostility toward African Americans, and unwilling to risk censure and ostracism by championing the cause of racial equality, he concluded—perhaps not surprisingly—that little could be done for blacks in America. But given his evangelical conviction that no sin was impervious to the transforming power of the Gospel, his admission that blacks could not be raised to the level of whites is startling. One explanation for this concession is that he did not view racial prejudice as a sin of a magnitude that warranted sustained efforts to eradicate or alter it, as he did with intemperance. Another is that, in ruling out the possibility of significantly altering racial attitudes, he subscribed to what George M. Fredrickson has characterized as a protoracist form of biological determinism. Although he, like Lyman Beecher, Ebenezer Baldwin, and some other northern colonizationists, condemned racial prejudice as "a malignant and persecuting spirit," he was by no means free of racial bias. For example, at times he referred to blacks' "barbarous lineage" and to "the sphere in which Providence has placed" them in American society. Indeed, unlike Philip Hay, a northern colonizationist who acknowledged that he shared the prevailing racist assumptions among white Americans, Bacon could never bring himself to admit his own prejudice.[46] In all, his racism, as well as his reluctance to challenge aggressively the prevailing racial attitudes among white Americans, effectively negated his benevolent impulse to advance the interests of free blacks who remained in the United States.

Yet Bacon and many other colonizationists, especially in the North, were not unequivocal racists who believed in the inherent and unalterable inferiority of blacks. Winthrop Jordan has argued that whites who observed the degraded condi-

statements, see Philip C. Hay, *Our Duty to our Coloured Population. A Sermon for the Benefit of the American Colonization Society, Delivered in the Second Presbyterian Church, Newark, July 23, 1826* (Newark, 1826), 10–11, 13; *African Repository and Colonial Journal,* II (July, 1826), 152–54; Ebenezer Baldwin, *Observations on the Physical, Intellectual, and Moral Qualities of Our Colored Population: With Remarks on the Subject of Emancipation and Colonization* (New Haven, 1834), iii–iv, 8, 13, 43–44.

46. Thompson, "Lyman Beecher's Long Road to Conservative Abolitionism," 96; Fredrickson, *The Black Image in the White Mind,* 18; Hay, *Our Duty to Our Colored Population,* 8; Leonard Bacon, "The Free People of Color," *Quarterly Christian Spectator,* 3rd series, IV (June, 1832), 318.

tion of free blacks increasingly came to question whether black mental, moral, and psychological characteristics were the result of environmental factors, thus leading to the "collapse of the environmentalist temple" in early-nineteenth-century America. But Bacon, Calvin Colton, Ebenezer Baldwin, Frederick Freeman, and Lyman Beecher, among others, as well as the ACS in its official pronouncements, provide supporting evidence for George Fredrickson's contention that, while environmentalism began to erode after 1810, until the late 1830s many colonizationists held that the degradation of African Americans was the result of circumstances, not inherent traits.[47]

Bacon was one of the most outspoken proponents of the environmental theory. He was convinced that black Americans would thrive and prosper in Africa, even going so far in a July 4, 1830, sermon as to draw an analogy between repatriation and the Puritan migration to New England and the movement of settlers to Ohio and Illinois. In Africa, unlike America, he declared in the 1828 Connecticut Colonization Society report, the African American would become "a member of a community in which he is not only free, but equal. There he stands up to be a man."[48]

The repatriation of blacks, in the opinion of Bacon, Lyman Beecher, and other New England clergymen, was not merely a means of elevating blacks; it was also a vehicle for exporting evangelical Protestant institutions and values to Africa, thereby hastening the advent of the millennium. Bacon's most forceful endorsement of colonization as a civilizing and Christianizing agent came in *A Plea for Africa,* an oration he had originally presented in Boston in 1824 and repeated in New Haven soon after his ordination. In this speech, which was published in 1825, he combined the concepts of American mission, disinterested benevolence, and the impending millennium to mobilize support for the cause. While he sought to enlist the sympathies of benevolent Christians by maintaining that Africans had the "instincts of humanity" and "the bearing of manhood," he echoed other colonizationists' claims that they were barbarians. With the return of Africa's "exiled children," he believed, that continent would be covered with "institutions of civilized freedom, and fill it with the light and knowledge and religion, and the whole negro race is raised in a moment from its hopeless depth of degradation."[49]

47. Jordan, *White over Black,* 533–38; Fredrickson, *The Black Image in the White Mind,* 2; Baldwin, *Observations on the Physical, Intellectual, and Moral Qualities of our Colored Population,* 44, 49; F. Freeman, *A Plea for Africa, Being Familiar Conversations on the Subject of Slavery and Colonization* (Philadelphia, 2nd ed., 1837), 169; Thompson, "Lyman Beecher's Long Road to Conservative Abolitionism," 95; American Colonization Society, *A Few Facts Respecting the American Colonization Society, and the Colony at Liberia,* 12.

48. Sermon of July 4, 1830, in Bacon Family Papers; *An Address to the Public, by the Managers of the Colonization Society of Connecticut,* 9.

49. Bacon, *A Plea for Africa,* 8, 10, 15; see also Thompson, "Lyman Beecher's Long Road to Conservative Abolitionism," 96; *New York Observer,* June 23, 1828; Lewis Tappan, *The Life of Arthur Tappan* (New York, 1970 reprint), 141.

Some historians have questioned the logic of the environmental theory. If African Americans were in fact as degraded as the colonizationists claimed, they ask, how could they possibly redeem Africa? And if Africans were even more depraved than blacks in America, how could the emigrants avoid being corrupted by the native population? For Bacon and other colonizationists who pinned their hopes for the redemption of Africa on the establishment of an African seminary in America, no such contradictions existed. Their espousal of an African seminary in America was a classic statement of the environmental theory. They held to the environmentalist conviction, shaped above all by the death of Samuel Mills in Africa in 1818, that whites could not survive the African climate. Thus, they reasoned, it was necessary to send African Americans as missionaries, teachers, and administrators for the purpose of bringing stability and enlightened leadership to the Liberian colony, and civilization and Christianity to the entire continent. They were also motivated by the environmentalist belief that, if isolated from negative influences in American society that degraded them, a select group of African Americans could be educated in America for leadership positions in Africa.[50]

Throughout the 1820s Bacon was a leading advocate of an African seminary. When he initially recommended such a school in 1823, the ACS's board of managers rejected his proposal that it establish an institution modeled on the American Board of Commissioners for Foreign Mission's school in Cornwall, Connecticut. Despite this setback, he remained enthusiastic about the plan. "Indeed," he informed Edward D. Griffith, a supporter of the idea, "it seems to be a project indispensable to their successful operation in Africa."[51]

Bacon's plan was quite ambitious. At a time when most whites resisted the idea of providing even a rudimentary education for blacks, he envisioned a liberal arts college with an independent board of trustees. A number of colonizationists— including Griffith, Gurley, Loring D. Dewey, Sidney E. Morse, and Robert G. Harper—acted on his initiative in 1824 and founded a committee to explore the possibility of establishing a seminary. This committee's deliberations led Bacon, Gurley, Theodore Freylinghuysen, and other supporters to organize the Society for the Education of African Youth in 1826.[52] Following the failure of this society,

50. See Fredrickson, *The Black Image in the White Mind,* 16; Friedman, "Purifying the White Man's Country," 8–10. For arguments on behalf of an African seminary, see Bacon, *A Plea for Africa,* 18; Bacon, "Review on African Colonization," 469; *Fifteenth Annual Report of the Vermont Colonization Society* (Montpelier, Vt., 1834), 14: *American Spectator and Washington City Chronicle,* November 19, 1831; Edward D. Griffith to Bacon, January 21, 1824, in "Records of the Society of Inquiry Respecting Missions."

51. Bacon to Ralph R. Gurley, February 28, 1823, Bacon to Edward D. Griffith, 1823, in "Records of the Society of Inquiry Respecting Missions"; Bacon, "The Reports of the American Society for Colonizing the Free People of Colour of the United States," 545.

52. Bacon to Ralph R. Gurley, February 28, 1823, Bacon to Edward D. Griffith, July 22, 1824, Loring D. Dewey to Bacon, June 12, 1824, Circular of the Society for the Education of African Youth,

those who believed that a national organization was required to mobilize support for a school that would teach "sober and industrious habits" to twenty or thirty black males each year founded the African Education Society in Washington in 1829. Although he was unable to attend the founding meeting, Bacon strongly supported the society's efforts and served with John Tappan, Nathaniel Lord, Francis Wayland, and other benevolent activists as an agent for the organization.[53]

The African Education Society's adherents were guided by somewhat contradictory assumptions regarding blacks. On the one hand, they viewed African Americans as degraded and tended to blame the failure of earlier attempts to establish a seminary on the dearth of suitable students, not the lack of funding from or interest of white people. Moreover, they planned to recruit only a select group of black men who showed special promise and pledged to emigrate to Liberia. On the other hand, they denied that African Americans were less capable than the white yeoman class of achieving moral and intellectual improvement through education and urged assistance for those blacks who might prefer to remain in the United States.[54]

Despite the efforts of Bacon and other African Education Society activists, the organization received little support in New England and the South, and its funding was never sufficient to operate a seminary. Even many colonizationists who sympathized with the idea of educating blacks for service in Africa doubted its feasibility. Consequently, a few warm friends of the society, including Freylinghuysen, concluded that it must either emphasize education in the colony or settle for creating a common school in the United States that would concentrate on mechanical pursuits. It is apparent that Bacon and a small cadre of African Education Society stalwarts stood in advance of most colonizationists on the question of whether a liberal education should be offered to African Americans, even if it involved only a relatively few males slated for repatriation.[55]

August 16, 1826, in "Records of the Society of Inquiry Respecting Missions"; *Religious Intelligencer,* August 12, 26, 1826.

53. *American Spectator and Washington City Chronicle,* May 7, 1831; *Report of the Proceedings at the Formation of the African Education Society: Instituted at Washington, December 28, 1829. With an Address to the Public, by the Board of Managers* (Washington, D.C., 1830), 7, 15–16; Vincent P. Franklin, "Education for Colonization: Attempts to Educate Free Blacks in the United States for Emigration to Africa, 1823–1833," *Journal of Negro Education,* XLIII (1974), 93–94.

54. Loring D. Dewey to Bacon, June 12, 1824, Circular of the Society for the Education of African Youth, August 16, 1826, in "Records of the Society of Inquiry Respecting Missions"; *American Spectator and Washington City Chronicle,* May 7, 1831.

55. *Report of the Proceedings at the Formation of the African Education Society,* 14; David Greene to Bacon, February 1826, in Bacon Family Papers; Theodore Freylinghuysen to Ralph R. Gurley, February 3, 1827, March 15, 1828, Gerrit Smith to Ralph R. Gurley, October 10, 1827, in American Colonization Society Papers; Kwando M. Kinshasa, *Emigration v. Assimilation: The Debate in the African American Press, 1827–1861* (Jefferson, N.C. 1988), 32–33; Franklin, "Education for Colonization," 96, 100–101.

Bacon was especially hopeful that many of the students at the proposed seminary would be emancipated slaves. He was confident that this experiment would show southerners that their slaves could be educated and improved in a proper environment. In addition, he believed that the example of a redeemed Africa and the guarantee of repatriation for manumitted slaves would not only arouse the slaveholders' benevolent impulses but also calm their fears that the former slaves would join other degraded free blacks in America.[56]

In a broader sense, Bacon and many other northern colonizationists considered repatriation a means to the end of abolition.[57] Bacon stood forth as one of the most outspoken antislavery colonizationists. At the same time that he helped to found the African Improvement Society in 1825, he was also instrumental in establishing, with the assistance of Woolsey, Twining, and other friends, the New Haven Antislavery Association, which investigated means of ending slavery in the United States. A year later, on the fiftieth anniversary of American independence, he delivered his harshest and most sweeping indictment of slavery in a speech at Center Church. He chose this auspicious occasion to single out slavery as the most urgent moral and political question of the day and to contrast the rejoicing of Americans in their freedom and independence with the plight of two million blacks held in bondage. The thought of these slaves, he told his audience, "is enough to pour darkness over the exulting spirit of the patriot." Yet he was confident that the system would disappear. "God never made this fair land," he asserted, "to be polluted and trampled into worthlessness forever" by an institution that represented "a criminal invasion of the rights of man." Much as he had stated in his 1823 report to the Society of Inquiry, he called upon every Christian citizen "to promote, by all means in his power, the gradual and legal abolition of slavery."[58]

In emphasizing that slavery was a "national evil" that both northerners and southerners must strive to eradicate, Bacon echoed the thoughts of Joshua Leavitt, then a minister in Stratford, Connecticut, who at times exchanged pulpits with him and whose articles on slavery appeared in the *Christian Spectator* shortly after Bacon came to Center Church. Like Leavitt, Bacon was especially concerned about the negative impact of slavery on whites. The system, he charged, rendered the nation vulnerable to external threat and slave insurrection, nearly bankrupted the South,

56. See Bacon, "Reports of the Colonization Society," 366–67; Bacon, "Review on African Colonization," 463, 477–79; Bacon, *A Plea for Africa*, 16–17; *An Address to the Public by the Managers of the Colonization Society of Connecticut*, 7.

57. See, for example, American Colonization Society, *A Few Facts Respecting the American Colonization Society, and the Colony at Liberia*, 12; New York *Observer*, June 23, 1828; Senior, "New England Congregationalists and the Anti-Slavery Movement," 39–41, 48–51.

58. Diary entry for July 6, 1825, sermon of July 4, 1826, in Bacon Family Papers; *Religious Intelligencer*, July 8, 1826.

and prevented the United States from having close diplomatic ties with Haiti and the South American republics that had abolished slavery. In all, he maintained, slavery was an evil that "will ere long explode beneath us, scattering in fragments the fabric of our institutions, and send over the wide land the fiery waves of a volcanic flood." During the next several years, in sermons and *Christian Spectator* articles, he reiterated various themes contained in this searing condemnation.[59]

Yet Bacon continued to be torn between two opposing instincts: his hatred of slavery and his hope that "not many scores of years" would pass before it disappeared, on the one hand, and, on the other, his attachment to ideological moderation and his belief that African Americans could not be substantially elevated in the United States. Because his fears of racial violence and his cautious, pragmatic instincts ultimately prevailed over his sense of moral outrage, he chose not to launch a vigorous assault on slavery and the racial prejudice that helped to perpetuate it. Colonization, he now concluded, as he had in 1823, was the only reasonable means of ending slavery as well as promoting sectional peace, purifying America, and atoning for the guilt of slavery and prejudice. Because he was convinced that repatriation ultimately would persuade masters to free their slaves, Bacon counseled both northerners and southerners to avoid "indignant invective." He agreed with George Bourne, Benjamin Lundy, and other "friends of liberty" on the goal of abolition. But even though these opponents of slavery were not immediatists and were few in number, he heartily dissented from what he considered their desire to "fan the flame of excitement."[60]

Bacon and other antislavery colonizationists believed that it was necessary to pursue a moderate, cautious course directed toward gradually altering public opinion on the slavery issue. He stated only months before William Lloyd Garrison established the *Liberator* on January 1, 1831, that in the final analysis, people of "sound judgment, sterling minds, and acknowledged weight of character" must provide leadership if slavery was to be abolished.[61] Many of the men and women who launched the abolitionist crusade in the early 1830s certainly did not meet Bacon's standards of moderation and respectability. During that decade Bacon would stand at the center of a wide-ranging and often bitter debate between the antislavery colonizationists and the immediatists on the issues of race and slavery.

59. Sermon of July 4, 1826, in Bacon Family Papers; see also Prospectus of *Christian Spectator,* December, 1828; Bacon, "Review on African Colonization," 473–76; Leonard Bacon, "Review of Speeches by Hayne and Webster," *Quarterly Christian Spectator,* 3rd series, II (September, 1830), 525–26.

60. Vol. 16 of Dissertations, pp. 11–13, in "Records of the Society of Inquiry Respecting Missions"; Bacon, "Review on African Colonization," 473.

61. Bacon, "Review on African Colonization," 479.

5

ANTISLAVERY COLONIZATION, RACE, AND ABOLITIONISM

HISTORIANS have long sought to explain why some opponents of slavery came to embrace the doctrine of immediate emancipation while others did not. During the 1830s, the abolitionists and those colonizationists—including Bacon, Ralph R. Gurley, Lyman Beecher, Theodore Freylinghuysen, and Joseph Tracy—who hoped that the removal of slaves and free blacks to Africa would eventually end slavery waged a bitter struggle to persuade the northern public that their position on the race and slavery issues was correct. Bacon stood in the center of the storm, engaging in a wide-ranging debate with William Lloyd Garrison, Gerrit Smith, James G. Birney, Elizur Wright, Simeon Jocelyn, and other immediatists. In the course of this debate he presented a sweeping critique of the abolitionists' ideology and tactics. Indeed, he remained one of their harshest and most persistent critics throughout the antebellum era.[1]

The men and women who launched the abolitionist crusade in the early 1830s reflected emerging aspirations for the liberation of the individual from historical and institutional limitations. They articulated the message of renunciation of the sin of slavery which necessitated its immediate abolition. Slavery, they argued, prevented blacks from being free moral agents ultimately accountable to God. The immediatists charged that colonizationists such as Bacon served to deepen racial prejudice by seeking to rid America of all blacks and to protect slavery by refusing to condemn it openly. Further, they ridiculed repatriation as impractical and decep-

---

1. This chapter is adapted from Hugh Davis, "At the Crossroads: Leonard Bacon, Antislavery Colonization, and the Abolitionists in the 1830's," in Randall M. Miller and John R. McKivigan, eds., *The Moment of Decision: Biographical Essays on American Character and Regional Identity* (Westport, Conn., 1994), copyright © 1994 by Randall M. Miller and John R. McKivigan. Reproduced with permission of Greenwood Publishing Group, Inc., Westport, Conn.

tive, maintaining that few African Americans had been colonized—largely because nearly all free blacks rejected emigration—and that colonizationists had no real desire to elevate blacks.[2]

Throughout the early and middle 1830s, Bacon vigorously defended the colonization cause from the immediatists' assaults and stood forth as one of its leading theoreticians and activists. As Gurley noted in 1834, Bacon's influence in the movement was "very great" and his efforts were crucial to its success in the North. In articles that appeared in the *African Repository and Colonial Journal,* the *Journal of Freedom,* the *Christian Spectator,* and other publications, in correspondence with prominent colonizationists in the North and South, and in speeches at the annual meetings of the American Colonization Society and the Connecticut and other state colonization organizations,[3] he acknowledged the diversity of opinion among colonizationists on matters relating to race and slavery. But he emphatically denied that the ACS accepted or condoned slaveholding or simply wished to rid the United States of free blacks. "Let it not be forgotten by every friend of colonization" he insisted, "that the 'chief end' of this enterprise is to *improve the condition of the emigrants.*"[4]

Yet the abolitionists' charges and the mounting defections by antislavery northerners from the colonization ranks represented only two of several problems experienced by the ACS in these years. The movement was also divided on matters relating to its fundamental objectives, its management, and its base of support. In the midst of this growing crisis, Bacon often found himself caught between contending factions while seeking to maintain a tenuous middle ground that would enable the cause to thrive, or at least to survive. One problem that continued to plague the American Colonization Society was the hostility with which most free blacks regarded it. Demanding inclusion in American society, they denounced colonization as a racist fraud and sought to mobilize public opinion against the movement.[5]

2. See, for example, Leonard I. Sweet, *Black Images of America, 1784–1870* (New York, 1976), 35–68; John L. Thomas, *The Liberator: William Lloyd Garrison* (Boston, 1963), 114–54; Merton L. Dillon, *The Abolitionists: The Growth of a Dissenting Minority* (DeKalb, Ill., 1974), 35–46; William Lloyd Garrison, *Thoughts on Colonization* (Boston, 1832), 155–56, *et passim.*

3. See, for example, *Religious Intelligencer,* May 18, 1833; New York *Observer,* May 18, July 18, 1833; Leonard to Lucy Bacon, July 26, 1834, in Bacon Family Papers; *Fourth Annual Report of the Managers of the Colonization Society of Connecticut,* 2–6; *Fifteenth Annual Report of the American Society for Colonizing the Free People of Colour of the United States* (Washington, D.C., 1832), 57.

4. See Bacon, "The Free People of Color," 324–25; Bacon, "Slavery and Colonization," *Quarterly Christian Spectator,* 3rd series, V (March, 1833), 148–49; *Journal of Freedom,* September 17, October 22, November 8, 15, 22, 1834.

5. For free blacks' denunciation of the colonization movement, see Sweet, *Black Images of America,* 37–68; *Liberator,* February 12, 1831; Floyd Miller, *The Search for a Black Nationality: Black Emigration and*

Consequently, only 169 of 2,886 emigrants to Liberia between 1820 and 1833 were northern blacks; and while the slave population grew by a half million and that of free blacks by 90,000 during the 1830s, the number of emigrants steadily declined from a peak of 796 in 1832.[6]

Bacon was disturbed by the free blacks' rejection of colonization. At the ACS's 1832 annual meeting he conceded that African Americans "look upon our undertaking with disaffection." Yet he had difficulty coming to grips with the depth of feeling that underlay their denunciation. Despite clear evidence to the contrary, he remained confident that free blacks, with whom he had limited contact by the late 1820s, would eventually gravitate to the movement once they realized that the ACS sincerely wished to provide a haven for them in Africa and that the abolitionists' propaganda was misleading.[7]

At the same time, opposition to colonization had intensified for several years in the South as slaveholders came to resent the antislavery pronouncements of Gurley, Bacon, and other northern activists. By the 1830s, many southerners considered the movement a threat to slavery. In 1832 the Virginia legislature indeed sought to strengthen the system by providing funding for the removal of free blacks, not slaves. At the 1833 ACS meeting, which Bacon was unable to attend, an angry debate occurred on this issue. As John H. B. Latrobe, a Maryland colonizationist, informed Bacon, the question that divided northern and southern colonizationists was *"shall slavery be extirpated or perpetuated through the agency of the Colonization Society?"*[8] The colonizationists' differences on how to deal with the slavery issue, as well as the concerted opposition of abolitionists, free blacks, and most slaveholders to the cause of antislavery colonization, sorely tested Bacon's and his associates' conviction that intelligent men of character and good will could constructively manage social change and improve society. Indeed, their opposition doomed the cause to failure.

Bacon believed that the fate of the cause hinged on its relationship to slavery. Realizing that he and other antislavery colonizationists were caught between the abolitionists and southern defenders of slavery, he sought to stake out a workable middle ground between those who wished to push the ACS in a more antislavery

---

Colonization, 1787–1863 (Urbana, 1975), 54–55, 89–90; C. Peter Ripley, ed., *The Black Abolitionist Papers,* vol. III, *The United States, 1830–1846* (Chapel Hill, 1991), 3–12.

6. Bruce Rosen, "Abolition and Colonization, the Years of Conflict: 1829–1834," *Phylon,* XXXIII (Summer, 1972), 192; *Fifteenth Annual Report of the American Society for Colonizing the Free People of Colour of the United States,* x.

7. *Fifteenth Annual Report of the American Society for Colonizing the Free People of Colour of the United States,* viii–ix; Bacon, "The Free People of Color," 326.

8. Fredrickson, *The Black Image in the White Mind,* 25–26; John H. B. Latrobe to Bacon, June 29, 1833, in Bacon Family Papers.

direction and those who sought more explicit attacks on the abolitionists. In a lengthy letter to Gurley that was published in the *African Repository* in 1833, he attempted to reassure southerners that the American Colonization Society had nothing official to do with slavery except as it "may be affected by the existence and growth of our African Colonies." Yet in a bow to northern antislavery sentiment he essentially contradicted himself by declaring that the ACS should state clearly that "voluntary and peaceful abolition" was "one of the ultimate results of its labors."[9]

These divisions on the slavery issue were exacerbated by the ACS's declining revenues and growing debt, which resulted from the mounting abolitionist defections and declining support among southerners. These ominous developments sparked vigorous criticism of the national officers and the colony's leaders by Elliott Cresson, Robert Finley, Latrobe, and other prominent colonizationists. The mismanagement of the national society, as well as its refusal to declare emancipation as one of its principal objectives, led the Maryland Colonization Society in 1833 to end all but a formal connection with the ACS. With a pledge of $20,000 from the Maryland legislature over ten years, the society sought eventually to make Maryland a free state by means of forced repatriation of manumitted slaves. This explicit linkage of emancipation with emigration, Latrobe assured Bacon, would do more for liberty than "the scattered, and feeble, because scattered" efforts of the ACS.[10]

The rift between the Maryland Colonization Society and the ACS, as well as the Maryland organization's plan for the forced removal of slaves, placed Bacon in a difficult position. Once more, he was pulled in different directions. He was especially close to Gurley and was opposed to any development that might weaken the national society, yet he was also disturbed by the seeming inability of the ACS to put its house in order. Likewise, while he applauded the Maryland society's plan to rid the state of slavery and believed that its approach might well be the only way to counteract the abolitionists' assaults, he was concerned about its insistence upon forced emigration.[11]

In 1833 and 1834 Bacon acted on several fronts to deal with the crisis that confronted the movement. Most important, he met with several leading colonizationists in New York, Baltimore, and Washington in late 1833 and made plans to attend the 1834 ACS meeting. He was convinced that the society's problems were rooted

9. Bacon to Ralph R. Gurley, March 19, 1833, in American Colonization Society Papers; *African Repository and Colonial Journal,* IX (December, 1833), 309–11.

10. Staudenraus, *The African Colonization Movement,* 222–23; Ralph R. Gurley to Bacon, April 30, 1833, Circular of the Maryland Colonization Society, April 30, 1833, John H. B. Latrobe to Bacon, July 29, 1833, in Bacon Family Papers.

11. See Leonard to Lucy Bacon, July 26, 1834, Robert J. Breckinridge to Bacon, July 15, 1834, in Bacon Family Papers; Bacon to Gerrit Smith, July 5, 1834, in Gerrit Smith Miller Collection, Syracuse University.

in the executive committee's excessive size and lack of accountability and the inadequate assistance for Gurley at headquarters. A fundamental reorganization, he optimistically predicted, would "infuse new vigor into all our movements and secure new triumphs for our cause." After meeting with Henry Clay, Daniel Webster, Theodore Freylinghuysen, and other friends of colonization, he concluded that, while the struggle to reorganize the society might destroy it, "without reform we are ruined."[12]

As a member of a committee charged with reforming the ACS, Bacon successfully urged a cessation of emigration until the society's $45,000 debt was paid. He also advocated more controls on the colony's government, cutbacks in funds allotted for the *African Repository* and traveling agents, a drastically reduced board of managers, and support for Gerrit Smith's plan to raise money for the organization. Yet as was often the case, he sought to balance his criticism of the national officers' policies with efforts to placate disgruntled factions within the movement. For example, he attempted to mollify the old board members by urging that some of them be reappointed and southerners by calling for one of them to be hired as an assistant to Gurley.[13]

Bacon emerged from the 1834 American Colonization Society meeting with renewed confidence in the cause. But other colonizationists were less sanguine about the movement's prospects. Samuel M. Worcester and Robert Finley, among others, despaired of meaningful improvements at the ACS headquarters. Robert J. Breckinridge was gloomy in his assessment of the cause in New England, declaring: "Colonization is dead, in all this region; and the principles of our parent society, will never revive here any more."[14]

Breckinridge made this statement while on a tour of New England to raise money for the Maryland Colonization Society, which actively sought to gain Bacon's support. Latrobe assured him that the organization did not wish to rid the state of free blacks or to strengthen slavery, and Breckinridge argued that it was better to force slaves "*to go and be free* than force them *to stay in bondage*." Although Bacon declined the society's offer to serve as its agent in the North, he applauded

12. Bacon to Thomas H. Gallaudet, March 18, 1833, Lucy Bacon to Sarah Wisner, August 26, 1833, Thomas H. Gallaudet to Bacon, November 29, 1833, Bacon to Ralph R. Gurley, January 3, 1834, Leonard to Lucy Bacon, January 16, 20, 1834, in Bacon Family Papers.

13. *Seventeenth Annual Report of the American Society for Colonizing the Free People of Colour of the United States* (Washington, D.C., 1834), iii, xv–xxiv; Staudenraus, *The African Colonization Movement,* 224–25; *Colonizationist and Journal of Freedom,* March, 1834; Bacon to Ralph R. Gurley, February 25, March 24, 1834, in American Colonization Society Papers.

14. *Colonizationist and Journal of Freedom,* March, 1834; Samuel M. Worcester to Bacon, February 19, 1834, Robert Finley to Bacon, February 20, 1834, in Bacon Family Papers; Robert J. Breckinridge to Charles Hodge, July 31, 1834, in Breckinridge Family Papers, Library of Congress.

what appeared to be a clear manifestation of antislavery colonization and joined representatives of the Maryland society for a fund-raising effort in Boston. Nevertheless, his concern that the society's policy of forced repatriation would be exploited by the abolitionists and would make it even more difficult to gain the support of free blacks for emigration, combined with his fear that it would irreparably divide the colonization cause, ultimately led him to stand aloof from it.[15]

In the midst of the crisis in the colonization movement, Bacon decided to establish a weekly newspaper devoted to both colonization and antislavery principles. Unlike the abolitionists, who successfully employed the press as a vehicle for disseminating their ideology, the colonizationists, who enjoyed rather easy access to the columns of many newspapers and journals, only peripherally relied upon printed propaganda in their operations. Bacon was convinced that if "*right* material of thought and discussion" were not disseminated by antislavery colonizationists, others would influence the public "to the great disadvantage of the cause of justice and righteousness." For this reason he founded the *Journal of Freedom* in May, 1834. At first he insisted that his connection with the weekly newspaper, which was published in New Haven until June, 1835, when low circulation levels forced him to sell it, be kept secret from the public. While his brother, David, was listed as editor, Bacon confided to Gerrit Smith that the editorials would be written "under my eye and in full accordance, I doubt not, with my views."[16]

The *Journal of Freedom,* which Garrison suggested should be named the *Journal of Despotism,* articulated the views of antislavery colonizationists, such as Elliott Cresson, Ralph R. Gurley, Gerrit Smith (until his defection to abolitionism in 1835), and Lyman Beecher, who espoused what Bacon termed "moderate antislavery" and "rational colonization." The paper, he informed Smith, would be "rationally Colonizationist, and in the true sense of the word, Abolitionist," and therefore would, it was hoped, convince readers that abolition was "practicable and safe." In line with the paper's motto, "Speaking the Truth in Love," he pledged to avoid controversy with all except those who defended slavery. He hoped to appeal especially to those who were not identified closely with either the American Colonization Society or the American Anti-Slavery Society, but he clearly was motivated by the desire to counteract the abolitionists' inroads among antislavery northerners

15. John H. B. Latrobe to Bacon, October 11, 1833, July 18, 1834, Ralph R. Gurley to Thomas H. Gallaudet, June 30, 1834, Ralph R. Gurley to Bacon, July 2, 1834, Robert J. Breckinridge to Bacon, July 15, 1834, in Bacon Family Papers. In 1835 the Philadelphia Colonization Society asked Bacon to be its general agent, but he declined the offer. Elliott Cresson to Bacon, August 13, 1835, in Bacon Family Papers.

16. Staudenraus, *The African Colonization Movement,* 214–16; *Journal of Freedom,* December 2, 1834; Bacon to Gerrit Smith, March 20, 1834, in Gerrit Smith Miller Collection; Thomas Buchanan to Bacon, July 28, 1835, in Bacon Family Papers.

and to show that immediatism was by no means the only approach. Although he made a point of declaring that the paper was independent of the ACS, he believed that the colonization cause ought to be sustained for the sake of Africa and for those African Americans who wished to emigrate.[17]

Bacon was moved to found the *Journal of Freedom* in part by his doubts concerning the adequacy of colonization as a means of abolishing slavery. In fact, he agreed with the abolitionists, in some respects, on the race and slavery issues. Historians have pointed to a variety of life experiences and beliefs that led some opponents of slavery—a number of whom had supported the colonization cause—to embrace the doctrine of immediate emancipation. These converts to abolitionism, historians argue, tended, among other things, to have parents who emphasized moral uprightness and the ability to improve the world, to be driven by a youthful idealism, to have experienced crises related to career choices in the 1820s, and to adhere to evangelical doctrines which called upon converts, as free moral agents, to act immediately to eradicate sin in the world.[18]

However, there is the danger of exaggerating the differences that set the pioneer abolitionists apart from critics of slavery such as Bacon, who never became immediatists. Bacon and the abolitionists indeed shared, in varying degrees, important experiences and beliefs. His parents were missionaries who emphasized a strict morality and good works. He was an idealistic youth of twenty-one when he became active in the colonization movement in 1823, believing that it would uplift African Americans, eventually end slavery, and civilize and Christianize Africa. Moreover, he had nearly been dismissed from his pastorate at Center Church in the mid and late 1820s. Finally, he believed that the individual was a free moral agent and that opposition to slavery should become part of the evangelical witness.[19]

More important, Bacon had long been interested in the plight of blacks throughout the world. Indeed, Gerrit Smith claimed in 1835 that "no man in our country

17. *Journal of Freedom,* May 17, December 2, 1834; Bacon to Gerrit Smith, March 20, 1834, in Gerrit Smith Miller Collection; Ethan A. Andrews to editors of the *Journal of Freedom,* May 30, 1834, in Bacon Family Papers. For Garrison's comment, see *Liberator,* April 20, 1834.

18. See, for example, Bertram Wyatt-Brown, "Conscience and Career: Young Abolitionists and Missionaries," in *Anti-Slavery, Religion, and Reform: Essays in Memory of Roger Anstey,* ed. Christine Bolt and Seymour Drescher (Folkestone, Eng., 1980), 185–90, 194–95; Lawrence B. Goodheart, *Abolitionist, Actuary, Atheist: Elizur Wright and the Reform Impulse* (Kent, Ohio, 1990), 4–15; Victor B. Howard, *Conscience and Slavery: The Evangelistic Calvinist Domestic Missions, 1837–1861* (Kent, Ohio, 1990), 6–7; Donald M. Scott, "Abolition as a Sacred Vocation," in *Antislavery Reconsidered: New Perspectives on the Abolitionists,* ed. Lewis Perry and Michael Fellman (Baton Rouge, 1979), 62–67.

19. Evidence of these experiences and beliefs is found in David to Leonard Bacon, June 26, 1803, Alice to Dr. Leonard Bacon, July 1, 1802, Alice Bacon to Bacon, November 28, 1817, November 1, 1818, W. Shedd to Bacon, September 30, 1826, Bacon to Charles G. Finney, April 12, May 30, 1831, Bacon to Asahel Nettleton, July 29, 1835, in Bacon Family Papers.

has written so much as you have on the subject of the interests of that race. No man in our country understands those interests as well as you do." During the 1830s, the abolitionists' assaults on colonization, Bacon's growing sensitivity to the plight of blacks resulting from contact with them, and free blacks' continuing rejection of repatriation moved him to criticize those colonizationists who urged the removal of blacks because they considered them threats to a moral and orderly society.[20]

Bacon also concurred with the abolitionists' contention that state laws which oppressed blacks were "repugnant to the spirit" and would someday be declared contrary to the United States Constitution. Moreover, he emphatically endorsed Garrison's claim that blacks "can be improved in the United States and *ought to be*," as well as his advice that they compete economically with whites by working for lower wages. He even sent his children to an integrated school in New Haven and urged other whites to do the same. In 1834 he went so far as to state: "It has long been a settled principle with me that a colored man should be treated with the same kindness and consideration which would be due to him, if he were a white man."[21]

In addition, Bacon, like many other antislavery colonizationists, shared with the abolitionists a deep and abiding hatred for slavery.[22] Throughout the 1830s he reiterated his earlier condemnation of slavery as a system that was "simply and utterly sinful" and had no basis either in nature or in the Bible. Furthermore, he expressed respect, albeit conditionally, for the abolitionists' sincerity, consistency of principle, and devotion to duty and liberty, and he defended the right of all critics of slavery to speak their minds freely and openly. He was especially contemptuous of those northerners who participated in, or condoned the actions of, the antiabolitionist mobs, whose "hushing rebukes" he considered "too preposterous to need an answer in this country."[23]

Yet in the final analysis, Bacon not only refused to cross the line from antislavery colonization to immediatism but stood forth as one of the abolitionists' most vocal critics. The personal and professional milieu in which Bacon moved as well as his temperament and belief system help explain why he made these decisions at this critical juncture.

20. Gerrit Smith to Bacon, February 6, 1835, in Bacon Family Papers; Bacon, "The Free People of Color," 334; Bacon, "Slavery and Colonization," 167; *Journal of Freedom*, May 17, October 22, 1834; *African Repository and Colonial Journal*, VIII (August, 1832), 174–75.

21. See Bacon, "The Free People of Color," 316, 318, 322, 327; Leonard Bacon, *Exposition of the Objects and Plans of the American Union for the Relief and Improvement of the Colored Race* (Boston, 1835), 3–15; *Journal of Freedom*, September 24, 1834.

22. See, for example, *Colonizationist and Journal of Freedom*, December, 1833; Boston *Recorder and Religious Herald*, April 26, 1834, December 18, 1835; *Address of Joseph R. Ingersoll at the Annual Meeting of the Pennsylvania Colonization Society, October 25, 1838* (Philadelphia, 1838), 21–22; *Religious Intelligencer*, January 12, October 12, 1833, July 22, 1837.

23. See Bacon, "Review on American Colonization," 474–75; *Slavery Discussed*, 23–32, 54–55, 101–105; *Journal of Freedom*, May 17, December 8, 15, 1834, March 11, 1835.

Bacon had developed close emotional and organizational loyalties to the colonization cause at a formative stage of his life—as a twenty-one-year-old student at Andover Theological Seminary and throughout the 1820s as a leading spokesman for the northern wing of the movement. By the time Garrison threw down the gauntlet against colonization in 1831, Bacon was a highly respected figure in the cause, with both a personal and a professional stake in defending it against its critics. He especially resented those who had recently embraced immediatism and who considered that to be the only legitimate stance on the slavery issue. This resentment was grounded in part in his conviction that many abolitionists were not sufficiently respectful of those who had long spoken against slavery and urged the elevation of blacks. For example, he caustically reminded Garrison in 1832 that he had favored a "complete education" for blacks, without condition of sending graduates to Africa, "long before Mr. Garrison was an enemy - nay, before he was a friend of the American Colonization Society."[24]

As pastor of the most prestigious church in Connecticut, and as a writer whose pamphlets and articles reached a broad evangelical audience, Bacon was respected in benevolent and ecclesiastical circles when he voiced his opinion on a wide range of issues. He was a proud, sensitive, and, at times, arrogant man who did not easily brook criticism. He clearly looked down on a man such as Garrison. In an 1833 article, for example, he suggested that because Garrison exhibited deficiencies in framing arguments and discussing principles, he should avoid controversy and employ his talents as a poet to advance the antislavery cause.[25]

As a spokesman for the colonization cause Bacon believed that he stood in the vanguard of efforts to prepare the world for the coming of the millennium. Consequently, the abolitionists' accusations shocked and angered him. These attacks were often quite pointed and personal, as when Garrison, his harshest critic, charged in 1833 that "no writer in the United States, no slaveholder in the South, has uttered or published more excusatory, corrupt, and blasphemous sentiments as regards slavery" than Bacon. Bacon genuinely detested Garrison and seemed to place little credence in his barbs. However, he was deeply hurt and offended by a personal rebuke from the acerbic Elizur Wright, a childhood friend, who angrily exhorted him to "take my advice and come out like a man—like a true Christian and confess your sin . . . with up and down honesty, against everlasting hairsplitting and equivocation." Stung to the quick by Wright's assault on his character, Bacon responded that he was "sorry to see that you have so bad an opinion of me."[26]

24. *Liberator,* April 27, 1833; Bacon, "The Free People of Color," 320.
25. Bacon, "Slavery and Colonization," 156.
26. Wendell Phillips Garrison and Francis Jackson Garrison, eds., *William Lloyd Garrison, 1805–1879. The Story of His Life Told by His Children,* vol. I, *1805–1835* (4 vols.; New York, 1885), 303n; Elizur Wright to Bacon, April 27, 1837, in Bacon Family Papers; Bacon to Elizur Wright, May 1, 1837, in Elizur Wright Papers, Library of Congress.

Bacon often sought to act as a mediator and conciliator within the colonization movement as well as the broader antislavery constellation. Yet he could, at times, hurl epithets with the best of them. For example, he labeled Garrison a "willful incendiary who would smile to see conflagration, rapine, and extermination sweeping with tornado-fury over half the land." Indeed, he acknowledged to Simeon Jocelyn that he occasionally became "unduly excited" by the immediatists' attacks. The emotion he invested in these and other charges and countercharges goes far to explain why it was so difficult for him even to consider seriously the invitations by various abolitionists—especially Smith, the only convert to immediatism with whom he remained on friendly terms—to join their ranks.[27]

Bacon's repudiation of immediatism was also grounded in his social and ecclesiastical milieu. Center Church, the city of New Haven, the Congregational Church, and the state of Connecticut all provided an atmosphere friendly to colonization and hostile to abolitionism and blacks. With the exception of a few ministers— including Joel Hawes and three New Haven clergymen, Jocelyn, Charles Cleaveland, and Henry G. Ludlow—the Congregational clergy in the state overwhelmingly supported colonization. Throughout the 1830s the Connecticut General Association, in which Bacon played a prominent role, heartily endorsed the cause. Moreover, clergymen continued to occupy important positions in the Connecticut Colonization Society, which met annually but raised little money and generated few publications.[28]

In addition, many of Bacon's closest associates and friends in New Haven, including Nathaniel Taylor and Benjamin Silliman, were dedicated colonizationists. Procolonization sentiment was also widespread in Center Church. With the blessing of certain pillars of the church, such as members of the Hotchkiss, Whittlesey, Trowbridge, Sheffield, Bradley, and other mercantile and manufacturing families that depended, in varying degrees, on the southern market, Bacon continued regularly to appeal to his congregation for contributions to the American Colonization Society. Moreover, his near dismissal in the late 1820s must have remained fresh in his mind. He clearly loved his work and wished to remain at Center Church. In

27. Bacon, "The Free People of Color," 333; *Slavery Discussed,* 58; *Journal of Freedom,* October 8, 1834; Bacon to Elizur Wright, May 1, 1837, in Elizur Wright Papers; Gerrit Smith to Bacon, January 9, 1835, January 22, 1836, in Bacon Family Papers.

28. Simeon Jocelyn to Elizur Wright, May 24, 1833, in Elizur Wright Papers; R. B. Hall to William Lloyd Garrison, February 14, 1833, in William Lloyd Garrison Papers, Boston Public Library; *Manual of the First Church in New Haven, 1860* (New Haven, 1860), 4–5; New Haven *Record,* May 23, 1840; John R. McKivigan, *The War Against Proslavery Religion: Abolitionism and the Northern Churches, 1830–1865* (Ithaca, 1984), 48; Lucy to Leonard Bacon, January 20, 1834, Bacon to Joel Hawes, March 22, 1836, in Bacon Family Papers; Senior, "New England Congregationalists and the Anti-Slavery Movement," 27–28, 44–45, 73–74, 158, 160.

declining an offer in 1834 to be the agent for the ACS in New England, he said of his pastorate: "I am not conscious of any gift or endowment which I cannot use advantageously for the church, for my country, for the world, just where I am."[29] The fact that he was settled in a career may well have reinforced his tendency to pursue a cautious course on the race and slavery issues. To have embraced the highly controversial abolitionist cause or to have appeared to endorse the concept of racial equality could have seriously jeopardized his position in both his church and the community; at the very least, it would have made his efforts to maintain harmony among the varied interests within his congregation much more difficult.

Antiabolitionist and antiblack sentiment reached a boiling point in New Haven in 1831, when Jocelyn, Garrison, Arthur Tappan, and a group of blacks proposed the creation of a college for black males. In June of that year the first Negro Convention, held in Philadelphia, pledged twenty thousand dollars to launch the institution. Citing New Haven's "friendly, pious, generous and humane" residents, its trade with the West Indies, and its literary and scientific character, the convention endorsed it as the site.[30]

Unfortunately, the great majority of New Haven whites proved far less hospitable to the idea than the school's supporters had anticipated. Frightened by the involvement of immediatists in the scheme (especially in the wake of the Nat Turner revolt), concerned about the reaction by southern students at Yale and by southern consumers of New Haven products, and opposed to providing a college education for African Americans and attracting more blacks to the community, a large number of white New Haveners held a mass meeting, at which they condemned the proposal by a vote of 700–4 and declared that the college would be resisted "by every lawful means." With their excitement stimulated by fiery speeches, an angry mob then shouted obscenities at blacks and stoned Tappan's home, which stood only a few doors from Bacon's residence.[31]

Bacon's response to the meeting's actions, like that of many moderate antislavery newspapers, was quite ambivalent. He expressed "mortification and sorrow" with

29. Mead, *Nathaniel William Taylor,* 236; George P. Fisher, *Life of Benjamin Silliman* (2 vols.; London, 1866), II, 47–48, 238–39; Simeon Jocelyn to Elizur Wright, May 24, 1833, in Elizur Wright Papers; *African Repository and Colonial Journal,* VIII (August, 1832), 169–72; *Seventh Annual Report of the Managers of the Colonization Society of Connecticut,* 23; *Patten's New Haven Directory, For the Years 1841–2. Number 2* (New Haven, 1841), 18, 25, 56–57, 77, 82, 86, 96, 101; Bacon to Ralph R. Gurley, August 12, 1834, in Bacon Family Papers.

30. *Connecticut Journal,* October 4, 1831; *Liberator,* June 18, November 12, 1831; Tappan, *The Life of Arthur Tappan,* 257; *Minutes and Proceedings of the First Annual Convention of the People of Colour* (Philadelphia, 1831), 5–7.

31. *Religious Intelligencer,* September 17, 1831; Tappan, *The Life of Arthur Tappan,* 148–50; Simeon S. Jocelyn, *College for Colored Youth. An Account of the New-Haven City Meetings and Resolutions, With Recommendations of the College, and Strictures on the Doings of New-Haven* (New York, 1831), 4.

"the *spirit* which we have seen a sober and christian community (or one so reputed) rush together to blot out the first ray of hope for the blacks" and emphasized his support for "a complete education" for blacks in the United States. Because Bacon did not own property at this time, he probably could not speak or vote at the public meeting. But in truth, he had never endorsed the proposed college. Indeed, he, as well as other colonizationists who supported black education, acknowledged that the college's opponents were justified in rejecting the proposal. He would support such an institution, he noted in 1832, "whenever it shall be proposed in a form which will give us reason to believe that the control of it shall be entrusted to discreet men, and that the course of instruction shall not be calculated to exasperate the pupils and their colored brethren against the institutions and the population, and to fill them with the spirit of wrath and insurrection."[32] If Bacon had been at all tempted to join the incipient abolitionist crusade prior to this incident, the sound and fury that erupted in the city certainly helped him to resist the urge.

In truth, New Haven whites' attitudes on race and slavery merely reflected the attitudes of most white residents of Connecticut. The state's relatively homogeneous population, its attachment to tradition and a sense of exclusiveness, and its economic ties with the South bred a distrust of rapid social change, especially that urged by the immediatists. Connecticut's ratio of mob actions to antislavery auxiliaries in the early and middle 1830s was more than twice as high as that of any other New England state, and its black population suffered more overt discrimination than elsewhere in the region.[33] Perhaps the best known antiabolitionist and antiblack incident in Connecticut in these years occurred in Canterbury in 1833. When Prudence Crandall sought to conduct a school for black girls, angry residents, led by local colonizationists who praised New Haven's actions two years earlier, forced the school to close. Their appeals to the state legislature led to the passage of a law that prohibited the establishment of any school for blacks who were not residents of the state and forbade their instruction without the approval of local authorities.[34]

While some abolitionists charged that all prominent Connecticut colonizationists were either actively involved in these efforts to prevent the elevation of African Americans or remained silent in the face of injustice, William Jay, an immediatist,

---

32. Bacon, "The Free People of Color," 320; *Religious Intelligencer,* September 17, 1831; Theodore Dwight Bacon, *Leonard Bacon,* 201.

33. Lawrence Bruser, "Political Antislavery in Connecticut, 1844–1858" (Ph.D. dissertation, Columbia University, 1974), 14–19, 51–55, 57–59; Leonard L. Richards, *"Gentlemen of Property and Standing": Anti-Abolition Mobs in Jacksonian America* (New York, 1970), 40.

34. Philip S. Foner, "Prudence Crandall," in *Three Who Dared: Prudence Crandall, Margaret Douglass, Myrtilla Miner—Champions of Antebellum Black Education,* ed. Philip S. Foner and Josephine F. Pacheo (Westport, Conn., 1984), 5–40; Susan Strane, *A Whole-Souled Woman: Prudence Crandall and the Education of Black Women* (New York, 1990), 34–65, 73–90, *et passim.*

probably included Bacon among those "pious and respectful colonizationists" in the state who in fact opposed the Canterbury outrage. Indeed, in a *Christian Spectator* article Bacon praised Crandall as "heroic and immortal" and condemned the legislature's actions as "dishonorable to the state; and still more so that popular passion under which it was enacted."[35] Yet much as with the New Haven incident, he never actually endorsed Crandall's school. His denunciation of what he considered excessive and illiberal reactions to these efforts on behalf of black education did not obviate his concern that to advance African Americans too rapidly would not only produce social disorder but also provide few real benefits for blacks. Perhaps above all, his response to these racial incidents indicates that he was unwilling to jeopardize his standing in Center Church, New Haven, and the colonization and other benevolent societies by directly confronting the pervasive racist sentiment among white Americans or by supporting institutions for black improvement that counted abolitionists among their active proponents. Given the fact that few whites other than the immediatists were committed to establishing such schools and that Bacon himself refused to take a bold stand in favor of the proposed college, his expression of support for black education, particularly at the college level, seems little more than an empty gesture.

Indeed, Bacon's differences with the abolitionists on both the race and slavery issues were substantial. Historians have noted that white abolitionists often depicted African Americans in abstract terms, expected them to adopt the abolitionists' middle-class values and to be meek in the face of persecution, and were, at times, blatantly racist in their assumptions and behavior. By the late 1830s, immediatists tended to react to antiabolitionist and antiblack mobs by focusing more on the civil liberties of whites than on the fundamental rights of blacks.[36] Yet one must not overstate the abolitionists' racism, for their call for African Americans to acquire knowledge and cultivation was rooted more in their middle-class social prejudices than in racial prejudice. Particularly during the 1830s many abolitionists expressed a commitment to racial justice and condemned racial discrimination and prejudice as extensions of slavery. As concerned slavery and racism, neither one nor the other, they insisted, could be eradicated unless both were. Bacon had periodically argued this point in the 1820s. In fact, he was, on the whole, less overtly racist than colonizationists such as Robert J. Breckinridge and Isaac Orr and less inclined to empha-

35. *Liberator,* June 15, 1833; William Jay, *Inquiry into the Character and Tendency of the American Colonization and American Anti-Slavery Societies* (6th ed., rev.; New York, 1838), 48; Bacon, "Mrs. Child's Appeal in Favor of the Africans," *Quarterly Christian Spectator,* 3rd series, VI (September, 1834), 449.

36. See Leon Litwack, "The Abolitionist Dilemma: The Antislavery Movement and the Negro," *New England Quarterly,* XXXIV (1964), 50–73; Friedman, *Gregarious Saints,* 160–95; William H. Pease and Jane H. Pease, "Antislavery Ambivalence: Immediatism, Expediency, Race," *American Quarterly,* XVII (1965), 689–92, 695.

size the need for a racially homogeneous America than Lyman Beecher. But he was far less willing than many abolitionists to challenge, aggressively and directly, the pervasive racism in America.[37]

Stung by the abolitionists' charges that the colonizationists, including many clergymen and lay leaders, were thoroughly racist toward blacks, and seemingly intent upon salving the conscience of northern whites, Bacon tended increasingly to minimize both the extent of white racism and the impact of white racism on free blacks. While he conceded that some Christians were prejudiced, he denied that they treated African Americans with "utter dislike." Moreover, he categorically rejected the immediatists' contention that northerners were more racist than southerners. He was especially defensive about the people of Connecticut, maintaining that the state's Black Law and the racial incidents in New Haven and Canterbury were aberrations created by "peculiar and we trust temporary causes.[38]

Bacon also retreated from his earlier statements that white racism was perhaps the dominant factor responsible for fastening poverty on most free blacks. By 1834, he had come to place much of the responsibility for poverty and low-wage jobs on blacks themselves. Citing the example of a wealthy black man who lived near him, Bacon asserted: "Whatever may be the cause which makes so many colored men shoe-blacks and waiters, it is not the mere prejudice of the white people." He even claimed that "so far as our observation has extended, colored men are judged each one by his own merits, as truly as white men." He did not abandon the environmental theory or come to believe, in the main, that African Americans were inherently inferior to whites; but as the implacable black opposition to repatriation became increasingly undeniable—a point illustrated by the coolness that many black New Haveners displayed toward Bacon—he seemed less inclined than he had been in the 1820s to give them the benefit of the doubt when explaining their plight.[39]

Bacon also disagreed with the immediatists on how discriminatory laws should be countered. Unlike many abolitionists, he believed that laws could not be changed until the prejudice that shaped them was diminished significantly; and he had grave doubts that this would occur for many years. Convinced that prejudice could be eradicated if exposed and attacked, a number of leading abolitionists urged

37. *African Repository and Colonial Journal,* IX (January, 1834), 310; *American Spectator and Washington City Chronicle,* February 12, April 2, 1834; Thompson, "Lyman Beecher's Long Road to Conservative Abolitionism," 104. The evidence indicates that one must qualify Timothy J. Sehr's assertion that Bacon considered blacks and whites "brothers and inherently equal." See Timothy J. Sehr, "Leonard Bacon and the Myth of the Good Slaveholder," *New England Quarterly,* XLIX (1976), 206.

38. Bacon, "The Free People of Color," 318, 321; "Mrs. Child's Appeal in Favor of the Africans," 446–47, 449.

39. Bacon, "The Free People of Color," 316, 318; *Journal of Freedom,* September 17, October 22, 1834.

agitation and confrontation; whereas Bacon and many other colonizationists, who lacked a sense of urgency and feared the consequences of a direct assault on racial discrimination, counseled patience, moderation, and Christian meekness. If black men feared God, worked hard, and were "unassuming towards those whom custom or the constitution of society regards as his superior," he stated, they eventually would gain the respect of whites. On the other hand, in advising blacks to avoid "an arrogant, assuming, disrespectful behavior," Bacon implied that those who aggressively sought equal rights or were critical of discrimination were partly responsible for the mob action that proliferated in the North.[40]

Bacon was especially critical of the abolitionists for challenging existing racial taboos. In the wake of the 1831 New Haven mob action, he accused Garrison of helping to provoke the escalating "vulgar malignity" against blacks by "filling them with delusive hopes." Whites, he argued, must refrain from challenging barriers in the color caste system that could not, and perhaps should not, be breached in the foreseeable future. As he warned Gerrit Smith in the midst of violent antiabolitionist and antiblack mob action in 1834: "If we undertake to force a change—if we undertake to develop these persons in rank faster than the progressive and self-manifested elevation of their character will carry them—if we make a violent assault upon existing prejudices—we shall make matters worse rather than better."[41] Thus, he clearly believed that free blacks had not yet developed their value system and standards of behavior sufficiently to warrant a standing in American society equal to that of most whites.

Bacon's response to the aspirations of African Americans and to agitation on their behalf by white abolitionists was shaped by a blend of racism and elitism. At times, he was blatantly racist, as when he speculated that the differences between whites and blacks in America were due in part to blacks' "barbarous lineage." Moreover, like many middle-class Americans of the time, Bacon was elitist in his attitudes toward both the white working class and free blacks. Despite the fact that elements of the northern middle and upper classes were involved in many of the race riots of the time and were largely responsible for the discriminatory legislation directed against free blacks, he blamed the "vulgar prejudice" of "low-bred" white workers for much of the racial conflict in society. Having risen from a "respectable" poverty, he consciously distanced himself from the white working class, which he viewed as disorderly and lacking in those character traits necessary for respectability and suc-

40. Bacon, "The Free People of Color," 322–23; *Journal of Freedom,* October 22, 1834. For similar sentiments by northern colonizationists, see Catharine E. Beecher, *An Essay on Slavery and Abolitionism, With Reference to the Duty of American Females* (Philadelphia, 1837), 29–31; Boston *Recorder and Religious Herald,* May 24, 1834.

41. Bacon, "The Free People of Color," 332; Bacon to Gerrit Smith, December 10, 1834, in Gerrit Smith Miller Collection.

cess. But as David Roediger has noted, notions of race were also shaped within the developing class formation of the time. As a member of the emerging professional middle class, which considered itself both culturally and morally superior to the working class, Bacon was inclined to view free blacks in an even more negative light, for they occupied the lowest level of northern society and suffered from an unfavorable racial stereotype. Thus, both class and racial considerations shaped his conviction that free blacks were not only partly responsible for their plight but were also unwitting pawns in the hands of the abolitionists and did not know what was best for themselves. White Christians, he wrote in 1834, should not ask blacks what needed to be undertaken for their welfare; rather, it was "for other wisdom than they [blacks] are masters of in their present circumstances, to inquire by what great system of measures . . . good can be effected in their behalf."[42]

Much as Bacon believed that free blacks were not capable of achieving equality with many whites in America, he was also certain that neither slaves nor whites were prepared for immediate emancipation. On one level, his prolonged debate with the abolitionists appears to have been little more than petty quibbling over semantics—what Elizur Wright had contemptuously termed "everlasting hairsplitting." For example, he claimed that they would have displayed a less "pugnacious, denunciatory attitude" had they described their organizations not as abolitionist societies but as societies for promoting freedom or for the emancipation of the enslaved, or even for the abolition of slavery.[43]

In addition, historians have shown that abolitionists did not agree on precisely what "immediate emancipation" meant. Many probably did not interpret it literally to mean the immediate liberation of slaves, though they insisted that emancipation precede any debate on a temporary guardianship for the freedmen. Moreover, he admitted that the process leading to total abolition must begin immediately. "As for the thing, which they describe as the meaning of immediate abolition," he stated, "we hold it to be not only practicable and safe, but the very first thing to be done, for the safety of a slaveholding country."[44]

Yet Gerrit Smith erred when he argued that Bacon's letters, which appeared in

42. Bacon, "The Free People of Color," 323–24; *Journal of Freedom,* October 22, December 15, 1834; David R. Roediger, *The Wages of Whiteness: Race and the Making of the American Working Class* (London, 1991), 55–57. This view was echoed by the *American Spectator and Washington City Chronicle,* April 2, 1831; Boston *Recorder and Religious Herald,* May 24, 1834.

43. Elizur Wright to Bacon, April 27, 1837, in Bacon Family Papers; *Journal of Freedom,* December 15, 1834.

44. See Anne C. Loveland, "Evangelicalism and 'Immediate Emancipation' in American Antislavery Thought," *Journal of Southern History,* XXXII (1966), 172–88; David B. Davis, "The Emergence of Immediatism in British and American Antislavery Thought," *Mississippi Valley Historical Review,* XLIX (September, 1962), 209–30; Bacon, *Slavery Discussed,* 71–72.

the *Journal of Freedom,* "show that you do not know yourself, and that you are in fact an immediatist." Bacon believed that the dispute over words was extremely important. The problem, he insisted to Smith, was that the abolitionists had one meaning in their definitions and another in their denunciations and popular harangues: "Immediate emancipation, however it may be defined in argument and in order to evade objections, will always be understood to mean in declamation, an immediate and instantaneous conversion of the slave, not merely into a 'person,' but into a person who is his own master invested like every other adult citizen with the power of self-control. . . . The *immediate duty* of emancipation is one thing; the duty of *immediate emancipation* is another thing. I go for the former, but not the latter."[45]

Bacon's rejection of immediate emancipation, however, was based upon more than a concern about the meaning and consequences of that doctrine. While he and many other opponents of slavery—including Albert Barnes, John Tappan and his brother Charles, and Joseph Tracy—agreed with the immediatists that the system was inherently sinful, they denied the abolitionists' claim that slaveholding was prima facie evidence of sin and, therefore, should be grounds for exclusion from Christian communion. To embrace such a doctrine, he informed Jocelyn, "is to outrage common sense, and to do violence to the Scriptures." Bacon and other gradualists clung to the belief that slavery would not survive the cessation of evil practices associated with the system, while the abolitionists feared that piecemeal improvement in the slaves' condition would deaden the slaveholders' consciences. The antislavery moderates also drew a second set of distinctions: between sinful and innocent slaveholders, faithful and unfaithful churches, and southern law and the southern people.[46]

Bacon believed that a master who bred slaves for profit, treated them like animals, sold family members, or did not take care of his slaves' physical and spiritual needs should be ostracized as a "heathen and a publican." Yet throughout the antebellum era he repeatedly set forth conditions—such as inheritance, the need to do what was necessary for the slaves' welfare under existing circumstances, the establishment of an apprenticeship leading eventually to emancipation, and state laws

45. Gerrit Smith to Bacon, August 27, 1835, in Bacon Family Papers; Bacon to Gerrit Smith, October 24, 1834, Gerrit Smith Miller Collection; *Journal of Freedom,* December 8, 1834. For similar criticism of the abolitionists' concept of immediate emancipation, see John H. Cocke to Thomas H. Gallaudet, July 15, 1834, in Thomas Hopkins Gallaudet Papers; *Colonizationist and Journal of Freedom,* May, 1833; Joseph Tracy, *Natural Equality. A Sermon Before the Vermont Colonization Society, at Montpelier, October 17, 1833* (Montpelier, Vt., 1833), 11, 14.

46. Albert Barnes, *An Inquiry into the Scriptural Views of Slavery* (Philadelphia, 1846), 260–72, 340–75; Bertram Wyatt-Brown, *Lewis Tappan and the Evangelical War Against Slavery* (Cleveland, 1969), 134–37; Sehr, "Leonard Bacon and the Myth of the Good Slaveholder," 196–97.

that often rendered it difficult to manumit slaves—which he believed absolved "good slaveholders" from guilt. Even the purchase of a slave, he stated, should not always be considered a crime, for one must take into account "the purposes and views with which the purchase is made."[47]

In addition, Bacon disagreed with the abolitionists on the issue of compensation for masters and slaves. The immediatists rejected any compensation for masters on the grounds that this would reward a sinful practice. In an 1826 sermon Bacon had asserted that the slaves' interests must take precedence over those of the master. But in the face of the abolitionists' onslaught and the South's mounting intransigence, he retreated from that position in the 1830s, warning that because emancipation might well impoverish masters and bring about the economic collapse of the South, slaveholders should be compensated by the state. Conversely, he rejected arguments by Jocelyn and Garrison that the freedmen deserved to be compensated for the labor they had performed as slaves. Although he acknowledged that some indemnity was legitimate, he denied that it should be a claim on the wealth of the nation. Instead, he maintained that whites owed all blacks a debt of love in the form of efforts to uplift them.[48]

During the 1830s, both Bacon and the abolitionists placed their faith in moral suasion as a means of effecting total abolition. But while the immediatists declared that masters could be brought to free their slaves only if confronted with the sin of slaveholding, Bacon called for gentle persuasion and Christian forbearance toward southerners. He was convinced that the abolitionists' single-minded fervor and harsh accusations alienated southern Christians, and particularly "good slaveholders"—the very people who must lead the way to abolition.[49] If the abolitionists were naive in believing that they could persuade masters to undertake immediate emancipation, Bacon certainly engaged in wishful thinking when he contended that an indeterminate number of slaveholders in fact wished to end slavery.

But the abolitionists' agitation, according to Bacon, did more than pit North against South and stiffen southern resistance to the abolition, or even the amelioration, of slavery. It also threatened social order and endangered the general welfare. He feared that the mounting violence and social discord—manifested most starkly in Nat Turner's revolt, the Nullification Controversy, and the escalating antiabolitionist and antiblack riots in numerous northern towns and cities in the 1830s— would destroy the delicate equilibrium of society. At times, he came close to expressing an apocalyptic vision of America's future. No matter how much the aboli-

47. See Bacon, *Slavery Discussed*, 50, 53.

48. Sermon of July 4, 1826, in Bacon Family Papers; *Journal of Freedom*, December 8, 1834; *Religious Intelligencer*, September 10, October 8, 15, 1836.

49. Bacon, *Slavery Discussed*, 86–87. Bacon discussed his concept of the "good slaveholder" in *Journal of Freedom*, August 20, September 17, 1834; Bacon, *Slavery Discussed*, 76–79.

tionists explained and declaimed their doctrines, he warned Gerrit Smith in 1834, immediate emancipation would necessarily lead to "misapprehension, misrepresentation, confusion, wrath, denunciation, hatred, violence, tumults" and, quite possibly, "convulsion, bloodshed, and revolution."[50]

Like many of his fellow antislavery moderates, Bacon valued social stability, abhorred violence, and respected order and propriety. In his reform endeavors he was ever mindful of reformers' limited ability to improve society quickly. He was especially alarmed by the perfectionist reformism evident in the immediatists' ideology. To him, the abolitionists resembled the drunkard or the sinner in that they appeared to lack internal controls and to be impervious to external restraints. Bacon and other evangelicals had long equated public order with harmony and had sought to foster liberty without jeopardizing social stability. The clergy, they believed, must labor to safeguard the order, morality, and self-restraint so necessary for the enjoyment of true freedom.[51]

Bacon and other critics of the abolitionists were convinced that the immediatists violated these precepts by seeking, among other things, to inject public measures into the political realm. This seemed especially evident in the petitions campaign that the abolitionists launched in the mid-1830s. Although most immediatists in fact repudiated third-party action during the thirties, Bacon was certain that they sought to create a political party, which he feared would further divide American society. Abolitionism, he charged in 1834, was "a low-minded, quarrelsome spirit of faction, the same that has already made the name of politics so infamous—born of self-conceit and nourished by jealousy and envy."[52]

Above all, Bacon and many northern clergymen were concerned that the abolitionists' agitation would divide and disrupt the churches. But at the same time, they believed that the clergy and congregations were unduly imposed upon by itinerant preachers and lecturers espousing temperance, anti-Catholicism, various theological doctrines, and other causes. Thus, Bacon and Lyman Beecher met in New Haven in 1836 to discuss how this situation could be rectified. From their meeting emerged a series of resolutions that they took to various New England Congregational General Associations. The Connecticut association unanimously adopted the so-called Norfolk resolutions, which defended freedom of speech but denied that churches were obligated to admit all speakers to their pulpits; declared that itinerant agents and lecturers who propounded particular doctrines, "*without the advice and consent of*

---

50. *Journal of Freedom,* December 8, 1834.

51. Scott, *From Office to Profession,* 97–98, 101–103; see also Streifford, "The American Colonization Society," 204–206; John L. Thomas, "Romantic Reform in America, 1815–1865," *American Quarterly,* XVII (1965), 656–81.

52. See *Journal of Freedom,* August 20, 1834. For concerns similar to those expressed by Bacon, see *Religious Intelligencer,* January 25, 1834; Boston *Recorder and Religious Herald,* December 18, 1835.

the pastors and regular ecclesiastical bodies," posed a threat to the authority and rights of the stated ministry and the "peace and good order of the churches"; and stated that itinerant evangelists who were devoted "especially to the business of excitement, and to the promotion of revivals" endangered the stability of the stated ministry, the harmony of the churches, and the influence of the Gospel.[53]

At first glance it seems strange that Bacon and Beecher, both proponents of revival activity, would seek to bar revival preachers from Congregational pulpits. Vincent Harding argues correctly that, particularly in the third resolution, they sought to limit access to the churches by Asahel Nettleton, a conservative Calvinist who was a thorn in the side of those who identified with the New Haven theology. Some historians have insisted that Bacon and Beecher acted solely against the abolitionists. The evidence, however, clearly indicates that they hoped to accomplish a dual objective: to keep both Nettleton and the immediatists out of New England Congregational pulpits. Bacon made this clear when, in a defense of the resolutions, he told Smith that their focus was "self-sent religious teachers and ones from associations for the reform of opinion or morals."[54]

The immediatists certainly assumed that Bacon and Beecher had specifically targeted them; thus, the Norfolk resolutions unleashed a barrage of abolitionist criticism. "Pray, what are such great men as you and Dr. Taylor and Dr. Beecher, etc. good for," Elizur Wright sarcastically asked Bacon, "if you cannot meet heretics and interlopers, on a fair field and put them to flight by the artillery of your brains?" William Goodell, a New York immediatist, indeed feared "that the Grand Ecclesiastical Combination throughout the country, of which Bacon appears to be the nucleus, the Center, and the spokesman, will succeed in effecting . . . severe legislative enactments throughout the country against us."[55]

In his defense of the Norfolk resolutions, Bacon posed as a friend of human freedom, religious liberty, and ecclesiastical order. He denied the abolitionists' charges that the resolutions served the interests of the South and noted that, in accordance with the principle of congregational independence, the association had upheld the right of each local church to decide who would have access to the pulpit. Yet the abolitionists seem partially justified in branding him a hypocrite and the Norfolk resolutions "Connecticut's gag law," for Bacon indeed was prepared to place significant limits on free speech so that ecclesiastical order might be main-

53. Harding, *A Certain Magnificence,* 415; Theodore Dwight Bacon, *Leonard Bacon,* 251; *Proceedings of the General Association of Connecticut, June, 1836* (Hartford, 1836), 8–9.

54. Harding, *A Certain Magnificence,* 415–16, 522n; Bacon to Gerrit Smith, June 3, 1837, in Gerrit Smith Miller Collection.

55. Elizur Wright to Bacon, April 27, 1837, in Bacon Family Papers; William Goodell to Amos A. Phelps, April 24, 1837, in Amos A. Phelps Papers, Boston Public Library.

tained.[56] At the very least, his attempt to embrace conflicting principles seriously compromised his commitment to the principle of liberty.

Bacon's angry confrontation with the abolitionists further underscores the fact that he and they approached the matter of means and ends from very different directions. On the one hand, the immediatists maintained that the need to prick the conscience of Americans and, thereby, to persuade them to rid society of slavery at once was so urgent that it more than compensated for any short-term social disorder that might ensue. On the other hand, Bacon was so disturbed by the conflict and division generated by the abolitionists' demands that he was even prepared to abridge their fundamental rights. "Nothing is justice," he declared in 1835, "which does more harm than good." Much later in his life, in a eulogy to Joshua Leavitt, he charitably conceded that "while my judgment was swayed by the certainty of proximate effects, he looked to the ultimate result and was sure that, whatever might be the reaction and whatever disasters might come, there would be victory at last for justice and liberty."[57] Nevertheless, throughout the antebellum era Bacon sincerely believed that the abolitionists' methods and rhetoric were both extremely dangerous and thoroughly counterproductive.

This does not mean that Bacon was a social conservative determined to maintain an orderly society at all costs. In fact, he considered proslavery southerners and antireform northerners to be terribly misguided and unenlightened in their opposition to the antislavery cause. He condemned in scathing language the "self-constituted guardians of peace and liberty" in both sections. At times, he despaired of ever persuading southerners to take meaningful steps toward abolition, and his relationship with southern colonizationists deteriorated significantly in the early and middle 1830s. At the same time, he had nothing but contempt for northerners such as James Watson Webb, editor of the New York *Courier and Enquirer,* whose "reckless" attempts to arouse popular passions against the abolitionists, he believed, "all good men of every party must deprecate."[58]

Bacon considered himself an enlightened and benevolent man who stood in the vanguard of efforts to create a moral, Christian republic. Yet he could not accept the

---

56. *Proceedings of the General Association of Connecticut, June, 1836,* 8; *Religious Intelligencer,* September 10, 1836, March 18, May 6, July 10, 1837; Bacon to Gerrit Smith, February 24, June 3, 1837, in Gerrit Smith Miller Collection.

57. *Journal of Freedom,* January 29, 1835; *Independent,* February 6, 1873.

58. *Journal of Freedom,* May 17, September 27, 1834; Bacon, *Slavery Discussed,* 85. On the growing breach between Bacon and southern colonizationists, see Leonard Bacon, "Gurley's Life of Ashmun," *Quarterly Christian Spectator,* 3rd series, VII (June, 1835), 332; James R. Stirn, "Urgent Gradualism: The Case of the American Union for the Relief and Improvement of the Colored Race," *Civil War History,* XXV (1979), 311–14; *Journal of Freedom,* October 22, 1834.

abolitionists' solution to the slavery question. Perhaps above all, their moral fervor and intensity seemed alien and frightening to him. He could never bring himself to view immediatism as a personal quest for piety or, in the words of Elizur Wright, a great struggle between "religious sincerity and hypocrisy." William Lloyd Garrison was not far from the mark when he said of men such as Bacon and William Ellery Channing, "They are polite men—they are cautious men—they are accommodating men; and they cherish a sacred horror of fanaticism, and do not like irritation, and love to sail beneath a cloudless sky upon an unruffled stream."[59]

At times, Bacon expressed considerable pride in his ability to carve out and maintain a middle ground between the conservatives and the abolitionists on the slavery issue, and many people who shared his moderate instincts looked to him for leadership. But his determination to occupy a centrist position was not without a price. He complained to Jocelyn in 1836: "I am so unfortunate as to put myself between the opposing fires of two furiously contending parties, and to make myself fully obnoxious to both. Southern lovers of oppression hate me, and if they had me in their power, would hang me, as an abolitionist. Anti-slavery agitators pour out their wrath upon me as an 'ecclesiastical defender of slavery.'" (To which Jocelyn replied coldly that southerners probably would not hang Bacon, because he never acted on his principles.)[60] In addition to feeling the relentless attacks by the immediatists and the conservatives, in consciously seeking to avoid leaning too far toward either ideological extreme, yet realizing that in doing so he might hopelessly obfuscate his professed antislavery principles, he must have experienced considerable inner tension.

Nowhere were these risks more evident than in the American Union for the Relief and Improvement of the Colored Race, which Bacon and other antislavery moderates founded in 1835. These men—most of them New England Congregationalists, including Ethan A. Andrews, Joseph Tracy, Bela B. Edwards, and Samuel M. Worcester—feared that many moderate opponents of slavery had been lost to the abolitionist movement because they desired some antislavery action. However, the American Union's founders also believed that large numbers of moderates were disgusted with the bitter struggle between the colonizationists and the immediatists. They deeply resented the abolitionists' increasingly harsh attacks on the churches and the clergy. Yet while involved in the colonization cause, they were disenchanted with repatriation as a means of ending slavery. In staking out a middle ground between these contending forces, Bacon and other founders of the American

59. Goodheart, *Abolitionist, Actuary, Atheist,* 37; *Liberator,* January 17, 1835.

60. *Religious Intelligencer,* September 10, 1836. For similar complaints by other antislavery moderates, see Boston *Recorder and Religious Herald,* August 30, 1839; Senior, "New England Congregationalists and the Anti-Slavery Movement," 117.

Union hoped to develop, in the name of "urgent gradualism," a "rational plan of emancipation" that would unite all antislavery Americans, facilitate a dialogue between northerners and southerners, and elevate blacks everywhere in the world.[61]

Bacon and one hundred other delegates from ten states met in Boston in January, 1835, to found the American Union. The delegates chose to ignore the abolitionists, but they fully realized that they must persuade both northerners and southerners of the efficacy and necessity of urgent gradualism if the organization was to survive. The society's executive committee, convinced that Bacon's experience and knowledge as well as his ability to unite antislavery moderates in all parts of the nation were essential to the organization's success, urged him to become its general agent at a salary of $1,800.[62]

Lucy Bacon was not anxious to move to Boston. Living expenses were higher there than in New Haven, and with the birth of Francis in 1831 and Theodore in 1834, she and Leonard now had five children and little money. Moreover, since at least 1831 she had periodically been bedridden with a lung disease. Bacon seriously considered the American Union's offer but ultimately declined it. Once again, he was unwilling to uproot himself for a better-paying position that did not offer security. Yet he regarded the American Union with "great interest and a strong hope of their success," and he agreed to write the prospectus for the society.[63]

In his *Exposition* Bacon sought to justify the union's existence and to provide a focus for its operations. He left no doubt that the union desired the ultimate abolition of slavery. The relief and improvement of blacks, he argued, would never be accomplished while slavery existed. Yet Bacon and his fellow antislavery moderates consciously stood apart from the immediatists. They focused upon relief and improvement, not abolition, and they assumed that piecemeal improvement would excite, not deaden, the slaveholder's conscience. Indeed, Bacon's powerful plea for religious instruction of the slaves, which was part of the union's attempt to advance

61. Ethan A. Andrews to Bacon, May 30, 1834, January 7, 1835, in Bacon Family Papers; Stirn, "Urgent Gradualism," 310–13; Bacon, *Exposition of the Objects and Plans of the American Union for the Relief and Improvement of the Colored Race,* 23; Boston *Recorder and Religious Herald,* December 26, 1834, May 1, 29, 1835.

62. Bacon, *Exposition of the Objects and Plans of the American Union for the Relief and Improvement of the Colored Race,* 1–2; Garrison and Garrison, *William Lloyd Garrison,* I, 470; Ethan A. Andrews to Bacon, January 7, 26, 1835, executive committee of the American Union to Bacon, January 21, 1835, Bela B. Edwards to Bacon, January 31, 1835, in Bacon Family Papers.

63. Lucy Bacon to Sarah Wisner, April 26, 1834, January 26, 1835, Leonard to Lucy Bacon, May 20, 1831, Alice to Leonard Bacon, November 3, 1831, Leonard to Alice Bacon, July 23, 1832, Bacon to Sarah Wisner, February 21, 1835, Bacon to executive committee of the American Union, February 14, March 20, 1835, Ethan A. Andrews to Bacon, February 28, 1835, in Bacon Family Papers; Baldwin, *Bacon Genealogy,* 279–80; *Rebecca Taylor Hatch, 1818–1904: Personal Reminiscences and Memorials* (New Haven, 1915), 40.

missionary activities in the South, was the only specific mode of direct action that he explicitly recommended.[64]

Bacon sought to assure his readers that there was "no essential repugnance" between the American Colonization Society and the American Anti-Slavery Society. Yet he was certain that much had not been done, or was likely to be accomplished, by these societies for the improvement of blacks, for each movement focused upon a single object. Thus, he argued, there was ample room for antislavery moderates in both sections to prevail upon slaveholders to ameliorate the system and to urge the gathering of statistical data regarding the condition of slaves. The truth that would emerge from "the steady and cautious researches of science," he hoped, would convince northerners and southerners alike that gradual emancipation was the wisest policy.[65]

Bacon also called for the abrogation of all laws that oppressed or denied equal opportunity to people of color. Citing blacks' "embarrassment and impositions" as well as their ignorance, lack of thrift, and vices, he especially emphasized—as he had at the time he founded the African Improvement Society ten years earlier—the "duty of combined and systematic local efforts" for black improvement. Yet his commitment to changing racial attitudes and putting in place institutions and practices capable of advancing the interests of northern blacks remained limited. The only concrete proposal for elevating blacks that he presented in his *Exposition* was to gather data regarding the condition of free blacks—a recommendation similar to the one that he had made in his 1823 report to the Society of Inquiry at Andover. Arthur Tappan spoke for most immediatists when he pointed out that enough was already known about the condition of blacks and that more information about their poverty would only deepen whites' contempt for them.[66]

To these antislavery moderates' consternation, neither the immediatists nor the southerners were willing to consider the union's ideology and rather vague proposals. From the beginning the society became embroiled in an angry confrontation with Garrison and other abolitionists. Their assaults, and the lack of support for the union by the AASS executive committee, quickly forced Tappan to retreat from his advocacy of the society. Moreover, the students and faculty at Andover as well as other potential northern converts, who feared that the union would create even more division within the antislavery ranks, chose to stand apart from the organization. Even more disturbing to Bacon and other union members was the cool reception that southerners, including most moderates, accorded it. In truth, the society's

64. Bacon, *Exposition of the Objects and Plans of the American Union for the Relief and Improvement of the Colored Race*, 9–10.

65. *Ibid.*, 6–10, 14–16; *Journal of Freedom*, April 23, 1835.

66. Bacon, *Exposition on the Objects and Plans of the American Union for the Relief and Improvement of the Colored Race*, 2, 6–11, 14–16; *Journal of Freedom*, April 23, 1835; *Liberator*, January 17, 1835.

founders sought information on slavery largely because they distrusted southern accounts of the treatment of slaves and were increasingly perplexed by the emerging "positive good" defense of the system. In the final analysis, the union was out of step with the confrontational mood of the time. Bacon's moderate plea, capable and sincere as it was, could not bridge the chasm between southerners and antislavery northerners, and southern intransigence made it difficult for moderates to compete with the abolitionists. His pronouncements about the need for men of moderation, good sense, and patriotic instincts came to nothing, for he enjoyed neither influence nor credibility with groups in both sections that increasingly set the tone of the debate on slavery. Unable to hire a general agent or to raise sufficient funds, the union scarcely became operational and disappeared in the late 1830s.[67]

Bacon never again joined an antislavery society. But the demise of the union did not lessen his interest in the slavery issue or his conviction that abolition would lead to the elevation of all blacks. He remained extremely critical of slavery and paid close attention to the course of British emancipation in the West Indies, which he believed would illustrate the superiority of free labor and benefit all members of society.[68] In addition, notwithstanding his conviction that abolitionist lecturers should not be permitted to create division and disorder in the churches, he continued to defend the right of opponents of slavery, such as Lewis Tappan, to speak out on the issue. He also bitterly attacked the congressional gag laws and supported Elijah Lovejoy's defense of his press against a proslavery mob.[69]

On occasion, Bacon was even able to make common cause with the immediatists. For example, he played a peripheral role in the *Amistad* case in the late 1830s and early 1840s. Anxious that the Mendi captives, who were held in a jail in New Haven while their case moved through the courts, become missionaries once they returned to Africa, Bacon and others supplied them with Bibles. More important, at the request of Lewis Tappan, Jocelyn, and Leavitt, who constituted the Amistad Committee that defended the Africans, he spoke and wrote on behalf of the cause, discussed strategy with various abolitionists, and testified in opposition to the jailer's attempts to continue using the young female captives as domestic servants. Al-

67. *Liberator,* January 17, 1835; Bacon, *Exposition of the Objects and Plans of the American Union for the Relief and Improvement of the Colored Race,* 5–6, 16; Stirn, "Urgent Gradualism," 313–14, 327–28; *Annual Report of the Executive Committee of the American Union for the Relief and Improvement of the Colored Race* (Boston, 1836), 5–6; Ethan A. Andrews to Bacon, November 24, 1836, in Bacon Family Papers.

68. Arthur Granger to Bacon, December 1, 10, 1837, in Bacon Family Papers; Leonard Bacon, "Emancipation in the West Indies," *Quarterly Christian Spectator,* 3rd series, X (September, 1838), 442–43; New Haven *Record,* August 3, 24, 1839.

69. Leonard to Lucy Bacon, January 20, 1839, in Bacon Family Papers; Leonard Bacon, "Memoir of Lovejoy," *Quarterly Christian Spectator,* 3rd series, X (June, 1838), 299–300; "Emancipation in the West Indies," 467.

though not involved in any organization devoted to elevating blacks following the demise of the American Union, he also remained interested in their plight in New Haven and elsewhere. For example, when Amos G. Beman, pastor of the Temple Street African Congregational Church in New Haven, was prepared to resign his pastorate in 1843 because he could not pay his debts, Bacon sought to raise money to build a new church and to pay the salary Beman's church owed him.[70]

Nevertheless, Bacon continued to condemn the abolitionists' ideology and methods and to defend the "good slaveholder" concept. Moreover, despite his serious doubts about the efficacy of the troubled colonization cause, he served into the 1840s as a vice president and manager of the Connecticut Colonization Society, and in 1841 he attended the ACS's annual meeting, where he co-chaired and wrote the report for a committee that investigated the colony's difficulties.[71]

By the mid-1830s, Bacon's interest in colonization focused above all on the state of the Liberian colony. In 1836 he proposed that Americans invest private capital in, and eventually take control of, the colony. And in 1837 he and a number of friends of colonization—including Gallaudet, Anson Phelps, and Theodore Freylinghuysen—founded and served as trustees of the American Society for the Promotion of Education in Africa. This organization, which was endorsed by the American Colonization Society but remained independent of it, emphasized providing assistance for the colony, especially by educating the colonists rather than transporting blacks to Africa.[72]

Bacon remained heartily opposed to the view that colonization must accompany emancipation, but he also doubted that repatriation would lead to abolition. Those doubts were intensified by reports of the sad state of affairs in Liberia that he received from his brother, David, who served as a physician there. He was not entirely candid when he informed David in 1839 that "I have taken no part in Colonization

70. New Haven *Record,* September 14, November 9, 1839; Lewis Tappan to Bacon, October 4, 1839, Charles Cleaveland to Bacon, October 26, 1840, diary entries for March 15, 17–19, 1841, in Bacon Family Papers; entries for March 8, 1839, September 28, 1841, Amos Gerry Beman to Bacon and others, January 5, 1843, Amos Gerry Beman to Colored Congregational Church and Society of New Haven, April 1, 1843, in Amos Gerry Beman Papers, Beinecke Library, Yale University, New Haven, Conn.

71. Leonard Bacon, "Valedictory Remarks," *Quarterly Christian Spectator,* 3rd series, X (December, 1838), 682; *Eleventh Annual Report of the Managers of the Colonization Society of Connecticut* (New Haven, 1838), 3, 15; *Annual Report of the Connecticut State Colonization Society* (Hartford, 1844), 2; Thomas H. Gallaudet to Bacon, April 14, 21, 1838, Bacon to Samuel Wilkeson, June 28, 1839, diary entries for January 15–16, 20–22, 1841, in Bacon Family Papers; Staudenraus, *The African Colonization Movement,* 238–39.

72. Gerrit Smith to Bacon, June 10, 1836, Reuben D. Turner to Bacon, April 5, 1837, in Bacon Family Papers; Bacon to Ralph R. Gurley, February 9, 1837, in American Colonization Society Papers; *Tenth Annual Report of the Managers of the Colonization Society of Connecticut,* 6–7.

movements for a long time past." But his involvement in the cause was minimal after 1835.[73]

With the failure of the American Union and the cessation of the *Journal of Freedom* and the *Christian Spectator,* Bacon lacked, for a time, a ready forum for his moderate antislavery views. Not until the territorial issue and the debate on the missionary societies' relationship with slavery burst upon the American scene in the mid-1840s would he again become actively engaged in the slavery debate. Yet even as he was embroiled in the controversy relating to race, slavery, and colonization, the temperance movement and numerous other benevolent causes, as well as responsibilities related to Center Church and his growing family, occupied his attention. Moreover, he played a pivotal role in the escalating struggle between the supporters of the New Haven theology and the conservative Congregationalists in Connecticut.

73. Bacon to C. S. Henry, May 14, 1838, Leonard to David Bacon, July 19, 1839, Bacon to Seth Terry, November 12, 1836, in Bacon Family Papers; Bacon to Gerrit Smith, February 24, 1837, in Gerrit Smith Miller Collection.

6

TEMPERANCE, REVIVALISM, AND THEOLOGICAL CONTROVERSY

DURING the 1830s, no public issues occupied more of Bacon's time and energy than those concerning race and slavery. Yet even in the midst of his colonization efforts and his battles with the abolitionists, he focused much of his attention on matters relating to his ministry and the Congregational Church. As a clergyman he also felt obligated to remain actively involved in a variety of benevolent causes, including the temperance movement. Lucy was concerned, with good reason, that his unremitting schedule and work ethic eventually would exact a heavy toll. "I cannot help feeling," she warned in 1839, "that you do not stop long enough to know how great is the wear and tear of your body and mind."[1]

In addition to his work, Bacon's growing family and Lucy's deteriorating health placed demands on his time. He believed that the family was the cornerstone of society. Much as Horace Bushnell would argue a decade later, he maintained, in a series of sermons he delivered in 1839, that the family was "a little church" where children were instructed in godliness and prepared for useful membership in the church and society. He shared with most Americans of the time the view that the father was "the anointed ruler and priest" in the family, while the mother was "the light of purity, comfort, and love," whose appointed sphere was the domestic arena. But he also preached that the husband's authority must be consistent with his wife's gentleness and love, which had "dominion" over him. Leonard and Lucy often expressed affection for each other. She frequently referred to him as her "best beloved," and he told her how much he missed her whenever they were apart. While he valued her opinion on many matters, and Lucy made most decisions regarding the household, within the family he appears to have considered himself the final

---

1. Lucy to Leonard Bacon, March 22, 1839, in Bacon Family Papers.

arbiter on decisions regarding finances, career choices, and the children's education.[2]

Bacon was especially concerned that parents mold their children into productive, moral adults. He, like many other evangelical Christians, was convinced that children inherited a perverse and selfish nature and were beset by a myriad of temptations in a corrupt world. Thus, he believed that it was incumbent upon parents to employ strict authority and *"a steady hand, guided by love"* to make good citizens out of "disobedient, headstrong, unmanaged children." Although his pastoral duties, writing, and organizational activities occupied much of his time, Bacon devoted considerable attention to his children, who, with the birth of George in 1836 and James in 1838, numbered seven. At times, he was responsible for much of the care of the children, for Lucy's advancing tuberculosis periodically kept her bedridden for weeks at a time or recuperating at her sister's home in Andover, Massachusetts. During the winter of 1837–1838, and again the following winter and spring, she lived with friends in Florida and Georgia in the hope of recovering her health in a warmer climate.[3]

Lucy's absences and illness created difficulties in the household. She and Leonard searched, with mixed success, for young women to serve as live-in maids to assist with cooking, cleaning, and child care. On occasion, her younger sister, Elizabeth, lived with them and helped with household tasks. Bacon conceded much of the daily childrearing responsibility to Lucy and others, admitting that it was "a work out of my proper calling." At various times one or two of the older children lived with Lucy's sister Sarah Wisner and attended an academy in Andover, while a few of Leonard's nephews periodically lived with the Bacons and paid rent. Bacon constantly worried about money and often felt that he was living on the edge of financial disaster. Although his congregation raised nearly $1,200 in 1838 to pay off his outstanding debts, at no time during the thirties did he own a home or land, and his salary proved inadequate for his large family.[4]

2. Sermons of June 16, 23, 30, 1839, Lucy to Leonard Bacon, February 19, 1838, Leonard to Lucy Bacon, January 11, February 10, 1839, in Bacon Family Papers. For treatments of the concept of separate spheres in the modern middle-class family, see Barbara Welter, "The Cult of True Womanhood, 1820–1860," *American Quarterly*, XVIII (1966), 131–75; Kathryn Kish Sklar, *Catharine Beecher: A Study in American Domesticity* (New Haven, 1973), 151–67.

3. Sermons of August 4, 1833, June 16, 23, July 7, 28, 1839, Leonard to Lucy Bacon, May 20, 1831, September 2, 1833, March 6, April 14, 1839, Leonard to Rebecca Bacon, March 18, 1837, Lucy to Leonard Bacon, February 19, December 14, 1838, Bacon to Sarah Wisner, April 1837, in Bacon Family Papers. The evangelical middle class's views regarding childrearing are discussed in William G. McLoughlin, "Evangelical Childrearing in the Age of Jackson: Francis Wayland's Views on When and How to Subdue the Willfulness of Children," *Journal of Social History*, IX (1975), 21–34.

4. Leonard to Lucy Bacon, November 22, 1838, January 20, February 28, March 6, 22, April 14, 1839, Bacon to W. J. Forbes, March 2, 1838, in Bacon Family Papers.

Yet for all of his family concerns, Bacon devoted much of his energy to his pastorate and related activities, including a number of benevolent enterprises. He remained convinced that the reward for benevolence was the knowledge that one lived under the government of God and did good for others. With constant prodding by Bacon, his congregation contributed generously to numerous benevolent causes throughout the decade.[5]

Some of the endeavors that Bacon was involved in, such as the peace movement, were essentially secular in nature. Although he never opposed the principle of self-defense or defensive war against aggression, he believed that human progress, liberty, and Christianity were antithetical to war. In the mid- and late 1830s he also served on the executive committee of, and wrote articles on a variety of subjects for, the American Society for the Diffusion of Useful Knowledge, which published pieces on the political economy of the nation, education, public morals, and American history.[6]

Bacon, like many other evangelical Protestants of the time, feared the effects of rapid social and economic change in a society where traditional controls were weakening and values were being altered. The influx of immigrants, partisan politics, the spirit of ultraism, the growing evidence of corruption at all levels of society, the "outcry against the wealthy and educated, and the bitter hostility to morals, worth, and reform," he complained in a review of Lyman Beecher's *Plea for the West* in 1835, "are among the painful indications that a broader struggle is before us."[7] He concurred with Beecher's warning that massive emigration by largely uneducated people to communities in which few social controls had been established might well produce chaos in the West. Thus, he urged easterners to assist in creating churches, schools, and colleges in the West, and even to migrate there themselves. He and Beecher, as well as many other eastern evangelicals, were particularly alarmed by the potential for Catholic influence in the western areas. Deeply committed to

5. Leonard Bacon, "Voluntary Associations," *Quarterly Christian Spectator,* 3rd series, VI (March, 1832), 163 *et passim;* Leonard Bacon, "Sketch of the Life and Character of Hon. James Hillhouse," *Quarterly Christian Spectator,* 3rd series, IV (June, 1833), 247; sermon of March 24, 1839, Leonard to Lucy Bacon, November 11, 1838, March 10, 1839, in Bacon Family Papers.

6. Leonard Bacon, *The Hopefulness of Efforts for the Promotion of Peace. A Discourse, Pronounced in the Center Church in Hartford, at the Celebration of the Anniversary of the Hartford County Peace Society, on the Evening of the Lord's Day, June 10, 1832* (Hartford, 1832), 9–10, 12–19; Gorham D. Abbott to Bacon, October 12, 1836, March 26, September 19, 1837, April 14, 1838, John Gilchrist to Bacon, March 6, 1838, report of the American Society for the Diffusion of Useful Knowledge, September 25, 1837, in Bacon Family Papers.

7. Leonard Bacon, "Beecher's Plea for the West," *Quarterly Christian Spectator,* 3rd series, VII (September, 1835), 481–82. Historians who emphasize the evangelical Protestants' fear of rapid social change include Bodo, *The Protestant Clergy and Public Issues,* 52–53, 253–54, and Charles I. Foster, *An Errand of Mercy: The Evangelical United Front, 1790–1837* (Chapel Hill, 1960), 3–10.

extending Protestantism throughout the world, and contemptuous of the Catholic ritual and hierarchy, they viewed Catholicism as an obstacle to religious liberty, human progress, and even the achievement of the millennium. Bacon was also convinced that Catholic immigrants, who had begun to arrive in New Haven and other northeastern cities in large numbers during the 1830s, were partly responsible for the urban unrest of the time, and he shared the nativist conspiracy theory that Catholic schools were part of a grand design to convert Protestant children and establish papal supremacy in the United States. In his private life his anti-Catholic feelings even moved him to refuse to hire a young Irish woman as a maid because she was Catholic.[8]

Notwithstanding his deep-seated anti-Catholicism, Bacon was in fact something of a moderate among American nativists. He was especially critical of such seasoned Catholic-baiters as George Bourne and W. C. Brownlee, whom he considered "perfectly rabid from the dread of popery." His opposition to these anti-Catholic extremists was based in part on his belief that their shrill rhetoric was "abhorrent to the bible and to humanity." On a more practical level, he was convinced that such nativist attacks rendered the conversion of Catholics to Protestantism far more difficult than if they were treated with kindness and patience.[9]

Yet Bacon's social concerns at this time were not limited to the perceived dangers of the Catholic presence in the cities and the West. He also feared that excessive materialism and individualism among the middle and upper classes endangered the moral vitality of the nation. On a number of occasions he warned his congregation of the dangers of their widespread preoccupation with accumulating material goods and pursuing ambition. He was also critical of economic speculation, which he blamed for the Panic of 1837 and the ensuing depression. Perhaps because he had struggled during his entire life to make ends meet, he was dismayed that wealth, which religion often sanctioned, increasingly appeared to be the principal criterion for status in society and that "luxurious and profligate habits of expenditure" were so prevalent.[10]

8. Bacon, "Beecher's Plea for the West," 482, 485–89, 492–99. For similar arguments, see Leonard Bacon, "Encouragements to Effort, for the Speedy Conversion of the World," *Quarterly Christian Spectator,* 3rd series, VII (March, 1835), 2–3; Leonard Bacon, *A Manual for Young Church-Members* (New Haven, 1833), 63. On anti-Catholic sentiment in this era, see Ray Allen Billington, *The Protestant Crusade, 1800–1860: A Study of the Origins of American Nativism* (Chicago, 1964), 41–108.

9. Bacon, "Maria Monk and Her Impostures," *Quarterly Christian Spectator,* 3rd series, IX (June, 1837), 263, 268–72, 282; W. C. Brownlee to Bacon, July 26, 31, 1837, Bacon to W. C. Brownlee, July 28, 1837, sermons of July 7, 1833, October 27, 1835, Bacon Family Papers.

10. See sermon of August 13, 1837, in Bacon Family Papers; *Religious Intelligencer,* June 3, 1837; Leonard Bacon, "The Present Commercial Distress," *Quarterly Christian Spectator,* 3rd series, IX (June, 1837), 331–35.

Bacon's denunciation of greed and selfishness, however, did not mean that he questioned the capitalist system, private property ownership, or inequalities of wealth in society. Like most middle-class Americans, he believed that the unequal distribution of wealth was one of God's laws and that workers' well-being depended upon their employers' prosperity. Moreover, he echoed the sentiments of many middle-class Americans in holding that, while even the "vicious and profligate" should not be allowed to starve, such assistance must not be permitted to destroy one's incentive to work.[11]

Bacon was especially concerned about "the multiplied means of vicious indulgence" that he believed threatened the moral and spiritual welfare of young men in cities such as New Haven. Throughout the 1830s he continued to point to intemperance as a significant cause of moral decay, social disorder, and poverty. He played an important role in the temperance movement, serving on the executive committees of the Connecticut Temperance Society and its New Haven County auxiliary in the mid-1830s and frequently writing and speaking on the subject. During these years, temperance activists debated strategy at length. While most of them came to adopt the principle of total abstinence from all beverages that intoxicated, they did not agree on how to achieve victory over intemperance. With encouragement from the American Temperance Union (formerly the American Temperance Society), Connecticut and several other states passed local option laws; Connecticut's law, passed in 1832, made it illegal to sell less than ten gallons of wine or liquor in one transaction without a license granted by a majority vote of a town meeting. Yet subsequent legislatures frequently modified the law, and this experiment in local prohibition was often difficult to enforce, in part because of the close proximity of no-license towns to others where licenses were granted.[12]

Upwardly mobile entrepreneurs, the clergy, and their evangelical allies generally were in the forefront of these efforts to regulate the liquor trade, which they believed corrupted the morals of the community. Like many other temperance advocates in the 1830s, Bacon was not certain what mix of moral suasion and government regulation was both appropriate and necessary. Although concerned that temperance pledges provided false estimates of success and often were too rigid, he insisted, as he had in the 1820s, that public opinion be "made right" in order for

11. Bacon, "The Present Commercial Distress," 328, 339; sermons of June 2, 1833, November 24, 1836, December 29, 1839, in Bacon Family Papers.

12. Sermon of March 19, 1837, speech before the New Haven County Temperance Society, February 26, 1833, in Bacon Family Papers; *Report of the Executive Committee of the Connecticut Temperance Society Presented to the Society, at Its Third Anniversary, in New Haven, May 16, 1832* (Middletown, Conn., 1832), 6; *Religious Intelligencer*, May 19, 1832, October 1, 1836. On the temperance movement's strategy, see Ian R. Tyrrell, "Temperance and Economic Change in the Antebellum North," in *Alcohol, Reform, and Society: The Liquor Issue in Social Context*, ed. Jack S. Blocker, Jr. (Westport, Conn., 1979), 47; Morse, *A Neglected Period of Connecticut's History*, 213–14.

temperance reform to be effective. The existence of numerous liquor licenses in New Haven, he conceded in 1836, showed that that had not occurred. Nevertheless, he continued to maintain that, with the exception of "some lawful and proper use"—that is, medical and illumination purposes—the temperance cause must rely above all on individuals' decisions to abstain from all intoxicating beverages. Only this, he believed, would effectively preserve families, produce a more equitable distribution of wealth and a more moral society, and strengthen religious institutions.[13]

Yet at the same time, he supported government regulation of dram shops and even the groceries whose retail activities, though legal, he considered a "public wrong." Even bitter criticism from New Haven grocers, many Democrats, much of the working class, and some socially prominent people in New Haven did not deter him from supporting the local option law as the legitimate product of the public's right to persuade officials to protect the community's interests.[14]

Bacon was certain that his work on behalf of various benevolent causes, as well as speaking out on slavery and other public issues, was a natural extension of his ministry. But he considered the responsibilities and activities related directly to Center Church and the interests of evangelical religion and Congregationalism absolutely central to his calling. The many and varied facets of his professional career were the source of much satisfaction. Yet as he noted in his *Concio ad Clerum,* which he delivered at Yale in 1840 as the clergyman designated that year to address members of the Connecticut General Association on theological issues, they also absorbed a great deal of time and fragmented his concentration.[15]

Bacon was an influential member of the Connecticut General Association. For example, he served as chairman of a committee formed in 1837 to develop a new edition of the Saybrook Platform, the foundation of the Connecticut form of Congregationalism. He also revised one hymnbook and compiled another during the decade. By adding numerous modern hymns, approximately half of them by American authors, to the rather outdated collection originally compiled by Timothy Dwight, he infused new life into the hymnal, which enabled it to retain its popularity well into the 1840s. Later in the thirties he and a Northampton, Massachusetts, minister jointly compiled a hymnbook that Bacon hoped would replace Asahel Nettleton's *Village Hymns for Social Worship,* which he considered unsuitable for use in prayer meetings and revivals.[16]

13. See Krout, *The Origins of Prohibition,* 225–30; *Religious Intelligencer,* October 1, 1836; sermons of April 1, 1836, February, 1837, in Bacon Family Papers; Leonard Bacon, *A Discourse on the Traffic in Spiritous Liquors, Delivered in the Center Church, New Haven, February 6, 1838* (New Haven, 1838), 4–5, 7–8, 12–17, 24–25, 27–29.

14. Bacon, *A Discourse on the Traffic in Spiritous Liquors,* 7, 51, 53–54; New Haven *Record,* December 7, 1939, May 23, 1840.

15. *Concio ad Clerum,* August 19, 1840, in Bacon Family Papers.

16. Bacon to Allen McLean, July 27, 1837, J. Mitchell to Bacon, December 13, 1838, Leonard to

Bacon also occasionally delivered lectures on church government and discipline at Yale Theological Seminary and took the pulpits of other clergymen throughout Connecticut and neighboring states. Yet he never doubted that preaching the Gospel and moving his parishioners toward a religious experience were his highest priorities. Whatever reservations he harbored about the heavy reliance on revivals within evangelical Christianity, he fully understood that many people judged him largely on his ability to generate religious excitement. The year 1831 would prove to be fruitful for his church as well as many others, as revivals swept across the land. In New Haven he and other Congregational clergymen and professors, at times acting in concert with local Episcopalian, Baptist, and Methodist ministers, addressed revival meetings, including one at Center Church attended by 1,200 people. During the revival, Bacon's church received more than 100 new professions of faith, which increased its membership to more than 600. There was widespread optimism that the religious excitement would sweep all before it.[17]

In the midst of the revival Bacon, acting on behalf of a number of New Haven clergymen, invited Charles G. Finney to assist them. Bacon expressed their confidence in Finney's theological views, assuring him that on doctrines and measures "they are our views with one exception." That exception was their belief that it was not advisable to call upon impenitent sinners to pledge themselves by standing before the congregation. Notwithstanding their desire that nothing be done in the revival meetings "to create surprise or startle prejudice," Bacon and his associates were prepared to welcome Finney with open arms. "We want you to come as *our* man, our brother, invited by us, 'true yoke-fellow,'" he assured Finney. He hoped not only that Finney would spur the revival onward but also that his visit would bring together Finney and Taylor, whom he termed "those two great champions of innovation."[18]

Bacon's theological views were in fact quite similar to Finney's. Both men rejected the idea that religion consisted largely of abstract points to be debated or was a passive experience, and both sought to harmonize human responsibility with the doctrine of absolute sovereignty. All people, they agreed, were voluntary moral agents who could choose whether or not to turn to God. Moreover, they believed that enthusiasm in religion was necessary for an awakening, but that it should not be allowed to develop without consideration of limits. Bacon also assured Finney that

Lucy Bacon, February 20, April 3, 1839, in Bacon Family Papers; *Minutes of the General Association of Connecticut at Their Meeting in New Milford, June 1837* (Hartford, 1838), 6–7; *Independent,* May 12, 1881.

17. George E. Day and others to Bacon, August 15, 1837, Leonard to Lucy Bacon, March 10, 1839, in Bacon Family Papers; *Religious Intelligencer,* March 26, April 19, September 10, 1831; *Leonard Bacon: Pastor of the First Church in New Haven,* 172, 192.

18. Bacon to Charles G. Finney, April 12, 1831, Bacon to Benjamin B. Wisner, March 31, 1831, in Bacon Family Papers; Timothy Dwight to Finney, March, 1831, in Charles G. Finney Papers, Oberlin College, Oberlin, Ohio.

the New Haven clergymen who invited him called for immediate repentance at every inquiry meeting and believed that no one sinned prior to the act of sinning.[19]

To Bacon's dismay Finney declined to come to New Haven. In turning down the offer, Finney, then occupied in revival activity in upstate New York and bombarded with numerous requests for assistance by other evangelical clergymen, made little mention of Bacon's muted concerns regarding revival measures. Rather, he noted that Bacon's letter had not conveyed the impression that there was any "special necessity" for his presence, and he brushed aside Bacon's concern about conservative opposition to Taylorism and Finneyism. The time was rapidly passing, he declared, when "the idle prattle about *isms* can frighten people."[20]

Thoroughly exhausted by their revival labors, Bacon and his colleagues were disappointed by Finney's response to their plea. But Bacon was deeply impressed and heartened by the progress of the revival, believing that it surpassed anything he had ever witnessed. The Connecticut General Association indeed claimed that in 1831 over one hundred Congregational churches in the state, as well as Yale Theological Seminary, experienced revivals, with at least eight thousand people converted. Nevertheless, by 1833 the level of revival enthusiasm had begun to decline dramatically. Only thirty-three converts were added to Center Church in 1832, and only twenty-one in 1833. In fact, with the minor exception of 1837, little excitement was evident in the church during the remainder of the decade, and the membership dropped from 583 in 1838 to 549 in 1840.[21]

Even as the revivals reached a peak in the early 1830s, both the Congregational and Presbyterian churches were becoming increasingly divided. The Old School Presbyterians—many of whom were Scotch-Irish from Pennsylvania and the Upper South—viewed with alarm the influx of Congregationalists into the Presbyterian ranks under the Plan of Union. They attacked what they considered doctrinal errors, especially in the interdenominational missionary societies, in the new measures revivals, and in the Presbygational churches, many with ministers trained at Andover and Yale.[22]

Bacon came into conflict with the Old School Presbyterians in 1831 as a delegate

---

19. For Bacon's views on these doctrines in the 1830s, see, for example, Leonard Bacon, *Thirteen Historical Discourses, on the Completion of Two Hundred Years, From the Beginning of the First Church in New Haven* (New Haven, 1839), 210; sermons of August 15, 1830, October 23, November 20, 1831, October 7, 1838, Bacon to Benjamin B. Wisner, March 31, 1831, in Bacon Family Papers. Finney's theology is treated in James E. Johnson, "Charles G. Finney and a Theology of Revivalism," *Church History,* XXXVIII (1969), 338–58; Keith J. Hardman, *Charles Grandison Finney, 1792–1875: Revivalist and Reformer* (Syracuse, 1987), 46–48, 82–86, 198–211, 229–33.

20. Charles G. Finney to Bacon, April 22, 1831, in Bacon Family Papers.

21. Bacon to Charles G. Finney, May 4, 1831, Bacon to Center Church congregation, 1839, in Bacon Family Papers; *Proceedings of the General Association of Connecticut, June 1832* (Hartford, 1832), 13–15; *Minutes of the General Association of Connecticut* (1837), 29, (1838), 19, (1839), 17, (1840), 24.

22. Sydney E. Ahlstrom, *A Religious History of the American People* (New Haven, 1972), 462–65.

from the Connecticut General Association at the Presbyterian General Assembly held in Philadelphia. By this time, conservative Presbyterians were alienated from the New School group, which shared with many evangelical Congregationalists a commitment to moral reform, revivalism, evangelical piety, and interdenominational cooperation. At the 1831 General Assembly meeting the conservatives brought Albert Barnes, a New School minister, to trial on heresy charges. Bacon was appointed to a special committee to whom the Barnes case was referred in the hope of avoiding a contentious trial. At the same time, the Old School forces sought to have the Presbyterian Church break with the interdenominational missionary societies.[23]

In the end, the New School forces prevailed on both the Barnes and missionary issues. Asahel Green, the editor of an Old School journal, later accused Bacon of committing "a great indelicacy" by agreeing to serve on the General Assembly committee. Bacon denied that he had acted as a partisan or that, as an honorary member, he had even voted in the committee, though he acknowledged that he had spoken frequently at the proceedings. Yet he clearly believed that, under the Plan of Union, New England Congregationalists had a real stake in the outcome of the Barnes case. He vigorously supported Barnes's theological views, and was distressed by the Old School's attacks on both Barnes and the interdenominational missionary organizations.[24]

Bacon's advocacy of interdenominational benevolent activities, however, did not mean that he doubted the superiority of the Congregational form of church government to that of all other denominations. In the 1830s he began a lifelong labor of love that would include an extensive exploration of the history of Congregationalism and a detailed explanation and defense of the church's polity and practices. Williston Walker, a late-nineteenth-century historian of American Congregationalism, stated at the time of Bacon's death that "to no man was the reentrance of our churches upon their heritage more due than to Dr. Bacon." His first major historical study was *Select Practical Writings of Richard Baxter,* a prominent seventeenth-century English Congregational divine. This two-volume work, published in 1831, was based largely on Baxter's narratives and was intended to educate the general public, and particularly Congregationalists, about the struggles and sacrifices of the early church leaders.[25]

---

23. Theodore Dwight Bacon, *Leonard Bacon,* 86–87, 125–26; George M. Marsden, *The Evangelical Mind and the New School Presbyterian Experience: A Case Study of Thought and Theology in Nineteenth-Century America* (New Haven, 1970); Leonard to Lucy Bacon, May 20, 1831, in Bacon Family Papers.

24. *Religious Intelligencer,* December 10, 1831; Bacon to Robert J. Breckinridge, September 22, 1838, in Bacon Family Papers.

25. Walker, *Ten New England Leaders,* 423, Leonard Bacon, *Select Practical Writings of Richard Baxter, With a Life of the Author* (2 vols.; New Haven, 1831).

Bacon was especially interested in informing young converts of the nature of the Congregational Church and the duties and relations of its members. In his *Manual for Young Church-Members,* which he initially presented as a series of lectures to youth groups at Center Church in 1833, he sought to guard against the errors that young, uninformed members often fell into. But his detailed treatment of Congregational forms and practices was also designed to underscore the advantages of an ecclesiastical system in which local churches enjoyed a large degree of autonomy. Finally, in praising New England as "the chief fountain of intelligence and thought for the nation," he sounded a theme of regional superiority that he would reiterate on many occasions in his numerous historical studies and contributions to newspapers and magazines.[26]

Yet Bacon was quick to disclaim any intention of awakening "the spirit of sectarian controversy." Although he did not foresee a time when all Christians would unite in one church, he looked forward to the day when "the theological literature of each denomination shall be the common stock of all." He was especially critical of the sectarian tendencies of the Old School Presbyterians and other like-minded groups, which he believed produced "a stagnancy of intellectual action on the subject of religious truth."[27]

Bacon was confident that because there was "no ecclesiastical power to stimulate the zeal of factions, and no mitred dignity to waken clerical ambition," the Congregational system of church government acted to prevent serious conflict within the church. Yet he was overly sanguine, for by the early 1830s the dispute between Nathaniel Taylor, Eleazur Fitch, and other Yale Theological Seminary professors and conservatives such as Bennet Tyler and Leonard Woods had already begun to divide the ranks of New England Congregationalists. Bacon often consulted with Taylor during the Taylor-Tyler exchange in the columns of the *Spirit of the Pilgrims,* and he clearly aligned himself with the New Haven group. But he was also in the forefront of efforts to devise a truce between these parties. In the fall of 1830 he met with the Andover Theological Seminary professors, Edward and Lyman Beecher, Asahel Nettleton, Calvin Stowe, Jeremiah Day, and a few other leading New England Congregationalists in Ebenezer Porter's study to discuss the issues that divided the evangelical clergy. Following extended debate, Bacon moved that all further controversy on issues that divided the evangelical ministers of New England should "cease from this time, on both sides." With strong support from Lyman Beecher, his motion passed without a dissenting vote. But the conservatives, determined to repudiate the New Haven theology and the *Christian Spectator,* and possibly to drive

26. Bacon, *A Manual for Young Church-Members,* esp. 6–8, 14–27, 131–32, 156–60, 165–66.

27. Bacon, "Voluntary Associations," 144, 162–64; also sermon of June 28, 1835, in Bacon Family Papers.

Taylor's supporters from the church, managed to eviscerate Bacon's attempt at reconciliation either by leaving the meeting early or by abstaining from voting.[28]

If anything, the lines that divided Connecticut Congregationalists became more
sharply drawn in 1833, when a group of conservatives headed by George A. Calhoun and Asahel Nettleton established the Pastoral Union for the purpose of opposing "prevailing error in doctrine and practice." Soon thereafter, they founded the
Theological Institute of Connecticut in East Windsor, which they hoped would
train "sound and faithful ministers." These men were especially critical of the New
Haven group's emphasis on individuals as free moral agents and their views on the
doctrines of divine imputation, regeneration through grace, and election.[29]

The guiding spirit within the conservatives' ranks was Nettleton, an acerbic
revivalist who for years had vigorously attacked both Finneyism and Taylorism.
Bacon considered Nettleton both a nuisance and a threat to progressive Christianity
and Christian unity. In an extremely caustic response to an angry letter from Nettleton in 1835, he accused Nettleton of being "unbalanced" and a liar and condemned him for impugning Taylor's "moral and Christian character" and attempting to destroy Yale Theological Seminary. His anger, and that of Beecher,
toward Nettleton's contentious ways while functioning as an itinerant evangelist
goes far to explain the tenor of the Norfolk resolutions that they pushed through
the Connecticut General Association in 1836.[30]

Bacon, Joel Hawes, Noah Porter, and other Connecticut Congregational clergymen who favored conciliation rejected the conservatives' insistence on what
Bacon termed "a perfect identity of opinion on every point of doctrine." In an
attempt to bring about peace between the warring factions, they circulated a
"Pledge for Peace" in the mid-1830s in which they sought to gain agreement on
essential doctrines that they believed both parties subscribed to. The conservatives,
however, were not deterred by these efforts. As conflict escalated between the conservatives and the advocates of the New Haven theology, who constituted a large

28. Sermon of September 30, 1832, Leonard to Lucy Bacon, September 10, 1832, Leonard Woods
to Bacon, February 27, 1837, Bacon to Leonard Woods, March 3, 1837, in Bacon Family Papers; Rev.
George A. Calhoun, *Letters to the Reverend Leonard Bacon, In Reply to His Attacks on the Pastoral Union
and Theological Institute of Connecticut* (Hartford, 1840), 48. On the Taylor-Tyler controversy, see Mead,
Nathaniel William Taylor, 222–32; Curtis Manning Geer, *The Hartford Theological Seminary, 1834–1934*
(Hartford, 1934), 36–43.

29. Geer, *The Hartford Theological Seminary,* 26–27, 31–32, 39–41; Harding, *A Certain Magnificence,*
310–11, 321.

30. Bennet Tyler, *Memoir of the Life and Character of Rev. Asahel Nettleton, D.D.* (Boston, 1850), 195,
297–301; John F. Thornbury, *God Sent Revival: The Story of Asahel Nettleton and the Second Great Awakening* (Grand Rapids, 1977), 211–17; Bacon to Asahel Nettleton, July 29, 1835, in Bacon Family Papers;
Leonard Bacon, *Views and Reviews. No. I. January, 1840. Seven Letters to Rev. G. A. Calhoun* (New Haven,
1840), 57–58.

majority of the Congregational ministers in Connecticut and other New England states, Bacon became more openly critical of the conservatives in both the Congregational and Presbyterian churches. Although he acknowledged in his eulogy at Taylor's funeral in 1858 that he had never been able to accept certain points of Taylor's philosophy, he agreed with much of the system of theology that Taylor had developed. Indeed, according to Curtis Geer, during the 1830s Bacon was "probably next to the Yale Faculty in his ability as an exponent of the New Haven view." Bacon was motivated to speak out forcefully in part by his conviction that the conservative Calvinists acted recklessly in charging the proponents of progressive orthodoxy with heresy. The Old School's excision of the New School Presbyterians and their abrogation of the Plan of Union in 1837 certainly confirmed his fears.[31]

With a formal division between the New Haven and East Windsor groups seemingly imminent, Bacon decided in 1839 to initiate a public debate with George A. Calhoun, president of the Pastoral Union. His letters, and Calhoun's rejoinders, were published in 1839 and 1840 in the columns of the New Haven *Record,* a weekly religious newspaper that he helped to found and often contributed to following the cessation of the *Religious Intelligencer,* and then in pamphlet form as *Views and Reviews.*[32]

Bacon engaged in this protracted debate with Calhoun, and later with Bennet Tyler in private correspondence, not as a theologian but as a defender and interpreter of progressive orthodoxy, as a controversialist, and as a mediator. He had a solid grasp of the intricacies of the dispute between Taylor and his critics; indeed, he would serve for several years as professor of theology at Yale following his retirement from the ministry in the mid-1860s. But he never developed a system of theology or, for that matter, wrote widely on purely theological subjects. He entered into his debate with Calhoun for a variety of reasons. He claimed that for several years he and other younger ministers had hoped to learn from the doctrinal disputes between Taylor and his adversaries. But as the conservatives had moved toward ever harsher attacks on Taylor and his supporters, he finally concluded that he could no longer be a spectator. Thus, he sought to defend, in a definitive manner, the New Haven forces from unfair charges and to show that the conservatives' "mischievous" actions were guided by "errors of judgment." He admitted that he relished the opportunity to exchange ideas, to challenge, and hopefully best, his opponents, and perhaps to resolve outstanding differences. "I love to see difficulties resolved, and

31. Sermon of June 22, 1835, Bacon to Horace Woodruff, n.d., sermon at Taylor's funeral, 1858, Bacon to Bennet Tyler, November 14, 1835, in Bacon Family Papers; Geer, *The Hartford Theological Seminary,* 18; Leonard Bacon, "The Revolution in the Presbyterian Church," *Quarterly Christian Spectator,* 3rd series, IX (December, 1837), 545–46, 659–60; Bacon, *Views and Reviews, No. I.,* 69–75.

32. Bacon, *Views and Reviews, No. I,* 3; Leonard Bacon, *Views and Reviews. No. II. May, 1840. An Appeal Against Division; With an Appendix of Notes on Mr. Calhoun's Letters* (New Haven, 1840), 84–85.

objections baffled," he noted. "I love to see abstruse analysis and sharp discrimination; and I want to catch whatever argument may help to 'vindicate the ways of God to man.'" Yet he was also motivated to engage in debate in part by his conviction that the warring camps in fact shared much in common and must reach a peaceful accord.[33]

In his letters Bacon defended not only Taylor's theological views but also the Connecticut General Association's decision to side with the New School group at the 1838 Presbyterian General Assembly and to seat only those delegates from the New School at the 1838 and 1839 General Association meetings. As he often would do on issues that he cared about deeply, Bacon went on the attack by condemning the Pastoral Union for remaining silent in the face of the Old School Presbyterians' "unjust" excision of its opponents. He acknowledged that differences existed between the contending Congregational parties on the nature of sin and regeneration and other theological issues. Further, while he conceded that the New Haven group's arguments were not entirely correct, he insisted that it had "altogether the advantage in the controversy," for the East Windsor theology was "surely wrong . . . in the false principles on which their reasonings against human responsibility and God's character and government are founded, and from which such reasonings derive all their plausibility."[34]

Calhoun was not prepared to accept Bacon's arguments. He bitterly criticized Bacon for his attacks on the Theological Institute of Connecticut, the Pastoral Union, and Nettleton. But he especially held Taylor responsible for fomenting division among Connecticut Congregationalists, contending that the Pastoral Union had merely defended itself against Taylor's "dangerous errors" that were "at war with God's word."[35]

Despite Bacon's harsh criticism of the conservatives' actions and his acknowledgment that theological differences separated the opposing groups, however, he ultimately denied that those differences warranted a schism in the ranks of Connecticut Congregationalism. The errors that Calhoun and other members of the Pastoral Union had cited in their Protest, he stated, resulted largely from "misconstrued" extracts from Taylor's writings. The differences between Taylor and his critics, he believed, were more philosophical than theological: Taylor's attempts to explain his interpretation of the orthodox creed, not the doctrines that he adhered to, had led to misunderstanding by his opponents. While Bacon's reasoning may well have escaped the conservatives, he was essentially correct in arguing that both

33. Bacon, *Views and Reviews. No. I,* 3; Bacon, *Views and Reviews. No. II,* 10, 34.

34. Bacon, *Views and Reviews. No. I,* 9–14, 19–20, 38–42, 78–83; Bacon, *Views and Reviews. No. II,* 44–54, 57; New Haven *Record,* August 31, 1839.

35. Calhoun, *Letters to the Rev. Leonard Bacon,* 3, 5–6, 7–9, 12–15, 20–24, 29–34, 38; Bacon, *Views and Reviews. No. I,* 81, 85.

groups adhered to the *"great elements"* of Christian doctrine. Searching for a middle ground in this struggle, much as he had done in espousing urgent gradualism on the slavery issue, he insisted that most members of both parties shared an emphasis on the inspiration and supreme authority of the Bible as well as the belief that, among other things, God's purposes were consistent with human liberty and human agency and that the Congregational system was superior to that of other churches.[36]

Convinced that Congregational clergymen were divided only on "certain abstruse questions of metaphysical theology," he concluded that the central issue was whether their minor differences should be grounds for excision. He firmly believed that whatever potentially dangerous doctrinal errors each side subscribed to would best be rectified by regular contact with the other party. Division, he warned, with the Presbyterian schism in mind, would produce litigation and conflict and would weaken the entire church. Moreover, he sensed that people were growing tired of the seemingly interminable debate that centered on fine distinctions and definitions of doctrine. In one of his letters to Calhoun, he noted: "Metaphysical theology is not without its charms for me; but I often hear its discussions with the feeling that they are as old as the origins of evil, and that probably the same points will be argued with the same zeal (may it be with a better temper!) a thousand years hence."[37]

Yet it was in fact Bacon who had initiated the public debate with Calhoun, and indeed it was complaints from readers of the New Haven *Record* about the number of columns devoted to the exchange, not Bacon's or Calhoun's decision to end their lengthy correspondence, that eventually brought the series to a conclusion. Neither Bacon nor the conservatives seemed willing to terminate the contentious debate. Much as in Bacon's battles with the abolitionists, the combative part of his personality, which compelled him to press onward with the struggle and to underscore his adversaries' faults, often conflicted with his genuine desire for reconciliation. When he reminded Calhoun that each faction's pride, interests, and passion stood in the path of peace and cooperation, he referred in part to the struggle that occurred within himself.[38] Indeed, at times his urge to prevail in such debates and to show his opponents just how misguided or wrong they were made it impossible to achieve the very rapprochement between contending forces that he professed to desire.

The conservatives clearly were prepared to continue the debate. In 1840 Bennet Tyler, president of the Theological Institute of Connecticut, berated Bacon for charging that he was guilty of a "plain falsehood" in his disputes with Taylor and for his "unfair" attacks on Nettleton. Tyler also reiterated the conservatives' longstanding accusation that widespread doctrinal errors persisted among Connecticut

36. Bacon, *Views and Reviews. No. I*, 36–43, 56, 58, 96–99, also 52–54, 125–26.
37. Bacon, *Views and Reviews, No. II*, 62, 72–75, 33–34; Geer, *The Hartford Theological Seminary*, 42.
38. New Haven *Record*, April 25, 1840; Bacon, *Views and Reviews. No. I*, 56.

Congregationalists. Bacon chose to keep the debate going by responding to every one of Tyler's charges, though he did not publish any part of the lengthy correspondence that extended over several months. Once again, he went on the offensive, condemning Tyler for "arraigning and denouncing" Taylor, himself, and other proponents of the New Haven theology.[39]

Much as he had done with Calhoun, Bacon ultimately backed off somewhat from his angry exchange with Tyler, expressing an interest in "peace, confidence, and the healing of wounded affections." Following Tyler's rejection of his call for mutual concessions, the exchange bogged down into a contest as to who would be first to retract his charges in public. In the end, each man proved to be too proud, angry, and tenacious and too sensitive to what he perceived as unwarranted attacks on himself and his close friends to give up the struggle unilaterally. Finally, in late 1840, perhaps concluding that nothing more was to be gained from their charges and countercharges, they ended their correspondence.[40]

Bacon emerged from his lengthy and, at times, acrimonious debate with the conservative Congregationalists convinced that party disputes within the church involved their "own particular mode of splitting a hair"—an ironic observation in light of the abolitionists' frequent criticism of him for hairsplitting. More important, he believed that this internecine conflict threatened the welfare of Congregationalism. Thus, in his 1840 *Concio ad Clerum* at Yale he urged each of the assembled clergymen to "be a Bible man, and not the man of an ecclesiastical or theological faction." Despite his considerable influence in Connecticut Congregational affairs, he had not gained concessions from the conservatives, and they had categorically refused to reconcile with the New Haven group. Nevertheless, his repeated calls for peace between the contending parties did play a decisive role in averting a schism in the Connecticut Congregational Church. At the same time, Bacon could take some comfort in the fact that, by the end of the 1830s, the drift of Congregationalists in the state toward Arminianism and Taylorism was quite evident.[41] As time passed he came to view the theological issues so fiercely debated from the late 1820s until the early 1840s as less and less relevant to the spiritual needs of Christians. When he again came into conflict with the conservative Congregationalists in the late 1840s, it would be as a defender of Horace Bushnell, who not only rejected the conservatives' position but also questioned important features of the revival theology propounded by his mentor, Nathaniel Taylor.

39. Bennet Tyler to Bacon, July 25, August 15, 1840, Bacon to Bennet Tyler, July 25, 28, 1840, in Bacon Family Papers.

40. Bacon to Bennet Tyler, August 27, September 25, November 18, 1840, Bennet Tyler to Bacon, September 2, October 20, November 24, 1840, in Bacon Family Papers.

41. *Concio ad Clerum*, August 19, 1840, in Bacon Family Papers; Timothy L. Smith, *Revivalism and Social Reform in Mid-Nineteenth-Century America* (New York, 1957), 88–92.

7

NEW HAVEN SCHOLARSHIP AND FAMILY CONNECTIONS

EVER since his undergraduate days, Bacon had displayed a penchant for social activism, believing that it was the obligation of all Christians to act upon their religious beliefs and not simply to engage in metaphysical speculation. But at the same time, he was drawn powerfully to the world of ideas. Acting more as a popularizer than an original thinker, he sought to influence a predominantly evangelical audience by interpreting and explaining the major social, economic, political, and intellectual developments of the time. He wrote and spoke widely in part because he assumed that he had important things to say on a broad range of subjects. He was also motivated by the need to supplement his salary. Perhaps above all, he felt obliged, as a clergyman and an educated man, to inform and guide the American people and to advance desirable social change. Because the minds of liberally educated men had been disciplined and expanded, he told the Phi Beta Kappa Society of Dartmouth College in 1845, they must serve as "good neighbors" on behalf of Christian benevolence and social progress. Moreover, they should always be scholars, for "whatever your profession may be . . . it will increase your capacity of usefulness to your country and to your race, whether in your particular profession, or in your relations as a citizen and as a man."[1]

Bacon practiced what he preached. Throughout his life he sought to extend his influence far beyond the boundaries of New Haven and to bring the world to his congregation and community. He maintained extensive contacts with intellectuals and activists throughout the North. But his primary source of intellectual stimulation was always the Yale faculty and the professional classes in New Haven. In founding the Club, in conjunction with Theodore Dwight Woolsey, then a professor of Greek at Yale, in 1838, he moved to facilitate the exchange of ideas among

---

1. Leonard Bacon, *Oration, Before the Phi Beta Kappa Society of Dartmouth College, Delivered July 30, 1845* (Hanover, N.H., 1845), 5–6, 13, 15, 19–20.

educated gentlemen, to restate and reaffirm common values and beliefs, and to con-
nect the members to the national world of scholarship. He and Woolsey were joined
at this time by a few other professional men in their thirties and forties—Henry
White, an attorney and deacon of Center Church; the Congregational minister
Henry G. Ludlow; Henry Tomlinson, a physician; and Josiah Gibbs, a professor of
linguistics at Yale. These men modeled the Club on the Bread and Cheese Club in
New York City, a literary organization that included among its members William
Cullen Bryant and James Fenimore Cooper.[2]

The membership of the Club grew from six to thirty over the next few decades,
with the percentage of ministers declining and that of Yale faculty growing. It
never had a formal organization, constitution, or officers, and no records of its
proceedings were kept until 1856. The Club met twice each month at one of the
members' homes, where they ate a light meal and decided on the next topic to be
discussed. Then they held an open dialogue, with each person expressing his views
on questions relating to theology, literature, science, politics, international relations,
slavery, and other subjects. Bacon took a particular interest in social and political
topics, and was perhaps the most assertive member, leading more discussion groups
than any other member during the Club's first four decades.[3]

All of the members of the Club were Yale graduates. Indeed, Bacon's connections with Yale were many and varied. He was close friends with the faculty as well
as with President Day, and a number of faculty members belonged to Center
Church. In 1839 Yale offered him the position of professor of rhetoric and oratory
at a salary of $1,200, which was less than he was receiving from Center Church at
this time. He was quite tempted by this offer, and chose to place it before the members of his church's Ecclesiastical Society for their consideration. In his letter to the
society he emphasized his "entirely and mutually affectionate" relationship with
the congregation and his desire to remain at Center Church. Yet he also pointed to
the close ties that existed between Center Church and Yale and the stake that all the
people of New Haven and the state had in preventing the college, as "one of the
great defences of Christian truth," from being corrupted or weakened. More disin-
genuously, and somewhat arrogantly, he also noted that his congregation might wish
to hire a minister who was "burthened with fewer public cares and labors," for
"there is no other Church in the State, whose pastor is so much the servant of the
Church at large and the public at large, as the pastor of this Church."[4]

2. Alexander M. Witherspoon, *The Club: The Story of Its First One Hundred and Twenty-five Years,
1838–1963* (New Haven, 1964), 8, 10–12; James T. Callow, *Kindred Spirits: Knickerbocker Writers and American Artists, 1807–1855* (Chapel Hill, 1967), 12–17.

3. Witherspoon, *The Club,* 7–8, 32–36, 51, 57–70; Louise L. Stevenson, *Scholarly Means to Evangelical
Ends: The New Haven Scholars and the Transformation of Higher Learning in America, 1830–1890* (Baltimore,
1986), 22–23.

4. Meeting of August 20, 1839, "Records of the Yale Corporation," Sterling Library, Yale Univer-

Not surprisingly, some members of Center Church concluded that he in fact desired the Yale position, while others were not certain. Following a meeting with President Day and Benjamin Silliman, however, the Ecclesiastical Society unanimously refused to dismiss him from his pastorate. Indeed, despite the lack of major revivals in Center Church during the late 1830s and the 1840s, Bacon enjoyed the confidence of most of his parishioners. In his weekly sermons he continued to emphasize the individual as a rational, free agent who chose either to sin or to turn to God. He also appealed to members of his congregation to conduct themselves in a moral and ethical manner. As New Haven grew steadily, becoming a commercial and industrial city of nearly twenty thousand people by the 1840s, he expressed growing concern that excessive concentration on wealth and material objects would produce selfishness and irreligion. Consequently, he urged his parishioners to find employment that was useful and would advance the welfare of the family and the community. He, like many other clergymen of the time, also espoused a regimen of self-education and self-culture for the purpose of strengthening one's mental powers and self-discipline, and he called upon people to observe the Sabbath and to avoid amusements, profanity, and alcoholic beverages.[5]

This message of free will, self-culture, and moral conduct appealed to many of his largely middle- and upper-class congregation, who sought to assuage whatever uneasiness they experienced in their pursuit of material success and status by adhering to the concepts of Christian benevolence, self-improvement, and the general welfare. Although the occupation of every adult male parishioner at Center Church cannot be known, some idea of the social makeup of the congregation can be gained. An analysis of 96 of the approximately 160 adult male members of his congregation (out of a total membership that ranged from 560 to 610 in the early and middle 1840s) shows that a few men were farmers and common laborers, while 20 (21 percent) were skilled craftsmen who worked as bakers, tailors, masons, printers, silversmiths, blacksmiths, joiners, shoemakers, coach trimmers and painters, and cabinet makers. But 66 (69 percent) of these 96 men (or more than one-third of all adult male parishioners) were either in professional occupations, such as lawyers, physicians, school teachers and administrators, college professors, and book and newspaper publishers, or were entrepreneurs, including merchants, manufacturers, wholesale grocers, and bankers. Throughout the 1840s, the number of members remained quite stable, even though there was a steady outflow to new Congrega-

sity; Bacon to Ecclesiastical Society of Center Church, 1839, in Bacon Family Papers; *Leonard Bacon: Pastor of the First Church in New Haven,* 23–24.

5. Leonard Bacon, "What It Is to Become a Christian," *National Preacher,* V (June, 1840), 144–48; special meeting of the First Ecclesiastical Society, September 2, 1839, Leonard to Catherine Bacon, September 4, 1848, sermons of October 24, 1841, April 10, 1842, October 26, 1845, March 5, 1848, March 18, July 29, November 11, 1849, lyceum lecture of March, 1841, in Bacon Family Papers; Warner, *New Haven Negroes,* 13–14.

tional churches established in the city and to other denominations, and approximately 1,500 people regularly attended Sunday services.[6]

Bacon respected and admired the members of his congregation. He valued the fact that, unlike many other churches, there was little conflict among his parishioners. He also expressed appreciation, in his twentieth-year sermon delivered in 1845, for the widespread desire for intellectual stimulation and moral guidance shown by "men of superior order of professional and general information." Although somewhat self-conscious about his general inability to produce stirring sermons, he nonetheless was convinced that his parishioners preferred "the plain thoughtful serious inculcation of the great truths and duties of religion."[7]

The Ecclesiastical Society's refusal to dismiss Bacon so that he could accept the Yale post did not lessen his involvement in, or concern about, the affairs of the college. Less than two months later, he was elected to the Yale Corporation. During the next seven years, he served on a number of committees, including the Prudential Committee, which dealt with such matters as tuition, room and board, use of space, budget, and faculty hiring and salaries. Indeed, he was so respected by people associated with Yale that when Jeremiah Day resigned as president of the college in 1846, Bacon, as a minister in his forties, with solid intellectual credentials and a widespread reputation in reform and ecclesiastical circles, was seriously considered for the position. A number of faculty and alumni, however, believed that he was too much of a controversialist, especially on the slavery issue, and questioned whether he had sufficient administrative ability. Consequently, the corporation turned to Woolsey, whom Bacon had strongly recommended. Bacon then resigned from the corporation in order to make room for Day. In doing so he cited the need for Day's "experienced wisdom" and the fact that he was "overwhelmed with the multiplicity of the toils and strifes to which I am accustomed on every side."[8]

Beyond his membership in the Club and his service on the Yale Corporation, Bacon's ties to the college extended to intimate intellectual and social relationships within an informal group that Louise L. Stevenson has termed the New Haven

6. *Patten's New Haven Directory, For the Years 1841–2* (New Haven, 1841), *passim; Benham's New Haven City Directory for 1846–7. No. 7* (New Haven, 1846), *passim; Minutes of the General Association of Connecticut* (1842), 31, (1844), 30, (1845), 30, (1847), 34; sermons of March 16, 1845, October 15, 1848, in Bacon Family Papers.

7. Henry G. Ludlow to Bacon, April 19, 1842, sermon of March 16, 1845, in Bacon Family Papers.

8. See meetings of October 23, 1839, October 20, 1846, "Records of the Yale Corporation"; meetings of December 18, 1839, August 4, 19, 1840, December 30, 1845, August 4, 1846, "Records of the Prudential Committee of the Yale Corporation," Sterling Library, Yale University; Bacon to Sarah Wisner, April 16, August 24, 1846, Leonard Woods to Bacon, February 7, 1846, Bacon to the President and Fellows of Yale College, September 18, 1845, in Bacon Family Papers; Timothy Dwight, Jr., *Memories of Yale Life and Men, 1845–1899* (New York, 1903), 182–83; Kelley, *Yale,* 171.

scholars. Over the years this group included Woolsey, White, and Gibbs, as well as S. W. S. Dutton, a Congregational minister, and a number of Yale professors. These men were evangelical Congregationalists whose families interacted on a regular basis and who, in a number of cases, were either related to each other by marriage or, as with Woolsey, Twining, and Bacon, were old friends from college days.[9]

As scholars, these men were committed to employing the most advanced learning of the age, especially in the form of the German historical and philological methods to which Bacon had been introduced by Moses Stuart at Andover. Even though New Haven stood on the periphery of the national intellectual mainstream, they viewed themselves as cosmopolitan members of a larger scholarly community and rejected the arguments of the more conservative Congregational clergy, who preached dogmatically, read the Bible literally, and repudiated the new currents of thought from Germany. Although they were, in important ways, successors to Nathaniel Taylor and the New Haven theology, Bacon and other New Haven scholars also came to believe that the conflict between the Taylorites and their conservative critics served to weaken the evangelical efficacy of the church. Indeed, at the 1850 Yale commencement Bacon reportedly referred derisively to the Taylor-Tyler controversy of the 1830s as having rested largely upon the additional letter in the former's surname.[10]

But the New Haven scholars' differences with the Taylorites transcended their aversion to sectarian squabbling. By the 1840s, they were disturbed by the tension between intellectual life and faith created by the hostility that many Taylorites directed toward discoveries in the natural sciences. Taylor, for example, insisted on the absolute truth of the Bible and rejected geologists' discovery of fossils and geological formations that challenged the Genesis story. Bacon, on the other hand, was a devoted proponent of scientific research. Because he believed that such research was "one of the great interests of a free people," he clearly disagreed with Taylor's resistance to finding common ground between religion and science. In a memorial to Congress on behalf of the Connecticut Academy of Arts and Sciences in 1846, he praised the federal government for funding a scientific expedition that he was convinced would extend the boundaries of knowledge for the benefit of all people.[11]

The subject of the role of scientific knowledge in Christian revelation was "a

9. Stevenson, *Scholarly Means to Evangelical Ends,* 1, 21–22; Witherspoon, *The Club,* 10–12.

10. See Stevenson, *Scholarly Means to Evangelical Ends,* 1–2, 5–9, 15–20; Laura Hadley Moseley, ed., *Diary (1843–1852) of James Hadley: Tutor and Professor in Greek in Yale College, 1845–1872* (New Haven, 1951), 89–90.

11. Draft of Connecticut Academy of Arts and Sciences Memorial to Congress, March 10, 1846, in Bacon Family Papers. For the Taylorites' views regarding scientific discoveries, see Stevenson, *Scholarly Means to Evangelical Ends,* 19–20; Mead, *Nathaniel William Taylor,* 236.

great one," he informed his mother, and he approached it with "something like temerity." In a sermon he presented at the inauguration of Woolsey as president of Yale in 1846, he sought to answer attacks by Taylor and other members of the theological faculty on Woolsey's lack of ministerial experience and his mastery of the philological methods of research taught at German universities. In doing so he recognized the difficulties involved in exploring the effects of Christian revelation on the progress of science, yet he forged ahead, telling the dignitaries assembled at the inauguration that, because Christianity and the natural sciences were so closely linked, a reformation in Christianity must precede one in science. Christianity, he asserted, was a religion of "reverent inquiry" as well as faith. "This is the very spirit of true science," he noted, "that finds truth in facts—God's truth in God's facts." Because Christianity must encourage science to advance the welfare of mankind, it should be enthroned in the university. By the same token, the university must not inhibit inquiry and examination, for its "vital element" was intellectual freedom and its message to the world was that one must prove all things. In an 1850 sermon at Center Church, attended by Benjamin Silliman, the eminent Harvard scientist Louis Agassiz, and other members of the American Association for the Advancement of Science, he even more directly challenged those Taylorites who resisted discoveries in the natural sciences. A modification of prevailing interpretations of the Scriptures, he stated, was necessary in order to "answer the demands of science."[12]

Yet as religious men, the New Haven scholars sought to infuse the past, present, and future with religious meaning and to show that all parts of the visible world revealed divine truth. They vigorously affirmed God's presence in human affairs and viewed the imminent Christian millennium as integral to true scholarship. The theistic system that they posited was intended to serve evangelical ends and rejected both the mechanistic Enlightenment world view and the abstract social theories of the French rationalists.[13]

As one of America's earliest historians, Bacon sought to blend the past and the present as well as scholarship and evangelical religion. In preparing his *Thirteen Historical Discourses,* a chronicle of Center Church and New Haven over the past two hundred years, which he initially presented in Sunday evening lectures in 1838, he engaged in extensive research not only in histories of New England and the United States but also in a variety of primary sources. Much like other Americans of the time who were active in founding and sustaining state historical societies—several of which elected him as a member—he wished to preserve historical records

12. Leonard to Alice Bacon, October 3, 1846, in Bacon Family Papers; Gabriel, *Religion and Learning at Yale,* 117; *Discourses and Addresses at the Ordination of the Rev. Theodore Dwight Woolsey,* 24–28, 30–34; Stevenson, *Scholarly Means to Evangelical Ends,* 20.

13. Stevenson, *Scholarly Means to Evangelical Ends,* 3–4.

and to further human knowledge. In a speech to the Connecticut Historical Society in 1843, he praised the organization for constituting "a bond of union for those who love old records, old books and documents, old customs and traditions," as well as for making members aware and supportive of others' research and the public appreciative of knowledge.[14]

These historical societies, however, did not diminish Bacon's fear of Americans' losing a connection with the past, a fear grounded in a recognition of the attractiveness of the present. Indeed, it was his eagerness to embrace many of the innovations of the time that ironically may have deepened his interest in and concern for knowing what had gone on before. (In this respect he was much like his contemporary, Abraham Lincoln.) The present, Bacon wrote in *Thirteen Historical Discourses,* "is the best age, the age in which it is the greatest privilege to live." Although concerned about the disorder and corruption that was part of modern American life, he could not accept the conservatives' gloomy forecasts. Nevertheless, the rapid pace of change in antebellum America seemed, at the same time, to render more difficult the task of preserving historical documents and memories.[15]

For all his emphasis on scholarship and technological, social, and economic progress in the modern age, however, Bacon was convinced they must serve evangelical ends. His interest in the history of the Puritan fathers was rooted largely in the hope that knowledge of their courage and piety would advance the cause of evangelical religion. "I trust that the book," he wrote Lucy while preparing *Thirteen Historical Discourses,* "is calculated . . . to exhibit and recommend evangelical religion." He, like other New Haven scholars, believed that history could only be understood within the context of God's plan for the human race. "The scheme of Divine Providence," he argued, "is one, from the beginning to the end, and is ever in progressive development. Every succeeding age helps to unfold the mighty plan."[16]

Bacon's didacticism manifested itself in still other ways. Like many other histori-

14. Bacon, *Thirteen Historical Discourses,* iii, 5–19, 223; David D. Van Tassel, *Recording America's Past: An Interpretation of the Development of Historical Studies in America, 1607–1884* (Chicago, 1960), 95–100; Leslie W. Dunlap, *American Historical Societies, 1790–1860* (Madison, 1944), 10–13; Thomas Day to Bacon, March 21, 1843, in Bacon Family Papers; Leonard Bacon, *A Discourse on the Early Constitutional History of Connecticut, Delivered Before the Connecticut Historical Society, Hartford, May 17, 1843* (Hartford, 1843), 3. Partly as a result of his *Thirteen Historical Discourses,* he was granted an honorary doctorate by Hamilton College in New York in 1842. *The Congregational Year-Book, 1882* (Boston, 1882), 18–19.

15. This irony is treated in Lewis Perry, *Boats Against the Current: American Culture Between Revolution and Modernity, 1820–1860* (New York, 1993). For Bacon's positive view of the present and future, see Bacon, *Thirteen Historical Discourses,* 286–87; Leonard Bacon, "The New Earth," *New Englander,* VII (February, 1849), 3–13.

16. Leonard to Lucy Bacon, February 3, 1839, in Bacon Family Papers; see also John Davis to Bacon, July 9, 24, August 12, 1838, in National and Local Historical Figures Collection, New Haven Colony Historical Society, New Haven, Conn.

ans in the early nineteenth century, his reverence for his Puritan ancestors often prevailed over historical objectivity. He acknowledged, for example, that he emphasized the virtues more than the faults of New Haven's leaders over the past two hundred years because he believed that their positive features were imperfectly understood. He also frequently engaged in historical presentism. As a matter of fact, by associating Asahel Nettleton with those revival preachers in the First Great Awakening who he was certain had spread "denunciation, calumny, contention, spiritual pride, and confusion," he probably contributed to the sectarian squabbling that he so often criticized.[17]

Bacon's interpretation of history was also shaped by an enduring attachment to a romantic nationalism. On numerous occasions he called for the development of an "American character," particularly through the creation of an indigenous literature. In an article that appeared in the *American Biblical Repository* in 1840, he argued that a truly American literature must manifest a national spirit, not "a faint and cheap imitation of foreign models," by celebrating equality before the law, patriotism, republican virtues, simplicity, and Christianity. Likewise, in his history of New Haven he lauded the Pilgrims' and Puritans' escape from the evils of the English monarchy, the nobility, and the Anglican Church.[18]

Above all, Bacon tended to view the American experience from a New England perspective. He was convinced that the true heritage of the United States was molded by the New England settlers. Only in that region, he proclaimed in a speech before the Phi Beta Kappa Society of Yale in 1839, could one find "the true operation, the demonstrated tendency of the American structure of society," which was built on the theory of equal rights brought to America by the Pilgrims. That theory, he and other New Haven scholars insisted, was rooted most deeply in the Congregational form of church government, which produced the individual freedom that was so prevalent in America. At times his attachment to New England took a chauvinistic turn, as when he declared that "when Yankee emigration scaling the Rocky Mountains, shall have established those institutions of New England, the district school, the Church, and the town-meetings, on the shores of the Pacific, the chartered boundaries will have been restored."[19]

Bacon, along with several of his fellow New Haven scholars—including

17. Bacon, *Thirteen Historical Discourses,* iii–iv, 15–16, 198, 208–209, 240–41, 285–86.

18. Richard Hegel, *Nineteenth-Century Historians of New Haven* (Hamden, Conn., 1992), 1–2; Leonard Bacon, "The Proper Character and Functions of American Literature," *American Biblical Repository,* n.s., III (January, 1840), 1–7, 10–23; *A Discourse on the Early Constitutional History of Connecticut,* 17–24.

19. Van Tassel, *Recording America's Past,* 91; Leonard Bacon, *The Proper Character and Functions of American Literature. A Discourse Before the Society of Phi Beta Kappa, in Yale College, August 20, 1839* (New York, 1840), 16; Bacon to Committee of the New England Society of New York City, November 20, 1840, in Bacon Family Papers; Stevenson, *Scholarly Means to Evangelical Ends,* 5–7.

Woolsey, Noah Porter, Joseph P. Thompson, and S. W. S. Dutton—further sought to interpret and explain the American experience from a New England evangelical, Congregational perspective when they founded the *New Englander,* a quarterly journal, in 1843. In 1842 he had persuaded these men, as well as Horace Bushnell, Joel Hawes, and others, of the need for a magazine that would treat "in a popular way a pretty large variety of topics generally neglected in Journals which have anything of a religious character." He served on the *New Englander*'s editorial committee from 1843 until 1863, and during the journal's first thirty-eight years contributed at least a hundred articles—more than any other person.[20]

In some respects the *New Englander* was the successor to the *Christian Spectator,* and Bacon clearly was the central transitional figure between the two journals. The tenor of the *New Englander,* however, was different from that of the *Christian Spectator;* this illustrates how far he and other New Haven scholars of his generation had moved from many of Nathaniel Taylor's generation. The *New Englander* was, overall, more liberal and secular in intention and practice than the *Christian Spectator* had been. Its columns were filled with lengthy reviews of current books on science, politics, and scholarly affairs, connecting its readers with a network of American and European scholars based in the colleges; whereas the *Christian Spectator* had been, above all, part of a transatlantic evangelical connection.[21]

This did not mean that the editors of the *New Englander* were uninterested in religious matters, for they intended to appeal to intelligent, "free Christian men" in order to teach them to be godly while also participating in public life. In addition, they promised to stand "on the side of order, of freedom, of progress, of simple and spiritual Christianity, and of the Bible as the infallible, sufficient and only authority in religion." At the same time, they stood against both "a mystical, pantheistic infidelity" and "a picturesque, enthusiastic superstition," whether in history, philosophy, poetry, romantic fiction, or socialist theories. Indeed, a number of articles in the early years of the *New Englander* were devoted to theology, and many topics clearly had a religious or moral cast.[22]

Yet the editors chose to devote little attention to the theological issues that had been so thoroughly debated in the columns of the *Christian Spectator.* In their prospectus Bacon, Woolsey, Porter, Thompson, and the other editors asserted that, while they might disagree among themselves, they would not include in the *New Englander* the views of those who wished to contradict or dispute them for the sake

20. Stevenson, *Scholarly Means to Evangelical Ends,* 41; Biographical Sketch of Bacon, Bacon to Alexander C. Twining, March 26, 1842, in Bacon Family Papers; Leonard Bacon, "Prospectus," *New Englander,* I (January, 1843), 2–3.

21. Stevenson, *Scholarly Means to Evangelical Ends,* 43–45.

22. Leonard Bacon, "Prolegomena," *New Englander,* I (January, 1843), 8; Bacon, "Prospectus," 2–3; also Frank Luther Mott, *A History of American Magazines, 1850–1865* (Cambridge, Mass., 1938), 312.

of controversy. To engage in doctrinal debate, they maintained, would not only undermine evangelical unity and alienate their lay audience but also draw them "further into the field of scientific and metaphysical theology" than they desired and would divert both the contributors and the readers from those matters "to which the progress of the age is giving more prominence and more of present importance."[23] The message, stated less discreetly, was that the fierce debates of the 1830s were both irrelevant and divisive.

From the journal's inception, Bacon wrote on a number of prominent social, political, and economic issues. He strongly supported the right of people to buy, sell, work, and produce in a free market and urged the United States to follow the lead of Britain in adopting a free-trade policy. As a proponent of free trade, he also espoused postal reform based upon the new system in Britain. At a time when the drive for reform of the postal system, with its high letter rates and glaring inefficiencies, was gaining ground, he called for a system that would provide unlimited access and rapid delivery, be uniform in its operation, and charge the lowest possible rates. Sweeping reforms, he asserted in an 1843 *New Englander* article, would have both moral and economic benefits for the American people and would cement the ties of family and states within the nation.[24]

Following Congress' passage of some reforms in 1845, Bacon urged the American people to insist upon a "thorough reform," with each user paying an equitable share of the postal department's expenses. Only then could the greatest number of customers be accommodated. Nearly a decade later he continued to call for a "radical and complete" reform of the system, which he believed must be a public convenience, not a tax, for the benefit of all Americans. Consequently, he espoused a drastic reduction of rates to two cents for letters weighing under a half ounce, which he believed would advance knowledge, enterprise, morals, and education.[25]

Another subject that Bacon frequently discussed in the columns of the *New Englander* was the need to extend New England ideas and institutions to the West. The Society for the Promotion of Collegiate and Theological Education at the West, which he helped to found in 1843 and was actively involved in for much of the rest of his life, sought above all to achieve this objective. He was moved to launch this society in part by his belief that a liberal, Christian education was neces-

23. Bacon, "Prospectus," 1–2.

24. Leonard Bacon, "The State of Political Parties," *New Englander,* V (April, 1847), 311–12; Leonard Bacon, "The Post Office System as an Element of Modern Civilization," *New Englander,* I (January, 1843), 14–25. On the American postal reform movement in the 1840s, see Daniel C. Roper, *The United States Post Office: Its Past Record, Present Condition, and Potential Relation to the New World Era* (New York, 1917), 60–62.

25. Leonard Bacon, "The New Post-Office Law," *New Englander,* III (October, 1845), 537–48; Leonard Bacon, "The New Post-Office Law," *New Englander,* XII (October, 1854), 537–40, 542–46, 548.

sary for the survival of a free society. Thus, colleges must be supported in order to make them affordable to all qualified young men. Yet a more conservative and restrictive impulse also moved him to support this organization: the conviction that it was especially vital to train an educated ministry, primarily for service in the West, which would Christianize the region and serve to counter the disorder and irreligion so prevalent in western settlements.[26]

Bacon, along with Lyman Beecher, Albert Barnes, Horace Bushnell, Theron Baldwin, and other evangelical Congregationalists and New School Presbyterians, was concerned that many western colleges and seminaries would collapse without systematic and adequate support from eastern churches. Such a development, Bacon warned, would leave the field either to state universities, which sought to unite all shades of moral and religious opinion and to placate all parties and sects, or to institutions controlled by a "corrupted, superstitious, hierarchical Christianity." Convinced that the practice of having each institution send its own agents to the East to solicit funds was a failure, he and other founders of the SPCTEW foresaw an eastern-based society to which western educational institutions would make a united appeal. As a member of the executive committee, headed by Baldwin, Bacon helped to distribute over one million dollars to fourteen colleges and theological seminaries across the country—including Wabash, Knox, Western Reserve, Marietta, and Illinois colleges and Lane Seminary.[27]

Yet Bacon viewed the Society for the Promotion of Collegiate and Theological Education at the West as more than an agent of education and civilization in the West. He also considered the society a powerful means of combating the Catholic influence in that region. If a reasonable number of evangelical Protestant colleges and seminaries were sustained, he wrote in 1844, "the Jesuit may pack up his relics and pictures, and go back to Rome." Bacon was a religious bigot who had little but

26. Leonard Bacon, "Beecher on Colleges," *Quarterly Christian Spectator*, 3rd series, VIII (September, 1836), 389–93; Leonard Bacon, "What Must Be Done to Provide an Educated Christian Ministry?" *New Englander*, I (January, 1843), 126–31; *First Annual Report of the Society for the Promotion of Collegiate and Theological Education at the West* (New York, 1844), 26. For treatments of the guiding motives of the SPCTEW's founders, see, for example, James Findlay, "Agency, Denominations and the Western Colleges, 1830–1860: Some Connections Between Evangelicalism and American Higher Education," *Church History*, L (1981), 73–78; Hermann R. Muelder, *Fighters for Freedom: The History of Anti-Slavery Activities of Men and Women Associated with Knox College* (New York, 1959), 247–48.

27. Leonard Bacon, *Christianity and Learning: A Discourse Preached in the Second Presbyterian Church in Troy, October 26, 1847, Before the Annual Meeting of the Society for the Promotion of Collegiate and Theological Education at the West* (New Haven, 1848), 4; James W. Fraser, *Pedagogue for God's Kingdom: Lyman Beecher and the Second Great Awakening* (Lanham, Md., 1985), 151–55; Findlay, "Agency, Denominations and the Western Colleges," 73n, 74–78; Edward Beecher to Bacon, September 21, 1843, in Bacon Family Papers. Colleges that did not support revivals, as well as Oberlin, with its perfectionist beliefs, did not receive assistance. Fraser, *Pedagogue for God's Kingdom*, 156.

contempt for the Catholic Church and its leaders. He was certain that its hierarchy was engaged in a "gigantic scheme for the extension of the papal dominion" to the United States, and he found Catholic doctrines and rituals repugnant.[28]

In response to the strident anti-Catholicism of the extreme nativists, however, he maintained, much as he had in the 1830s, that Protestants must be tolerant toward Catholic immigrants in America. He conceded that Catholicism contained some truth, along with obvious errors, and that it was possible for Catholics to be saved and for a priest to be an honest man. He also felt that Catholics must be treated according to their individual character and emphasized that most Catholic immigrants in fact had fled from oppression. Any social proscription directed against them by hostile Protestants, he feared, might well move them to reject all authority in a Protestant-dominated society and to become the dupes of demagogues. Such pronouncements were unacceptable to extreme nativists, such as Samuel F. B. Morse, Charles Sparry, and Robert J. Breckinridge, who frequently warned of an imminent Catholic takeover of American society and ridiculed Catholic immigrants as intemperate and disorderly paupers and criminals who lowered the moral tone of communities. But Bacon believed that the militant Protestants' "anti-popery panic" was unjustified, for Catholics constituted a small minority of the population and few Protestants had converted to Catholicism.[29]

His commitment to the principle of religious liberty, as well as his desire to extend Protestantism throughout the world as a means of ensuring the coming of the millennium, were the guiding forces behind a number of anti-Catholic organizations that Bacon helped to establish and sustain during the 1840s. The Philo-American Society, founded in New York City in 1842, sought to rally Protestants under a common banner in order to "revolutionize the Papacy" and to achieve religious liberty in the Catholic countries of Europe. In 1843 Bacon headed a committee of this society that was charged with developing a plan of attack against papal influence in the Catholic nations, and he served as the society's corresponding secretary.[30]

28. Leonard Bacon, "Romanists and the Roman Catholic Controversy," *New Englander,* II (April, 1844), 233–35, 237, 239, 242, 245–46, 250–51. An excellent treatment of the anti-Catholic conspiracy theory is David Brion Davis, "Some Themes of Counter-Subversion: An Analysis of Anti-Masonic, Anti-Catholic, and Anti-Mormon Literature," *Mississippi Valley Historical Review,* XLVII (September, 1960), 205–24.

29. Bacon, "Romanists and the Roman Catholic Controversy," 234, 236–42, 245; sermons of November 26, 1843, February 11, 1844, November 27, 1845, in Bacon Family Papers; New York *Evangelist,* January 27, 1848; Billington, *The Protestant Crusade,* 168–70, 182–85, 194–98. For an analysis of the Protestant perception of Roman Catholicism in antebellum America, see Jenny Franchot, *Roads to Rome: The Antebellum Protestant Encounter with Catholicism* (Berkeley, 1994).

30. Leonard Bacon, "The Day Approaching," *National Preacher,* XVI (October, 1842), 222–25; Carroll John Noonan, "Nativism in Connecticut, 1829–1860" (Ph.D. dissertation, Catholic University of

When the Christian Alliance absorbed the Philo-American Society in 1843, Bacon, George B. Cheever, and Edwin Holt were chosen as its corresponding secretaries. In their address to the public, Bacon and Cheever asserted that the political revolutions of the past twenty-five years indicated that many people in Italy, as well as Italians living in other parts of the world, were "liberally disposed and ready to receive new ideas" regarding religious liberty and Protestantism. Bacon believed that the Christian Alliance could best serve as a clearinghouse for bringing together all who espoused the "universal emancipation of Christianity from 'every false yoke.'" From the alliance's inception, Bacon did his utmost to advance its interests, presenting a series of public lectures on Italy, writing a letter to Pope Gregory XVI, and addressing several of the society's annual meetings. He was certain that religious liberty would eventually triumph in Europe because economic development and progress in the areas of literature, science, and transportation would overwhelm censorship and despotism. Nevertheless, the society had little money, enjoyed meager support among the clergy (who found it difficult to identify with a crusade against papal influence in European countries), and employed no agents in Europe. Consequently, it largely faded from the scene by 1847.[31]

One of the factors contributing to the demise of the Christian Alliance was the founding of the Evangelical Alliance in 1846, which Lyman Beecher, Bushnell, Bacon, and other Protestant leaders in the United States and Britain envisioned as an international movement to combat Catholicism. Bushnell, an outspoken anti-Catholic activist, urged Bacon to attend the founding meeting in London and asked Bacon's parishioners to pay for the trip. Bacon seriously considered attending the convention and then traveling in Europe for several months. But in the final analysis, his responsibilities toward Center Church and his family convinced him to remain in New Haven.[32]

Bacon's ministerial obligations continued to occupy much of his time. He made a concerted effort to see each of his parishioners himself rather than sending his

America, 1938), 106; Horace Bushnell to Bacon, April 18, 1843, Theodore Dwight, Jr., to Bacon, April 29, May 5, 20, 25, 1843, in Bacon Family Papers; *Circular of the American Protestant Society* (New York, 1847), 1–3, 16.

31. *The Christian Alliance: Its Constitution, List of Officers, and Address* (New York, 1843), 3, 5–6, 9–13; *Address of the Rev. L. Bacon, D.D., and Rev. E. N. Kirk, at the Annual Meeting of the Christian Alliance, Held in New York, May 8, 1845, With the Address of the Society and the Bull of the Pope Against It* (New York, 1846), 5, 8–9; Bacon to Joseph P. Thompson, June 28, 1846, A. L. Barginni to Bacon, April 10, 1845, Joseph P. Thompson to Bacon, June 18, 1846, sermon of November 27, 1845, in Bacon Family Papers; Bacon, "Romanists and the Roman Catholic Controversy," 254–55; Noonan, "Nativism in Connecticut," 107–109.

32. J. F. Maclear, "The Evangelical Alliance and the Antislavery Crusade," *Huntington Library Quarterly*, XLII (Spring, 1979), 144–45; Horace Bushnell to Bacon, June 11, 1845, Leonard to Benjamin Bacon, July 1, 14, August 29, 1845, William H. Bidwell to Bacon, July 7, 1845, in Bacon Family Papers.

deacons. In addition, he followed the standard weekly regimen adhered to by clergymen, including meeting with the deacons and Sunday school teachers and leading prayer meetings, and he devoted at least two days a week to study for, and the writing of, the sermons he preached twice each Sunday. He also remained active in the Connecticut General Association, serving as its moderator in 1845 and heading a Committee on Psalmody that devoted considerable labor in the mid-1840s to the preparation of a hymnbook for use in Congregational churches. *Psalms and Hymns, for Christian Use and Worship,* which contained over 700 hymns, including 70 that were new to the United States and 5 that he composed, represented an important addition to American hymnody.[33]

While Bacon's pastoral labors followed a rather predictable rhythm, his family life during these years was filled with volatility and uncertainty. His family grew steadily and experienced a number of tragedies and difficulties. One of the most devastating personal losses of Bacon's life was the death of his son James in 1840 at the age of two following a brief illness. Although he sought comfort in the belief that his son was in God's hands, Bacon was deeply saddened by the loss. James, he noted in his diary, "so tenderly and dearly beloved by us all, with all the light and bloom of his gay existence—has been taken away from our sight. The way has been opened from my fireside to the grave. That way will be kept open—will be trodden again and again till all are gone."[34]

There were also joyous occasions, such as the birth of Lucy in 1841 and of Edward Woolsey in 1843. But during the early 1840s his wife's health continued to deteriorate. By 1844, she was too ill to travel, and Delia and Rebecca had to take over much of the care of the youngest children. Following Lucy's death from consumption in November, 1844, Bacon once more sought solace in his faith. He frequently asked himself why she had died, but invariably concluded that all people must learn the "lesson of simple and absolute acquiescence in the will of God." Not only did Lucy's death deal a heavy emotional blow to Bacon and his seven children; it also created real difficulties in terms of care for his children, who ranged in age from one to eighteen years. Rebecca, the oldest child, was enlisted to take care of her younger siblings—a task that she would commit herself to for many years, at the expense of marriage and, until later in her life, a career. With his busy schedule, Bacon was unable to devote much time to daily child care, but he provided affection and advice and dealt with numerous matters related to his children's education and upbringing. Although he could be flexible in his expectations regarding his sons' training and career planning, he was a strict disciplinarian and frequently chided his

33. *Minutes of the General Association of Connecticut* (1842), v; *Minutes of the General Association of Connecticut* (1843), 5–6; Bacon to Oliver Henry Percy, January 17, 1844, in Oliver Henry Percy Papers, Connecticut Historical Society, Hartford, Conn.; Leonard to Catherine Bacon, September 4, 1848, sermon of March 2, 1845, in Bacon Family Papers; Foote, *Three Centuries of American Hymnody,* 213.

34. Diary entry for February 19, 1841, in Bacon Family Papers.

children for not devoting themselves sufficiently to their studies or to spiritual matters.[35]

Bacon's life changed dramatically in 1847, when he married Catherine Terry, the daughter of Nathaniel Terry, a wealthy Hartford businessman and congressman. Although he was concerned that his children might not accept her as their step-mother, and although Rebecca was reluctant to give up control over household affairs, Leonard and Catherine's marriage proved to be a happy one. Their first child, Katherine, was born in 1848. Unfortunately, in that year Bacon's son Benjamin, a recent Yale graduate, died of consumption. During the weeks prior to Benjamin's death, Bacon devoted much of his time to caring for his son. Again, he could not easily express his feelings of grief openly and freely. His son Leonard Woolsey Bacon recalled many years later that his father was "a man of singular reserve and self-repression, at times when his feelings were most profoundly affected."[36] Although Bacon undoubtedly felt deeply the deaths of his children and his wife, he, like many other Victorian-era men, found it difficult to express his emotions. For Bacon, this reticence, which the culture deemed appropriate for males, may have been intensified by his attempts, during his teens and twenties, to deal with his father's death and his mother's fragile emotional state.

At the same time that Bacon experienced these joys and sorrows, he also had to cope with numerous problems his mother and siblings were having. His sister Susan lived in poverty following the death of her husband, and Julia's two children died suddenly in the early 1840s. Every two or three years Bacon was able to visit his sisters and mother in western New York, and his mother occasionally came to live with him in New Haven. Although hard-pressed to sustain his family, and unable to buy a home until 1841, he periodically sent money to Susan and his mother, and in 1845 he traveled to Tallmadge, Ohio, in an attempt to settle a claim for land that had belonged to his parents. Yet Alice often complained, much as she had since his teenage years, that she seldom saw her son. Still adept at guilt manipulation, she as much as accused him of devoting all of his love to his church and his immediate family.[37]

35. Baldwin, *Bacon Genealogy*, 280; Leonard to Rebecca Bacon, July 17, 31, 1844, July 12, 1845, March 2, 1848, Bacon to children, August 1, 1844, Leonard to Lucy Bacon, August 8, 1844, sermon of December 8, 1844, Rebecca to Leonard Bacon, September 18, 1845, May 25, 1846, Leonard to Catherine Bacon, September 28, 1849, Bacon to Sarah Wisner, November 6, 1845, Leonard to Benjamin Bacon, July 14, 1845, October 13, 1847, in Bacon Family Papers; Bacon to Theodore Dwight Woolsey, January 22, 1846, in Woolsey Family Papers.

36. Bacon to Catherine Terry, May 27, 1847, Leonard to Benjamin Bacon, June 8, 1847, Rebecca Bacon to Catherine Terry, May 31, 1847, Leonard to Alice Bacon, March 14, May 30, 1848, Leonard Woolsey Bacon, introductory note to "Light Out of Darkness: Three Sermons of Consolation and Instruction," in Bacon Family Papers.

37. Alice to Leonard Bacon, September 10, 1844, April 22, 1847, Susan B. Hodges to Bacon, December 8, 1842, Leonard to Lucy Bacon, July 28, 1843, September 4, 1844, Rebecca to Benjamin Bacon,

Bacon also sent money to his brother David, who was already showing signs of depression and alcoholism and was in dire financial straits. Yet in spite of the magnitude of David's problems, the most serious difficulty by far that Bacon experienced with his family of origin concerned his sister Delia, who had periodically lived with him and Lucy since the late 1820s. A strong advocate of education for women, Delia had gained a considerable reputation as a teacher of young women and a lecturer on history and literature. But she was also a complex and rather eccentric person.[38]

During the mid-1840s, the termination of Delia's relationship with Alexander MacWhorter, a young, wealthy graduate licentiate at Yale Theological Seminary who lived in Nathaniel Taylor's home, created a scandal in New Haven, nearly led Bacon to leave the city, divided Connecticut Congregationalists and the Yale faculty, and deeply alienated Bacon from his old friend Taylor. A writer for the *Literary World* in New York may have been correct in terming this "a squabble in a country town," but to Bacon and his sister, to Taylor, to Catharine Beecher, and to others it was a serious matter involving honor, morality, and power.[39]

Neither Bacon nor his mother approved of Delia's relationship with Mac-Whorter, and both Catharine Beecher, Delia's former teacher, and Harriet Beecher Stowe, who observed MacWhorter pursuing Delia for ten weeks during a stay in Brattleboro, Vermont, felt much the same way. The Beecher sisters assumed that the couple were engaged, but were subsequently informed that MacWhorter did not wish to be. Indeed, his friends soon charged that Delia was a love-starved spinster who had no self-respect or modesty. Word of these developments infuriated Bacon, who was determined to protect her honor and reputation. His father's death nearly thirty years earlier had impressed upon him the obligation to defend and assist his siblings whenever possible. Even though he now had seven children of his own, he believed that he must act as Delia's surrogate father. He was also motivated to act in her defense by a stern code of morality, which he felt MacWhorter had violated with impunity. Consequently, he confronted MacWhorter on the streets of New Haven and demanded to know whether his intentions were honorable. Receiving no satisfactory reply, he denounced MacWhorter as a charlatan and a fool. Bacon hoped that Delia's "annoying relationship" had been "got rid of," but that was not the case, for MacWhorter proceeded to circulate Delia's love letters among his friends and to deny that he had ever proposed to her. All of this created considerable

---

September 30, 1845, Leonard to Benjamin Bacon, September 26, 1845, Leonard to Rebecca Bacon, September 16, 1845, in Bacon Family Papers.

38. David to Leonard Bacon, May 6, October 9, 1849, Leonard to David Bacon, August 5, 1849, Bacon to Hubbard Winslow, February 25, 1847, in Bacon Family Papers; Hopkins, *Prodigal Puritan*, viii.

39. Milton Rugoff, *The Beechers: An American Family in the Nineteenth Century* (New York, 1981), 191.

gossip in New Haven, which humiliated Delia and threatened her reputation. To make matters worse, Taylor sided with MacWhorter, asking Bacon to assist in containing the scandal and telling Delia that the episode must be closed.[40]

Bacon, however, was determined to see justice prevail, and angrily confronted Taylor. Yet he was acutely aware of the possible ramifications of this incident; on the eve of his marriage to Catherine Terry, he even offered to release her from a connection that might embarrass her. Indeed, he was prepared to leave New Haven if MacWhorter was not forced to prove his charges against Delia. "I will not live here," he defiantly informed Catherine. "This makes me independent." Encouraged by her brother's conviction that the cause was just and by the support of Benjamin Silliman and other friends, Delia overcame her sense of shame and fear of publicity and reluctantly concurred with Bacon's decision to press charges against MacWhorter in the New Haven West Association of the Congregational Church.[41]

At the association's meeting in May, 1847, Bacon accused MacWhorter of "disgraceful conduct" and urged that his license to preach be revoked. Taylor responded by denying that any evidence of misconduct existed. An acrimonious two-day debate ensued, in which Bacon alternately appealed to the members' sense of justice and threatened to read MacWhorter's letters to Delia. Taylor and a few older members of the association, whom Bacon sarcastically characterized as "foolish enough to think that excitement would be suppressed by their attempting to suppress inquiry," opposed an investigation. But many of the younger country ministers, as well as Woolsey, Cleaveland, and Day, supported Bacon's position. Ultimately, his motion carried by a decisive majority, and a three-man committee, which he hoped would give him a fair hearing, was formed.[42]

This committee asked both Bacon and MacWhorter's lawyer to provide written statements in preparation for a trial. Tired of what he termed "that miserable MacWhorter business," Bacon nevertheless traveled to Brattleboro to question Catharine Beecher and other witnesses. He also implored his mother to testify at the trial, where he was confident of "putting MacWhorter very low-down." Though angry with MacWhorter for his treatment of Delia, Alice nonetheless begged her son not to seek revenge, for she understood how daring it was for a woman to call to account even a licentiate in the church. Yet, as he so often did when he believed he was right or had been treated unfairly, Bacon grimly forged ahead. Fearing that some of the

40. Hopkins, *Prodigal Puritan,* 72, 75–76, 78–80, 84, 87, 90–91, 93–94; Catharine Beecher's testimony in the MacWhorter case, 1848, pp. 1–2, Leonard to Alice Bacon, January 5, 1847, in Bacon Family Papers; Caskey, *Chariot of Fire,* 97, 189–90.

41. Hopkins, *Prodigal Puritan,* 94–98; Bacon to Catherine Terry, April 22, 29, 1847, in Bacon Family Papers.

42. Leonard to Delia Bacon, May 26, 1847, Bacon to Catherine Terry, May 27, 1847, Leonard to Alice Bacon, May 30, 1847, in Bacon Family Papers.

leading men in New Haven, including Taylor, would never be able either to forget what they had done in this matter or to believe that he had forgotten, he once more seriously considered leaving New Haven.[43]

At the ecclesiastical trial, Bacon, his mother, Catharine Beecher, and Harriet Beecher Stowe testified on Delia's behalf. In his lengthy testimony Bacon again charged that MacWhorter had disgraced the ministry and had trifled with Delia's affections and grossly slandered her by claiming that she had relentlessly pursued him. Although the committee trusted Bacon's motives and was not pleased with MacWhorter's conduct, a majority ruled that the charges of falsehood and misconduct were not sufficiently sustained. Therefore, they merely admonished him for "imprudence." Delia was devastated by the decision, and Bacon was furious, believing that it restored MacWhorter's reputation at her expense. Nonetheless, a slim majority of the association, who hoped that this nasty affair could be put behind them, voted to sustain the committee's report. Bacon, however, was not willing to accept the verdict. Tenacious to the end, he, along with eight other members of the association, filed a protest, which was placed in the body's records. Their protest was fiercely debated at the association's 1848 meeting, where Bacon and Taylor, driven in part by their desire to determine who would control the association, once more exchanged angry barbs.[44]

In the end, the association did not sustain the protest, and Bacon had to admit defeat. For one who believed that a person could, by employing reasonable arguments, persuade others to act in a judicious and considerate manner, this must have been a humbling experience. Not only had he failed to convince MacWhorter, Delia, Catharine Beecher, and Nathaniel Taylor to behave responsibly and rationally; he ultimately had been unable to count on sympathetic allies and friends such as Jeremiah Day and Theodore Dwight Woolsey to stand by him in defense of honor and justice.

Nevertheless, Bacon was relieved that the affair, which had been extremely time-consuming, stressful, and distracting for him, was now finally behind him; he never again mentioned the possibility of leaving the city. He also hoped that Delia would be able to get on with her life, but she was deeply depressed by the experience. His patience obviously wearing thin, Bacon complained to his mother in 1848 that to hope for Delia's recovery, "one might as well wait for a river to run

43. Bacon to Catherine Terry, July 23, 24, 1847, Leonard to Alice Bacon, July 26, 1847, Alice to Leonard Bacon, August 1, 1847, Bacon to Joseph P. Thompson, October 1, 1847, in Bacon Family Papers.

44. Rugoff, *The Beechers,* 191; Moseley, ed., *Diary (1843–1852) of James Hadley,* 313; Hopkins, *Prodigal Puritan,* 103, 108–15; George Thacher to Bacon, November 9, 1847, S. H. Elliot to Bacon, November 10, 1847, in Bacon Family Papers.

dry." Tired of Delia's "completely morbid" state of mind, he ultimately gave her eighty dollars to facilitate her move to New Orleans to teach school.[45]

Yet neither Bacon's nor his sister's troubles had ended, for Catharine Beecher, deeply resentful of the double standard for men and women and frustrated at women's loss of status compared with men in politics and society, was determined to expose the hypocrisy and venality of Taylor and a number of other men associated with Yale and the clergy. She also perhaps hoped to reestablish her position as Delia's mentor. Bacon, his sisters, and many members of the Beecher family pleaded with her not to publish her diatribe. But despite these pleas, Beecher published *Truth Stranger Than Fiction,* a lengthy indictment of Taylor, Yale, and the clergy for employing their power to destroy a defenseless woman. However, the book also, ironically, dwelt on Delia's character defects while defending her.[46]

If Bacon and Taylor agreed on anything in this protracted struggle, it was their feeling that Beecher's book was excessively harsh toward Yale and the Congregational clergy. Even Bacon's anger toward those who he believed had wronged his sister, it seems, could not match the intensity of his loyalty to his alma mater and his professional associates. Over the years Bacon's relationship with Taylor and other Yale professors who had stood against Delia gradually improved. Indeed, as already mentioned, in 1858 he delivered the eulogy at Taylor's funeral, and during and after the Civil War he again served as a member of the Yale Corporation. But during the years immediately following the Delia-MacWhorter episode, he remained angry and resentful toward these men.[47]

As distracting and enervating as this struggle was for Bacon, he remained active on numerous fronts during the mid- and late 1840s. Perhaps the most important of these was the escalating debate within the Congregational Church and other denominations on the relationship between the home and foreign missionary societies and slavery, as well as the sectional controversy reignited by the territorial issue. After nearly ten years, during which he had devoted little attention to the slavery question, he now moved into the thick of the debate as an outspoken advocate of the moderate antislavery position.

45. Austin Putnam to Bacon, November 9, 1847, Leonard to Alice Bacon, May 30, 1848, in Bacon Family Papers.

46. Rugoff, *The Beechers,* 191–92; Caskey, *Chariot of Fire,* 97–98; Moseley, *Diary (1843–1852) of James Hadley,* 41; Catharine Beecher, *Truth Stranger Than Fiction: A Narrative of Recent Transactions, Involving Inquiries in Regard to the Principles of Honor, Truth, and Justice, Which Obtain in a Distinguished American University* (Boston, 1850); Sklar, *Catharine Beecher,* 188–95.

47. Stuart C. Henry, *Unvanquished Puritan: A Portrait of Lyman Beecher* (Grand Rapids, Mich., 1973), 277; Hopkins, *Prodigal Puritan,* 127–29; Moseley, *Diary (1843–1852) of James Hadley,* 287.

8

"GOOD SLAVEHOLDERS," MISSIONS, AND THE TERRITORIAL ISSUE

URING the early 1840s, Bacon scarcely noted in his writings the rise of political abolitionism, the controversy surrounding the gag on anti-slavery petitions in Congress, and the expansionists' efforts to annex Texas. Nevertheless, he remained steadfastly opposed to slavery. In 1840 and 1843, for example, he was instrumental in pushing through the Connecticut General Association resolutions that urged slaveholders to begin immediately to free their slaves and called upon the churches to exert their "appropriate influence for the emancipation of all the enslaved in this land and throughout the world."[1]

With the advent of sustained debate within the American Board of Commissioners for Foreign Missions regarding its relationship with slavery, as well as the escalating controversy surrounding the territorial issue, Bacon once more became a significant participant in the debate on slavery. Much as he had done during the early and middle 1830s, he adopted a moderate antislavery position, standing in opposition to the abolitionists in addition to southerners and their conservative northern allies. He and other northern moderates remained convinced that the immediatists' uncompromising demands exacerbated social conflict and alienated southerners, who alone could end slavery. At the same time, he rejected not only the southern defense of slavery but also the argument by conservative northern clergymen that because slavery was a political issue, not a purely religious matter, the churches should subordinate it to the cause of evangelicalism, if not ignore it altogether.

Bacon had long been a vocal advocate of foreign missions, which were overseen by salaried secretaries and a board of managers appointed by several Protestant groups that contributed to the movement. Convinced that the missionary move-

---

1. *Minutes of the General Association of Connecticut* (1840), 8, (1843), 8.

ment stimulated cooperation among Christians and diffused intelligence, benevolence, and salvation throughout the world, he often urged his parishioners to contribute to the cause and invited missionaries to address the congregation. In 1842 he
became a corporate member of the ABCFM, which gave him voting rights at its
annual meetings.[2]

The debate that erupted at the ABCFM's 1845 meeting was the product of the
abolitionists' prolonged efforts to force the society to sever its ties with the Cherokee and Choctaw mission churches that included slaveholders. The missionaries'
use of slave labor exposed the society to charges that it was proslavery. But while
troubled by the immediatists' threats to withhold support from the board, its officers
above all feared that the slavery issue would hinder efforts to convert Native Americans. The abolitionists' protests came to a head at the ABCFM's 1844 meeting,
where antislavery memorials were referred to a committee; its report precipitated
the board's first full-scale debate on slavery at the 1845 meeting held in Brooklyn.
The committee staked out a moderate antislavery position, calling for the "speedy
and universal termination" of slavery but also declaring that the missions' primary
objective was conversion, not emancipation, and that the missionaries in the field,
not the board, must decide who was truly converted. It also insisted that the board
could not refuse slaveholders as converts because slaveholding was "not *such* a sin as
to warrant an immediate expulsion from the church."[3]

In response to this report Amos A. Phelps, a Boston abolitionist who spoke for
the American and Foreign Anti-Slavery Society, demanded a categorical condemnation of slaveholding as sin *per se*. The board, he charged, deemed slavery an "atro-
cious thing, but he who is guilty of it may persist in it unrebuked, and be counted
unworthy of discipline." Thus, he called upon the board to brand both slavery and
slaveholding "a great moral evil" and to withdraw support from all churches that
included slaveholders, as it did with drunkards and gamblers. Slaveholders, he insisted, should be condemned for having the power to oppress, not simply for acts
of oppression.[4]

Prior to the board's 1845 meeting, Phelps had expressed to Bacon the hope that
the abolitionists and antislavery moderates could find common ground. But sup-

2. Sermons of October 22, 1848, December 23, 1849, in Bacon Family Papers; *The Congregational
Year-Book, 1882,* 18.

3. Robert T. Lewit, "Indian Missions and Anti-Slavery Sentiment: A Conflict of Evangelical and
Humanitarian Ideals," *Mississippi Valley Historical Review,* L (1963), 39, 41–42; McKivigan, *The War
Against Proslavery Religion,* 113; American Board of Commissioners for Foreign Missions, *Report of the
Committee on Anti-Slavery Memorials, September, 1845* (Boston, 1845), 3–4; Leonard Bacon, "The Ameri-
can Board and Slavery," *New Englander,* VII (May, 1849), 273–74.

4. New York *Evangelist,* September 18, 1845.

porters of the ABCFM's policy regarding slavery had very different expectations. For example, David Greene, a member of the board's committee on slavery, urged Bacon to attend the meeting, arguing that he would be an effective voice of reason who could challenge the "ultra views on both sides." Indeed, at the meeting, where he, Calvin Stowe, and Edward Beecher led the charge against the abolitionist critics of the board, Bacon consciously sought to occupy a middle ground on the slavery question. He could not accept the claims by southerners and their northern allies—including Nathaniel Lord, Gerard Hallock, Parson Cooke, Sidney E. Morse, and Amasa Converse—that the slavery issue should be entirely subordinated to the conversion of Indians and the evangelical independence of the missionaries in the field. During the forties and fifties, he frequently chided the conservatives for their "old habits of temporizing and compromising on any issue remotely connected with slavery." He was especially disgusted by their belief that "abolitionism and not slavery is the great danger and sin in our country and the great evil above all others against which all Christian men are bound constantly to testify."[5]

Bacon in fact agreed with the abolitionists on several points concerning slavery and the missions to the Native Americans. He regretted that slavery had been introduced to the Cherokees and Choctaws and believed that the board's cooperation with southern churches was not desirable. He also shared their conviction that slaveholders should not be appointed as missionaries and conceded that the board had made too much of the "one great object" of converting the heathen. Finally, although he informed Phelps that "as a Congregationalist, I would stand for the independence of the churches gathered upon missionary grounds," he acknowledged that the board could, if it wished, insist that its missionaries preach the antislavery message in their churches, or be dismissed.[6]

But the differences between Bacon and the immediatists were substantial. While he chided the conservatives for their fear of being termed abolitionists, he exhibited much the same concern. Following a conference with Bacon and Edward Beecher prior to the 1845 meeting, George W. Perkins, a Connecticut abolitionist, informed Phelps: "They both wish, and honestly so, that the Board should take different ground from that on which they [the officers] now stand. But they are both afraid of being among the 'abolitionists' and would avoid any course which will compel them to seem to act in unison with such men as you; indeed they almost so said in express terms."[7]

5. Amos A. Phelps to Bacon, August 25, 1845, David Greene to Bacon, July 14, 1845, in Bacon Family Papers; Tise, *Proslavery,* 282–83; *Independent,* October 4, 1849, October 5, 1854.

6. Bacon to Phelps, August 29, 1845, in Amos A. Phelps Papers; Amos A. Phelps, *Letters to Professor Stowe and Dr. Bacon on God's Real Method with Great Social Wrongs in Which the Bible Is Vindicated from Grossly Erroneous Interpretations* (New York, 1848), 129.

7. Bacon to Phelps, August 29, 1845, George W. Perkins to Phelps, August 30, 1845, in Amos A. Phelps Papers.

Perkins may well have engaged in wishful thinking, for Bacon in fact was critical of the board's committee report for stating that a person could be a better Christian if he gave up slaveholding. Rather than attempting to placate abolitionist critics by implying that slavery could be equated with slaveholding, he told the assembled members of the society, the board should have stated unequivocally that the immediatists' call for the expulsion of all slaveholders from the churches was "a miserable, paltering, juggling sophism that can have no better effect than to mislead and madden enthusiastic minds, and to irritate the passions of the slaveholder while it sears his conscience." In a series of resolutions, which he acknowledged were less antislavery in spirit than the committee report, he reiterated his longstanding hatred of slavery. But he also insisted that the "mere relation" of a master to a slave should not in all cases warrant expulsion from the churches.[8]

Most northern antislavery moderates adhered to the concept of the "good slaveholder"; Bacon was perhaps its foremost proponent. While he conceded that the apostles had not sanctioned slavery and had demanded that masters treat their slaves with kindness and justice, he insisted that slaveholders had been subject to rebuke in the New Testament churches only if they committed specific wrongs against their slaves. Thus, he was convinced that slaveholding was "consistent, on the whole, with a Christian profession."[9]

Unlike the immediatists, he favored "censuring and excommunicating sinners, not for having the power to do wrong, but for doing wrong, not for standing in a certain constitutional relation toward his servants, but for his conduct toward them in that relation." Only those masters who bought and sold slaves for gain, refused to recognize their "dignity and worth" and the "divine sanctity" of their marriages and families, and failed to render to their slaves "that which is just and equal" should be investigated and, if found guilty of these transgressions, excommunicated. He even went so far as to inform a friend that he would invite a slaveholder to his pulpit if that person showed he was a "good slaveholder,"[10] though there is no evidence that he ever did this.

Much as they had in the 1830s, Bacon, Beecher, Francis Wayland, and other

---

8. Bacon, *Slavery Discussed,* 134, 145–46, 157; New York *Evangelist,* September 18, 1845.

9. New York *Evangelist,* September 18, 1845, March 19, 1846; Bacon, *Slavery Discussed,* 180–81. On northern antislavery moderates and the concept of the "good slaveholder," see, for example, John Harvey Gossard, "The New York City Congregational Cluster, 1848–1871: Congregationalism and Antislavery in the Careers of Henry Ward Beecher, George B. Cheever, Richard S. Storrs, and Joseph P. Thompson" (Ph.D. dissertation, Bowling Green State University, 1986), 28–29; Clifford E. Clark, Jr., *Henry Ward Beecher: Spokesman for a Middle-Class America* (Urbana, 1978), 139–42.

10. New York *Evangelist,* September 18, 1845; Bacon to Phelps, August 29, 1845, in Amos A. Phelps Papers; Bacon, *Slavery Discussed,* 243–44; Sehr, "Leonard Bacon and the Myth of the Good Slaveholder," 194–213. For Edward Beecher's and Calvin Stowe's views on "good slaveholders," see New York *Evangelist,* September 18, 1845.

antislavery moderates frequently drew distinctions between sinful and innocent slaveholders and southern state laws and the southern people. They also set forth numerous conditions that they believed absolved "good slaveholders" of guilt for participating in a sinful system. For instance, Bacon maintained that a person might be required to own slaves "for the very purpose of giving to those placed in his possession that which is just and equal. Oppression he may not practice for an hour; but it may be his duty to stand between them and the law which oppresses them."[11]

At the 1845 ABCFM meeting, Bacon's resolutions in defense of this position were sent to a new committee, on which he served. Although most members of this committee approved of his resolutions, they feared that to append them to the original report would make it appear that the board sought to infringe upon the prerogatives of various ecclesiastical bodies. Bacon denied that this would happen. But in the end, he acquiesced in the decision of the majority of the committee and joined the other seventy-four corporate members of the ABCFM in adopting the original report.[12]

Passage of the committee's report on slavery did not end the society's concern about the issue, nor did it signal an end to Bacon's debate with both the abolitionists and the conservatives. At the 1846 meeting, held in Bacon's Center Church, pressure from the antislavery forces led the board to urge its missionaries to cease hiring slave labor. And though the Prudential Committee announced in 1848 that it could not exercise direct control over either the missionaries or the mission churches, growing resistance to the board's policy by the missionaries led the ABCFM's corresponding secretary, Selah B. Treat, to direct them to preach against the sin of slavery. In a move that marked a turning point in the relations between the board and its missions to the Indians, Treat was then dispatched to investigate the Cherokee and Choctaw missions.[13]

As the ABCFM moved slowly toward a more explicit antislavery position, the debate between Bacon and the board's critics continued. For example, the Philadelphia Christian Observer, a proslavery New School Presbyterian newspaper, charged that Bacon's condemnation of slavery and his call for the excommunication of those who did not fit his description of a "good slaveholder" were "indiscriminate and abusive." The abolitionists were no less critical of his position. In a pamphlet published shortly after the Brooklyn meeting, Phelps ridiculed Bacon's "singularly confused and self-contradictory" views on the relationship between the churches and slavery and denounced the "good slaveholder" doctrine as "essentially and necessar-

11. See, for example, New York Evangelist, September 18, 1845; James H. Moorhead, American Apocalypse: Yankee Protestants and the Civil War, 1860–1869 (New Haven, 1978), 88–89.

12. Bacon, Slavery Discussed, 147–57.

13. New York Evangelist, September 17, 1846; Bacon, "The American Board and Slavery," 274–76; Lewit, "Indian Missions and Anti-Slavery Sentiment," 43–44, 48–49.

ily impotent." Moreover, he charged that, in "viciously" attacking the abolitionists, Bacon had "really out-Baconed Bacon." More scathing yet was the criticism from Joshua Leavitt, editor of the *Emancipator,* who, pointedly referring to the apparent inconsistency of Bacon's views, claimed that among an important group of religious leaders in America who had "put forth their anti-slavery sentiment as an apology for acting against abolition . . . no one has from the beginning come nearer to abolition without hitting it" (*i.e.,* nearer to occupying the abolitionist position without being an immediatist) than Bacon. Angered by Bacon's and the ABCFM's refusal to embrace the immediatists' doctrine of slaveholding as a sin *per se,* George Whipple, Lewis Tappan, Phelps, and other Christian abolitionists, who hoped to reform the society by drawing away contributions, created the rival American Missionary Association in 1846.[14]

At times, Bacon was philosophical in the face of such attacks. He noted, for example, that experience had shown him that whenever he wrote on slavery, "I must make up my mind to encounter reproach from the most opposite quarters." More often, however, he was defiant. He rejected the conservatives' claims that his condemnation of slavery was an unwarranted attack on all slaveholders; and, in response to the immediatists' assaults, he complained that "it seems not to enter into the thoughts of those writers that a man who differs from them on this most complicated theme, may possibly be honest." Because he drew back from absolutist thinking, he, unlike the abolitionists, was reluctant to draw sharp lines within the antislavery ranks. Much as he had done when he espoused the American Union for the Relief and Improvement of the Colored Race in the 1830s, he emphasized the need to follow one's own path toward abolition. "When conscientious men differ conscientiously, and neither of them can convince the other," he informed Phelps. "The best thing they can do is to differ."[15]

Yet because Bacon was convinced that his position on the slavery issue was correct, he was by no means prepared to cease speaking "what seems to me to be the truth, important and timely." During the late 1840s, he indeed continued to write frequently on slavery and the churches. Especially important was a series of letters that appeared in early 1846 in the New York *Evangelist,* the organ of the New School Presbyterian Church, in which he defended the ABCFM's policy and the "good slaveholder" concept. He wrote these letters at the invitation of the *Evangelist's* editors, William Bradford and William H. Bidwell, in the hope of clarifying the

14. Phelps, *Letters to Professor Stowe and Dr. Bacon,* 128–31, 146; *Emancipator,* October 24, 1845; Wyatt-Brown, *Lewis Tappan and the Evangelical War Against Slavery,* 293, 313–14; Clifton Herman Johnson, "The American Missionary Association, 1846–1861: A Study of Christian Abolitionism" (Ph.D. dissertation, University of North Carolina, 1958), 273–74, 279–80, 283–85.

15. New York *Evangelist,* October 23, 1845; Bacon, *Slavery Discussed,* 233–35; Bacon to Phelps, August 29, 1845, in Amos A. Phelps Papers.

differences between the ABCFM and the abolitionists and influencing a large number of readers. These letters marked the beginning of a three-year association with the *Evangelist,* during which he wrote numerous articles and unsigned editorials for the paper.[16] The popularity of his letters on foreign missions and slavery soon led him to include them, along with a few of his pieces on slavery that he had written in the 1830s, in a collection titled *Slavery Discussed,* which was published in 1846.

In his *Evangelist* articles and editorials Bacon was sanguine about the presence of "good slaveholders," though both the numbers and the exact criteria were rather elusive. At various times he claimed that "the entire people of the South," "thousands of Southerners," and "the more intelligent Southerners" were "a great deal better than their laws are." At one point he even implied that those who merely taught their slaves to read the Bible were "good slaveholders." He also sought to buttress his argument by citing, as the epitome of this type, an anonymous Georgia slaveholder (who, in fact, was Thomas Clay, whose plantation Bacon had visited in the early 1840s while Lucy was recuperating from her illness). According to Bacon, Clay had inherited one hundred slaves; because state law prohibited manumission on the spot, he had chosen to "do the best he could" for them in bondage. Bacon painted a rosy picture of slave life on Clay's plantation, pointing to a flexible task system, a joint stock company in which slaves could sell goods they produced in their free time, a school for slave children, a church, and a system resembling trial by jury. Yet despite his effusive praise for Clay's Christian benevolence, he was not without doubts. Most revealing was his confession that Clay was a "voluntary slaveholder" who profited from his ownership of slaves, maintained order through strict discipline, and might well err in judgment in refusing to free his slaves and send them to the North. More generally, he acknowledged that such "good slaveholders" as Clay probably were rare and that, given the growing number of proslavery mobs and treatises, he had to "try very hard" to retain his optimism on the issue. Notwithstanding his doubts, even about a slaveholder he considered enlightened and kind, in the final analysis he insisted that Clay and other such slaveholders were not guilty of "specific crimes" and, therefore, should not be excommunicated.[17]

Not surprisingly, Bacon's eagerness to excuse and defend a slaveholder such as Clay elicited scorn and anger from abolitionists. An anonymous correspondent, for example, pounced upon Bacon's admission that Clay punished his slaves. "I rather suspect, Dear Doctor," wrote "Mercator," "that the slaveholding Christian bamboozled you. . . . Did you witness a Christian flagellation—laid on according to

16. See William H. Bidwell to Bacon, March 2, April 1, 1846, in Bacon Family Papers. Bacon's nine letters appeared in the *Evangelist* between February and April, 1846.

17. New York *Evangelist,* October 23, 1845, February 11, March 4, April 1, 8, 1847; Bacon, *Slavery Discussed,* 201–202; S. W. S. Dutton to Phelps, March 27, 1846, in Amos A. Phelps Papers.

apostolical sanctions? . . . It is important to the peace of such men to get the sanction of some Northern Doctor of Divinity to the practice."[18]

Bacon's tenacious defense of the "good slaveholder" concept clearly ensnared him in an illogical argument and stretched the definition of the "good" master nearly to the breaking point. This theory included so many conditions and was so difficult to verify that it left its proponents with little credibility. In fact, most masters who might have fallen within this indeterminate group had no desire to free their slaves. Equally important, Bacon exerted no influence on either the abolitionists, who accused him of excusing slaveholders under virtually all circumstances, or the slaveholders and their allies, who categorically condemned his antislavery views. Thus, in his desperate attempt to maintain a sensible middle ground between the ideological extremes, he ended up defending an unrealistic and meaningless concept.

The illogical nature of his arguments—underscored, ironically, by his use of Thomas Clay as a model slaveholder—was not the only problem with Bacon's position. He was also forced to confront the difficult matter of how to discipline those who were not deemed "good slaveholders" and what effect that would have on the Congregationalists' relations with the Presbyterians. He realized that the argument on behalf of Clay and other such masters was worthless unless ecclesiastical bodies investigated their practices and applied appropriate discipline. He assured Phelps that "if a church refuses to exercise discipline upon such offenses, that is a sufficient reason for other churches, after admonition, to withdraw communion from that church." He especially had the Presbyterians in mind. Although the Old School Presbyterians included many slaveholders among their members and refused to condemn slavery, they maintained official correspondence with most of the Congregational ministerial associations.[19]

Bacon and many other Congregationalists were especially troubled by the New School's position on slavery, for they had long felt a close theological affinity with the New Schoolers and interacted with them in the Plan of Union and the benevolent empire. Although the editors of the New York *Evangelist* and most other northern New School Presbyterians subscribed to the concept of "good slaveholders," they were eager to prevent a secession by their southern colleagues, and thereby to maintain a national church in the wake of the 1837 Presbyterian schism. Consequently, they did little more than periodically make vague, and at times contradictory, statements regarding slaveholding in the church. They sought to apply enough

18. "Mercator" to Bacon, March 20, 1846, in Bacon Family Papers.

19. Bacon to Phelps, August 29, 1845, in Amos A. Phelps Papers; Linda Jeanne Evans, "Abolitionism in the Illinois Churches, 1830–1865" (Ph.D. dissertation, Northwestern University, 1981), 171–72; Irving S. Kull, "Presbyterian Attitudes Toward Slavery," *Church History,* VII (1938), 101–14.

pressure to move southern New Schoolers, who represented only 10 percent of all members of the church, to act against slavery but ultimately drew back from any action that might drive the southern wing from the New School.[20]

Many Congregationalists, particularly in the West, became increasingly impatient with the New School's failure to take concerted action against slavery in its midst. Often influenced by Oberlin perfectionism, which emphasized a life of perfect holiness and freedom from sin, and having broken away from the Presbyterian Church rather than defend the ecclesiastical status quo, these westerners sought to use the antislavery appeal to draw members of the Presbygational churches into newly established Congregational churches. They were more inclined than Bacon and other eastern brethren—many of whom had formed a deep attachment to the moderate antislavery position in the 1830s in response to Garrisonian abolitionism—to convert their social leadership into aggressive activism and their independent tradition and theology of individual accountability into a righteous separation from slaveholders. During the mid- and late 1840s, a number of local and state Congregational associations in the midwestern states severely criticized Presbyterians for their refusal to condemn slavery in the church.[21]

Bacon shared the western Congregationalists' frustration. In his *Slavery Discussed* he complained that a "great scandal" had been developing within the Presbyterian Church for twenty years. The northern churches, he maintained, must be concerned about discipline in the southern churches. He believed that the southern synods in the Presbyterian Church were accountable to the General Assemblies, which must conduct an inquiry and then impose the requisite discipline. If either General Assembly failed to take measures for the removal of this scandal, he argued, Congregationalists should inform Presbyterians of their "unchristian neglect of discipline" and soon move to end all correspondence with them. He recognized that any forthright action might compel the southern synods to secede from the Presbyterian Church, but he believed that this should not be regretted. In fact, however, he was optimistic that secession would not ultimately occur, for he held tenaciously to the assumption that some southern Christians would rejoice in the opportunity to defend themselves against imputations; those who did not strengthen discipline would be disgraced and, subsequently, would begin to reform their practices.[22]

20. Hugh Davis, "The New York *Evangelist,* New School Presbyterians, and Slavery, 1837–1857," *American Presbyterians,* LXVIII (Spring, 1990), 18–19; Marsden, *The Evangelical Mind and the New School Presbyterian Experience,* 98, 188.

21. See Evans, "Abolitionism in the Illinois Churches"; Frederick Irving Kuhns, *The American Home Missionary Society in Relation to the Antislavery Controversy in the Old Northwest* (Billings, Mont., 1959), 13–14, 17–22, 25.

22. Bacon, *Slavery Discussed,* 217–25.

As a delegate from the Connecticut General Association at the 1846 New School General Assembly meeting, Bacon endeavored, with considerable success, to persuade the various factions within the Congregational church to support a full investigation of slaveholders in southern Presbyterian churches. During the same year, he reported optimistically, in his capacity as head of a committee on slavery of the Connecticut General Association, that the New School had forcefully testified against slavery and had exhorted masters to use every means in their power to end the system. No hard evidence was forthcoming regarding discipline of slaveholders by either the Old School or the New School, however. Thus, in 1848 the association admitted that it was "in the dark" on this matter, and a committee of three, which included Bacon, was appointed to collect facts and make inquiries on the subject. Other eastern Congregational associations went even further. For example, by 1850 the General Associations of Massachusetts, New York, and Rhode Island had moved to end fraternal relations with the New School General Assembly.[23]

Yet during the late 1840s Bacon was prepared to give both the Presbyterians and the slaveholders the benefit of the doubt, even if it meant that Connecticut Congregationalists would lag behind popular opinion among a growing number of Congregationalists in the nation. Speaking in 1849 for the majority of the Connecticut General Association committee on slavery, he claimed that "common fame" (that is, popular rumor or report) of slaveholding abuses among southern Presbyterians had been exaggerated by abolitionists intent upon "agitating the public mind." Thus, he concluded, in his usual cautious manner, that more information was required before judgment could be rendered. Once more, when confronted with a situation that appeared to warrant decisive action, which he earlier had seemed prepared to undertake, he retreated to a tepid position that left the issue unresolved and the slaveholders untouched. Pulled by his desire to investigate slaveholding practices and to break with "bad" masters and those who attempted to shield them, yet hopeful that, in the name of interdenominational unity, a rupture between the Congregationalists and the New School Presbyterians could be avoided, he prevaricated. His unwillingness to act on his convictions left him in an untenable middle ground, with neither the means of initiating a meaningful investigation nor the will to end relations with churches that included "bad" slaveholders. In his minority report George W. Perkins was far less charitable than Bacon toward the Presbyterians, charging that because they had done nothing to rebuke or question slave-

23. Bacon to Henry White, May 28, 1846, in Bacon Family Papers; *Minutes of the General Association of Connecticut* (1846), 16, (1848), 9; Calvin Montague Clark, *American Slavery and Maine Congregationalists: A Chapter in the History of the Development of Anti-Slavery Sentiment in the Protestant Churches of the North* (Bangor, 1940), 123–28; Samuel C. Pearson, Jr., "From Church to Denomination: American Congregationalism in the Nineteenth Century," *Church History,* XXXVIII (1969), 83–84.

holders, they were "deeply implicated in the guilt of upholding and sanctioning slavery."[24]

Yet even as Bacon studiously avoided offending New School Presbyterians and held out the hope that pressure by well-meaning northern Christians would somehow move "good slaveholders" to free their slaves, the Mexican War and the emerging territorial issue steadily weakened his faith in the slaveholders' willingness to consider such action. Indeed, he was energized to speak out forcefully against the Mexican War and on behalf of the Wilmot Proviso primarily by his fear that the slave interests were intent upon capturing the West, subverting the Constitution and the Union, and threatening the fundamental rights and interests of northern whites.

The escalating sectional controversy thrust Bacon into the center of the national debate. During the mid- and late 1840s, he expressed his views in a number of forums, including his pulpit, the *New Englander,* and especially the New York *Evangelist.* His numerous signed articles and anonymous editorials, which appeared in the *Evangelist* until late 1848, permitted him to influence a large number of evangelical Protestants in the Middle Atlantic states and the Midwest. His contributions on slavery and related matters were much appreciated by the paper's editors. As William H. Bidwell wrote in 1848, "I do not believe that any single pen has done as much as yours to influence public opinion aright on this important subject."[25]

Even before the territorial issue burst upon the scene in the mid-1840s, Bacon was prepared to draw a line in defense of rights and interests that he believed were endangered by the slave interests. One must not refrain from condemning slavery in order to prevent sectional conflict, he told his congregation even prior to the Mexican War and the advent of the territorial debate, for this would enable the slaveholding class to make all other Americans subservient to its interests. The responsibility for sectional hostilities, he insisted, rested with the slaveholders, not those who resisted their designs. He clearly had moved rather far from his earlier admonitions, expressed as recently as the late 1830s, that one must temper one's attacks on the slaveholders so as to avoid a dangerous confrontation between the North and the South. When the annexation of Texas occurred, he joined a chorus of antislavery critics in warning that this act would bring war not only with Mexico but also Britain. War with Mexico, he declared in an 1844 sermon, would be "a war without a shadow of excuse" and one that, above all, would establish as the "one great policy" of the United States the protection and perpetuation of slavery.[26]

The annexation of Texas and President Polk's efforts to force Mexico to cede

24. *Minority Report of a Committee of the General Association of Connecticut, on the Sin of Slavery. Presented, June, 1849, at the Meeting of the Association, at Salisbury, Connecticut* (n.p., 1849), 2–20; *Minutes of the General Association of Connecticut* (1849), 6.

25. William H. Bidwell to Bacon, October 4, 1848, in Bacon Family Papers.

26. Sermons of August 7, 1842, April 5, 1844, in Bacon Family Papers.

New Mexico and California indeed precipitated armed conflict. The northern churches were deeply divided on the war. While many Methodists supported the war effort and Old School Presbyterians were split, most Baptists, New School Presbyterians, and Congregationalists opposed it. Many New England ministers rejected the notion of a "covenanted" people marching off to war for land or against the forces of Romanism. For example, in 1847 the Connecticut General Association testified against "certain principles, or modes of reasoning," that required Americans "to support human government whether right or wrong."[27]

Bacon's criticism of the war was harsher and more wide-ranging than this. He was not a pacifist, for he considered wars of defense to be justifiable. The Mexican War, in his opinion, however, was a war of aggression that would enrich the "purse-proud aristocracy" in both sections while imposing higher taxes on workers. As a vocal proponent of the Congregational system of church polity, he also identified with a system of government that provided for extensive states' rights and local prerogatives within the framework of a federal Union. With the war, such a system, he warned in 1847, would give way to "a consolidated empire in which all law and all power proceed from the center." He was equally troubled by the mounting war spirit that he observed among the American people. But he ultimately came to emphasize the moral dimension of the war above all others. To him and many other northern reformers, the Mexican War symbolized the desecration of the ideals of the American Republic. In their rush for territory and nationalistic pride, Bacon argued, Americans ignored the higher question of truth and justice; moral sense showed clearly that precipitating and prosecuting an unjust war, especially for the purpose of spreading slavery into the new areas of the West, was "the most horrible of all crimes."[28]

When the Treaty of Guadalupe Hidalgo was finally signed in 1848, Bacon was outraged. He was convinced that Americans had no right to the territory taken from Mexico, for the Mexican people were not a party to the treaty. It was, therefore, little more than "conquest and national robbery," which placed the United States on a level with the European imperialists, Turks, Goths, and Romans. "One improvement may lead to another," he wrote, with obvious sarcasm, "and who can

---

27. *Minutes of the General Association of Connecticut* (1847), 11. For treatments of the northern churches and the Mexican War, see Clayton S. Ellsworth, "American Churches and the Mexican War," *American Historical Review,* XLV (1940), 301–26; Mark Y. Hanley, *Beyond a Christian Commonwealth: The Protestant Quarrel with the American Republic, 1830–1860* (Chapel Hill, 1994), 66–68.

28. Leonard Bacon, "The War with Mexico," *New Englander,* V (October, 1847), 604–13; sermons of July 10, 1847, April 21, 1848, in Bacon Family Papers; New York *Evangelist,* February 25, September 23, October 21, 1847. On protest against the Mexican War, see John H. Schroeder, *Mr. Polk's War: American Opposition and Dissent, 1846–1848* (Madison, 1973), 20–32, 99–106; Robert W. Johannsen, *To the Halls of Montezuma: The Mexican War in the American Imagination* (New York, 1985), 276–79.

tell that ultimately there may not be found some way of conducting wars of invasion and conquest 'upon Christian principles?' "[29]

Most disturbing to large numbers of northerners, including many clergymen, was the alliance that appeared to exist between the federal government and southern interests for the purpose of spreading slavery into the territory taken from Mexico. This effort, many antiwar and antislavery northerners feared, would discourage northern white settlers from migrating to the West and would provide additional proslavery votes in Congress and the electoral college. Following its promulgation in 1846, the Wilmot Proviso attracted widespread support in the North.[30]

Bacon's editorials and articles in the New York *Evangelist* and the *New Englander* in 1847 and 1848 helped to mobilize northern public opinion on the territorial issue. He was not a radical on the slavery issue, if by that term one means a person who consistently refused to compromise with the South on any question. Instead, he remained essentially an antislavery moderate who espoused caution and gradualism and rejected the abolitionists' rhetoric and tactics. Indeed, especially Garrisonians considered the Wilmot Proviso a totally inadequate measure. Yet by the mid and late 1840s, growing numbers of political abolitionists were coming to espouse the proviso as a means to the end of emancipation; few northerners spoke out more forcefully on its behalf than Bacon.[31]

Bacon constantly reminded his readers that twenty years before the war Mexico had abolished slavery in the territory taken by the United States; thus, Congress had both the unquestionable power and the obligation to exclude slavery from this territory. Congress, he argued, had never imposed slavery on an area where it did not then exist; to do so would be unconstitutional. Much like Salmon P. Chase, Joshua Giddings, and other proponents of the Wilmot Proviso, he insisted that because slavery was the creature of municipal law, the federal government must divorce itself from the institution.[32]

Bacon and many other antislavery northerners frequently appealed to southern nonslaveholders, who they maintained would not benefit from the expansion of slavery. These southerners, they hoped, would soon learn that, as Bacon stated, the

29. Leonard Bacon, "Peace—And What Next?" *New Englander,* VI (April, 1848), 292–94.

30. See Eric Foner, "The Wilmot Proviso Revisited," *Journal of American History,* LVI (1969), 262–79; Chaplain W. Morrison, *Democratic Politics and Sectionalism: The Wilmot Proviso Controversy* (Chapel Hill, 1967), 60–73.

31. Richard H. Sewell, *Ballots for Freedom: Antislavery Politics in the United States, 1837–1860* (New York, 1976), 132–38; Hugh Davis, *Joshua Leavitt, Evangelical Abolitionist* (Baton Rouge, 1990), 233–36, 240–42.

32. See New York *Evangelist,* January 28, February 11, March 25, 1847. Chase's and Giddings' views are discussed in Frederick J. Blue, *Salmon P. Chase: A Life in Politics* (Kent, Ohio, 1987), 51–60; James Brewer Stewart, *Joshua R. Giddings and the Tactics of Radical Politics* (Cleveland, 1970), 70–71, 128–31.

burden of slavery had been created by a "class of lordlings to domineer in the name of democracy." But as the crisis surrounding the territorial issue deepened, his rhetoric took on a decidedly antisouthern tone. He especially blamed the slaveholders and slave traders, whom he termed "an exacting and unscrupulous aristocracy," for pushing an aggressive expansionism. Yet he was perhaps most angered and disappointed by the strongly anti-Wilmot position assumed by southern religious leaders, for he had long looked to them as a potential source of antislavery action. "Nothing in the influence of slavery at the South," he complained, "is more painful to any right-minded American."[33]

As southerners mobilized against the proviso, Bacon became increasingly convinced that they were prepared "to trample down Constitutional precedents for the attainment of their needs, just as they trample down justice and humanity." He was especially contemptuous of John C. Calhoun's views on the Constitution and slavery, including his contention that slaves were property and that the Union should be dissolved if slavery were not allowed to spread into the new territories. The compromises of 1787, Bacon asserted, were not intended to sanction slavery or to make the Union "the subject matter of legitimate negotiation."[34]

In standing firmly in support of the Wilmot Proviso, Bacon, like many northern antislavery clergymen, transcended the arguments on behalf of a political balance between free and slave states, public safety, economic prosperity, national honor, and constitutional principles. He emphasized, above all, the moral dimension of the territorial issue. At the heart of the crisis, he informed his *Evangelist* readers in 1847, was the struggle between slavery and universal freedom. Congressmen who voted to impose slavery on an area where it did not exist, he insisted, would commit "a *crime* against God, and against those universal and immutable principles of right, which God will not permit to be violated with impunity."[35]

When a strong majority of the House of Representatives, with overwhelming support from northern members, adopted the Wilmot Proviso in early 1847, Bacon was encouraged. But the Senate's defeat of the measure, and the refusal by the Whigs and Democrats to endorse it for fear of losing southern votes, deeply angered and disappointed him. By the end of 1847, he predicted that both parties would attempt to get rid of the proviso by evasion. Bacon did not divulge his party preference, nor had he previously done so, either in his public statements or his private correspondence. But he, like many Connecticut Congregationalists who were part of the professional middle class and who regarded themselves as guardians of morality,

---

33. New York *Evangelist*, March 25, 1847, October 19, 1848.

34. *Ibid.*, February 13, March 4, December 30, 1847, July 6, 13, September 7, 1848.

35. *Ibid.*, March 4, 1847; Bacon, "Peace—And What Next?" 297–99; C. C. Goen, *Broken Churches, Broken Nation: Denominational Schisms and the Coming of the American Civil War* (Macon, Ga., 1985), 103.

social stability, and economic prosperity, probably had voted Whig. He had long been an admirer of Henry Clay; and like many Whigs who had opposed the annexation of Texas, he mistakenly blamed the Liberty party for helping to defeat Clay in 1844.[36]

Yet Bacon was by no means a Whig partisan. During the 1840s, he was critical of the party's attachment to the tariff and the national bank as well as its failure to stand firmly against the war and to end corruption and abuses in government. By 1848, however, the Mexican War and the crisis surrounding the territorial issue convinced him that matters such as peace, war, and the extension of slavery or freedom must take precedence over even economic issues and the personal character of candidates.[37]

Bacon's conviction that the major parties were unwilling to take a principled stand on the territorial issue prompted him to call upon voters to work for their dissolution. Like numerous other antislavery northerners who supported the free-soil position, he considered antiextension a morally responsible policy that would lead, albeit gradually, to abolition in the South. As a clergyman he did not feel that it was appropriate to engage in partisan politics, and no evidence exists that he explicitly endorsed the Free-Soil party or its candidate for president, Martin Van Buren. But he was convinced that new forces, such as the territorial question, would sever old party ties that had been maintained largely through patronage. Voters, he told his parishioners, must not be silenced by the voices of the multitude but should stand as witnesses for truth, duty, and God.[38]

Shortly after the election of 1848, in which the Free-Soil party received 10 percent of the vote, Bacon embarked upon a new venture that would prove to be one of the most important and fruitful of his life. In accepting the offer to serve as senior editor of the New York *Independent,* while continuing to function as pastor of Center Church, he gained a significant public forum for his views on the territorial issue and the mounting sectional crisis, as well as Congregationalism, home and foreign missions, theology, temperance, and numerous other matters.

36. New York *Evangelist,* March 4, December 2, 1847; Bruser, "Political Antislavery in Connecticut," 32–46, 69; Leonard Bacon, "The Ethics of the Right of Suffrage," *New Englander,* VI (July, 1848), 452; Vernon L. Volpe, "The Liberty Party and Polk's Election, 1844," *Historian,* LIII (Summer, 1991), 691–710.

37. Leonard Bacon, "Paul on Politics," *New Englander,* XV (August, 1857), 462–77; Leonard Bacon, "Public Affairs," *New Englander,* I (April, 1843), 300–301; Bacon, "The State of Political Parties," 313, 315; sermon of March 24, 1845, in Bacon Family Papers.

38. New York *Evangelist,* July 27, 1848; Bacon, "The State of Political Parties," 308–309; Bacon, "The Ethics of the Right of Suffrage," 447–50. On the Free-Soil party, see Bruser, "Political Antislavery in Connecticut," 76–77, 91–94; Frederick J. Blue, *The Free Soilers: Third Party Politics, 1848–1854* (Urbana, 1973), 122–23 *et passim.*

9

THE *INDEPENDENT*, SECTIONALISM, AND DENOMINATIONALISM

FOR nearly two decades Bacon had enjoyed a considerable reputation as an articulate and thoughtful commentator on, and advocate of, both Congregationalism and a moderate antislavery position. Thus, it is not surprising that when a number of antislavery Congregationalists in New York City considered founding a newspaper in the mid-1840s, they looked to Bacon as a possible editor. Joseph P. Thompson, a student of Nathaniel Taylor who for several years had been associated with Bacon as pastor of the Chapel Street Church in New Haven, a member of the Club, and an editor of the *New Englander* before moving to New York to become pastor of the Broadway Tabernacle, deserves much of the credit for the eventual founding of the *Independent*. In 1847 he spoke to David Hale, editor of the *Journal of Commerce,* who expressed interest in establishing a paper on the condition that Bacon, whom he earlier had unsuccessfully urged to accept a pastorate in the city as a means of extending the influence of Congregationalism against Presbyterian denominationalism, would leave New Haven and edit the paper. Bacon declined the offer. But Thompson persisted in his efforts and succeeded in organizing a group of merchants who agreed to bankroll the paper. Bacon again delayed a decision, in part because of his busy schedule at Center Church and with the *New Englander.* But, convinced that the paper would be an ideal forum for disseminating his views on a broad range of subjects, he soon consented to Thompson's request to serve as the New York *Independent*'s senior editor.[1]

The proprietors of the *Independent* were socially sensitive, pious Yankees who

1. Benjamin Lockwood to Bacon, December 2, 1844, David Hale to Bacon, October 16, 1839, in Bacon Family Papers; Louis Filler, "Liberalism, Anti-Slavery, and the Founders of the *Independent,*" *New England Quarterly,* XXXV (1954), 295; Gossard, "The New York City Congregational Cluster," 65–67.

wished to advance the benevolent empire and the antislavery cause and to make New York City the vortex of a national Congregationalism. By the early 1850s, the more cautious of the proprietors would sell their shares in the paper, and Henry C. Bowen, whose evangelical opinions and social outlook were quite similar to those of the editors, would progressively become the publication's driving force. Bacon, Thompson, and Richard S. Storrs, Jr., who served as editors from 1848 until 1861, were appropriate choices. All of them, and particularly Bacon, the oldest of the trio, had editorial experience and were prominent Congregational ministers. Thompson, an intense workaholic, supervised the paper's operations, including layout and composition, and, with Bacon, supplied much of the editorial comment. He was extremely close to Bacon, who considered him "a younger brother." Storrs joined the editorial staff less because of any proven journalistic ability than because several of the original proprietors were members of his Church of the Pilgrims in Brooklyn. At times during the 1850s, he limited his contributions to stated editorials and columns in the literary department.[2]

Although Bacon had often visited New York City to attend meetings and deliver speeches, he chose not to live there, for he was not comfortable with the fast pace of life in the city and was not prepared to resign his post at Center Church. Consequently, for thirteen years he conducted much of his business with the editorial office by mail, visiting Thompson and other members of the staff every few weeks for consultation. His many responsibilities in New Haven meant that he could not give the paper his undivided attention; nevertheless, he played a significant role in the paper's operations. Not only did he help to shape its layout and editorial position, but his associates often looked to him to resolve differences among the forceful personalities who shared the journal's columns and to speak for the staff when proprietorial and policy issues generated concern. Storrs, nearly twenty years younger than Bacon, regarded him as a mentor and stood in awe of his intellect. Yet Bacon was quick to admit that he was "jointly responsible" for the paper's content, and he rarely saw what Thompson and Storrs wrote before it appeared in the *Independent's* columns.[3]

2. Donald David Housley, "The *Independent:* A Study in Religious and Social Opinion, 1848–1870" (Ph.D. dissertation, Pennsylvania State University, 1971), 7–8, 17–18, 29–30; Mott, *A History of American Magazines, 1850–1865,* 369; Joshua Leavitt to Bacon, February 2, 1852, Richard S. Storrs, Jr., to Bacon, August 25, 1852, in Bacon Family Papers; *Independent,* January 2, July 15, December 4, 1852; *Leonard Bacon: Pastor of the First Church in New Haven,* 194–95; Gossard, "The New York City Congregational Cluster," 57–59.

3. Bacon to Elizur Wright, 1837 draft, Catherine to Leonard Bacon, August 19, 1851, Joshua Leavitt to Bacon, May 14, 1849, January 19, 1852, Richard S. Storrs, Jr., to Bacon, April 19, 1852, Henry C. Bowen to Bacon, February 3, 1852, Bacon to Nathaniel Hewit, December 16, 1853, diary entries for 1852–54, in Bacon Family Papers; *Leonard Bacon: Pastor of the First Church in New Haven,* 195.

The fourth member of the editorial staff during Bacon's years with the *Independent* was Joshua Leavitt, whom Bacon and Thompson had persuaded to serve as managing editor. Leavitt, who had extensive experience as a newspaper editor, influenced the tenor of the *Independent,* but this did not extend in any formal way to editorial policy. Indeed, the editors' concerns, as antislavery moderates, that Leavitt's reputation as an abolitionist might alienate the clergy and other potential subscribers led Bacon to announce to their readers that the editors, not Leavitt, were "responsible *solely* and *fully* for the character of the paper."[4]

During the first years of the paper's existence, the editors placed their names on the masthead in order to take responsibility for what it contained. Yet, hoping to avoid personal attacks, they generally refused to sign their editorials. From the *Independent*'s inception, they were also fiercely protective of their editorial autonomy. The paper, they asserted in 1850, had been given to them to be controlled and directed "as they should see fit," unless they controverted the principles and doctrines upon which the *Independent* was founded. For the most part the owners honored this desire for autonomy. The editors' insistence upon independence was also manifested in their adamant refusal to serve as spokesmen for any particular party or sect. In his inaugural editorial Bacon pointedly expressed the editors' conviction that, although they were Congregationalists, the *Independent* "was not established as the organ of any ecclesiastical body, or of any sect or party—new school or old school." Nor were they "the champions of any man's 'scheme' or metaphysical system, or of the views set forth from any chair of theology." Likewise, while the paper would stand forthrightly in favor of the free-soil principle and would speak to all questions that affected "great moral interests" in the nation, "no *political* party has any right or interest in our columns."[5]

The proprietors hired Henry Ward Beecher, George B. Cheever, Harriet Beecher Stowe, and other prominent Congregational clergymen and writers to make regular contributions to the *Independent*'s columns. The popularity of their columns helps to explain the *Independent*'s success in the highly competitive New York City market, which, in 1848, included fifty-two religious and secular papers. Bacon and his colleagues sought to appeal to a broad evangelical audience, especially among Congregationalists and Presbyterians who lived in New England, New York, and Ohio. The paper, Bacon announced in his inaugural editorial, would meet the pressing need for a "symposium" type of journalism that covered a wide variety of both secular and religious subjects. In doing so, the *Independent* set itself apart from

4. Davis, *Joshua Leavitt,* 252–54; *Independent,* December 21, 1848.

5. *Independent,* December 27, 1849, October 27, 1853, October 31, 1850, December 7, 1848; W. C. Gilman to *Independent* proprietors, May 29, 1852, Henry C. Bowen to Bacon, February 23, 1852, in Bacon Family Papers. Bacon's correspondence with his editorial associates and Bowen, as well as his diary entries, indicate many of the editorials that he wrote.

most other weeklies: it differed from religious journals in its strong and consistent interest in social reform, especially antislavery, and it differed from the reform and antislavery journals in the religious cast of its editorials and articles. This combination of religious sentiment and social reformism helped to make the *Independent* one of the most popular and influential religious newspapers in the United States by the mid-1850s.[6]

The *Independent's* growing popularity was also due in part to the editors' endorsement of traditional values, moral uprightness, and social responsibility. During a time of rapid industrialization, urbanization, and immigration, they constantly searched for principles and values that would maintain stability and lessen uncertainty. At the same time, however, they rejected calls for a return to an earlier, simpler time and expressed admiration for the social and economic progress of the age. Their response to change was nevertheless often cautious, and at times defensive of the status quo. They were not blind to the needs of an increasingly complex modern society, but their conviction that morality and spiritual uplift were essential to the regeneration of society sometimes made it difficult for them to propose workable prescriptions for the social ills of the time. For example, although they were disturbed by the growing evidence of poverty in the urban centers, they believed that only the "virtuous" poor deserved assistance and that Christians were especially obligated to preach the Gospel to the poor.[7]

Bacon remained thoroughly committed to the liberal principles propounded by Adam Smith and John Stuart Mill. The *Independent,* he stated in 1852, stood for *"Free Soil, Free Speech, Free Schools, Free Trade, Free Homes, Free Men, and Free Salvation."* He was convinced that both the individual and society would advance and prosper only if people enjoyed fundamental liberties and opportunities; thus, government action should be limited largely to protecting and enhancing liberty. He was confident that, by working hard and saving money, an American laborer could become an independent proprietor and accumulate wealth, and he cautioned that government must not attempt to regulate wealth or redistribute property. His defense of the emerging industrial capitalism in the North also represented a response to some southerners' charges that the condition of free laborers was worse than that of slaves. Indeed, he favorably compared skilled workers' comforts with those of many slaveholders.[8]

6. Clark, *Henry Ward Beecher,* 110–14; Richard S. Storrs, Jr., to Bacon, June 24, 1853, in Bacon Family Papers; *Independent,* December 7, 1848, January 2, 1851, May 20, 1852, November 24, January 5, 1854; Joan D. Hedrick, *Harriet Beecher Stowe: A Life* (New York, 1994), 227; Housley, "The *Independent*," 11; Mott, *A History of American Magazines, 1741–1850,* 370, 375.

7. Housley, "The *Independent*," 112–13; *Independent,* May 3, December 13, 1849, August 1, 1850, January 27, 1853, February 16, August 31, 1854, November 19, 1857; sermons of April 13, 1856, November 22, 1857, in Bacon Family Papers.

8. *Independent,* June 20, 1850, May 6, July 15, 1852, 1854, May 22, 1856, February 2, 1860; Leonard

Bacon's attachment to liberty, however, was selective. In the columns of the *Independent* and the *New Englander,* for example, he articulated the prevailing gender attitudes of the time. Holding firmly to the doctrine of separate spheres, he declared that women should be content to remain within the domestic circle, where "that refinement of taste, that delicacy of moral sensibility, and that exquisitely elevated and unworldly character" would exalt reform and uplift society. Thus, despite the fact that Harriet Beecher Stowe commented on public issues in the columns of the *Independent,* he cautioned women against engaging in political debate, or even speaking publicly on behalf of reform causes, and he was convinced that the right to vote was not essential to civil liberty.[9]

While Bacon and his fellow editors expressed many of the evangelical middle class's deeply held values and attitudes, their outspoken commitment to free-soil principles and especially their harsh criticism of the major parties for failing adequately to defend northern interests placed them in advance of many northern evangelicals. The *Independent* was founded at a time when the territorial issue was moving the nation inexorably toward a crisis that threatened the Union. During Bacon's tenure, the paper was consciously, and even proudly, antislavery at a time, especially in the early 1850s, when the conservative reaction following passage of the Compromise of 1850 made antislavery unpopular among many northerners. Although the editors were decidedly anti-Garrisonian, and repeatedly denied conservatives' charges that the *Independent* was an abolitionist paper, they were convinced that slavery fundamentally violated Christian principles and must be abolished throughout the United States.[10]

Bacon, Thompson, and Storrs, like many other editors of religious newspapers, believed that they were obligated to discuss issues that had a moral content. In response to criticism from conservative clerics and journalists, they frequently expressed their commitment to principles, not political parties. But they never doubted that, in appropriate ways, ministers must discuss the slavery issue.[11]

As the sectional crisis deepened in the late 1840s, Bacon joined a chorus of

---

Bacon, "The Application of Political Economy," *New Englander,* VII (August, 1849), 420–23, 482–36; Leonard Bacon, "The Southern Apostasy," *New Englander,* XII (November, 1854), 647–51.

9. See, for example, Leonard Bacon, *The Relation of Christianity to the Law and Government. A Discourse Before the Society of Phi Beta Kappa, in Harvard University, 17th July, 1856* (New Haven, 1856), 11–12; Leonard Bacon, *Discourse, Before the Literary Societies of Hamilton College, Clinton, July 27, 1847* (Utica, 1848), 25–26; *Independent,* February 16, 1854, February 16, 1860.

10. Smith, *Revivalism and Social Reform in Mid–Nineteenth-Century America,* 208–217; Gossard, "The New York City Congregational Cluster," 95–96, 99. For Bacon's views on abolition and the abolitionists, see *Independent,* April 18, July 4, 1850, May 20, October 21, 1852; Leonard Bacon, "The Question! Are You Ready for the Question?" *New Englander,* VIII (May, 1850), 292.

11. Chester Forrester Dunham, *The Attitude of the Northern Clergy Toward the South, 1860–1865* (Toledo, 1942), 10, 13–14; New York *Observer,* February 23, 1850; *Independent,* April 18, May 23, October 31, 1850, January 1, 1852.

antislavery northerners in accusing President Polk of "downright knavery" in seeking to impose slavery on California and New Mexico at the expense of future generations of slaves and settlers. He was so disturbed by the prospect that slavery might be fastened upon the territories that he warned of the possibility of an armed struggle against slavery and of God's destruction of the national government. Long an antislavery moderate who preferred compromise and forbearance to open conflict, he now believed that the line must be drawn, no matter the consequences. He remained convinced that slavery must be abolished and that a containment policy would eventually destroy the system. But like many other free-soil advocates, he regarded the territorial issue, which involved the integrity and morality of the national government rather than the need for state action against slavery, to be "infinitely more important" than abolition in the South.[12]

In this crisis Bacon and a growing number of northern clergymen emphatically declared for liberty and morality over preservation of the Union. He informed his *New Englander* readers that although Americans should pray that God would interpose and save the nation from its enemies, he would pray "*first* for the preservation of the law of the prophets, and *secondly* for the Union." Convinced that there was collective guilt for collective immorality, he fully expected that God's blessing to America would be withdrawn if divine principles were not respected. Yet in the final analysis, he was confident that because virtually all Americans were attached to the Union and the Constitution and because the free-soil position was the "embodiment of a great principle of justice and humanity," the Union probably would not be dissolved.[13]

For Bacon, anyone who sought to preserve the Union by giving demagogues what they demanded betrayed "a capacity of being used for purposes of treason utterly inconsistent with his pretensions to statesmanship." Consequently, he was highly ambivalent about Henry Clay's compromise package in 1850. Although he praised Clay's leadership, and especially his proposal for a free California, he criticized Clay's refusal to call for the abolition of slavery in the District of Columbia and condemned the proposal for returning fugitive slaves. He saved his harshest criticism for Daniel Webster, whose stirring speech in favor of sectional reconciliation rallied the forces of compromise. Like most other free-soilers, Bacon scoffed at Webster's and Stephen A. Douglas' reliance on the law of nature to exclude slavery from the territories, arguing that only laws of society would accomplish that end. Furthermore, contrary to Webster's position, he believed that threats of disunion

12. *Independent,* December 14, 1848, January 4, 25, February 15, 1849; Bacon, "The Question! Are You Ready for the Question?" 297–98, 310–11.

13. Bacon, "The Question! Are You Ready for the Question?" 293–94; sermon of April 6, 1849, in Bacon Family Papers; *Independent,* January 3, March 7, 1850.

were "a kind of constructive treason" that must not, under any circumstances, be met with compromise.[14]

As important as Bacon considered the crisis confronting the nation, and in the midst of the congressional debate, he nevertheless began a one-year sabbatical from his pastorate and editorship in order to observe the state of religion in Europe and to visit missionary stations in the Middle East. Having taken little time off from his work during the past quarter century, he looked forward to an extended absence that he hoped would expand his knowledge and usefulness. He had planned for some time to leave in mid-1850, but the birth of his son Thomas Rutherford and the illness of his mother placed his plans on hold. (When Alice died in the summer of 1850, Bacon delivered a stirring sermon that praised her spiritual faith and women's contributions to the family. Nearly all of his sermon, however, dwelled on his father's missionary work on the frontier. Although certainly an appropriate topic for a sermon, this also may well have reflected the anger that he felt toward his mother, who had often questioned whether he exhibited sufficient attention and caring.)[15]

Alice's death, as well as the Ecclesiastical Society's approval of the trip, the hiring of A. H. Eggleston as his replacement, and generous contributions by members of the church, freed him to leave New Haven with his eldest son, Leonard Woolsey, a recent graduate of Yale, in September, 1850. During his travels, Bacon maintained an editorial correspondence with the *Independent,* in which he primarily described the scenery and analyzed the social and economic systems that he observed. While in Scotland and England, he preached in several churches, spoke before temperance and other reform organizations, observed schools and asylums, and visited factories, universities, and castles. Following a leisurely trip across the Continent, Bacon and his son arrived in Beirut in January, 1851, where they spent a few weeks before traveling to Palestine, and then Asia Minor, to observe missionary stations for the American Board of Commissioners for Foreign Missions. Bacon thoroughly enjoyed his travels, comparing the Ottoman Empire's primitive conditions and mule trains with the Overland Trail to California and Oregon. But when he, his son, and Dwight Marsh, an ABCFM missionary, were waylaid and held hostage by a group of Kurds, the aura of quaintness began to dissipate. The Kurds, who were not interested in the pasha of Mosul's letter of protection that Bacon's party carried, hoped to arouse their compatriots to insurrection by provoking the imperial government to retaliate. Even after Bacon's party was freed following payment of a bribe, further

14. *Independent,* March 14, February 14, 28, July 4, 1850; Bacon, "The Question! Are You Ready for the Question?" 301, 307–308.

15. Bacon to First Ecclesiastical Society in New Haven, July 21, 1850, sermon of August 11, 1850, in Bacon Family Papers; Theodore Dwight Bacon, *Leonard Bacon,* 319; Baldwin, *Bacon Genealogy,* 280.

threats were made. Nevertheless, Bacon persevered and visited several missionary stations in eastern Asia Minor.[16]

Upon his return to England, Bacon visited numerous cities and villages. The highlight of his one-month stay in England was the Evangelical Alliance convention in London, which lasted for fifteen days. Although the alliance had been established in 1846 as an anti-Catholic organization, nearly from the beginning slavery had divided the Protestant groups that comprised its membership. Bacon had agreed with the American delegates at the 1846 meeting, who, in support of the "good slaveholder" concept, resisted British attempts to bar slaveholders from the convention. As an observer at the 1851 meeting, he again castigated British evangelicals for "pertinaciously" insisting that all slaveholders automatically be excluded from Christian communion. Their refusal to invite slaveholders to the meeting, he charged, was a "disputed and unscriptural dogma" that millions of antislavery Americans rejected unequivocally.[17]

Following the convention, which ended with British and American evangelicals still at loggerheads over slavery, Bacon returned to New Haven in October, 1851, thirteen months after his journey had begun. Over the next few months, he accepted numerous offers to write articles for journals, deliver public lectures, and present speeches before missionary and tract societies on matters related to his trip. He also moved immediately into his pastoral duties and his family life. As time had passed, Catherine had felt increasingly burdened, and even depressed, by the responsibilities of caring for their many children and overseeing the household finances during his absence. Although Bacon seemed sympathetic to her travails and was pleased to be back with his family, perhaps especially with the baby, Ruddy, who had no memory of his father, he quickly resumed his frenetic work schedule.[18]

Bacon felt compelled above all to relieve Thompson of some of the editorial responsibilities he had assumed during the past year. Although the *Independent* continued to lose money, by 1851 its subscription list had steadily climbed to 10,000,

16. First Ecclesiastical Society in New Haven to Bacon, July 22, 1850, Trowbridge Family to Bacon, August 2, September 2, 1850, Catherine to Leonard Bacon, September 23, 1850, Leonard to Rebecca Bacon, October 4, 1850, Leonard to Catherine Bacon, October 14, 1850, Bacon to family, February 4, 1851, lecture on Middle East trip, 1852, in Bacon Family Papers; *Independent,* November 7, 14, 21, 28, December 5, 12, 19, 1850; March 13, June 19, July 24, 31, 1851; *Leonard Bacon: Pastor of the First Church in New Haven,* 29–38.

17. *Independent,* August 14, September 4, 18, October 2, 1851; Leonard to Catherine Bacon, September 8, 1851, in Bacon Family Papers; Leonard Bacon, "Evangelical Alliance," *New Englander,* X (May, 1852), 309–12, 328–29, 323; Maclear, "The Evangelical Alliance and the Antislavery Crusade," 141, 143–45, 149, 153–59, 162.

18. See Edwards Park to Bacon, October 9, 1851, Bacon to Milton Badger, October 15, 1851, lecture on travels in the Middle East, 1852, Catherine to Leonard Bacon, August 19, October 31, 1851, in Bacon Family Papers.

including 1,500 ministers. While Bacon was away, however, the editors' response to the Fugitive Slave Act of 1850 had created a crisis that, for a time, threatened the paper's very existence. That law—which greatly increased the number of federal officials to hear claims by slave owners and grant certificates of removal, offered officials ten dollars if the accused black person was judged to be a fugitive and half as much if not, commanded Americans to aid in the execution of the law, and denied basic constitutional protection to those accused of being fugitives—exacerbated sectional tensions. Despite these flaws, many northerners, including some who disliked the law, were willing to support the compromise package because they desired peace and prosperity and an end to the sectional crisis. One expression of such support was the Castle Garden meeting in October, 1850, attended by New York City merchants, clergymen, politicians, and others who believed that those who condemned the Fugitive Slave Act endangered the Union, law and order, the Constitution, and trade with the South.[19]

Antislavery northerners, including pro–Wilmot Proviso Whigs and Democrats, however, viewed the law not as a question of Union or secession but as one that demanded complicity with slaveholders. Protests, involving both active and passive disobedience, spread across the North. As the battle raged, northern clergymen were deeply divided on the issue. Many subordinated their dislike for slavery and the Fugitive Slave Act to the need to preserve an orderly society that they believed was the best hope of mankind; others, though, including the editors of the *Independent,* joined the chorus of protest. As early as April, 1850, Bacon, Thompson, and Storrs had declared that Christians could not obey legislation that contravened God's laws. They were especially critical of the absence of due process, which they termed "a cruel mockery of justice." In perhaps his most provocative editorial following passage of the Fugitive Slave Act, Thompson called for passive nonviolent resistance by whites and fugitives alike.[20]

The reaction was not long in coming. Conservatives in Thompson's church nearly succeeded in dismissing him; and, in retaliation for the paper's editorial stance and the proprietors' refusal to sign the call for the Castle Garden meeting, half of the *Independent's* six thousand subscribers canceled their subscriptions. Frightened by the uproar, one of the owners, Simeon B. Chittenden, withdrew from the paper, and two others, Seth and Jonathan B. Hunt, sold their interest to

19. *Independent,* October 31, November 28, December 4, 1851. For treatments of the Fugitive Slave Act and its supporters, see Holman Hamilton, *Prologue to Conflict: The Crisis and the Compromise of 1850* (Lexington, Ky., 1964), 140, 142–43, 161–63; Thomas D. Morris, *Free Men All: The Personal Liberty Laws of the North, 1780–1861* (Baltimore, 1974), 131–53.

20. *Independent,* April 18, May 16, October 24, 1850. Northern opposition to the Fugitive Slave Act is treated in Morris, *Free Men All,* 153, 156–58, *et passim.* Clerical opinion on the law is discussed in McKivigan, *The War Against Proslavery Religion,* 132–36, 152–54, 160, 166, 168, 175.

Theodore McNamee and Henry C. Bowen. In addition, the *Journal of Commerce,* the New York *Observer,* and other conservative newspapers in the city bitterly accused the *Independent* of being an "ultra-abolition journal," and even of "encouraging Rebellion and Murder." These attacks, however, did not deter Thompson and Storrs. In a series of editorials in January, 1851, Storrs urged opponents of the law to disregard its provisions and counseled fugitives to defend themselves. His position, which differed little from what many abolitionists argued, provoked another onslaught from the conservative press. But many other northern newspapers applauded his arguments, and during the months following the Castle Garden meeting the *Independent* added five thousand new subscribers.[21]

Although Bacon was far removed from the controversy that swirled around the *Independent,* and neither Thompson nor Storrs solicited his views on the matter, he felt compelled to enunciate his position on the fugitive slave issue. While traveling through Italy on his way to the Middle East in December, 1850, he wrote an article for the *Independent* that was cautious and somewhat contradictory. Once again, when confronted with a controversial issue he sought to weigh a number of considerations and then to occupy a middle ground between what he considered extreme ideological positions. On the one hand, he pronounced the law unconstitutional, "unjust," and "severe," and therefore urged Americans to do no more than passively obey it. On the other hand, he set forth a number of conditions that, if heeded, would have seriously limited the options available to both fugitives and their potential rescuers. He specifically discountenanced violent resistance as "illegal and revolutionary" and even suggested that slaves "endure in meekness" until the opportunity to escape arose. Although his statement was rather contradictory and confusing, Thompson and Storrs quickly declared that Bacon's views were "manifestly just and impregnable; and in their logical applications they cover the whole ground" taken by the *Independent.* Yet even they conceded that he had not touched upon the slaves' right to defend themselves by force in order to avoid capture. By not clarifying this point, Bacon allowed conservatives to claim that he repudiated the "wild and fanatical radicalism" of Thompson and Storrs.[22]

When Bacon returned to the United States in late 1851, he chose not to elucidate his differences with his fellow editors. Instead, he defended the higher-law doctrine against attacks from its critics. In a Thanksgiving Day sermon later published in pamphlet form, he acknowledged that both magistrates and citizens were bound by the law, that the disorganization of society should not be attempted in the name of

21. Filler, "Liberalism, Anti-Slavery, and the Founders of the *Independent,*" 297; New York *Observer,* April 13, June 1, 8, December 7, 14, 1850, January 9, 1851; *Independent,* December 5, 1850, January 16, 30, February 20, 1851. The abolitionists' views on the higher-law doctrine, as well as their defiance of the Fugitive Slave Act, are discussed in Dillon, *The Abolitionists,* 177–89.

22. *Independent,* February 13, 1851; New York *Observer,* September 11, 1851.

Christian duty, and that individual conscience was liable to error. Nevertheless, he stated emphatically that "the rule of right and wrong, recognized by the human conscience as sanctioned and guarded by the righteousness of God, is the supreme principle of action for the individual man." Bacon's sermon circulated in many parts of the North and elicited widespread approval. For example, William Seward, who had defended the higher law in the United States Senate in 1850, wrote Bacon that his sermon "clears away a mass of sophistries, and places the subject discussed in a strong light." Others, however, including those members of Center Church who had adopted a resolution at the New Haven Union meeting in December, 1850, that condemned the higher-law argument, considered Bacon's position both radical and dangerous.[23]

Perhaps the harshest criticism of Bacon's views came from Gerard Hallock, editor of the *Journal of Commerce,* a conservative New York City newspaper that spoke for many northern merchants who feared losing profitable markets in the South. Throughout 1852 he and Bacon exchanged a series of angry letters that appeared in both the *Independent* and the *Journal of Commerce.* Hallock asserted that the Constitution, not divine law, was the highest law for political action. Thus, he argued, Bacon and others who called for defiance of the law of the land encouraged Americans to engage in "riot, insurrection, anarchy, and bloodshed" and manifested a fundamental disloyalty to the United States government.[24]

Bacon's letters clearly illustrate the gulf that separated advocates of the higher law from those who insisted upon obedience to the Constitution as the law of the land. He categorically rejected Hallock's distinction between moral and political action and repudiated his claim that people must obey a law no matter whether it was contrary to God's law. To follow Hallock's advice, he warned, would risk God's wrath, for the Fugitive Slave Act struck down "all the defenses of freedom" for fugitives and sought to compel northerners to protect slavery.[25]

Bacon's pledge to submit to the Fugitive Slave Act's penalties but not to obey its provisions, which was similar to the position occupied by the American and Foreign Anti-Slavery Society, certainly placed him in advance of public opinion. Yet on certain points he remained somewhat more cautious than Thompson and Storrs. For example, he never endorsed Thompson's statement in 1852 that God would favor the North if its refusal to enforce the Fugitive Slave Act led to the dissolution

23. *Independent,* January 1, 1852; Senior, "New England Congregationalists and the Anti-Slavery Movement," 263, 369–70; Roger Sherman Baldwin to Committee of New Haven Citizens, December 23, 1850, in Baldwin Family Papers, Sterling Library, Yale University.

24. *Journal of Commerce,* January 15, 29, March 20, October 16, 1852; also William H. Hallock, *Life of Gerard Hallock, Thirty-three Years Editor of the New York "Journal of Commerce"* (New York, 1869), 208–27, 229–33.

25. *Independent,* February 12, 26, June 10, July 8, December 30, 1852.

of the Union. And, in response to Hallock's charge that he helped to incite riots at Christiana, Pennsylvania, and Syracuse, New York, where opponents of the law employed force to protect fugitives, he at least implicitly rejected Storrs's position by repeatedly urging peaceful resistance by fugitives who sought to avoid capture.[26]

Nevertheless, Bacon seldom veered far toward the radical or conservative positions on the slavery issue. While his vigorous opposition to the Fugitive Slave Act and his defense of the higher law brought him into sharp conflict with northern conservatives, his defense of the home and foreign missionary societies and the "good slaveholder" concept placed him at odds with the abolitionists in the early and middle 1850s. He and other antislavery moderates continued to reject the immediatists' demands that the ABCFM exclude all slaveholders from the mission churches and tended to celebrate those occasions when the society took a firm stand on slavery. Yet he became progressively impatient as the board's missionaries to the Cherokees and Choctaws, most of whom were southern Old School Presbyterians, dragged their feet in implementing the ABCFM's decree that they show converts the injustice of slavery. As the impasse between the board and its missionaries deepened, he warned the society that if it alienated antislavery northerners, who were its principal contributors, it would be bankrupted.[27]

The debate on the missions' relationship with slavery declined in intensity in the aftermath of the Compromise of 1850. The peace was shattered in 1853, however, when a group of Choctaw slaveholders enacted a new set of codes prohibiting the education of blacks. Notwithstanding this provocative act, at the society's 1853 meeting in Cincinnati, where he served as chairman of the business committee, Bacon expressed confidence that Christianity was moving the tribe away from slavery and that the ABCFM was generally moving in the right direction. "We go for practical progress and reform," he lectured the abolitionists in 1854, "and leave abstractions to take care of themselves." Ever the pragmatist, he sincerely believed that a cautious, moderate policy would advance the interests of both the antislavery and the foreign mission causes. Unfortunately, in pinning his hopes on incremental reforms he pleased neither the radical nor the conservative faction within the ABCFM. Equally important, he was left with little choice but to react to what others did. As much as he wished to avoid another potentially divisive battle on the slavery question within the ABCFM, the Choctaw code ultimately forced a confrontation in which Bacon finally was forced to draw the line. At the 1854 ABCFM meeting in Hartford, he presented resolutions endorsing the board's order that slaves must be taught in the mission schools and that missionaries must preach

26. *Independent,* April 8, 15, 1852; Morris, *Free Men All,* 157–58.

27. See *Independent,* April 12, 26, June 7, 28, 1849, July 26, December 16, 23, 1852, June 23, August 25, 1853, October 25, 1855, August 21, 1856.

against slavery. Following passage of his resolutions, over the opposition of conservatives, he declared the subject of slavery in relation to the board to be "settled upon the eternal basis of right."[28]

This action prompted the exodus of most of the Choctaw missionaries to the Old School Presbyterian missionary board and effectively ended the debate on slavery within the ABCFM. But throughout the early and middle 1850s, Bacon and his editorial associates at the *Independent* were even more concerned about the New School Presbyterian Church's relationship with slavery, especially through its southern wing. This was bound to affect the Congregationalists' interaction with the American Home Missionary Society, which depended heavily upon both groups for funding and leadership. During the late 1840s, western Congregationists had been particularly critical of the society for continuing to subsidize southern churches that included slaveholders. This pressure gradually moved the AHMS away from its long-standing contention that it had no control over the churches it subsidized. Fearing the loss of antislavery contributions and facing growing defections to the American Missionary Association, the AHMS's officers urged their missionaries to expound antislavery principles and appointed no more slaveholders as missionaries. Yet because the society continued to accept contributions from slaveholders and to allow them to be members of the mission churches, many Congregational abolitionists left the AHMS anyway in the early 1850s.[29]

The slavery issue, especially as it related to home missions, was a major factor that drove both New School Presbyterians and Congregationalists inexorably toward denominationalism. New Schoolers, offended by the Congregationalists' criticism of their policy on slavery and resentful of the growing competition from Congregationalists in the West, established a Standing Committee on Home Missions, which was charged with planting new churches "in advance of all others." At the same time, Congregationalists' concerns about their contact with New School slaveholding churches subsidized by the AHMS helped to accelerate the development of a self-image characterized by a belief in a free church and a free gospel for free Americans.[30]

Bacon was ambivalent about these developments: he valued cooperation among various Protestant denominations but also sought to protect, and even advance,

28. Lewit, "Indian Missions and Anti-Slavery Sentiment," 51–52; *Independent*, September 8, 22, 1853, February 16, April 20, September 21, 28, 1854; Catherine to Frank Bacon, September 22, 1854, in Bacon Family Papers; Theodore Dwight Bacon, *Leonard Bacon*, 398–403.

29. Evans, "Abolitionism in the Illinois Churches," 195, 213–14; Howard, *Conscience and Slavery*, 48, 50–54, 100–107; *Report on the Relations of the American Home Missionary Society to Slavery. Adopted by the General Association of Michigan, June, 1853* (n.p., 1853), 26.

30. Davis, "The New York *Evangelist*, New School Presbyterians, and Slavery," 20; McKivigan, *The War Against Proslavery Religion*, 118–19.

Congregational interests, especially in the West. He had long been an outspoken critic of sectarianism, and therefore applauded the AHMS for refusing to give in to sectarian pressures. Yet he and his editorial associates also firmly believed that the Congregational Church's polity most closely resembled the primitive apostolic church as well as political democracy. The *Independent* contributed significantly to Congregationalism's move from a church to a national denomination. Although Bacon was unwilling to admit the consequences of his actions, he in fact had long been a driving force behind the denominational awakening that occurred in Connecticut and other New England states, which, in turn, paved the way for the creation of a national structure. As the Congregational Church moved beyond the protected and provincial religious environment of the region and interacted with other religious traditions, particularly those of the Presbyterians, Bacon and others not only developed a keener sense of the uniqueness of their church polity but also recognized that justification of the church's peculiar principles and practices was necessary if it was to expand and survive in the free market of theology.[31]

From the 1840s on, Bacon stood forth as something of an expert on Congregational practices and principles. He frequently received requests for advice on a broad range of matters, including the hiring and dismissal of ministers, the nature and functions of church councils, and the role of deacons. In numerous contributions to the *Independent* and the *New Englander,* he consistently championed the concepts of localism, freedom, and independence, which he believed formed the cornerstone of the Congregational way. Congregationalists, he believed, must be ever vigilant against domination by a "consolidated spiritual despotism," just as all Americans should defend the principle of local self-government in civil affairs. Although he emphasized the need for Christian fellowship with neighboring churches, he idealized the local Congregational church for its "inherent independence, self-subsistence, sovereignty, and reserved rights."[32]

Bacon especially underscored the differences between the Congregational and Presbyterian systems. While Presbyterians maintained conformity through creeds, constitutions, and ecclesiastical courts, he argued, Congregationalists thought for themselves and relied upon the Bible as the sole test of orthodoxy. He was also concerned that the New Schoolers, driven by a sectarian spirit, used the Plan of Union to benefit themselves at the expense of Congregational expansion in the

31. See *Independent,* December 7, 1848, December 4, 1851; Leonard Bacon, *The American Church. A Discourse in Behalf of the American Home Missionary Society, Preached in the Cities of New York and Brooklyn, May, 1852* (New York, 1852), 6; Leonard Bacon, "The Relative Character and Merits of the Congregational and Presbyterian Systems," *New Englander,* III (July, 1845), 438–39; Pearson, "From Church to Denomination," 79–87.

32. See *Independent,* August 12, 26, December 9, 23, 1852, March 3, 31, 1853; Leonard Bacon, "Hodge on Presbyterianism," *New Englander,* XIV (February, 1856), 17.

West. With Thompson and the New York General Association leading the way, the *Independent* initiated the call for a Congregational convention to discuss the growing tensions between the two churches regarding the AHMS, the slavery issue, and competition in the West, as well as differences between eastern and western Congregationalists on theology and slavery.[33]

Because of Bacon's position with the *Independent,* his influence in New England, and his standing as an authority on Congregationalism, his support for the convention was vital for its success. He ultimately endorsed the call for the meeting and, when Thompson fell ill, took charge of much of the preparation for the convention. Nevertheless, his deeply held belief in Congregational independence and localism, as well as his opposition to sectarianism, made him cautious. He especially warned against any attempt to create "some sort of mongrel Presbyterianism," emphasizing that the proposed convention must be "strictly an occasional meeting" for the purpose of consultation and mutual assistance.[34]

Some eastern Congregationalists had even more reservations about the meeting than did Bacon. While in Troy, New York, in September, 1852, to deliver the sermon at the ABCFM meeting, he met with Joel Hawes, Absalom Peters, and other easterners, who opposed the convention because they feared a break with the Presbyterians. They were also disturbed by the fact that many western Congregationalists adhered to the Oberlin theology, which held that only a perfectly holy person could hope to know exactly what God's will was and could live up to its demands. After a lengthy discussion, Bacon managed to persuade these men to attend the convention, which was to be held the following month in Albany, New York. While he believed that the idea of entire sanctification was far too optimistic a conception of human ability, he hoped that all Congregationalists would "meet as family and candidly and we may come to some safe and harmonious conclusion."[35]

The slavery question was potentially more explosive than the Oberlin issue. While many antislavery westerners believed that slavery must be the leading question at the convention, other Congregationalists feared that such a focus would damage the AHMS as well as relations with the New Schoolers. Bacon sought to act as a conciliator in order to maintain Congregational unity and to facilitate the church's expansion in the West. Although he was confident that the slavery issue

---

33. Bacon, "The Relative Character and Merits of the Congregational and Presbyterian Systems," 441–49; *Independent,* January 8, 15, February 19, 26, 1852, April 14, 1853; Pearson, "From Church to Denomination," 76–78, 85.

34. *Independent,* July 29, September 2, 1852; H. D. Kitchell, "The Congregational Convention," *New Englander,* XI (February, 1853), 72–75.

35. Senior, "New England Congregationalists and the Anti-Slavery Movement," 289–90; diary entry for September 8, 1852, sermon before the ABCFM, September 7, 1852, Bacon to Parson Cooke, September 29, 1852, in Bacon Family Papers.

would be disposed of "without much trouble," he foresaw an irreparable rift within the church if westerners pushed their "violent Antislaveryism" or if easterners determined that slavery should not be considered or opposed. Searching further for a middle ground upon which Congregationalists could unite, he condemned southern Christians for their apostasy on the slavery question, while also hoping "not to irritate them with modern doctrines and modern applications of Christian discipline."[36]

At the Albany Convention, held in October, 1852, 462 Congregational ministers and laymen met in the first general convention since the Cambridge Synod over two hundred years earlier. Bacon played a leading role in the convention's affairs, serving as chair of the business committee, which dealt with such important matters as the Plan of Union, church building in the West, the operations of the AHMS, and relations between eastern and western Congregationalists. He was convinced that many of the insinuations and charges of heresy in doctrine and disorder in practice leveled against western Congregationalists constituted "a great evil" that would not stand up under close scrutiny. While he acknowledged that he did not agree with some westerners on theological matters, he pointed out that easterners also differed among themselves. With strong support from western delegates, he presented resolutions, which were accepted with only one dissenting vote, that called for the rejection of all but specific allegations against fellow Congregationalists and for regular contact between easterners and westerners.[37]

Bacon, however, believed that easterners must go beyond merely tolerating the theological views and practices of their western brethren; they also should provide much-needed financial assistance for building new churches in the West. Despite opposition from those who feared that such assistance would weaken eastern churches, he presented a plan for raising $50,000 within six months, with $10,000 to be contributed by Bowen and McNamee, proprietors of the *Independent*. The proposal easily passed, and a central committee as well as a committee of three men in each state were formed to coordinate the fund-raising effort, with Bacon being appointed to the Connecticut group.[38]

In a related move that represented an even bolder expression of denominational sentiment, Bacon's committee proposed the repeal of the Plan of Union. By "virtually requiring" Congregational ministers settled over Presbyterian churches and Congregational churches having Presbyterian ministers to be connected with presbyteries, the committee charged, New School Presbyterians had rendered the plan

36. Bacon to Parson Cooke, September 29, 1852, in Bacon Family Papers.

37. *Proceedings of the General Convention of Congregational Ministers and Delegates*, 9–11, 13, 14, 53–60; *Independent*, October 14, 1852.

38. *Proceedings of the General Convention of Congregational Ministers and Delegates*, 16–17, 23, 64.

"unfavorable to the spread and permanence of the Congregational polity, and even the real harmony of these Christian communities." While Bacon and other members of the committee urged both denominations to exercise a "spirit of love," the delegates unanimously endorsed the call to end the plan and to "maintain vigilantly the Congregational privileges."[39] Though largely defensive in nature, this action represented a bold move toward denominationalism. Once again, Bacon and other like-minded Congregationalists could not decide whether to pursue denominational cooperation or competition.

The convention was not consistent in its actions, however, for at the same time that it embarked upon an aggressive building program and repealed the Plan of Union, it also unanimously endorsed the American Home Missionary Society, despite some western concerns that the society's operations favored the Presbyterians. But the convention was deeply divided over the AHMS's assistance to churches that included slaveholding members. Bacon moved that the matter be referred to a special committee on home missions, consisting of one representative from each state in attendance. This committee divided 9–6 in favor of a resolution that "slaveholding churches"—those which accepted masters who used slaves for profit—ought not to receive assistance from the society. The minority report, on the other hand, declared that because the Gospel tended to correct all social evils, the missionary societies must aid only those churches in the South that attempted to preach the Gospel in such a way as to mitigate the oppressions of slavery.[40]

Hoping to strengthen relations between eastern and western Congregationalists and to cement support for the AHMS, Bacon searched for a middle ground between the majority and minority reports, neither of which accepted the abolitionists' argument that slaveholding was a sin *per se*. He took considerable pride in the fact that he once again stood between contending forces on the slavery issue, noting that "I am somewhat in the habit of standing by myself . . . in a state of 'between-ity' in relation to parties on questions connected with slavery." Indeed, his search for a centrist position had become rather predictable, no matter the specific point debated. It was as if he weighed the competing arguments and came as close as he could to splitting the difference. He did not necessarily eschew principles; rather, he considered himself a principled pragmatist intent upon building a broad consensus for effective action by fashioning language that the largest possible number of antislavery Americans could support. In the Albany Convention debate on slavery he especially expressed his opposition to the majority report's reference to "slaveholding churches," believing, much as he argued in the ABCFM debate on the Choctaw missions, that the AHMS should focus its attention on the fitness

---

39. *Ibid.*, 19–20; *Independent*, October 14, 1852.
40. *Proceedings of the General Convention of Congregational Ministers and Delegates*, 20, 77–83.

and fidelity of the missionaries, not the state of discipline in the churches they presided over. If the churches must first end all connection with slavery, he warned, the missionaries could not preach to all listeners. Yet he also was not pleased with the language of the minority report, for it spoke only of the Gospel mitigating the effects of slavery, not leading to its abolition. Something "stronger and more definite" was required, he reasoned.[41]

The problem, in Bacon's opinion, was that while nearly all Congregationalists opposed slavery in the territories and favored abolition wherever the federal government had jurisdiction, they fundamentally disagreed on the question of church discipline as it applied to slavery. In order to establish common ground among the delegates, he presented a compromise resolution that narrowed the language of the majority report by stipulating that only masters who held slaves for profit should be excommunicated, but also strengthened the minority report by declaring that the Gospel would "speedily" end slavery and that the AHMS must provide aid only to churches that testified against the system. The matter was then recommitted to the committee that dealt with home missions, which reported a resolution close to Bacon's that the convention overwhelmingly supported.[42] Once again, he had wielded enormous influence within the Congregational Church.

Bacon's actions at the Albany Convention were instrumental in establishing a strong basis for cooperation between most eastern and western Congregationalists. During the months following the convention, he labored to help raise the fifty thousand dollars pledged for church building in the West and frequently insisted that Congregationalists had a right to establish churches wherever they wished without Presbyterians slandering or distrusting them. Angered by the New School Presbyterians' "party spirit" and by what he considered disproportionate assistance given to them by the AHMS, he even came to suggest that Congregationalists contribute to the AHMS on the condition that the funds go to Congregational churches.[43]

In addition, Bacon was the guiding force behind the founding of the American Congregational Union, which manifested, and served as a catalyst for, the further development of a denominational consciousness among Congregationalists. The ACU, with Bacon as its president for many years, gained broad support among Congregationalists, though some within the church charged that it sought to im-

---

41. *Ibid.*, 83–84; *Independent,* October 21, 1852.

42. *Proceedings of the General Convention of Congregational Ministers and Delegates,* 85–86; *Independent,* October 21, November 4, 1852.

43. Jonathan Blanchard to Bacon, October 7, 1856, Henry C. Bowen to Bacon, December 2, 1852, in Bacon Family Papers; *Independent,* January 6, April 14, 1853, June 15, 1854, July 12, 26, 1855; *Proceedings of the General Convention of Congregational Ministers and Delegates,* 92–93; Bacon, "Hodge on Presbyterianism," 22–29.

pose a centralized authority on local churches. Clearly defensive on this matter, Bacon consistently maintained that it was a nonsectarian organization that sought to preserve a record of the Congregational Church in America and to promote evangelical knowledge and the Congregational polity. In its early years, the ACU printed a yearbook that listed Congregational churches and ministers, but it struggled and nearly went bankrupt.[44]

Bacon's efforts at the Albany Convention and on behalf of the ACU certainly strengthened ties among Congregationalists, but they also helped to exacerbate tensions between Congregationalists and New School Presbyterians and to place the American Home Missionary Society in an awkward position. Because the churches the society subsidized were often Presbyterian, during the early and middle 1850s both eastern and western antislavery Congregationalists pressured the AHMS to declare that it would aid no churches with slaveholding members unless there was evidence that they temporarily held them under the "law of love." These developments further alienated New Schoolers, intensified their concentration on their own missions, and accelerated the southern New School churches' withdrawal from the AHMS.[45]

The home missionary society's gradual move toward firmer antislavery ground was deemed inadequate by many Congregational abolitionists, while it drove some conservatives in the church, including Gerard Hallock and Leonard Woods, into the Southern Aid Society, which subsidized slaveholding churches. Once again, Bacon occupied the middle ground. He, like a large majority of Congregationalists, remained steadfastly loyal to the AHMS and its definition of "free missions" as ones "where the missionary is free to follow his own judgment as to what the Scriptures teach concerning the proper method of abolishing slavery." Bacon, however, was deeply troubled by the refusal of southern New School churches to discipline slaveholders or to permit the General Assembly to investigate their practices. This failure to discipline masters, even for the "grossest oppression," he concluded in 1854, was "ever troublesome" and "growing more delicate and perplexing." Although he and his editorial associates acknowledged the difficulty that northern New Schoolers experienced in their attempts to investigate the practices of southerners, they repeatedly urged them to pressure their southern brethren to explain their practices and to accept secession if no action was forthcoming. When nothing happened, they chided New Schoolers for placing church unity and competition with the Old

44. N. E. Eggleston to Bacon, March 16, May 5, August 10, 1853, Joseph S. Clark to Bacon, May 21, 1853, sermon of October 29, 1854, in Bacon Family Papers; *Address of Rev. Drs. Edwards, Amasa Park, Truman Marcellus Post, and Leonard Bacon, at the Anniversary of the American Congregational Union, May, 1854* (New York, 1854), 127–31; *Independent*, May 4, 18, 1854, May 17, 1855.

45. Howard, *Conscience and Slavery*, 170–71; Griffin, *Their Brothers' Keepers*, 187–88.

School above forceful action against "concrete enormities" within the church.[46] It became increasingly clear to Bacon that he had precious little influence with the northern New Schoolers and none with their southern brethren. If anything, his sharp attacks on the New Schoolers' denominational tendencies and his aggressive advocacy of Congregational rights and interests made it increasingly difficult for him to gain a hearing with any Presbyterians.

In the final analysis, Bacon chose to criticize New School Presbyterians above all for holding to a system of church government that encouraged "timid declarations" against slavery out of fear that any fundamental differences on the issue would create agitation within the church's General Assembly. Because northern New Schoolers were compelled to recognize slaveholding southerners as members in good standing, however lax their discipline concerning slavery, it was, he wrote in 1852, "every way better . . . to separate from the New School Presbyterian Church because of its Presbyterianism, than to do so under the plea that its General Assembly has shown an unchristian reluctance to testify against the wickedness of slavery." Thus, notwithstanding his very real frustration with the New Schoolers on the issue of slaveholders in the churches, his own concern that Congregationalists might assume too dogmatic a stance on this matter prevented him from categorically condemning the New School for failing to take decisive action. The southern New Schoolers' secession from the church in 1857 redeemed it in the eyes of most Congregationalists, but this development did little to heal the denominational rift. Northern New Schoolers continued to leave the AHMS, which ultimately became a Congregational missionary society, and Bacon and other Congregationalists remained highly critical of New School Presbyterians for their sectarianism.[47]

Nevertheless, while Congregationalists were able to find considerable common ground on such matters as expanding the church in the West and combating the New School's denominational spirit and its failure to discipline slaveholders in its southern churches, they were at times deeply divided on issues relating to theology and church government. The controversy in Connecticut surrounding Horace Bushnell, a longtime friend and colleague of Bacon, is a case in point. Bushnell, pastor of North Church in Hartford, was perhaps the most influential mid-nineteenth-century critic of the prevailing evangelical emphasis upon revival activity and conversion. Although he never rejected the principal evangelical concepts,

46. *Independent,* January 12, 1854, June 12, 1856. For evidence of widespread support for the AHMS among Congregationalists, see *Report on the Relations of the American Home Missionary Society to Slavery,* esp. 19–27; Evans, "Abolitionism in the Illinois Churches," 194–95. The Southern Aid Society is discussed in Howard, *Conscience and Slavery,* 121–31. For Bacon's definition of "free missions," see Bacon to Dr. Pomeroy, January 18, 1855, in Bacon Family Papers.

47. *Independent,* December 16, 1852, January 20, 1853, June 9, 1859, June 7, 1860; *Minutes of the General Association of Connecticut* (1859), 20.

and indeed considered himself an orthodox Congregationalist, he criticized the formalized and ritualistic nature of revivals and denied that they should be equated with the whole of the Christian experience. In perhaps his most influential work, *Christian Nurture,* published in 1847, he called upon the church to return to its historic emphasis upon the organic relationship between parents and children and asserted that it was entirely possible for children to grow up as Christians and never know themselves to be otherwise. In his most controversial book, *God in Christ,* published in 1849, he urged Christians to abandon the idea of Unity and Trinity in favor of the simpler concept of Father, Son, and Holy Ghost. Moreover, while proclaiming the divinity of Christ, he argued that the doctrine of the Trinity was descriptive not of God's being but of the modes of self-disclosure by which God was made known.[48]

Because Bushnell drew from both conservative and liberal strands of evangelical thought, it is not surprising that his provocative views were criticized by Taylorites as well as Bennet Tyler, Joel Hawes, Nathaniel Hewit, and other conservative Congregationalists. Concerned that these men might seek to expel him from his pastorate, Bushnell turned to Bacon for assistance, assuring him that "when you become a heretic I will try to do as much for you." But confronted with a barrage of criticism from numerous clergymen and religious newspapers and journals, he was uncertain how even Bacon and his editorial associates at the *Independent* would respond to his ideas. "I hope," he wrote Bacon, "you are not all going to cast me out as a reprobate, if so let me know it."[49]

In fact, Bacon's theological views had been evolving over the years, and some of these changes carried him in the same directions that Bushnell was moving. Neither man had ever been entirely comfortable or successful in generating revivals in his church, and both were moving away from an emphasis on induced religious fervor. Moreover, they both wished to avoid a renewal of the doctrinal conflict of the 1830s, which Bacon termed a "passion for heresy-hunting," and increasingly disliked metaphysical expositions of Christianity. In a sermon marking his twenty-fifth year as pastor of Center Church, Bacon, much like Bushnell, disavowed any identification with a theological party. While Bushnell adhered to a progressive orthodoxy, Bacon stood forth, in a somewhat similar manner, as a flexible centrist. Sympathizing with innovations in theology while also seeking to avoid "disputable novelties," he occupied a position halfway between cautious evangelicals, such as Albert Barnes and George Duffield, and the radical perfectionism of Oberlin. He

---

48. For treatments of Bushnell's theology, see for example, Claude Welch, *Protestant Thought in the Nineteenth Century,* vol. I, *1799–1870* (New Haven, 1972), 262–65; William A. Johnson, *Nature and the Supernatural in the Theology of Horace Bushnell* (Lund, Netherlands, 1963), 12, 14, 18–24.

49. Smith, *Changing Conceptions of Original Sin,* 145–48; Horace Bushnell to Bacon, December 18, 1848, March 30, 1849, in Bacon Family Papers.

clearly shared Bushnell's willingness to accept change in the New England theology. In a *New Englander* article he maintained that such change was always filled with danger but was often beneficial in that "the vital truths of the evangelical system" were "contemplated in a clearer light and with a wider view of their relations, and that thus they are more adequately appreciated." Bushnell challenged widely held doctrinal interpretations; likewise, Bacon came to base his theology not so much on the standard systems of theology as on his own study of the Bible. Indeed, he hoped that his theology would become "exclusively Biblical."[50]

In response to widespread criticism of *Christian Nurture* and *God in Christ,* Bacon expressed confidence in Bushnell's intelligence, integrity, and piety. He believed that Bushnell's arguments represented an imaginative blend of New and Old School thought, and he rejected charges that Bushnell was a Unitarian. Moreover, he praised his friend for helping to turn evangelical Christians "from dogmas about Christ to Christ himself." Yet Bacon acknowledged that because he had, at one time, been concerned that Bushnell was drifting toward Unitarianism, he understood why Bushnell's "mysterious idiosyncracies" had led many people to doubt his orthodoxy. He was especially critical of what he considered careless speculation in *God in Christ,* which he believed created "all sorts of misapprehension and logical misconstruction." He considered Bushnell's theory regarding the Trinity particularly "unsatisfactory" and "painful to many a devout and not unintelligent reader."[51]

Bushnell reacted to this mixed appraisal of his work with equanimity, informing Bacon that "it is really refreshing to me to read something on my book that is intelligent." Relatively few people, however, joined Bacon in defending Bushnell's right to express his theological views within the bounds of orthodoxy. Hawes, for example, warned Bacon and his colleagues that if the *Independent* endorsed doctrines "directly subversive of the standard theology of our New England ministers and churches and all of evangelical Christendom," he and like-minded clergymen would cease to support the paper.[52]

Hawes and other conservatives were determined to bring Bushnell to trial for heresy. But it proved difficult for Bushnell's enemies to remove him from his pastor-

50. Bacon, *A Sermon to the First Church and Society in New Haven, 10th March, 1850,* 5–12; sermons of February 6, April 3, May 22, 1853, March 5, 1854, in Bacon Family Papers; *Independent,* January 8, 1849; Leonard Bacon, "Moses Stuart," *New Englander,* X (February, 1852), 52; Bacon, "Evangelical Alliance," 319–20.

51. Leonard Bacon, "Concerning a Recent Chapter of Ecclesiastical History," *New Englander,* XXXVIII (September, 1879), 701–705, 712; Leonard Bacon, "Review of Bushnell's 'God in Christ,'" *New Englander,* VII (May, 1849), 324–25; *Independent,* April 26, June 21, 1849.

52. Horace Bushnell to Bacon, May 14, 1849, Joel Hawes to Bacon, March 7, 1949, in Bacon Family Papers. See also Theodore T. Munger, *Horace Bushnell: Preacher and Theologian* (Boston, 1899), 142–44; John Wright Buckham, *Progressive Religious Thought in America* (Boston, 1919), 31–32.

ate, for his congregation was devoted to him and the Hartford Central Association refused to bring heresy charges. Despite harsh criticism from some *Independent* readers, Bacon was determined to support his friend in the name of maintaining harmony and tolerance within the church. Much as he did in defending western Congregationalists against charges of doctrinal irregularities, he now insisted that the Congregational polity was peculiarly adapted to the promotion of unity within diversity, rather than the rigid uniformity that he identified with Presbyterianism.[53]

During the early 1850s, the Fairfield West Association repeatedly attempted to bring Bushnell to trial. The issue came to a climax in 1853, when, in its third attempt, the association presented a demand, signed by fifty Congregational ministers in the state, that the Hartford Central Association be excluded from the state ecclesiastical body for protecting Bushnell and, thereby, sanctioning "a subversion of all vital and fundamental doctrines of Christianity." Bacon was deeply troubled by this action. Whatever his reservations concerning Bushnell's theological views, he was determined to resist what he considered an attempt by a "Presbyterianizing faction" to carry out a vendetta against Bushnell and his local association as a means of imposing Presbyterian forms on Connecticut Congregationalism. He was certain that the Saybrook Platform, which had opened the door for the creation of consociations in Connecticut, had never really been enforced and therefore was not binding on the General Association.[54]

At the 1853 meeting of the General Association, Bacon's view of the proper nature of the Congregational polity prevailed in a case that was only indirectly related to the Bushnell controversy. When the newly formed New Haven Central Association, of which Bacon was a member, petitioned for admission to the General Association, Nathaniel Hewit and others who opposed Bushnell argued that this local association was merely a group of congenial ministers, not a consociation of churches. The General Association ultimately accepted Bacon's contention that the Saybrook Platform could not limit local associations in connection with the state organization. The more crucial issue before the General Association, however, was whether the Saybrook Platform gave the state body jurisdiction over the Bushnell case. Following heated exchanges between Bushnell's critics and friends, Bacon, once more acting as a conciliator, adroitly offered a resolution that succeeded in bringing the debate to an end. The General Association, he stated, had no fellowship with the opinions imputed to Bushnell. But he added the proviso that the division between the Hartford Central and Fairfield West Associations in-

53. Horace Bushnell to Bacon, October 13, 1849, W. Clarke to Bacon, April 1, 1850, in Bacon Family Papers; *Independent,* November 1, 1849.

54. *Minutes of the General Association of Connecticut* (1850), 17–18, (1852), 8–9, (1853), 76–77; *Independent,* June 30, 1853, June 15, 1854.

volved differences of judgment on a question of fact and interpretation—whether Bushnell had so contradicted certain doctrines that there should be no fellowship with him—not essential differences of faith on great Christian truths. Because this question must be determined by appropriate evidence, he concluded, the General Association could not pronounce its opinion "without usurping that power of ju-dicial review and control over the particular Associations which has never been conceded to."[55]

The General Association's adoption of Bacon's resolution, with only one dis-senting vote, gave each of the contending parties a partial victory. Once again, Bacon had succeeded in shaping a resolution that enabled each group to conclude that it had carried the day on what really mattered. By explicitly rejecting the opin-ions imputed to Bushnell, it placated most conservatives, but it also satisfied Bush-nell's friends by implying that he in fact was not chargeable with the views for which he had been repudiated. For Bacon, the association's ruling represented a dual triumph: it vindicated his conviction that Connecticut Congregationalism was not even semi-Presbyterian in nature and prevented what he feared was an inexora-ble movement toward a permanent division among Congregationalists in the state.[56]

The resolution of the Bushnell case, however, did not presage a period free of controversy for Bacon. If anything, the mid- and late 1850s proved to be among the stormiest years in both his public and private life. As the nation moved ever closer to a violent sectional confrontation, his defense of northern interests and his attacks on the slaveholding class and its northern allies became increasingly harsh. In addi-tion, he stood at the center of a contentious campaign to force the American Tract Society to take a stand against slavery. Finally, he was compelled to deal with ex-tremely painful family problems involving his sister Delia and his brother David.

55. *Minutes of the General Association of Connecticut* (1853), 5–7; diary entry for June 22, 23, 1853, in Bacon Family Papers; *Minutes of the General Association of Connecticut* (1853), 11; *Independent,* June 30, 1853.

56. See *Independent,* June 20, July 21, 1853, June 15, 1854.

10

KANSAS AND THE
REPUBLICAN PARTY

T HE relative calm that followed the passage of the Compromise of 1850
was shattered in 1854 by the furor surrounding the Kansas-Nebraska Act.
Seeking to placate southerners, believing soil conditions and climate
would discourage the spread of slavery into the region, and desiring the economic
development of the vast trans-Mississippi area for the benefit of white settlers, Stephen A. Douglas proposed a bill that effectively repealed the Missouri Compromise.
Douglas hoped that by avoiding mention of the 1820 compromise line and by
couching the popular sovereignty doctrine in the language of grass-roots democracy, his bill would gain quick passage. But this was not to be. Indeed, Douglas'
proposal mobilized northern antislavery opinion more than the Fugitive Slave Act
had and completed the destruction of the Whig party. It also reinforced many of
the existing reasons for hostility to the expansion of slavery: moral antipathy to the
institution; the desire to limit the political power of the South and to extend the
free labor system to the West, thereby preserving the values of social mobility and
opportunity; economic self-interest; and the fear that blacks would be brought into
the territories.[1]

The religious community led the charge against the Kansas-Nebraska Act.
Within weeks of the bill's introduction, Bacon and other clergymen in New
England and New York delivered over three thousand anti-Nebraska sermons,
and religious newspapers, including the *Independent,* attacked the legislation as a

---

1. On the Kansas-Nebraska Act, see Robert W. Johannsen, *Stephen A. Douglas* (New York, 1973),
402–18; William W. Freehling, *The Road to Disunion,* vol. I, *Secessionists at Bay, 1776–1854* (New York,
1990), 536–65. On northern opposition to the Kansas-Nebraska Act, see Michael F. Holt, *The Political
Crisis of the 1850s* (New York, 1978), 148–49; Sewell, *Ballots for Freedom,* 257–60.

breach of Christian ethics. Even the conservative New York *Observer* warned that if the Missouri Compromise were set aside, it would be "the end of all compromises."[2]

Bacon was among the first northerners to speak out against the bill. During the fierce debate that extended through the first half of 1854, he harshly and persistently attacked it in speeches, published letters, sermons, petitions, articles, and editorials. He and his editorial associates condemned Douglas' proposal as unconstitutional and contrary to public safety and national prosperity. But they above all emphasized that it was "a religious question that concerns the progress of Christianity." For Congress to permit slavery to take root where it was not intended to exist, they angrily declared, would be a crime against humanity and Christianity that might well lead to the dissolution of the Union, civil war, and slave insurrection.[3]

During these months, Bacon also appealed directly to members of Congress to reject the Kansas-Nebraska Act. In a letter to Democratic senator Isaac Toucey of Connecticut, which was published in the *Independent* and other newspapers, he admonished Toucey that to vote for the bill would make him guilty of all the injustices associated with slavery. Henry Ward Beecher assured Bacon that his letter would bring the North "at last upon a firm, *united,* frank ground." Others, however, condemned him as a "consistent abolitionist" and a partisan Whig; Toucey, unfazed by Bacon's plea, warned that if the Whigs and abolitionists had their way, the South would secede and the federal government would be destroyed.[4]

Efforts by Bacon and other anti-Nebraska clergymen to petition Congress met with greater success. In mid-February Edward Beecher met with Bacon and a few other men in New Haven and asked them to mobilize ministers in the area in support of a mass petition. Ultimately, 3,050 clergymen from all the Protestant denominations in New England signed the petition, which was presented in the United States Senate by Edward Everett. Although Everett moved to table the petition, Douglas insisted that it be read, thus giving him an opportunity to assert that the clergy must preach immortal truths, not political principles, and that they were bound to respect the authority of the state. Most northern ministers, including Bacon, thoroughly disagreed with Douglas. While disclaiming any intention of

2. McKivigan, *The War Against Proslavery Religion,* 154–55; Edmund Emmett Lacy, "Protestant Newspaper Reaction to the Kansas-Nebraska Bill of 1854," *Rocky Mountain Social Science Journal,* VII (October, 1970), 63–66; New York *Observer,* February 16, 1854.

3. *Independent,* January 19, February 2, 9, April 6, 1854.

4. *Independent,* February 16, 1854; New Haven *Palladium,* February 28, 1854; Henry Ward Beecher to Bacon, February 18, 1854, Richard S. Storrs, Jr., to Bacon, February 18, 1854, in Bacon Family Papers; New Haven *Daily Register,* February 18, 1854; Isaac Toucey to Horace Salvin, October 28, 1854, in Isaac Toucey Papers, Connecticut Historical Society, Hartford, Conn.

meddling in issues that were "properly political," Bacon insisted that when the government acted unjustly and dishonorably, ministers had "no right to be silent or neutral." Thus, he ridiculed Douglas' outburst against the clergy's petitions as "too ludicrous to move our indignation."[5]

Although the minority in Bacon's church who were Democrats deeply resented his response to Douglas' speech, as they had his earlier attacks on Polk, the Compromise of 1850, and the Fugitive Slave Act, he persisted in his endeavor to arouse the northern public against what he considered "an intentional crime." He and several other New Haven pastors, as well as Woolsey, met at Bacon's home to plan a public meeting to be held in early March, for which he drew up resolutions. At the meeting held in Brewster Hall, Bacon, in the major speech of the evening, presented a pointed and sweeping indictment of both slavery and the Nebraska bill. Not only was slavery "a violation of inalienable human rights," he stated, but its extension into the territories would sacrifice the free laboring classes, destroy any hope of future compromise with the South, and defy the will of God. In a statement that foreshadowed his later efforts on behalf of the Emigrant Aid Society, he also warned darkly that antislavery northerners must be prepared to mobilize fighters who would go to the territories with the pioneer's axe in one hand and "the rifle in the other hand—the symbol of conflict with barbarism."[6]

As the vote in the Senate drew near, Bacon intensified his efforts to rally the anti-Nebraska forces. In a *New Englander* article he termed the situation more critical to the destiny of the nation than anything since the adoption of the Constitution. Resigned to the bill's passage, he ultimately came to argue that the North must act vigorously to counter the tyranny of the slave interests by electing representatives who would combat any attempt to nationalize slavery, by declaring all people in the territories to be free under the Constitution, and by passing personal liberty laws in the states.[7]

With the passage of the Kansas-Nebraska Act, Kansas became both a central

5. Diary entries for February 13–15, 1854, Edward Beecher to Bacon, February 16, 1854, sermon of March, 1854, in Bacon Family Papers; Robert Meredith, *The Politics of the Universe: Edward Beecher, Abolition, and Orthodoxy* (Nashville, 1963), 198–99; *Speeches and Other Proceedings at the Anti-Nebraska Meetings, Held in New Haven, Connecticut, March 8th and 10th, 1854* (New Haven, 1854), 15–16; *Independent,* March 23, 1854; Leonard Bacon, *Two Sermons Preached to the First Church in New Haven, On a Day of Fast, viz., Good Friday, the 10th of April, 1857* (New Haven, 1857), 30; Leonard Bacon, "Morality of the Nebraska Bill," *New Englander,* XII (May, 1854), 328, 330, 335.

6. Sermon of March, 1854, in Bacon Family Papers; *Speeches and Other Proceedings at the Anti-Nebraska Meetings,* 4, 10–17, 20. Bacon presented a similar speech in towns near New Haven. E. R. Gilbert to Bacon, March 1, 1854, diary entry for March 9, 1854, in Bacon Family Papers.

7. Bacon, "Morality of the Nebraska Bill," 304–306, 312, 314–17, 319–20, 326; *Independent,* June 8, July 20, 1854.

symbol of and an actual battleground in the conflict between the North and the South. Convinced that the struggle would determine the future of the West, and hence the nation, growing numbers of northerners now sought to assist the emigration of free settlers to Kansas. Numerous Kansas leagues and committees were formed under the auspices of the New England Emigrant Aid Society and other organizations to defend against the incursions into Kansas by the "Border Ruffians" from Missouri, who antislavery northerners believed threatened the lives of God-fearing northern freeholders. Eli Thayer, a leader of the New England organization, met several times in 1854 with Bacon, Woolsey, Silliman, and other antislavery New Haveners and spoke twice in Center Church in an effort to mobilize support for financing emigration to Kansas. In response to Thayer's pleas, Bacon and other leading men in the community founded the Charles B. Lines Colony, which initially consisted of seventy-nine well-armed men.[8]

Bacon addressed several meetings in New Haven in early 1856 that raised funds for people who had chosen to emigrate to Kansas but lacked weapons. At one of these meetings, held in North Church, Henry Ward Beecher eloquently appealed for rifles for the Kansas settlers. Bacon fully agreed with Beecher's contention that the free-soil forces had the right to arm themselves in self-defense, terming this "legitimate Kansas work." His position on this matter stands in marked contrast to his entreaties to whites, as well as blacks accused of being fugitives, to avoid violence, even in self-defense, in the aftermath of the Fugitive Slave Act. This apparent contradiction may be explained in part by the fact that in the early 1850s federal marshals, not proslavery ruffians from Missouri, would have been the targets of violence by those who acted in the name of self-defense. Perhaps more important for Bacon, much as for some abolitionists who increasingly espoused violent means to destroy slavery, Kansas appears to have deepened his frustration and rage as well as his sense that Americans were engaged in a desperate struggle in which freedom, constitutional rights, and God's laws were at stake.[9]

The continuing clashes between the proslavery and free-soil forces in Kansas

---

8. Ralph V. Harlow, "The Rise and Fall of the Kansas Aid Movement," *American Historical Review*, XLI (1935), 7; Eli Thayer, *A History of the Kansas Crusade: Its Friends and Its Foes* (New York, 1889), 55, 130–32, 188; James Dwight to Bacon, July 12, 1854, Edward E. Hale to Bacon, June 15, 1855, in Bacon Family Papers; Bruser, "Political Antislavery in Connecticut," 323–24. On the importance many Americans attached to the Kansas situation, see John Niven, *The Coming of the Civil War, 1837–1861* (Arlington Heights, Ill., 1990), 87–95, 104–109.

9. Fulton and Thomas, *Benjamin Silliman*, 259–60; Bruser, "Political Antislavery in Connecticut," 324; *Independent*, February 14, 1856; Leonard Bacon, "The Moral of Harper's Ferry," *New Englander*, XVII (November, 1859), 1071; see Jane H. Pease and William H. Pease, "Confrontation and Abolition in the 1850's," *Journal of American History*, LVIII (1972), 923–37; Dillon, *The Abolitionists*, 219–43.

kept emotions at a high pitch throughout the North. But the caning of Charles Sumner in the Senate chamber by a southern congressman perhaps generated even greater indignation among northerners than the incidents in the distant, sparsely settled territory, for it seemed to represent a direct attack on free speech. Bacon was so infuriated by this incident that prior to an indignation meeting at which he, the governor of Connecticut, and other prominent citizens spoke, Rebecca expressed the hope that her father would not "take the roof off." As he saw it, the Kansas depredations and the "murderous assault" on Sumner were mutually reinforcing. Resistance to these and other assaults of the slave interests were necessary prerequisites not only for a religious awakening but, he implied, for something akin to a religious war that would "purge the land of the guilt of oppression." He was confident, as he noted in a stirring speech in October, 1856, welcoming Governor Charles Robinson of Kansas, who was under federal indictment for refusing to acknowledge the legitimacy of the proslavery legislature, that God's law would ultimately vindicate right and justice in a struggle that might well culminate in massive bloodshed.[10]

The enactment of the Kansas-Nebraska Act and the escalation of violence in Kansas provided a powerful impetus for the formation of the Republican party. With the disintegration of the Second Party System in the early 1850s, Bacon and many other northerners were uncertain as to where to turn. Although Bacon tended to agree with the Democrats on the tariff and the National Bank issue, he saw no hope for them on the slavery question. But he also did not trust the Whigs, who he believed had been "thoroughly corrupted" by their compromises on slavery. Thus, as early as mid-1855 he urged the creation of a new antislavery party.[11]

Historians continue to debate the question of why growing numbers of northerners flocked to the Republican ranks in the mid- and late 1850s. Some point to northerners' dislike of the slaveholders and the South—especially as manifested in their emphasis upon the Slave Power conspiracy as the principal threat to republicanism—as the dominant factor motivating northerners to join the party. Others, however, point above all to the party's hostility toward slavery and its expansion as constituting the core of the party's ideology. Moreover, the party's identification with anti-Catholicism and its affinity with the antiliquor movement, according to

---

10. *Independent,* May 29, September 18, 1856; Rebecca to Frank Bacon, May 26, November 4, 1856, in Bacon Family Papers; New Haven *Morning Journal and Courier,* October 31, 1856. On the importance of the caning of Sumner in exacerbating sectional tensions, see Frederick J. Blue, *Charles Sumner and the Conscience of the North* (Arlington Heights, Ill., 1994), 93–98; William E. Gienapp, "The Crime Against Sumner: The Caning of Charles Sumner and the Rise of the Republican Party," *Civil War History,* XXV (1979), 218–45.

11. *Independent,* July 27, 1854, June 7, 1855.

some historians, projected an image of Protestant morality, middle-class respectability, and self-righteousness that appealed to many northern evangelicals.[12]

Bacon was drawn to the Republican party by all of these considerations, though some were clearly more compelling than others. For him, as with many other northerners, the rapid decline of the Whig party left little other choice but to join the fledgling Republican party, which appeared to embody their most cherished principles and values and to stand in opposition to developments they deemed most threatening to the nation's well-being. Like many northern evangelicals who joined the Republican party, he had long been a vocal temperance advocate. Frustrated by the failure of the no-license and local option efforts, these activists came increasingly to recognize the difficulty of devising legal solutions for intemperance. Many of them turned to the state governments for action, believing that prohibition would remove the aura of respectability from the licensing system and fundamentally reshape community sentiment. In Maine in 1851, and then in Connecticut and eleven other northern states by 1855, statewide prohibition laws were passed, which contained stringent search-and-seizure clauses and imposed heavy fines and imprisonment on offenders.[13]

In many of these states, including Connecticut, Free-Soilers and antislavery Whigs tended to be strongly prohibitionist; Bacon's editorial associates and many of his clerical colleagues in New Haven and in the General Association endorsed the cause. He did not, however, actively promote the passage of the Connecticut prohibition law, for he doubted that the people would accept the invasion of privacy that the legislation entailed. Once it was enacted, he acquiesced in the law and urged that it be rigorously enforced. Yet the Democrats' refusal to enforce its provisions when they came to power reaffirmed his longstanding conviction that "law must express the aggregate sense of the people, or it will be resented . . . as an invasion of their right of liberty, and the reaction will be greater than the benefit."[14]

Indeed, Bacon was far from consistent even in his support of the principle of total abstinence. Although he had long argued that moderate drinking led almost

12. See, for example, Holt, *The Political Crisis of the 1850s*, 189–90, 194–96; Eric Foner, *Free Soil, Free Labor, Free Men: The Ideology of the Republican Party Before the Civil War* (New York, 1970), 40–72 passim; Sewell, *Ballots for Freedom*, 262–65, 281–85, 292–95; William Gienapp, "Nativism and the Creation of a Republican Majority in the North Before the Civil War," *Journal of American History*, LXXII (1985), 529–59.

13. Tyrrell, *Sobering Up*, 240–43, 252–58, 260–65, 270–72.

14. William E. Gienapp, *The Origins of the Republican Party, 1852–1856* (New York, 1987), 52–55; *Independent*, November 14, 1851, August 3, 1854, March 29, 1855; J. Robert Lane, *A Political History of Connecticut During the Civil War* (Washington, D.C., 1941), 15, 18–21, 41–42; sermon of January 25, 1852, lecture, 1856, in Bacon Family Papers; *Letter to Rev. Leonard Bacon, D. D. of New Haven, Conn., from John Marsh, D.D.* (New York, 1865), 10–11.

invariably to intoxication, he now rejected the ultraist argument that consumption of alcohol in any degree or under any circumstances was sinful, stating that it exaggerated the distinction between the temperate person and the temperance advocate. He, in fact, purchased beer on several occasions in 1858, probably for his brother, David. If he evaded the law, he certainly was not alone, for many Connecticut residents who opposed prohibition came to disregard it. Because the prohibition laws were so controversial and divisive, the Republican leadership tended to downplay the issue wherever possible.[15] Certainly, the liquor issue was a minor consideration moving Bacon toward the party.

Many who joined the Republican party also held in common a deep-seated hostility toward Catholics, and the party effectively employed the nativist theme to recruit supporters in Connecticut and other northeastern states. The Know-Nothing movement's novelty and its rituals, as well as its assault on "alien" influences in American life, appealed to many people who feared job competition, Catholicism, and the immigrant vote. In the early and mid-1850s, the Know-Nothings swept to power in Connecticut and a number of other states; and in New Haven, whose foreign-born residents constituted approximately 25 percent of the total population, the nativists elected the mayor and most members of the Common Council.[16]

Bacon had remained active in the anti-Catholic cause, especially as it was directed against the papacy and in defense of religious liberty. In the late·1840s he had helped to found the American and Foreign Christian Union, which sought to proselytize American and European Catholics and to advance the cause of religious freedom, and in 1851 he welcomed Louis Kossuth, the Hungarian patriot, to New Haven as the representative of "true constitutional liberty" in opposition to Catholic despotism. He even attempted, quite unsuccessfully, to recruit Bishop John Hughes of New York to the cause of religious liberty.[17]

Bacon was by no means free of religious bigotry. In an 1854 sermon, for example, he termed many Catholics "mere infidels, bitterly prejudiced against the name

15. Leonard Bacon, "The Christian Basis of the Temperance Reformation," *American Temperance Preacher,* I (January, 1848), 1–11; diary entries for March 11, May 20, August 18, September 29, 1858, in Bacon Family Papers; Tyrrell, *Sobering Up,* 280–81, 304–305; Janice Law Trecker, *Preachers, Rebels, and Traders: Connecticut, 1818–1865* (Chester, Conn., 1975), 53.

16. On the rise of the Know-Nothings as a powerful political force, see Gienapp, "Nativism and the Creation of a Republican Majority in the North Before the Civil War," 529–59; Tyler Anbinder, *Nativism and Slavery: The Northern Know Nothings and the Politics of the 1850s* (New York, 1992), 104–105. On the Know-Nothings in Connecticut, see John Niven, *Connecticut for the Union: The Role of the State in the Civil War* (New Haven, 1965), 11.

17. *Questions Answered in Regard to the American and Foreign Christian Union* (New York, 1849), 2; *Independent,* May 9, 1850, November 27, 1851, May 13, 1852, May 12, 1853.

of Christianity." Yet he continued to be motivated by a complex mix of principle and expediency in opposing the extreme nativists. He urged Americans to welcome and seek to assimilate Catholic immigrants in the hope of accelerating their conversion to Protestantism, and he condemned the efforts of George B. Cheever and other nativists to impose the Protestant Bible on Catholics in the public schools as "unjust and impolitic" as well as contrary to the "great Puritan principle of religious freedom." He and his editorial associates were especially critical of the Know-Nothings. Although they were willing to accept a temporary exclusion of Irish immigrants from officeholding as a warning to "petty politicians who trade for votes"—a decidedly undemocratic proposal in its own right—they considered the Know-Nothing cause "virtually an order of *Protestant Jesuits*." More important, they believed antislavery to be far more significant than nativism as a basis for political action. They reminded their readers that the American party candidate, Millard Fillmore, would do nothing to protect freedom in the territories or in the entire nation, and repeatedly charged that the nativists sought to divert attention from the slavery issue. Ultimately, the immigrant and Catholic issues were relegated to a secondary place in the new Republican party; they clearly had little to do with Bacon's decision to become a Republican.[18]

For many northerners, including Bacon, slavery was the decisive factor that determined their political loyalty. In his *Independent* editorials he frequently pointed out that the central question to be decided was whether Americans were to fellowship with slavery. He shared with many other Republicans the belief that if the party came to power and abolished slavery wherever the federal government had jurisdiction, it would eventually generate a "moral influence" capable of ending slavery in the South.[19] As much as he wished to see slavery destroyed throughout the United States, however, he considered the fundamental question before the American people to be whether the institution would be legislated into existence in the territories, and perhaps throughout the nation. He also remained critical of what he considered the abolitionists' "indiscriminate invective."[20]

18. Sermons of May 23, 1852, August 27, November 30, 1854, Richard S. Storrs, Jr., to Bacon, June 24, 1853, in Bacon Family Papers; *Independent,* January 26, February 23, March 2, August 3, 31, October 19, 1854, June 26, 1856.

19. *Independent,* July 10, August 14, 1856, November 4, 1857; Bacon, *Two Sermons Preached to the First Church in New Haven, On a Day of Fasting,* 22–23; Leonard Bacon, *The Growth of the Kingdom of Heaven. A Discourse Before the Congregational Board of Education in the Tremont Temple, Boston, on the 26th of May, 1858* (Boston, 1858), 22–23; sermon of April 14, 1854, in Bacon Family Papers.

20. Leonard Bacon, "The President's Message," *New Englander,* XV (February, 1857), 25–27; Leonard Bacon, *The Jugglers Detected. A Discourse, Delivered by Request, in the Chapel Street Church, New Haven, December 30, 1860* (New Haven, 1861), 15–17; *Independent,* July 10, 1856, November 18, 1858, October 6, 1859, October 18, 1860, February 28, 1861.

Much like that of a growing number of Republicans, Bacon's rhetoric assumed an increasingly antisouthern tone during the mid- and late 1850s. Even as he refused to jettison the totally unrealistic "good slaveholder" doctrine, he insisted that all masters should be presumed guilty of sin until they proved otherwise. Instead of seeking to prove themselves "good slaveholders," of course, many masters defended the institution. Bacon praised James Henry Thornwell, a proslavery cleric and president of the University of South Carolina, who argued that the state might at least partially abolish slavery if masters remained antipaternalistic and thus anti-Christ. Yet at the same time, he could not accept Thornwell's defense of the system as a "permanent arrangement" sanctioned by the Bible. Indeed, during these years Bacon became ever more outspoken in his attacks on the southern churches, accusing them of having "apostacized from the first principles of righteousness."[21]

The distance that separated Bacon from the conservative Republicans, who tended to emphasize nativism, economic issues, party loyalty, and restoration of the Missouri Compromise line, was considerable. He shared with most Radicals and moderates in the party an abiding hatred of slavery and the Slave Power, as well as a growing animus toward the South. His career, like that of many moderate Republicans, had been shaped less by the slavery issue than had those of most Radicals. He also shared with the moderates an inclination to allow events to take a slower course toward emancipation than many Radicals desired. But in all, he stood with the Radicals in the pre–Civil War Republican party in consistently underscoring the moral dimension of the slavery issue, in viewing containment as a first step to universal emancipation, in emphasizing the need to denationalize the system, and in regarding the party as a means to the goal of liberty and demanding that it be abandoned if it did not seek to advance the antislavery cause.[22]

The *Independent* editors had long affirmed their attachment to principles and candidates rather than parties. They lauded the election of Nathaniel Banks as Speaker of the House of Representatives in 1856, and later that year they favored Salmon P. Chase, the darling of the Radicals, as the party's nominee. As John C. Frémont's stock rose within the party, however, they were prepared to endorse his candidacy so long as he was as resolute on the slavery issue as Chase, Banks, Sumner, and Seward. Once Frémont was nominated, they jumped on his bandwagon, proclaiming their attachment to "Free-soil, Free-speech, Free-men, and Frémont."

---

21. *Independent,* November 13, 1856; Leonard Bacon, "Thornwell on Slavery," *New Englander,* XII (February, 1854), 93–99; see Bacon, "The Southern Apostasy," 627, 633–34, 638–41, 644–45, 658–62; also *Independent,* December 29, 1853, March 3, 1854, December 31, 1857, December 22, 1859. For an analysis of Thornwell's criticism of defective paternalism among slaveholders, see William W. Freehling, *The Reintegration of American History: Slavery and the Civil War* (New York, 1994), 59–73.

22. On the ideological divisions within the pre–Civil War Republican party, see Foner, *Free Soil, Free Labor, Free Men,* 105–28, 139–41, 186–210, 310–13, *passim;* Sewell, *Ballots for Freedom,* 305–309.

While Bacon insisted that Frémont was "not a party candidate but really independent of all parties," he increasingly appealed to his readers as "fellow Republicans" and threw himself fully into the contest. He was, Rebecca noted, "driven—driven—driven—all the time" about the election, writing editorials, presenting speeches, and even inviting Frémont to stay at his home during Yale's commencement. In his final sermon prior to the election, he made the Democrats in Center Church "very mad," according to Rebecca, by urging his congregation to vote for the welfare of the nation, not for expediency or for sectional or business interests. During a torchlight parade for Frémont, factory workers stopped in front of Bacon's home, where they gave three cheers for him, and then three more when he came out the door.[23]

Although Democrat James Buchanan won the election, Bacon was buoyed by the fact that Frémont carried all but four northern states. Like many Republicans, he remained confident that southerners who opposed slavery and its expansion would somehow break free of the "bloody and ferocious despotism" that oppressed them, thus making the party truly national in scope. On a more ominous note, however, he feared that popular sovereignty would not permit the people to exclude slavery from the territories. Indeed, shortly after Buchanan's inauguration, the Supreme Court's southern majority declared in the *Dred Scott* case that the federal government could not prohibit slavery in the territories and that African Americans had no rights which whites were obligated to recognize. Because the race question tended to unite Democrats and divide Republicans, the Republican party devoted relatively little attention to the court's statement regarding blacks. But Bacon and his editorial associates were among those who strongly condemned this portion of the decision as both morally and legally wrong. Yet they were even more troubled by what they termed "this great outrage of judicial despotism," which Bacon warned would prevent the states from granting citizenship to free blacks and would make slavery national in its scope.[24]

Bacon held Buchanan partially responsible for the substance of the *Dred Scott* ruling, but he blamed the president even more for the continuing violence in Kan-

23. *Independent,* February 7, June 12, 19, 26, September 11, October 23, 1856; Leonard Woolsey to Rebecca Bacon, June 20, 1856, Leonard to Catherine Bacon, June 11, 1856, Bacon to John C. Frémont, June 27, July 31, 1856, Rebecca to Frank Bacon, November 11, 1856, sermon of November 2, 1856, in Bacon Family Papers.

24. Bacon, "The President's Message," 20, 22, 38; Leonard Bacon, "Buchanan on Kansas," *New Englander,* XV (November, 1857), 694; *Two Sermons Preached to the First Church in New Haven, On a Day of Fasting,* 32; *Independent,* November 13, 1856, March 12, 19, 26, April 9, 1857. On the Republican reaction to the *Dred Scott* decision, see Don E. Fehrenbacher, *Slavery, Law, and Politics: The Dred Scott Case in Historical Perspective* (New York, 1981), 230–43; Kenneth M. Stampp, *America in 1857: A Nation on the Brink* (New York, 1990), 104–109.

sas. Several months after the *Dred Scott* decision was rendered, he joined forty-two prominent Connecticut residents in sending a memorial that accused Buchanan of violating the Constitution by empowering Governor Robert Walker of Kansas to impose laws and magistrates upon an unwilling free-soil majority. Buchanan categorically rejected the memorialists' arguments and defended federal protection of the proslavery government in Kansas as well as Walker and the *Dred Scott* ruling. This, however, did not end the exchange, for Bacon was determined to add his voice to the dispute. In a *New Englander* article he condemned Buchanan as the central figure in "a traitorous conspiracy."[25]

Unlike his earlier advocacy of "urgent gradualism" and the "good slaveholder" concept, which had elicited the support of relatively few northerners or southerners, Bacon's wide-ranging assault on the Kansas-Nebraska Act had helped to rally large numbers of evangelical northerners to the cause of keeping the West free of slavery. The organization of the Republican party and its strong showing in the election of 1856 especially appeared to bode well for the antislavery forces. Nonetheless, there had been major setbacks along the way, including the enactment of the Kansas-Nebraska Act and the Supreme Court's decision in the *Dred Scott* case.

During these years, antislavery evangelicals also suffered a stinging defeat in their attempt to force the American Tract Society, one of the largest and most influential benevolent organizations in the nation, to speak out against slavery. Bacon had served as a director of the society since 1845, but it was not until the 1850s that he and other antislavery northerners began to challenge the ATS's leadership for failing to publish material related to slavery. In this struggle they achieved far less success than they had in the missionary society debates. Owing to the conservatives' control of the society's executive and publishing committees and their refusal to publish material that might offend any evangelical Christian, the groups that attempted to persuade the ATS to publish even mild criticism of slavery confronted nearly a hopeless task.[26]

Bacon excoriated the ATS especially for its refusal to criticize sinful practices that he believed so often characterized the master-slave relationship. By the mid-1850s, he had come to urge his readers to buy tracts from other organizations. There was, however, no simple solution to this problem, for the ATS had abundant capital and a sophisticated delivery system that made it virtually independent of outside pressure. In addition, the annual meetings were, as Bacon charged, "little more than a ceremony" and the election of officers "little less than a sham." Nevertheless,

---

25. Bacon, "Buchanan on Kansas," 682–92, 697; Horace Bushnell to Bacon, September 14, 1857, in Bacon Family Papers; *Independent,* October 1, 1857.

26. Leonard Bacon, "Responsibility in the Management of Societies," *New Englander,* V (January, 1847), 28–34; see also McKivigan, *The War Against Proslavery Religion,* 120–21.

because he feared that to establish a rival society would merely rid the ATS of the dissidents, he and many other dissatisfied northern evangelicals decided to work for reform within the society.[27]

Yet, much as he so often had done over the past three decades, Bacon instinctively used the ideological extremes as negative reference points in order to advance his argument in favor of moderation. The antislavery forces, he warned, must occupy a position between "Southern apostasy" and the doctrine of abolitionist come-outerism espoused by Parker Pillsbury. Nevertheless, he seemed especially sensitive to charges that he was a radical. For example, in response to harsh criticism from the New York *Observer* and other conservative newspapers, which labeled him an abolitionist and "a revolutionist," he denied any desire to replace the present ATS administration. This was not entirely a tactical move to disarm the society's supporters, for at the 1856 annual meeting he went out of his way to establish his conservative credentials. "I am not a disorganizer," he stated defensively. "I am not a radical reformer. I am a conservative man. . . . I wish to perpetuate and not paralyze the usefulness of this great institution." Indeed, Bacon was unwilling to give up on the ATS. Urged by William A. Hallock and other conservatives to save the society by resolving this conflict, at the 1856 meeting he offered a resolution to create an investigative committee that would report at the next meeting. Following a fierce debate, it passed overwhelmingly. Bacon and many other antislavery northerners were heartened by the committee's recommendation in 1857 that the ATS publish nonpolitical tracts which condemned evils associated with slavery. With his confidence in the society renewed, he now urged evangelicals to support the ATS. Southern protests, however, soon forced the organization to suppress circulation of a tract that merely encouraged masters to treat their slaves with Christian compassion.[28]

Outraged by the executive committee's reneging on its promise, Bacon called upon the directors to oust the committee. He saw a clear analogy between the ATS situation, the Kansas crisis, and the rupture within the New School Presbyterian Church. Both the American Tract Society and President Buchanan, he charged, showed themselves to be subservient to the Slave Power, while the southern influence on the ATS officers and the southern secession from the New School illus-

---

27. See *Independent*, August 5, 1852, June 23, 1853, August 24, December 21, 1854, February 22, March 15, November 15, 1855, April 3, March 27, 1856; Bacon, "The Southern Apostasy," 629, 633–34.

28. *Independent*, March 1, September 20, October 25, 1855, March 27, May 8, 15, June 12, 19, 1856, February 19, March 12, May 14, 1857; S. Guiteau to Bacon, January 17, 1856, William A. Hallock to Bacon, May 3, 1856, in Bacon Family Papers; McKivigan, *The War Against Proslavery Religion,* 120–21. For the conservatives' attacks on Bacon, see New York *Observer,* November 22, 29, 1855, May 27, July 23, 1857, April 15, May 20, 17, 1858.

trated that all attempts at ecclesiastical union between northerners and southerners, "however well intended, are disadvantageous to both parties."[29]

The conservatives' intransigence, John R. McKivigan notes, had finally forced antislavery moderates into "uncharacteristically strong counteraction." In a rare display of cooperation, Bacon, Thompson, Henry Ward Beecher, and other moderates met with a group of abolitionists to plan strategy for the 1858 tract society meeting. In a powerful speech at the society's meeting, which was echoed by William Jay and other abolitionists, Bacon condemned its officers as hypocritical, for though they denounced in their publications such practices as drinking and dancing, they refused even to mention slavery. Their actions, he told a hostile audience, represented "an attempt to degrade our evangelical Christianity to the lowest level of political and financial expediency."[30]

Despite the united effort by the antislavery forces, they were overwhelmingly defeated by those loyal to the executive committee, which successfully packed the 1858 and subsequent meetings with its conservative supporters. Moreover, the differences between Bacon and the abolitionists persisted. Growing numbers of immediatists joined the American Reform Tract and Book Society, formed by western abolitionists in 1851 to publish antislavery tracts, while many antislavery moderates threw their support to the Boston auxiliary of the ATS, which promised to publish mildly antislavery literature. Bacon applauded the Boston society's program. Nevertheless, motivated by a desire to redeem the ATS while "calmly and patiently enduring personal insult and wrong"—thereby showing that he had fought the battle to the very end—Bacon attended the 1859 and 1860 annual meetings, where he and other antislavery delegates were overwhelmed by the conservatives.[31]

Ironically, at the same time that abolitionists applauded Bacon for attacking the ATS's hypocrisy, George Cheever used the columns of the *Independent* to accuse him, Thompson, Henry Ward Beecher, and other antislavery moderates of being hypocrites themselves. Cheever maintained that the tract society was less culpable than the ABCFM, which they supported, because the former society, in refusing to condemn slavery as a sin, sinned by omission, while the latter, in sanctioning and supporting slavery among the Cherokee and Choctaw churches, sinned by commission.[32] He engaged in a degree of hyperbole, for by the late 1850s the ABCFM, encouraged by Bacon and other antislavery moderates, had largely abandoned the

29. *Independent,* July 9, October 15, 22, December 3, 1857, April 8, 1858.

30. McKivigan, *The War Against Proslavery Religion,* 122; *Independent,* May 20, 1858.

31. See *Independent,* May 5, 12, 1859, May 10, 17, 1860; Leonard to Catherine Bacon, May 9, 1860, in Bacon Family Papers.

32. *Independent,* November 18, 1852.

Indian missions in the South. The abolitionists certainly had been more aggressive than the moderates in applying pressure on the benevolent societies, but they would not have accomplished their objectives, especially in their struggle with the missionary societies, without the moderates' sustained, albeit conditional, support for antislavery action. At the same time, Bacon and the moderates had been far more committed to employing these societies in the struggle against slavery than the conservatives. Yet in the end, they failed, as did the immediatists, to move southern Christians toward abolition.

During the mid- and late 1850s, Bacon also experienced serious difficulties, as well as some satisfaction, in his family life, his ministerial career, and his connection with the *Independent*. Between 1852 and 1858, the last of his and Catherine's children were born—Alfred Terry in 1852, Ellen Brinley in 1856, and Alice Mabel in 1858. These were joyful occasions for the Bacons, but they were tempered by the sudden death of their daughter Lucy in 1854 at the age of thirteen. While his family continued to grow, several of Bacon's older children reached adulthood and launched their careers. Rebecca was the organist at the Chapel Street Church and remained in the family home to assist her mother in caring for the younger children; Leonard Woolsey graduated from Andover Theological Seminary and served as a minister in Rochester, New York, and later in Litchfield, Connecticut; Frank received his medical degree from Yale and became a surgeon in Galveston, Texas, and then in New York City; Theodore studied law and then established a practice in Rochester, New York; and George was a reporter and then a minister. Bacon took a great deal of interest in his children's lives. He especially directed a steady stream of advice toward his older sons, all of whom studied at Yale, as they began to pursue their careers. He was ever vigilant regarding their moral values, but also vigorously defended them when he believed they were unjustly attacked. For example, when Leonard Woolsey was sued for libel in 1860, Bacon warned that when he was finished with his son's accusers, they "shall one and all have a lesson which it will be easy for them to remember as long as they live."[33]

As Bacon's older sons completed their education and became self-sufficient, the financial burden was lightened somewhat. But additions to the family meant that several children lived at home at any given time during the 1850s. Despite an increase in his Center Church salary to $2,400 in 1858, throughout the decade Bacon and Catherine were saddled with a debt of approximately $1,500. As Catherine

33. Susan Hodges to Bacon, August 22, 1854, Leonard Woolsey to Frank Bacon, February 6, October 2, 1856, Leonard Woolsey to Leonard Bacon, October 24, 1851, May 29, June 7, July 12, 1855, April 25, 1859, April 4, 1860, Catherine to Frank Bacon, April 7, 1853, January 31, 1855, Leonard to Frank Bacon, May 2, 1853, November 16, 1854, Leonard to Leonard Woolsey Bacon, November 25, 1851, November 24, 1859, April 8, August 2, 1860, Rebecca to Frank Bacon, October 20, 1856, in Bacon Family Papers.

complained in 1855, "Could we ever have two cents to put in a money box and so 'we have this over when all our debts are paid' I should feel very rich." Indeed, in 1856 Rebecca asked her brother Frank for a loan in order to avoid the possibility of creditors taking the house, expressing the desperate hope that her father could break free of his debts and enjoy "'a tranquil old age' as the story book says." But, she complained bitterly, that would not happen as long as her father was forced "to throw money into the Atlantic Ocean" to help her "perverse and ungrateful" Aunt Delia.[34]

Delia's attempt to prove that the plays attributed to William Shakespeare in fact had been written by her ancestor, Sir Francis Bacon, and her agonizing descent into insanity, were some of the most painful experiences in Bacon's life. In the early 1850s Delia was a respected lecturer and tutor to the literary and business elite of Boston, and then Brooklyn. Yet even then she showed signs of instability and delusions, most profoundly in her belief that Catherine Bacon was bound to the service of the devil through his prime agent, Delia's and Leonard's brother, David. But her principal obsession was the theory regarding Shakespeare's plays, which came to possess her uncontrollably. As early as 1852 Bacon had urged her to give up "this delirious fancy," but instead she went to England for several years, where she sought to confirm her thesis.[35]

Delia's knowledge of Shakespeare's and Francis Bacon's works, as well as her intelligence and intensity, attracted support from such prominent writers as Thomas Carlyle, Ralph Waldo Emerson (even though he doubted the validity of her theory), and Nathaniel Hawthorne, who was also American consul in Liverpool and the brother of Delia's closest friend, Elizabeth Peabody. Both Emerson and Hawthorne sought to find a publisher for her work, while Bacon, his wife, and his sisters were more dubious of Delia's theory and feared that she was insane. But despite the family's dire financial straits, during these years they sent hundreds of dollars to Delia.[36]

Bacon's correspondence with Delia reveals a complex blend of compassion, love, condescension, and anger. He urged her to follow Hawthorne's advice and publish her findings in a series of articles rather than a book, but, with Hawthorne's assistance, she published her findings in *The Philosophy of the Plays of Shakespere Unfolded* in 1857. In counseling Delia to concentrate on the meaning of Shakespeare's com-

34. Rebecca to Frank Bacon, January 19, 1858, May 26, 1856, Catherine to Frank Bacon, March 28, 1855, in Bacon Family Papers.

35. *Independent*, February 10, 1853; Catherine to Leonard Bacon, December 16, 1850, Catherine to Rebecca Bacon, 1851, in Bacon Family Papers; Rugoff, *The Beechers*, 192.

36. Theodore Bacon, *Delia Bacon*, 60–72, 79–82, 161–70; Catherine to Frank Bacon, March 28, 1855, Elizabeth P. Peabody to Bacon, October 23, 1859, in Bacon Family Papers; Hopkins, *Prodigal Puritan*, 197, 199, 249.

positions, not their authorship, Bacon implicitly repudiated her theory. More bluntly, he urged her to use her "natural good sense" to escape "the enchanted wood" into which she had been led. He hoped that these remarks, however hurtful, might bring Delia, whom he suspected of being "hopelessly lost to usefulness and reason," to her senses. Not surprisingly, she was crushed by her brother's remonstrance. She never answered the letter containing these remarks, and she complained bitterly to Hawthorne about Leonard's "harshness and coldness." By 1856, it was quite apparent to the Bacon family as well as Hawthorne that Delia was insane and must return to the United States, but it was not until 1858 that she agreed to leave England with Bacon's son Theodore. Once back in America, she was placed in asylums in New York and then Hartford. Bacon continued to contribute as much as he could toward her care and occasionally visited her until her death in 1859.[37] Throughout this tragic episode, he attempted to do all that he could to assist Delia, at considerable emotional and financial cost.

Unfortunately, Delia's developing insanity and eventual death was not the only family tragedy that Bacon had to endure during these years. His sister Susan, with whom he was closest among his siblings, died suddenly in 1857. Even more emotionally draining was his brother David's advancing alcoholism and neurosis. David, like Leonard and Delia, was brilliant, intense, and driven. But while Leonard threw himself into his ministry and his writing and Delia became obsessed with her literary theory, David, increasingly haunted by his failure to realize his aspirations, first as a physician and then as a journalist, retreated into prolonged bouts of solitary drinking.[38]

By 1857, David's frequent movement between his brother's home and cheap New York City hotels, where he went on extended binges, elicited a stern lecture from Leonard. Like his admonitions to Delia, his warning to David that if he continued to drink heavily he would be better off dead manifested a stern righteousness. Yet Leonard in fact cared deeply about his brother's welfare and exhibited enormous patience, understanding, and compassion in the face of adversity. He frequently sent David to a doctor and for years endured his brother's drunkenness and insults while David lived in his home. Indeed, David's behavior became so intolerable that the Bacon children ceased to invite their friends to the house. The

37. Theodore Bacon, *Delia Bacon,* 248–50, 255–57, 267; Rebecca to Frank Bacon, May 26, 1856, Catherine to Frank Bacon, June 24, 1857, Elizabeth P. Peabody to Bacon, October 23, 1859, Bacon to Elizabeth P. Peabody, February 11, 1860, diary entries for February 19, 1855, August 20–28, September 2, 1859, Leonard to Frank Bacon, July 7, 1858, Leonard to Rebecca Bacon, August 24, 30, 1859, in Bacon Family Papers; Hopkins, *Prodigal Puritan,* 310, 314.

38. M. F. Hodges to Bacon, November 25, 1857, in Bacon Family Papers. David Bacon's descent into alcoholism is analyzed in Rorabaugh, *The Alcoholic Republic,* 165–66.

situation took a heavy toll on Bacon. "All the constant anxiety, watchfulness and disappointment," Rebecca complained to Frank in 1857, "have worn upon him very much." Yet, convinced that he was obligated to assist his siblings in whatever way he could and that he somehow could move his brother toward recovery, Bacon continued to allow David, penniless and nearly blind, back into the home whenever he returned from his benders.[39]

The combination of financial worries and anxieties regarding his brother and sister contributed to Bacon's lengthy illness in 1858. These concerns were exacerbated by the difficulties that the *Independent* experienced in the wake of the 1857 financial panic. In many respects the paper had flourished since its inception, with 50,000 subscribers by 1860. On the eve of the Civil War an Episcopalian newspaper, the *Quarterly Church Review,* claimed that the *Independent* had a larger circulation and more influence than any other religious newspaper in the United States. Yet the paper routinely lost money. The failure of Bowen's and McNamee's businesses following the 1857 panic dealt the *Independent* a severe blow, forcing the proprietors to cease paying the editors in advance. The popularity of Henry Ward Beecher's column, the revenue derived from additional space devoted to advertisements, and the managerial ability of Theodore Tilton, the new managing editor, finally turned a profit for Bowen. But Bacon was deeply concerned that Bowen's control of the paper would undermine the editors' independence and feared that the growing tendency to devote a large portion of the paper to advertisements would deduct more from the paper's value as a "first-class, family, religious newspaper" than it would add in revenue. Given the declining portion of the paper's space that was devoted to news and editorials, he offered to resign his post as senior editor.[40]

As disgusted as Bacon was by the space devoted to "rascally quack medicines," he did not follow through on his threat to resign. There were other problems, however, for he clashed with both Beecher and Cheever in the *Independent*'s columns. In the early 1850s Beecher's hymnbook, *The Plymouth Collection,* had come into competition with *Psalms and Hymns,* compiled largely by Leonard Woolsey Bacon and endorsed by the Connecticut General Association for use in the state's Congregational churches. The conflict centered around Beecher's indiscriminate appropriation of hymns from Leonard Woolsey's collection and his use of the columns of

39. Rebecca to Frank Bacon, February 26, March 23, 1857, January 19, 1858, Catherine to Leonard Bacon, September 10, 14, 1859, Julia Woodruff to Bacon, March 23, 1860, Frank to Leonard Bacon, January 17, 1860, in Bacon Family Papers.

40. Theodore Dwight Bacon, *Leonard Bacon,* 454; *Independent,* January 12, 1857, January 5, 1860; Henry C. Bowen to Bacon, February 3, 1852, J. H. Ladd to Bacon, October 14, 1857, Joshua Leavitt to Bacon, December 11, 1858, Bacon to Henry C. Bowen, December 18, 1858, in Bacon Family Papers; Housley, "The *Independent,*" 44–46.

the *Independent* to laud his own collection. The dispute escalated to the point where, by 1857, Bacon was forced to admonish both Beecher and his irascible son to calm down; eventually Beecher apologized for his actions.[41]

There was no such accommodation between Bacon and Cheever. In 1858 he and Thompson sharply rebuked Cheever on the editorial page for his derogatory remarks about the ABCFM, which Cheever interpreted as an attempt to stifle him. The debate continued in the paper's columns through 1859 and 1860, with Cheever denouncing the editors' defense of the missionary society and Bacon criticizing Cheever for being arrogant and "far too sweeping and indiscriminate" in his charges. During the late 1850s, they also clashed over a controversy that had erupted within Cheever's Church of the Puritans. A wealthy minority in Cheever's church, who disliked his abolitionist views, applied for dismissal to other churches, but Cheever and a majority of the congregation initiated disciplinary action against them. In 1859 the excluded members called for an *ex parte* council, headed by Bacon, which sided with the minority and chastised Cheever for his actions. By this time Bacon and Cheever heartily disliked each other, and they proceeded to fill several issues of the *Independent* with deeply personal attacks as well as their conflicting views on the merits of the council's report. Underlying this acrimonious exchange was the gulf that separated Cheever's abolitionist views and Bacon's moderate antislavery convictions. Finally, Bacon's editorial associates ran out of patience with Cheever and refused to publish any more of what Storrs termed his *"insufferable"* attacks.[42]

In the midst of the many concerns and responsibilities related to his family and his editorial position, Bacon remained extremely busy addressing ecclesiastical and benevolent society meetings and fulfilling his obligations as pastor of Center Church and as a leading figure in the Congregational Church. He also continued to be actively involved in the affairs of the Connecticut General Association and delivered the eulogy at the funerals of several church leaders as well as the fiftieth-anniversary sermon at Andover Theological Seminary. But he devoted the preponderance of his time to the preparation of sermons for his congregation. Both his pulpit presence and his preaching continued to receive mixed reviews. One observer noted not only his "singular" physical appearance—including "a head shaped

41. Bacon to Henry Ward Beecher, August 18, 1852, in Beecher Family Papers, Sterling Library, Yale University; *Minutes of the General Association of Connecticut* (1856), 10–13, (1857), 12; Leonard Woolsey to Frank Bacon, June 20, 1856, Leonard to Leonard Woolsey Bacon, December 19, 1856, January 1, 1857, Leonard Woolsey to Leonard Bacon, December 22, 1856, in Bacon Family Papers.

42. *Independent,* October 14, 1858, February 24, November 17, 1859, July 12, 26, 1860; Robert M. York, *George B. Cheever, Religious and Social Reformer, 1807–1890* (Orono, Maine, 1955), 157–59; George B. Cheever to Henry Cheever, November 25, 1859, in Cheever-Wheeler Papers, American Antiquarian Society, Worcester, Mass.; Richard S. Storrs, Jr., to Bacon, March 4, 1859, in Bacon Family Papers.

as a hatchet"—and an "uninviting demeanor," but also his "few graces of oratory." Yet he quickly added that when Bacon preached one of his great sermons, "he astonishes you with the colossal proportions of his understanding—you feel the presence of a giant, and sit awe-struck in the shadow of his greatness!"[43]

Bacon was somewhat defensive about his preaching, noting that in New Haven there was "a constant demand not for the flashy oratory which is in some places called popular preaching, but for the clear, thoughtful, serious inculcation of the great truths and duties of religion." Nevertheless, he realized that his sermons were not his forte. In his thirtieth-year sermon in 1855, he acknowledged that their preparation was "even now, the most difficult and depressing of literary labors," while his many other writing endeavors had long constituted "almost wholly my recreation." It was, he explained, not the learning, logic, imagination, or rhetorical skill required but, rather, the "direct address to the conscience and the religious sensibility of common minds" that made this task "the great labor" of his life.[44]

Much of Bacon's congregation appears to have tolerated the rather inconsistent quality of his sermons and to have supported his antislavery, antiextension, and antisouthern views. They also clearly identified with his strong attachment to evangelical Congregationalism and took pride in his many accomplishments, both within the Congregational Church and the larger society. Yet in 1859 a crisis developed within Center Church that nearly led to his resignation as pastor. The problem was that many members owned and rented pews, while one-third of the property of the church was reserved for the Ecclesiastical Society. Increased expenses had led the society to sell the remaining pews. This, Bacon complained, had made the church "a house of merchandise" and excluded the poor. Prodded by Bacon, the society eventually voted to impose an assessment on all pews and to buy back some of them, but by that time Bacon was so upset by the controversy in the church that he threatened to resign. In the end, his threat moved the opposing forces to reach an accommodation on the issue.[45]

While Bacon was dealing with these various difficult issues, he did not ignore the question of slavery. He became increasingly alarmed that commercial and party

---

43. See *Minutes of the General Association of Connecticut* (1854), 13, (1859), 14; Leonard Bacon, "A Burning and a Shining Light," *National Preacher and Village Pulpit*, n.s., II (January, 1859), 1–8; David Q. Mears, *Life of Edward Norris Kirk, D.D.* (Boston, 1877), 334–35; Bacon to Theodore Dwight Woolsey, August 1858, in Woolsey Family Papers; diary entries for May 24–28, June 3, 1854, June 17–18, 20, 23–24, 1857, September 4–10, 1858, September 3–11, 1860, description of Bacon, June 1852, in Bacon Family Papers; also Sigma, "Pulpit Portraits; Or, Sketches of Eminent Living American Divines: Rev. Leonard Bacon, D.D.," *Holden's Dollar Magazine*, V (January, 1850), 54.

44. Sermon of March 11, 1855, in Bacon Family Papers.

45. Sermons of December 26, 1858, July 1859, March 11, 1860, Leonard to Catherine Bacon, July 14, 1859, in Bacon Family Papers.

interests might succeed in reopening the African slave trade, and was convinced that the slave interests were intent upon acquiring Cuba and establishing a protectorate in Mexico in order to expand slavery. All of this, he warned, would fasten slavery on the territories and possibly the entire nation, maintain southern and Democratic control of the federal government, and carry the *Dred Scott* decision beyond the borders of the United States.[46]

But, rather curiously, after devoting enormous space in the columns of the *Independent* to the Kansas situation over the past three and a half years, Bacon and his editorial associates scarcely mentioned the bitter debates in Kansas and Washington regarding the proslavery Lecompton Constitution. It appears that, for whatever reason, Bacon, Thompson, and Storrs concluded that the ongoing tract society dispute and other matters were of greater relevance to their readers' lives than the outcome of the Kansas issue. In fact, not until John Brown's raid on the Harpers Ferry arsenal in the fall of 1859 did Bacon and his editorial colleagues once more devote considerable attention to the slavery issue and the sectional controversy. Brown's assault caused a sensation throughout the North and South. Northern Democrats and southerners angrily denounced Brown's audacious act as an inexcusable outrage and blamed it on the Republicans' inflammatory rhetoric. Many Republicans also initially denounced the raid as a counterproductive act of a madman, but as Brown's trial progressed, they increasingly tended to praise his courage and integrity in attacking an evil institution.[47]

Bacon's assessment of Brown and his raid followed somewhat the same course as that of many antislavery northerners, though from the beginning his response was quite ambivalent. As children, he and Brown had attended school together in Hudson, Ohio, and Brown had visited his home twice in 1857. Yet despite their shared antipathy toward slavery and their mutual desire to defend the free-soil cause in Kansas, Bacon could not condone Brown's violent attempt to instigate a slave rebellion. He initially termed the raid "the height of madness" and "a wild and absurd enterprise" characterized by "intrinsic lawlessness." His stand was based in part, as it had been regarding the Fugitive Slave Act, on his opposition to any attempt "to take up arms against a government because of its injustice in legislation and administration." Even though the state made war on slaves, and people could rightly refuse to obey wicked laws, he wrote in the *New Englander,* any resort to violence "usurps the function of government."[48]

46. *Independent,* December 4, 25, 1856, October 21, December 16, 1858, January 27, February 10, June 2, August 4, 1859.

47. See *Independent,* December 3, 1857, January 28, February 11, 25, March 4, 1858. On the reaction to Brown's raid, see Robert W. Johannsen, *Lincoln, the South, and Slavery: The Political Dimension* (Baton Rouge, 1991), 96; Stephen B. Oates, *To Purge This Land with Blood: A Biography of John Brown* (New York, 1970), 310–11, 331–36, 353–57.

48. Bacon to Henry A. Wise, November 14, 1859, in Bacon Family Papers; *Independent,* October

Yet almost immediately after the raid, Bacon contended that Brown was a brave man whose act must be judged in light of extenuating circumstances. Quite apart from his philosophical opposition to violent acts against constituted authority, he declared that Brown's raid was unwarranted especially because of its "sheer impracticality." Moreover, he was convinced that Brown was insane and that his madness was the result of acts committed by the slave interests. He therefore urged Governor Henry A. Wise of Virginia to take the effects of Brown's "conflict and sorrows" into account when he weighed his fate. In his *Independent* editorials Bacon was far more blunt, charging that the outrages of the proslavery forces in Kansas, the evils of slavery, and the precedent of armed proslavery adventurers in Cuba, Mexico, and Nicaragua had transformed Brown from "an honest, sturdy farmer, into a lawless brigand." Indeed, he considered Brown's act to be God's warning of retribution against the nation for the sins associated with slavery. More important, even sooner than many antislavery northerners he praised Brown's motives and character, lauding him for his "singular devotion" to the cause of freedom and insisting that this "brave old man" would awaken the nation's "sluggish moral sense, and the almost forgotten memories of the heroes of the Revolution."[49]

Like most northern editors, Bacon doubted whether Brown should be hanged. "John Brown, swinging upon the gallows," he warned, would "toll the death-knell of slavery," but it also would further strain sectional relations. Brown's courage and eloquence during his trial and his eventual execution indeed served as a rallying point for antislavery northerners as they moved toward the 1860 presidential election. At the same time, his raid, and the praise heaped upon him by Bacon and other northerners, convinced many southerners that the Republicans were bent on destroying slavery by any means possible. Bacon and his *Independent* associates did not doubt that slavery would be the dominant issue in the 1860 contest. They also condemned racial segregation in the North as "not only unchristian and wicked, but unmanly and mean." But above all, they pledged to endorse any Republican candidate who called for the denationalization of slavery, while warning that because the contest was "a naked question of right and wrong," continued support for the party depended upon its remaining a thoroughly antislavery instrument.[50]

Notwithstanding the conditions they attached to their party loyalty, there was

---

20, November 3, 10, December 8, 1859; Leonard Bacon, *Established in Righteousness. A Discourse to the First Church and Society in New Haven, On a Day of Public Thanksgiving, November 24th, 1859* (New Haven, 1859), 10–11, 17; Bacon, "The Moral of Harper's Ferry," 1076–77.

49. Bacon to Henry A. Wise, November 14, 1859, in Bacon Family Papers; *Independent,* October 20, 27, November 3, 10, 1859; Bacon, "The Moral of Harper's Ferry," 1071–75; Bacon, *Established in Righteousness,* 17–18.

50. *Independent,* November 24, September 22, 1859, January 5, February 23, March 15, 29, April 5, May 10, 24, July 5, September 6, 27, 1860; Leonard Bacon, "The Crime Against the Right of Suffrage," *New Englander,* XVIII (May, 1860), 453–54.

little doubt that Bacon, Thompson, and Storrs would ultimately support it so long as the candidate expressed "a decided and uncompromising opposition to slavery" wherever it existed. At first they tended to favor Seward, whom they considered the most steadfast in the long struggle against the encroachments of slavery. But Seward suffered from having too radical a reputation and too uneven a record on the slavery question, and many nativists disliked him for his criticism of the anti-Catholic movement. Bacon and his editorial associates were disappointed that Seward was not nominated, but they soon came to support Abraham Lincoln as an honest and capable man who was true on the territorial issue.[51]

Indeed, when Lincoln was elected, the *Independent* editors were ecstatic. "The power of the slave-interest at Washington is broken," they proclaimed, and "the crisis is over." Yet within a few weeks of Lincoln's victory South Carolina left the Union, and several other southern states soon followed its lead. Bacon and his editorial associates had long believed that southerners, fearful of insurrection, armed invasion intended to free the slaves, economic collapse, and subjugation by a foreign power, would never secede. Now that secession had occurred, Bacon, like many other northerners, sought to maintain certain fundamental principles while also calling for a spirit of conciliation and forbearance.[52]

As the crisis deepened, Senator James Dixon of Connecticut, a moderate Republican, asked Bacon whether he thought the party was perhaps mistaking "stubborn adherence to a dogma" for principles. In his response to Dixon's inquiry, Bacon acknowledged that he, too, did not know where events would lead the nation. He hoped that the federal government would avoid any violent collision with the seceded states and that the Union might emerge from this crisis stronger than before. Yet he, like many Radical Republicans, was unyielding in his conviction that any attempt to arrest secession through additional compromises would place northerners in "perpetual subjection to agitators and terrorists." The rights of all Americans, guaranteed by the Declaration of Independence, he informed Dixon, must not be sacrificed in order to restore the Union.[53]

---

51. *Independent,* March 8, 15, 29, 1860. On Seward's political difficulties in 1860, see John M. Taylor, *William Henry Seward: Lincoln's Right Hand* (New York, 1991), 116–18; Glyndon Van Deusen, *William Henry Seward* (New York, 1967), 220–22; *Independent,* May 24, 31, August 30, 1860. On Lincoln and the slavery issue in 1860, see Johannsen, *Lincoln, the South, and Slavery,* 30–31, 33–34, 59–67; Phillip Shaw Paludan, *The Presidency of Abraham Lincoln* (Lawrence, Kans., 1994), 17–18.

52. *Independent,* November 8, 15, 1860, January 3, 31, February 14, 1861; sermon of November 29, 1860, in Bacon Family Papers; see also Moorhead, *American Apocalypse,* 32–34.

53. James Dixon to Bacon, December 12, 1860, Bacon to James Dixon, December 14, 1860, diary entry for December 31, 1860, in Bacon Family Papers; also Bacon, *The Jugglers Detected,* 20–22, 24. On Dixon as a moderate Republican, see Allan G. Bogue, *The Earnest Men: Republicans of the Civil War Senate* (Ithaca, 1981), 35, 96–98.

Bacon feared that civil war was virtually inevitable. But he was certain that secession was a "crime against liberty and the welfare of the human race, hardly surpassed by any other crime which history has recorded." Thus, he heartily disagreed with Seward's efforts at compromise with the South, warning that if the Republican party accepted such compromises, a new antislavery party would arise. The question, he declared, was no longer simply Union or disunion, slavery or antislavery, but government or anarchy—and lawlessness must be quelled. Yet Bacon, like Horace Greeley and a number of other leading Republicans, did not wish to drag the South forcefully back into the Union. Such willingness to allow peaceful secession was grounded in part in the hope that the South would soon come to its senses and accept the will of the majority on the slavery issue. Equally important, in Bacon's opinion, was the concern that any attempt to coerce the South to return to the Union would involve "indiscriminate slaughter" and would have a deleterious effect on "moral habits." Consequently, he wrote in late March, 1861, "Let them go, to work out their own destiny by themselves."[54]

Throughout the secession crisis, Bacon and his editorial colleagues commended Lincoln's steadfastness and urged him to maintain the constitutional authority of the federal government in the southern states.[55] The Confederates' assault on Fort Sumter ended Bacon's and the Republicans' search for a means of avoiding war while also refusing to compromise in the face of secession. Once the war commenced, Bacon was determined to pursue the struggle until the Confederacy was vanquished. Convinced that God was on the side of the Union and the cause of freedom, he stood forth as an outspoken supporter of the Lincoln administration, the war effort, and emancipation. During the war years, Bacon also experienced important changes in his personal and professional life, as three of his sons served in the military, his connection with the *Independent* ended, and he became a regular columnist for the *Congregationalist*.

54. Sermon of January 1861, in Bacon Family Papers; Bacon, *The Jugglers Detected*, 145–47, 157–59; *Independent*, December 6, 13, 20, 27, 1860, January 3, 17, 24, February 7, 14, 21, 28, March 14, 21, 1861. On the concept of peaceful secession, see Jeter Allen Isely, *Horace Greeley and the Republican Party, 1853–1861: A Study of the New York Tribune* (New York, 1965), 304–13. For a discussion of abolitionists who assumed this position, see George M. Fredrickson, *The Inner Civil War: Northern Intellectuals and the Crisis of the Union* (New York, 1965), 56–59.

55. *Independent*, January 10, March 21, 28, April 4, 11, 1861.

II

THE CIVIL WAR YEARS

THE Confederate attack on Fort Sumter brought to a violent end the near paralysis that had gripped the nation since the inception of the secession crisis. The wave of excitement and anger that swept across the North represented not only an emotional release from months of agonizing uncertainty but also a determination to no longer submit to the Slave Power. Bacon was caught up in the agitation and anticipation of the moment, telling an enthusiastic meeting at Music Hall in New Haven that northerners must singlemindedly devote their energies to the great struggle that lay ahead.[1]

Bacon, like many other northern Protestant clergymen, placed the war within the broader context of God's plan for the human race and His punishment for the sins of both the North and the South. "Our pride, our luxury, our habit of self-assertion, Sabbath-breaking, infidelity, our increasing complicity as a nation with the crime of slavery," he editorialized in the *Independent*, "all this has accumulated upon us as a weight of guilt that calls for judgment." The war would not end, he warned in an 1862 discourse, until God had "sufficiently purified us in the furnace of this great calamity."[2]

Yet Bacon had no doubt that God favored the Union cause. He and other ministers frequently employed religious imagery in their sermons and writings, asserting

---

1. Diary entry for April 22, 1861, in Bacon Family Papers. See Phillip Shaw Paludan, *"A People's Contest": The Union and Civil War, 1861–1865* (New York, 1988), 3–13; James M. McPherson, *The Struggle for Equality: Abolitionists and the Negro in the Civil War and Reconstruction* (Princeton, 1964), 47–50.

2. *Independent*, September 12, 1861; Bacon, *Conciliation. A Discourse at a Sunday Evening Service, New Haven, July 20, 1862* (New Haven, 1862), 17. For treatments of the Protestant clergy's emphasis upon the Civil War as judgment for the sins of Americans, see Moorhead, *American Apocalypse*, 42–47; Charles Stewart, "Civil War Preaching," in *Preaching in American History: Selected Issues in the American Pulpit, 1630–1967*, ed. De Witte Holland (Nashville, 1969), 185–92.

that the northern war effort would advance the cause of Christianity. He believed that the New Testament condoned righteous wars for the defense of a nation. Thus, he assured his congregation, the present struggle was "simply the armed power which a legitimate government is wielding, in the name of God's justice, for the punishment of evil-doers and the protection and safety of them who do well."[3]

Bacon expressed the view of many northerners that this was an irrepressible conflict between fundamentally antagonistic ideas and social systems. The war, much like the Puritan wars of the seventeenth century, he wrote in 1862, involved "the most elementary principles of social order and government, of justice and morality, and of religion itself." Perhaps above all, it was a war to preserve the government, the Union, and the Constitution, for defeat would sound the death knell of popular self-government by constitutional majorities. Convinced that America stood in the vanguard of the struggle for liberty and democracy, he and other clergymen sought successfully to inject a sense of moral purpose into the Union war effort.[4]

In this great crisis many northern clergymen, intellectuals, and others called upon all true patriots to rally to the defense of the nation. Some northerners, such as Joseph Thompson and Francis Lieber, argued that the right of revolution was at best conditional, while Horace Bushnell and Henry W. Bellows came close to demanding that citizens give unconditional loyalty to their government. Bacon never became the passionate nationalist that Bushnell was. Before the war, he had employed the higher-law argument to attack the Fugitive Slave Act and the *Dred Scott* decision, and he remained wary of giving too much power to the federal government. But with the government now in Republican hands and the nation threatened by a massive rebellion, he moved rather quickly toward Bushnell's position. Believing that the Union and the cause of Christianity were inextricably connected, he came to view the nation as a divinely ordained instrument of God that must be supported, even by those who doubted the government's course of action.[5]

Because of his conviction that the war was one of the "hinges on which the destiny of nations and ages" turned, Bacon rejected any thought of compromise or negotiation with the Confederacy. All patriotic Americans, he maintained, must

---

3. Sermon of June 6, 1861, in Bacon Family Papers. For similar sentiments, see *Independent,* June 6, 1861. See also Donald G. Jones, *The Sectional Crisis and Northern Methodism: A Study of Piety, Political Ethics and Civil Religion* (Metuchen, N.J., 1979), 69–96.

4. Leonard Bacon, "The War of the Lord," *New Englander,* XXI (January, 1862), 134; *Independent,* April 18, 1861; sermon of February 16, 1861, in Bacon Family Papers; Moorhead, *American Apocalypse,* 38–41; Earl J. Hess, *Liberty, Virtue, and Progress: Northerners and Their War for the Union* (New York, 1988), 1–3.

5. Fredrickson, *The Inner Civil War,* 76, 131–50; Moorhead, *American Apocalypse,* 44–51; sermons of November 27, 1862, March 25, 1864, in Bacon Family Papers.

bear whatever sacrifices were necessary to realize victory. In his sermons he often acknowledged the separation and death that were part of this "sore calamity," and he turned to the Bible to console those who suffered and to assure them that God reigned in the interest of righteousness. At the same time, he urged his congregation to be thankful and humble, for submission to the traitorous conspirators would be "a greater evil than war, even if war should end in defeat." The Union soldiers, as well as their families and friends, he believed, must know that "to die for a good cause in the spirit of self-sacrifice may be a blessed privilege."[6]

During the initial months of the war, Bacon disseminated his views on the causes and meaning of the war in a number of forums, including the editorial columns of the *Independent*. But his connection with the paper ended abruptly in December, 1861, when he, Thompson, and Storrs resigned their editorial posts. Henry C. Bowen had experienced financial problems since the 1857 panic, and with the onset of the war, the failure to collect debts owed by southern creditors pushed Bowen, Holmes and Company into bankruptcy. When Lewis Tappan, Bowen's father-in-law and a prominent abolitionist, to whom the paper had been transferred in order to avoid losing it in a bankruptcy proceeding, criticized Bacon's position on possible English recognition of the Confederacy, the editors reacted to what they deemed unwarranted interference by hastily submitting their resignations.[7]

Bowen praised the editors for their labors over the years, but neither he nor Tappan sought to persuade them to reverse their decision. Attempting to put the best face on the situation, Bacon informed Henry M. Dexter, editor of the *Congregationalist*, that he was relieved to have been released from a responsibility that had become "increasingly irksome for me for some time past."[8] In fact, however, he had been forced out of a position that for thirteen years had enabled him to influence a large number of northern Protestants. His labors, and those of his editorial associates, had succeeded in transforming a struggling journal with a rather small circulation into a mass-circulation newspaper for the general reader who had a religious orientation. The paper had spoken out forcefully on a number of crucial issues during the tumultuous decade of the 1850s. While the editors had often fallen short

6. *Independent*, August 22, 1861; Bacon, *Conciliation*, 8, 9–17; sermons of November 28, 1861, February 16, 1862, April 3, 1863, in Bacon Family Papers. See also Hess, *Liberty, Virtue, and Progress*, 52–54; Fredrickson, *The Inner Civil War*, 80–82.

7. Diary entries for November 12, 14, 19, December 16, 1861, in Bacon Family Papers, Housley, "The *Independent*," 46–47.

8. Henry C. Bowen, Samuel P. Holmes, and Anthony Gilkison to Bacon, December 17, 1861, Lewis Tappan to Bacon, Joseph P. Thompson, and Richard S. Storrs, Jr., December 17, 1861, "Explanation," in Bacon Family Papers; Bacon to Henry M. Dexter, December 27, 1861, in C. A. Richardson Collection, Congregational Library, Boston, Mass.

of the abolitionists' mark, especially with regard to the relationship between the missionary societies and slavery, they had appealed to a growing number of northern Christians who increasingly disliked slavery and distrusted the designs of southerners and their northern allies. In vigorously defending the rights and interests of northerners, they had helped to steel the public for the secession crisis and the war that came in 1860–61.

While some old foes of Bacon and his colleagues welcomed their departure from the paper, Henry Ward Beecher, who succeeded them in the editorial chair, hoped that Bacon would continue to contribute to the *Independent* and praised the former editors for having "carried the banner of truth" in every controversy that had arisen since the paper's inception. When Beecher traveled to England in 1863 to speak on behalf of the Union, and Tilton replaced him as editor, however, Bacon, who had long resented Tilton's influence with Bowen, his abrasive style, and his outspoken abolitionism, refused to be associated with the *Independent*. He remained on friendly terms with Beecher, who asked him to officiate at his father's funeral in 1863, but he would not again contribute to the paper's columns until after the Civil War.[9]

As he often had done after leaving an editorial post, Bacon immediately searched for another forum from which he could communicate to the public his views on a broad range of issues. Ten days after his resignation from the *Independent,* he expressed a desire to write a column as the Connecticut correspondent for the *Congregationalist,* the leading denominational newspaper in the Congregational Church. C. A. Richardson, the office editor, soon welcomed Bacon's offer, and in early 1862 he began a connection with the *Congregationalist* that would last for several years. His columns, which appeared biweekly under the heading *Watch-Tower,* dealt with the war, emancipation, Reconstruction, the state of the Congregational Church, and many other matters of public concern.[10]

In the columns of the *Congregationalist,* as well as in other publications, public lectures, and sermons, Bacon urged his fellow northerners to support the Union cause with vigor and determination. From the outset of the conflict, his connection to the struggle was a very personal one. Rebecca and a number of her friends worked as volunteer nurses, tending to wounded soldiers in an army hospital in New Haven. In addition, Frank, who had studied medicine at Yale, became a sur-

9. William Lloyd Garrison to Oliver Johnson, December 22, 1861, in William Lloyd Garrison Papers; Joshua Leavitt to Bacon, December 25, 1861, diary entry for January 22, 1863, in Bacon Family Papers; *Independent,* December 19, 1861.

10. Bacon to Henry M. Dexter, December 27, 1861, in C. A. Richardson Collection; C. A. Richardson to Bacon, December 30, 1861, April 19, December 24, 1862, Henry M. Dexter to Bacon, January 7, 1862, in Bacon Family Papers.

geon with the 7th Connecticut Regiment. At the same time, Theodore came home from Europe, where he was teaching, and was made a captain in the army.[11]

In July, 1861, Bacon traveled to Washington to urge Senator Dixon of Connecticut and other members of Congress to provide adequate funding for the war effort. While in the nation's capital, he listened to the Senate debates on taxes for the war and met at length with Secretary of the Navy Gideon Welles and Attorney General Edward Bates, who took him to the White House to meet the president. He was also intent upon visiting his sons and other members of their regiment, who had recently seen action at Bull Run. Both young men had nearly been captured by the enemy and were exhausted. Although proud of his sons' bravery, he was profoundly shocked by the loss of life and the humiliating defeat.[12]

On a number of occasions during 1862 and 1863, Bacon sought either to advance or to defend his sons' interests. In these efforts he once more showed himself to be a father who was both tenaciously protective of and deeply committed to his children's well-being. For example, he frequently, and quite unsuccessfully, attempted to persuade Governor William Buckingham to promote Theodore in rank and to transfer him to another regiment, and he spoke personally to Theodore's commanding officer about the matter. Frank's situation was even more emotionally charged. While serving as superintendent of the St. Louis Military Hospital in 1863, he was charged by the New Orleans correspondent of the New York *Tribune* with favoring Confederate prisoners over Union soldiers and allowing Confederate women to sing secession songs in the hospital. Frank brought charges of defamation of character against the correspondent and Bacon angrily accused the *Tribune* editors of printing "unequivocally and basely false" charges against a patriot who was "a resolute and uncompromising enemy of secession, and of slavery." In the end, the paper refused to apologize to Bacon or his son, even though a provost court found the *Tribune* correspondent guilty of slander.[13]

Another of Bacon's sons, Edward, left Yale at the age of seventeen to enlist in the navy, and in 1863 was asked to serve as adjutant to the commander of a black regi-

11. Niven, *Connecticut for the Union,* 322–23; Edward Woolsey to George Bacon, May 11, 1861, in Edward Woolsey Bacon Papers, American Antiquarian Society, Worcester, Mass.; Theodore Dwight Bacon, *Leonard Bacon,* 465.

12. Joseph P. Thompson to Bacon, July 9, 1861, Leonard to Catherine Bacon, July 26, 27, 30, 1861, in Bacon Family Papers.

13. Leonard Woolsey to Leonard Bacon, September 15, 1862, Rebecca to Frank Bacon, June 24, 1863, Bacon to New York *Tribune,* September 21, 1863, Sidney Howard Gay to Leonard Woolsey Bacon, October 31, 1863, Frank to Leonard Woolsey Bacon, November 24, 1863, Frank Bacon to editor of New York *Tribune,* December 7, 1863, clipping from New Orleans *Era,* November 24, 1863, in Bacon Family Papers.

ment in Louisiana. Bacon, uncertain about Edward's health, sought to persuade the army not to take his son, but Edward joined the regiment as a major and saw action in several battles during the next two years. All of Bacon's sons survived the war; Frank and Theodore were discharged late in the war, and Edward led his black troops triumphantly into Richmond in April, 1865.[14]

Throughout the war Bacon displayed an unflinching devotion to the Union cause, even in its darkest moments. At times, his intense loyalty to the Union led him to question the patriotism even of those who merely opposed the government's conduct of the war. His confrontation with J. Halstead Carroll, pastor of South Church in New Haven, who frequently prayed for peace in the midst of the war, was especially protracted and bitter. Indeed, throughout the war neither man seemed willing to end the controversy. While Bacon called Carroll's character into doubt, Carroll, before he left New Haven in 1866 with his reputation severely tarnished, accused him of exhibiting "passion, prejudice, and rank, disreputable error" and of being a liar and a "self-righteous bully."[15]

Bacon was especially inclined to question the loyalty of Democratic politicians and editors. For example, he termed the Hartford *Times,* the New Haven *Register,* and other Democratic papers in the state "anti-republican, anti-liberty, and anti-Union" and charged that there probably were more traitors in New York City than in any southern city. Convinced that northerners must present a unified front against the forces of treason, he even criticized the "carping" Republican papers for their attacks on Lincoln. "The government," he insisted, "must either be maintained or opposed by all its subjects."[16]

This does not mean that Bacon unconditionally supported the administration's policies regarding civil liberties and other matters. Unlike Bushnell, he acknowledged that Lincoln's suspension of habeas corpus was vulnerable to abuse and warned that illegal violence against northern anti-Union protesters did more harm than good for the cause. Nevertheless, he, like most northerners, including constitutional experts, rallied behind Lincoln's resort to martial law and censorship as legitimate means of suppressing the rebellion and preserving the nation. Indeed, he

14. Edward Woolsey to Kate (Katherine) Bacon, July 6, 1862, Rebecca to Frank Bacon, November 21, 1863, in Bacon Family Papers; Edward Woolsey to Kate (Katherine) Bacon, July 24, August 30, October 8, November 7, 1864, March 31, 1865, obituary of Edward Woolsey Bacon, 1887, in Edward Woolsey Bacon Papers.

15. Bacon to Gideon Welles, April 8, 1861, in Gideon Welles Papers, Connecticut Historical Society, Hartford, Conn.; Hallock, *Life of Gerard Hallock,* 173–88, 192; J. Halsted Carroll, *A Letter to Rev. Leonard Bacon, D.D.* (New Haven, 1866), 3–4, 16, 24–26.

16. *Congregationalist,* March 27, July 31, 1863; *Independent,* July 11, August 1, 8, 1861; Leonard Bacon, "Reply to Professor Parker," *New Englander,* XXII (April, 1863), 192, 199.

managed to convince himself that the selective imprisonment of people and the suspension of newspapers sympathetic to the Confederacy actually preserved free speech under the Constitution.[17]

Bacon's criticism of people he deemed insufficiently supportive of the Union cause extended to the British as well. While he conceded that Americans tended to be overly sensitive to British opinion and he praised British industrial workers as well as Richard Cobden, John Stuart Mill, and other middle-class reformers for their pro-Union stance, he believed that the aristocratic forces and all too many evangelical elements were dominated by the "cotton interests." Even at the end of the war he continued to express shock and dismay at the general lack of British support for the Union, blaming it largely on jealousy, different social and political systems, and economic competition.[18]

Bacon's support for the war effort extended beyond writing and speaking. As an influential clergyman he also frequently joined political leaders in recruiting regiments and presiding at ceremonies that either bade farewell to troops going off to war or welcomed those returning. Moreover, he joined with other clergymen in early 1862 to found the Connecticut Chaplains' Aid Association. This organization sought to supplement the work of the United States Sanitary Commission, which labored to protect the health of the soldiers, and the tract and other benevolent societies, which attempted to infuse antidotes for vice into the army camps. By furnishing each Connecticut regiment with a chapel tent for worship, lectures, and singing, as well as secular and religious newspapers and books, the association hoped to insulate soldiers from "vicious intercourse and debauchery."[19]

While Bacon devoted considerable attention to the task of advocating and justifying the Union war effort, nearly from the outset of the conflict he concentrated on the relationship between this great struggle and the fate of slavery. Shortly after the war began, Radical Republicans reluctantly supported the Johnson-Crittenden resolutions, which declared that the sole aim of the war was the restoration of the Union. But, convinced that there could be no speedy end to the war or permanent peace without emancipation, the Radical Republicans agitated for an aggressive

17. *Independent,* July 25, August 29, 1861; *Congregationalist,* November 28, December 5, 1862. For an excellent treatment of Lincoln's policy on civil liberties, see Mark E. Neely, Jr., *The Fate of Liberty: Abraham Lincoln and Civil Liberties* (New York, 1991), 93–138 *passim.*

18. *Independent,* May 23, 1861; *Congregationalist,* May 2, 1862, January 16, 23, 30, August 14, 1863; *Debates and Proceedings of the National Council of Congregational Churches, Held at Boston, Massachusetts, June 14–24, 1865* (Boston, 1866), 323–26.

19. See Paludan, *"A People's Contest,"* 347–49; Edward Woolsey to George Bacon, May 11, 1861, in Edward Woolsey Bacon Papers; Osterweis, *Three Centuries of New Haven,* 320; Leonard to Catherine Bacon, January 21, 1864, in Bacon Family Papers; Hartford *Courant,* January 18, June 7, 1862.

war to expand liberty and grew increasingly frustrated with Lincoln's cautious policy regarding slavery. Indeed, Lincoln occupied a precarious middle ground on the issue. While he frequently cooperated with the Radicals on matters relating to the conduct of the war, and agreed with them on the end of ultimately ridding the nation of slavery, he did not wish to make the war a crusade for emancipation. Nearly until the moment he presented the Emancipation Proclamation, he supported a plan that combined colonization and compensated emancipation. In the final analysis, his proclamation linked both political expediency and ideological principle to the defense of the nation.[20]

In the early stages of the war, Bacon, like most other northern clergymen, emphasized the preservation of divinely established government, not the destruction of slavery, as the reason for waging war against the Confederacy. In a sermon he delivered a week after the war began, he maintained that the struggle was not one "of fanatical philanthropy for the abolition of slavery in States adhering to our Union, or in States beyond our jurisdiction." Throughout the first half of the war, he generally endorsed Lincoln's cautious approach to the slavery issue. In fact, during a visit to the White House by Joseph Thompson in 1864, Lincoln informed Thompson that Bacon's *Slavery Discussed,* published in 1846, "had much to do in shaping my own thinking on the subject of slavery"; Lincoln added, "He is quite a man."[21]

Bacon was convinced that both northerners and southerners instinctively felt that a Union victory would doom the institution that had caused the war, and he denounced as "a very sad and dangerous mistake" Lincoln's revocation of John C. Frémont's martial law decree that confiscated the Rebels' property, including slaves. Yet during the first year of the war, he and his colleagues in the Connecticut Gen-

20. See Hans L. Trefousse, *The Radical Republicans: Lincoln's Vanguard for Racial Justice* (New York, 1969), 168–202, 168–77, 203–10; Allan Bogue, *The Congressman's Civil War* (Cambridge, Mass., 1989), 132–39. On the historical debate regarding Lincoln and slavery prior to the promulgation of the Emancipation Proclamation, see, for example, George M. Fredrickson, "A Man but Not a Brother: Abraham Lincoln and Racial Equality," *Journal of Southern History,* XLI (1975), 39–58; James M. McPherson, *Abraham Lincoln and the Second American Revolution* (New York, 1990), 29–34. For treatments of the Emancipation Proclamation, see Mark Krug, "The Republican Party and the Emancipation Proclamation," *Journal of Negro History,* XLVIII (1963), 98–114; David Brion Davis, "The Emancipation Moment," in *Lincoln, the War President: The Gettysburg Lectures,* ed. Gabor S. Boritt (New York, 1992), 85–87.

21. Sermon of April 21, 1861, in Bacon Family Papers; also *Independent,* May 2, 9, 1861, *Congregationalist,* March 30, 1866. See also Leonard Woolsey Bacon, *A Discourse Delivered in the Memorial Presbyterian Church, Detroit, Michigan; On the Occasion of the Unveiling of a Tablet, in Memory of the late Leonard Bacon, D.D., December 24, 1882* (n.p., 1882), 8–9. The northern clergy's views on the war and emancipation in the early stages of the conflict are discussed in Moorhead, *American Apocalypse,* 97–101; McKivigan, *The War Against Proslavery Religion,* 185–86, 188–90.

eral Association seemed more inclined to wait patiently upon God's providence to end slavery by peaceful means "as soon as may be" than consciously to employ the force of arms to eradicate the system.[22]

As the war entered its second year, Bacon became increasingly favorable toward the notion that emancipation should be carried out in the name of military necessity, and he even hinted that constitutional scruples should not stand in the way of God's purpose. The Union's leaders, he argued, must not stand with their enemies against the slaves, and the slaves would doom the institution by continuing to choose liberty. But like many other northerners, he was quite unclear as to how slavery could or should be eradicated. As late as the summer of 1862, he predicted, for example, that slavery would not end as the result of insurrection, an act of Congress, or a presidential proclamation but, rather, through "the natural course of events."[23]

In his search for a means of ending slavery that would be constitutional, equitable, and irreversible, Bacon occupied a position that fell far short of that held by the Radicals. He shared with them a genuine abhorrence of slavery and a desire to see it abolished, a belief that the government should vigorously pursue victory, and a deep-seated hostility toward the South. But he differed with the Radicals on how and when slavery should be ended. His determination to avoid taking a radical stance on the issue of abolition placed him in a more moderate position than even the normally cautious Henry Ward Beecher, who by 1862 had come to insist that the war be a crusade for the abolition of slavery. Prior to the Civil War Bacon had lacked the abolitionists' sense of urgency; he now seemed willing to allow slavery to exist for at least another decade. Moreover, like Lincoln, he endorsed compensation as a means of making emancipation acceptable to the slaveholders. In the name of conciliation and compromise, which he believed would bring peace and prosperity to all Americans, he proposed, in an 1862 discourse, that all persons who took an oath of allegiance to the Union prior to May, 1863, and who liberated their slaves prior to July, 1876, would be paid at "fair valuation" by the United States Treasury, with 10 percent of that sum being given to the slaves at the time they were emancipated. In this way he hoped to shorten the war, save lives and money, and guarantee that abolition in fact would occur throughout the nation. Unlike many of the Radicals, he was also willing to accept colonization of the freedmen, though he opposed any government purchase of foreign lands for that purpose.[24]

22. Sermon of September 26, 1861, in Bacon Family Papers; *Independent,* May 9, July 18, October 24, November 14, 1861; *Minutes of the General Association of Connecticut* (1861), 12.

23. Bacon, "Noah's Prophecy: 'Cursed Be Canaan,'" *New Englander,* XXI (April, 1862), 356–58; Bacon, *Conciliation,* 18–20; *Minutes of the General Association of Connecticut* (1862), 16–17.

24. Leonard Bacon [Pacificator, *pseud.*], *The Nail Hit on the Head; or, the Two Jonathans Agreeing to Settle the Slave Question With or Without More Fighting, as the South Pleases* (New Haven, 1862), 6–20; Clark, *Henry Ward Beecher,* 153–55; *Congregationalist,* July 25, 1862. Some historians argue that many

Bacon also objected to the Radicals' agitation for federal abolition of slavery in the seceded states. Much as he had insisted upon a precise definition of terms in his debates with the abolitionists in the 1830s on immediate emancipation, he now called to task those who he believed mistakenly equated emancipation with abolition. While he wished to see abolition occur throughout the United States, he considered references to federal emancipation of slavery to be "pure nonsense." He emphasized this distinction because he believed that although the federal government could use its war powers to emancipate slaves, only the states could abolish slavery.[25]

Unlike such fervent nationalists as Horace Bushnell and Francis Lieber, as well as Radicals such as Charles Sumner and Thaddeus Stevens, Bacon was deeply concerned about the implications of a powerful national government. He was not entirely consistent in his thinking on this matter, however. He had upheld congressional authority to keep the territories free of slavery and in the secession crisis had embraced the concept of federal supremacy to defend the prerogatives of the national government. Moreover, during the war he supported, albeit within certain limits, Lincoln's suppression of civil liberties in the name of preserving the Union. But like many other Republicans, on the question of abolition he adopted what Herman Belz has termed a states' rights nationalism, which was rooted in both a strong feeling of nationalism and a desire to avoid a centralized American government. He was influenced in part by his attachment to the decentralized polity of the Congregational Church and by what he believed to be the excesses of a southern-dominated federal government in the 1850s. In addition, he opposed federal abolition because he did not consider the destruction of slavery to be the principal end of the war and he feared that it would be a divisive issue that might well impede efforts to save the nation. Perhaps most important, he had grave doubts about the constitutionality of federal abolition. Under the Constitution, he argued, no power was given to the federal government except that which was "absolutely necessary to our unity and stability as a nation." Thus, in all matters of internal police and governance not committed explicitly to the national government, each state was sovereign. Without such safeguards for the states' reserved rights and powers, he warned, "there is no security for liberty—no barrier against the perversion of our national government into a centralized despotism, under the name and form of democracy."[26]

---

moderate and Radical Republicans shared these beliefs. See, for example, Glenn M. Linden, "The Radicals and Economic Policies: The Senate, 1861–1873," *Journal of Southern History,* XXXII (1966), 188–99; Allan G. Bogue, "The Radical Voting Dimension in the United States Senate During the Civil War," *Journal of Interdisciplinary History,* III (Winter, 1973), 449–73.

25. *Congregationalist,* May 30, 1862.

26. *Congregationalist,* June 13, 1862; Herman Belz, *Emancipation and Equal Rights: Politics and Constitutionalism in the Civil War Era* (New York, 1978), xv.

In acknowledging the force of the states' rights barrier that surrounded slavery, Bacon left himself with little choice other than to pursue a circuitous, and extremely confusing, path to abolition. Ironically, his insistence upon state abolition led him to propose a plan that could well have required a greater use of federal power, and entailed a more dramatic restructuring of southern society, than the strategies devised by Thomas Ashley, George Julian, and other Radical Republicans. A new population and a new distribution of property in the South were necessary, Bacon wrote in mid-1862, in order to create "a new possibility of civilization and progress" and to pave the way for state abolition. Such a revolution in southern society, he asserted, would be accomplished by the expulsion of leading Confederates and the voluntary exile of others; by the forfeiture and sale of lands for unpaid taxes and the voluntary sale of other lands by impoverished or emigrating proprietors; by the emigration of "industrious and thrifty" northerners and foreigners to the South, who would purchase these lands and introduce new modes of industry and build new towns and cities; and by the reformation of opinion "in what may be left of the old population." As this process moved toward completion, he stated confidently, local laws that prohibited the teaching of slaves would be nullified and slaves would work for wages, acquire knowledge, and bear arms for the Union. Eventually, he believed, it would be possible to assemble conventions in each of the states that would "freely and gladly" abolish slavery. While Bacon did not make clear which level of government would carry out the various facets of this sweeping transformation of southern society, it seems quite likely that at least some of these policies would have been devised and implemented by the federal government.[27]

Although Bacon claimed that his plan would be acceptable to Lincoln, it in fact went much further than anything considered by the president. Given the radical nature of Bacon's proposal, as well as the time required to achieve state abolition, it is not surprising that neither moderate nor Radical Republicans considered his plan. Yet on the issue of emancipation Bacon continued to stand with Lincoln and most moderate Republicans in insisting on "emancipation for the war," which would advance Union military efforts in the South, not war for emancipation. As northern opinion shifted inexorably toward support for the argument based upon military necessity, he consciously stood, as he had so often done over the years, between the "sham conservatives," who he believed desired a Constitution as it was in order for the slave interests to dominate the nation once more, and the "anti-slavery destructives," whom he accused of seeking a new Constitution, created by presidential decree, which would forever take fundamental rights and duties from the states.[28]

---

27. *Congregationalist,* June 13, 1862. For Radical proposals early in the war for restructuring southern society, see McPherson, *The Struggle for Equality,* 238–40, 247–56; Herman Belz, *Reconstructing the Union: Theory and Policy During the Civil War* (Ithaca, 1969), 168–70.

28. *Congregationalist,* June 13, 20, September 5, 19, 1862; 1862 sermon, in Bacon Family Papers.

Lincoln's preliminary Emancipation Proclamation, presented in late September, 1862, received mixed reviews from northerners. Nearly all Democratic politicians and newspapers denounced it as unwise and unconstitutional, while some abolitionists criticized it for lacking in moral content and for urging both compensated emancipation and colonization. But eventually, most Republicans applauded the edict. Bacon waited nearly a month before commenting on the proclamation so as not to speak "inconsiderately." Although he doubted whether Lincoln should have waited as long as he did before issuing the decree and believed that the president probably should have indicated his dislike of slavery, he fully supported the president's right to present it and applauded his decision to base it upon military necessity. He also defended the proclamation against attacks from lawyers, arguing that the Constitution, like the Bible, must be interpreted by the common sense of the people.[29]

Bacon's October, 1862, *Congregationalist* column sparked a heated debate with Joel Parker, professor of constitutional law at Harvard Law School. In a series of letters that appeared in the Boston *Post* in late 1862 and early 1863, Parker condemned the Emancipation Proclamation as unconstitutional and dangerous, denounced Bacon's contention that the clergy, as well as the people, knew more about constitutional law than did lawyers, and charged that Bacon and other proponents of the proclamation were "willing to surrender all the liberties of the freemen of the United States . . . in order to subserve your favorite project of giving freedom to all the slaves."[30]

In a lengthy response to Parker's letters, Bacon deftly presented Lincoln's rationale for the Emancipation Proclamation. He maintained that because southern secession had unleashed such a vast rebellion, the president was invested with all belligerent rights, even though the Confederacy was not a belligerent nation. Consequently, he had "no shadow of a doubt" about Lincoln's constitutional right to issue the proclamation. Nor did he relent on his claim that all Americans had a right of private judgment concerning the meaning of the Constitution.[31]

Not only did Bacon heartily endorse the military necessity argument set forth by Lincoln, but he also welcomed the president's call for the recruitment of black troops. Moreover, he endorsed Lincoln's recommendation of compensation for slaves taken from loyal masters and for loyal states that abolished slavery, though he was careful to state that this was a matter of public policy and expediency, not of justice. While Lincoln and a growing number of Republicans quickly moved toward support for a constitutional amendment prohibiting slavery throughout the

29. *Congregationalist,* October 31, 1862. For northern reactions to the Emancipation Proclamation, see Victor B. Howard, *Religion and the Radical Republican Movement, 1860–1870* (Lexington, Ky., 1990), 35–36, 46–55; Franklin, *The Emancipation Proclamation,* 47–61, 68–78.

30. See Boston *Post,* November 29, December 8, 12, 20, 27, 1862, January 3, February 18, 1863.

31. Bacon, "Reply to Professor Parker," 195–97, 210–11, 219–32.

United States, Bacon continued to urge an act of Congress that would offer to every state a bonus pegged to the number of slaves at the date of the proposed abolition. Once again, he chose to pursue what he considered a practical course of action, even though it might well delay the achievement of an objective he very much desired. Such a "practicable" measure, he believed, would be more likely to be enacted than a constitutional amendment and would be preferable to meddling with the Constitution. He seemed less concerned than many Republicans, especially the Radicals, that a constitutional amendment was needed to preclude the possibility of repeal of the Emancipation Proclamation by a future president, Congress, or the Supreme Court, for he was confident that the federal government could never reenslave the freedmen. Yet perhaps because his plan for state abolition was so unrealistic and because, with Lincoln's support, the tide was running strongly toward passage of the Thirteenth Amendment, by late 1864 he told his congregation that the "question of right before God" dictated that the Constitution should prohibit slavery forever within the United States.[32]

Given his general support for Lincoln's policies regarding civil liberties, emancipation, and the conduct of the war, it was logical for Bacon to strongly endorse the president's bid for reelection in 1864. He never considered backing John C. Frémont, whom some Radicals supported, and he feared that a Democratic victory would mean that the "hopes of national unity will sink in endless night." The election, he told his congregation during the campaign, was "more momentous in its bearings on the destiny of the human race than the battle of Waterloo." Although McClellan carried New Haven by four hundred votes, Lincoln carried the nation. Convinced that the will of the people had declared against any compromise with the Confederacy and in favor of self-government, the supremacy of the Constitution, and the eventual destruction of slavery, Bacon was ecstatic.[33]

Bacon's endorsement of Lincoln's policies extended as well to his proposal for reconstructing the southern states. While the president and congressional Republicans agreed on a number of points, including the belief that Reconstruction should be accomplished without slavery, many Republicans in Congress and elsewhere questioned whether Lincoln's proposal for organizing loyal state governments in the South would adequately protect the rights of the freedmen and considered his 10 percent plan to be undemocratic. Congressional Republicans sought to expand

32. *Congregationalist,* January 2, September 11, 1863; Bacon, "Reply to Professor Parker," 254–55; Leonard Bacon, *A Historical Discourse Delivered at Worcester, in the Old South Meeting House, September 22, 1863: The Hundredth Anniversary of Its Erection* (Worcester, Mass., 1863), 29; sermon of November 1864, in Bacon Family Papers. The Republican party's movement toward passage of the Thirteenth Amendment is discussed in McPherson, *The Struggle for Equality,* 124–27, 192–97.

33. *Congregationalist,* October 28, 1864; sermons of November 1864, November 24, 1864, in Bacon Family Papers.

Congress' role in, and the national government's control over, the Reconstruction process, to delay the start of Reconstruction, to increase the standard of loyalty for participation in the new governments, and to guarantee equality before the law. They proceeded to pass the Wade-Davis bill in 1864, which Lincoln pocket-vetoed.[34]

Like many other Republicans during the war, Bacon was not entirely consistent in his thinking on Reconstruction. At times, he seemed to stand close to the more advanced Radicals. He firmly believed, for example, that if "a permanent peace, hearty peace, a true conciliation" were ever to be achieved, the leaders of the Confederacy must never again hold office and those who proved themselves implacable enemies of the nation should be forced into exile. Indeed, in 1862 he foresaw, as he had in his plan for state abolition, a massive transformation of the South that would have shaped it in the image of New England society. By confiscating the land of those who had committed treason, with much of the remaining land being sold to pay off debts, and by injecting new ideas, capital, methods, and men—from both the North and Europe—he hoped that loyal state governments would replace the old order with a society guided by small landowners, free laborers, a regenerated press and pulpit, and a democratic system of education. After a few years, he predicted, the South would be reconciled to the Union and the Constitution.[35]

This proposal clearly transcended the scope of Lincoln's ideas concerning Reconstruction, which sought largely to reestablish the states as they had existed prior to the war, except for the destruction of slavery. Yet as time passed, Bacon's views on Reconstruction moved much closer to Lincoln's than the Radicals'. He fully agreed with Lincoln that the union of the states was a "finality" and that the "pretended" secession constituted a rebellion by individuals, not by the states themselves. Thus, he categorically rejected the "state suicide" theory propounded by Charles Sumner, Thaddeus Stevens, and other Radicals. He in fact concluded that there was no need to reconstruct the national government, the Union, or the Constitution. Once legitimate state governments were established by the loyal people of the states, he declared in September, 1863, delegates would be elected to conventions, which would then write constitutions and submit them to the people. If Congress accepted these constitutions, representatives of the states would be admitted, thereby ending the federal government's role in the Reconstruction process. While he was uncertain whether Lincoln was a regular reader of his *Congregationalist* columns, he boasted in early 1864 that the president's Proclamation of Amnesty

---

34. For the historical debate on Lincoln, Congress, and the Reconstruction issue, see Belz, *Reconstructing the Union,* 126–32, 138–39, 155–67, 188–89, 198–99; Eric Foner, *Reconstruction: America's Unfinished Revolution, 1863–1877* (New York, 1988), 35–36, 61–66.

35. *Congregationalist,* November 14, 1862; sermon of July 30, 1862, in Bacon Family Papers.

and Reconstruction contained many ideas that he had included in his September, 1863, article.[36]

Bacon's views on where the former slaves would fit into the postwar southern society also closely resembled those of Lincoln (and many congressional Republicans, who did not include a provision for black suffrage in the Wade-Davis bill). Although he was not clear as to how far changes in southern race relations should carry, he believed that southern whites must swear to acknowledge the rights of all people, presumably including blacks. Yet he gave no indication that the nation was morally obligated to assist the former slaves. He clearly did not look toward either special treatment or social equality for them. Rather, he assumed—as did many other northerners—that blacks would come to occupy a decidedly subordinate category, as peasants, employees, or free servants.[37]

Many of Bacon's writings and speeches during these years quite naturally focused upon the national crisis and the thorny issues it raised. But he also continued to devote considerable time and energy to his family and his church, as well as the state of religion in America. His concerns about family extended beyond the anxieties associated with his sons who served in the military, for throughout the Civil War his brother's alcoholism worsened. By early 1862, David's health had deteriorated to the point where Bacon, with financial and moral support from all of his adult sons, was forced to admit him to the Hospital for the Insane in Northampton, Massachusetts, at a cost of three hundred dollars a year. Bacon had become increasingly pessimistic about his brother's prospects of recovery, warning David that if he did not make an earnest effort at rehabilitation, the alcoholism would "continue to degrade you and drag you down till you sink into your grave."[38]

Bacon's pessimism was well founded, for a few months after being admitted to the hospital David escaped and was caught by the police. Like his earlier efforts to rescue Delia, Bacon's sense of obligation to advise and protect a troubled younger sibling produced little but resentment. David responded angrily to Leonard's remonstrances (and those of his sisters), referring to his advice as "foolish, incoherent, and self-contradictory" and refusing to communicate with his siblings for the next two and a half years. Finally, in early 1865 David died in a New York City hotel.[39]

Bacon continued to be involved in a broad array of activities in the community and the nation. He remained extremely interested in the collection of historical

36. *Congregationalist,* September 11, 1863, January 8, 1864.

37. *Congregationalist,* January 8, 1864; Bacon, "Reply to Professor Parker," 254–55.

38. Day Book for March 26–27, 1862, Leonard to David Bacon, March 23, 1862, Leonard Woolsey to Leonard Bacon, April 2, 3, October 13, November 7, 1862, in Bacon Family Papers.

39. Dr. Henry Prince to Bacon, June 19, 1862, David to Leonard Bacon, August 12, 1862, Bacon to Jared Linsly, December 24, 1864, Joseph P. Thompson to Bacon, January 21, 1865, Marcus F. Hodges to Bacon, January 23, 1865, in Bacon Family Papers.

documents, helping in 1862 to establish the New Haven Colony Historical Society and serving as a director for many years. He was also active in a number of endeavors related to the Congregational Church and the expansion of evangelical religion, including the New Haven City Missionary Society, which sought to proselytize the growing immigrant population and to aid the families of soldiers, as well as the Connecticut General Association and the American Board of Commissioners for Foreign Missions. On many occasions he was also called upon to deliver commemorative addresses, lectures on Christianity and other subjects, and funeral eulogies for friends and dignitaries.[40]

In the midst of these responsibilities, Bacon also found time to write *Christian Self-Culture,* which the American Tract Society published in 1863. This book reflected a continuing emphasis in middle-class evangelical culture on self-examination, self-help, and self-improvement. It would, he hoped, serve to instruct and uplift "the intelligent youth of our land in the ways of righteousness," for the chief end of Christian life was self-culture, which extended to integrity, faith, enlightened commitment, charity, and self-government. His emphasis upon self-culture was a logical extension of his growing attachment to a Christ-centered theology based upon the authority of the Bible. If one came to know Christ, rather than adhering to a specific system of theological propositions, he asserted, one would take the first step toward knowing and receiving a true theology. Not surprisingly, he continued to hold to Horace Bushnell's emphasis upon Christian nurture as the key to spiritual salvation and a godly life.[41]

Just as Bacon eschewed adherence to any specific and narrowly defined theological system, he also remained an outspoken critic of sectarianism. When groups were compelled to recognize each other as "evangelical" and as holding essential doctrines in common, he stated in an 1863 discourse, "theology has made great progress in spite of the theologians; and men begin to see in what direction lies the path to viable unity among believers in Christ." Consequently, he reminded Congregationalists that the Congregational Church was "not a sect, but a principle." Yet Bacon continued to prefer the Congregational polity to all other forms of church government, and he clearly was unwilling to accept an actual union of

40. *Papers of the New Haven Colony Historical Society* (2 vols.; New Haven, 1865), II, 3–5, 9–27; Osterweis, *Three Centuries of New Haven,* 343–44; "Report of the Board of Managers of the New Haven City Missionary Society, 1862," Selah B. Treat to Bacon, June 6, 26, 1862, Leonard Woolsey to Leonard Bacon, December 6, 15, 1864, Israel P. Warren to Bacon, December 18, 1863, funeral sermon for Lyman Beecher, January 14, 1863, in Bacon Family Papers; *Minutes of the General Association of Connecticut* (1863), 56–57; *Congregationalist,* February 13, 1863.

41. Notice of Bacon's *Christian Self-Culture; or Counsels for the Beginning and Progress of a Christian Life,* in *New Englander,* XXII (April, 1863), 357–58; J. P. Warren to Bacon, April 14, 1863, sermons of December 4, 1864, February 2, 1865, in Bacon Family Papers; *Congregationalist,* April 22, 1865.

denominations under one church government, for he feared that such an arrangement would subvert Congregationalism's fundamental principles of liberty and "complete decentralization."[42]

As a result of Bacon's stature as an expert on Congregational polity and procedures, he was often asked either to provide advice regarding church councils or to serve on them. For example, a minority in George Cheever's Church of the Puritans, who opposed his abolitionist views and his insistence upon loyalty to his position, asked, as they had in 1859, to be dismissed from the church. They were suspended by Cheever's partisans, who called an *ex parte* council that unanimously sided with the opposition and recommended that other Congregational churches withdraw fellowship from the Church of the Puritans. The press, including the *Independent* and most of New York City's secular papers, stood against Cheever, but Horace Greeley and a number of abolitionists charged that Bacon and Thompson were aligned with a reactionary, wealthy clique in Cheever's church. Indeed, Bacon had been the council's guiding light; and, in a replay of his 1859 confrontation with Cheever, he chastised Cheever's congregation for ignoring the council's findings and categorically denied that the slavery issue had been involved in the controversy. In yet another instance, two years later, Bacon gave Charles Beecher advice concerning a council that had alleged doctrinal unsoundness, and he then defended Beecher before his association.[43]

Bacon's primary responsibility remained, as it had been since 1825, his pastorate at Center Church. As he approached his fortieth year as its minister, he retained the affection and confidence of the great majority of his parishioners. His blend of moralism, progressive evangelicalism, and antislavery moderation, as well as his stature in the community and the nation, were appealing and comforting to his largely middle- and upper-class congregation. Although Center Church had lost numerous members over the years as other Congregational churches were established in the city, its membership continued to stand at approximately 550–560, with an additional 1,000 people regularly attending Sunday services.[44]

---

42. Bacon, *A Historical Discourse Delivered at Worcester,* 49; *Congregationalist,* August 5, 1864, February 24, 1865, February 7, 21, March 7, 1862.

43. E. W. Chester to Bacon, April 10, 24, 1861, in Bacon Family Papers; York, *George B. Cheever,* 181–84; *Independent,* May 16, 1861; Charles Beecher to Bacon, June 19, 30, September 30, October 13, November 23, 1861, in Collections of American Literature, Beinecke Library, Yale University, New Haven, Conn.

44. *Minutes of the General Association of Connecticut* (1861), 53; *Leonard Bacon: Pastor of the First Church in New Haven,* 46, 84. Of the 66 adult male members at this time whose occupations are known, fifty-five (83 percent) were part of the business or professional classes, while eleven (17 percent) were farmers or skilled laborers. See *Benham's New Haven Directory and Annual Advertiser. Number Seventeen. 1856–7* (New Haven, 1856), *passim; Benham's New Haven Directory and Annual Advertiser. Number Twenty-two. 1862–1* (New Haven, 1861), *passim; Benham's New Haven Directory and Annual Advertiser for 1865–6. Number Twenty-six* (New Haven, 1865), *passim.*

Although Bacon loved his work as pastor and suffered from no serious illness, he became increasingly conscious of his advancing age. On his sixtieth birthday, in 1862, he calculated that he had only ten years of life remaining. His son Leonard Woolsey urged him to seek an assistant for a year or two, which would free him for literary work. But he did not follow this advice, and on his sixty-third birthday he remained convinced that the last seven years of his life would be ones of "decadence and decay," pushing him toward "the front rank of old men who have out-lived their generation." Bacon's belief that his life was nearing an end, though quite mistaken, ultimately convinced him that it was time to retire from the ministry. On the fortieth anniversary of his ordination at Center Church, in March, 1865, he announced that, as the oldest pastor in Connecticut who had not partly or wholly withdrawn from his work, he would retire as soon as a successor could be hired. Thereafter he would teach at Yale Theological Seminary.[45]

Having declared his intention of leaving a post that he had occupied since he was a young man of twenty-three, Bacon now faced a period of significant adjustment. As he came to a crossroads in his life, so, too, did the nation, for only a month after he announced his resignation the bloody Civil War came to an end. With the cessation of the conflict, the nation could begin to heal its wounds and ponder the shape of the postwar society. At a mass meeting on the New Haven Green, attended by five thousand people, Bacon expressed something of the ambivalence that many northerners felt toward the defeated enemy. While he emphasized the "duty of conciliation" toward those southerners who were willing to stand by the nation and the Constitution, he also reminded his audience of the "duty of justice against the authors of the rebellion."[46]

Bacon's uncertainty as to the exact shape that Reconstruction should assume was deepened by the assassination of Lincoln only days after Lee's surrender at Appomattox. Like most northerners, he was shocked and saddened by this tragedy. In a sermon at Center Church, he sought to explain how this horrible act could have occurred. Choosing to view it as a metaphor for the brutality and evil that had characterized the great struggle, he told his parishioners: "Perhaps this last and crowning crime of the rebellion was in some sort needed to complete and confirm forever the world's conviction of the wickedness which has characterized the rebellion from the first."[47] What sort of president Andrew Johnson would be, and where he would carry American society, were not of concern to Bacon or to many other northerners at the moment, but this would soon change.

And at a crossroads was where the Congregational Church stood, too. As the

---

45. Sermon of February 19, 1862, Leonard Woolsey to Bacon, September 1, 1863, in Bacon Family Papers; *Leonard Bacon: Pastor of the First Church in New Haven*, 67, 104, 111.

46. Dunham, *The Attitude of the Northern Clergy Toward the South*, 170–71.

47. *Ibid.*, 172; sermon of April 16, 1865, in Bacon Family Papers.

Civil War moved into its final months, Bacon was the guiding force in organizing the National Council of Congregational Churches, slated to meet in June, 1865. Anticipating new opportunities as well as mounting problems for the church as it entered the postwar era, he and other Congregational leaders believed that a national meeting was necessary in order to evangelize both southern whites and the former slaves and to make church polity and doctrines relevant to late-nineteenth-century realities.[48]

48. See *Congregationalist,* February 24, 1865; Ray Palmer to Bacon, March 1, 1865, in Bacon Family Papers.

12

THE RECONSTRUCTION EXPERIMENT AND EVANGELICAL THEOLOGY

A S Americans emerged from the Civil War, they began the difficult process of adapting to changes that had surfaced both before and during the conflict. New opportunities and challenges confronted not only the federal and state governments but also the churches and other institutions. Bacon both actively participated in and commented extensively on the debate surrounding important social, political, and theological issues that divided Americans in the wake of the Civil War.

Following decades of rapid expansion, the Congregational Church faced the challenge of defining itself in relation to other denominations and of determining the degree of centralization and uniformity that should exist within the church. Between November, 1864, when Bacon and other Congregational leaders met in New York City to plan the church's National Council, and June, 1865, when the council met in Boston, Bacon was the person most responsible for planning and organizing the most important American Congregational convention since the Cambridge Synod in the mid-seventeenth century. At the preliminary meeting in 1864, where he served as moderator, he and his colleagues decided to focus the council's attention on the evangelization of the South and West, church building, theological education, and, above all, the expediency of issuing statements of Congregational polity and faith.[1]

One of the most hotly debated issues at the National Council concerned the Declaration of Faith. On this matter, Bacon sought to strike a balance between an emphasis upon the nonsectarian nature of Congregationalism and the need for a fresh statement of received tradition that would be relevant to nineteenth-century

---

1. *Debates and Proceedings of the National Council of Congregational Churches,* 4–8; Ray Palmer to Bacon, March 1, 1865, William W. Patton to Bacon, March 15, 1865, in Bacon Family Papers; *Congregationalist,* February 24, 1865.

Christians. Because some people believed that the church stood for "nothing in particular," he told the delegates, a positive creedal statement, without any hint of forced adherence or the exclusion of other Christians, was necessary in order that members knew what they shared in common and that missionary efforts could be aggressively undertaken among millions of former slaves in the South. But Joshua Leavitt, speaking for a minority of the committee that developed the Declaration of Faith, expressed the fear that references to Calvinism would prevent other Protestants from attaching themselves to the Congregational Church. After revisions and further debate, the delegates concluded that taking a vote would seriously divide the council. Consequently, Alonzo Quint further revised the statement; and at a special meeting held at Burial Hill in Plymouth, Bacon's motion that the compromise language, which deleted the word *Calvinism,* be accepted passed unanimously.[2]

The other major issue debated by the National Council related to Congregational Church polity. As chairman of the committee on church polity, Bacon, with assistance from Quint, wrote a lengthy treatise for the council's consideration. Once more, he sought to occupy a middle ground between traditional principles and usages and present-day needs as well as between localism and centralization. While he looked to the Cambridge Platform for guidance, he noted that the committee had "freely departed" from it for the sake of clarity and relevance. He also insisted that local churches retain their essential autonomy and that church councils had no legislative or judicial power. But at the same time, he made it clear that all churches had mutual duties that grew out of obligations of fellowship. Leavitt again filed a minority report, arguing that a less denominational orientation, which illustrated the effect of Congregational principles on religious and political liberty in the United States, would serve to create a broad-based ecumenical brotherhood. Ever mindful of the bitter clashes between the Congregationalists and Presbyterians in the 1850s, Bacon, however, underscored the need to highlight the differences that existed between the groups' forms of church government. Following extended debate, the delegates adopted the report, with amendments offered by Edwards Park, who succinctly enunciated the distinctive characteristics of Congregational polity as localism, mutual fellowship, and the absence of a hierarchy. Yet because there was insufficient time to consider the full treatise, the council appointed a committee of twenty-nine, including Bacon and Quint, to prepare a full statement, with explanatory material. Over the next seven years, he and other members of the committee labored diligently on this report. Finally, in 1872, they completed the "Boston Platform," but because of its length and complexity it was never widely adopted.[3]

2. Bacon to William W. Patton, April 7, 1865, in Bacon Family Papers; *Debates and Proceedings of the National Council of Congregational Churches,* 135–47, 350–52, 354–57, 363–64, 400–404; Atkins and Fagley, *History of American Congregationalism,* 203–205.

3. *Debates and Proceedings of the National Council of Congregational Churches,* 103–104, 114–22, 129–33, 430–37, 445–46, 448–55, 463–64; Williston Walker, *A History of the Congregational Churches in the*

Issues relating to church doctrine and polity were not the only matters that divided the National Council. Debate also erupted on the prohibition question, and Bacon's outspoken criticism of the Maine Law during the council's deliberations precipitated a bitter controversy that continued for months after the meeting adjourned. Even prior to the Civil War, enthusiasm for the prohibition statutes enacted in the 1850s had begun to wane and beer and liquor consumption had risen. While many northerners continued to believe that legal action could suppress drinking, many others evaded the law, and enforcement was spotty or nonexistent. Although Bacon was disturbed by the reappearance of drinking habits that had been prevalent when he entered the ministry, at the National Council he declared that it would be "unfortunate, and to an extent disastrous" for the council to commit itself to the Maine Law, for "the quackery of such legislation has been the ruin of the cause, from which it cannot be rescued until we cut ourselves clear of the whole scheme of legislating alcohol out of the creation of God." Contrary to his expectation, his motion to delete the words relating to prohibition was overwhelmingly accepted by the council. Bacon and the other delegates were not alone in questioning the efficacy of the Maine Law; even such stalwart prohibitionists as John Gough and Edward Delevan had come to urge that greater emhasis be placed on moral suasion campaigns.[4]

Bacon's criticism of the Maine Law infuriated many prohibition advocates, including John Marsh, secretary of the American Temperance Union. In several letters that appeared in the *Independent* in 1865, Marsh pointedly asked whether Bacon favored prohibitory, permissive, or no legislation. Marsh acknowledged that the prohibition laws had not achieved the objectives expected by their proponents, but he largely blamed liquor dealers, unscrupulous politicians, and passive clergymen for the shortcomings and insisted that these laws had informed the public conscience. Above all, he rejected Bacon's claim that the temperance movement had been wrecked on the shoals of the Maine Law. In these attacks on Bacon, which at times became quite personal, and in similar attacks by Horace Greeley, Neal Dow, and others, Bacon's support for licensing laws was derided and he was accused of giving aid and comfort to the liquor dealers.[5]

As so often occurred when he was challenged or criticized, Bacon could not resist the temptation to defend and explain his position at great length. At times, he reacted angrily to his critics, terming them "professional agitators" and harshly

---

United States (New York, 1894), 399–401. Bacon discussed this issue in the *Congregationalist,* February 24, August 25, 1865.

4. Tyrrell, *Sobering Up,* 307, 316–29; Bacon, *Four Commemorative Discourses,* 32–33; *Debates and Proceedings of the National Council of Congregational Churches,* 481.

5. See *Letter to the Reverend Leonard Bacon, D.D. of New Haven, Conn., from John Marsh, D.D.,* 3–11, 14–15; *Independent,* August 3, 17, 31, September 7, 14, 1865; S. C. Rouse to Bacon, September 15, 1865, anonymous to Bacon, September 18, 1865, in Bacon Family Papers.

rebuking them for their "calumnious attacks on my personal character." In numerous letters that appeared in the *Congregationalist* and the *Independent* in 1865, he reminded Marsh that he had strongly supported the resolutions at the council which commended abstinence from the ordinary use of intoxicating drinks. This "original basis" of the temperance cause, he wrote, was the "simple and most defensible platform of voluntary association for mutual support in the course of benevolent, but easy self-denial." The issue, he pointed out, was not whether to renounce the aid of legislation but whether the Maine Law was "a wise and practicable method of securing the welfare of society." Clearly he believed that it was not.[6]

While Bacon conceded that licensing laws suffered from certain defects, he remained convinced that legislated prohibition would have little effect on drinking habits unless it reflected the moral sense of the people. Because prohibition was coercive rather than voluntary, it could not do this. Thus, the Maine Law was a "lamentable failure" and "an embarrassment" because many people opposed total abstinence and because judges and juries refused to enforce a law they considered excessively severe. When laws were not executed, he added, it taught contempt for the law. Bacon also criticized prohibition laws for being indiscriminate in their application in that they equated temperate drinking with drunkenness, failed to distinguish between liquor and beer, cider, and wine, and concentrated on liquor dealers and manufacturers and moderate drinkers while largely ignoring the drunkard. In the final analysis, he pursued—much as he had in his earlier debates with the abolitionists—a moderate and pragmatic, albeit not entirely consistent, course based upon distinctions and conditions which he believed would enable society effectively to combat a practice that he disliked and wished to eradicate.[7]

By the end of 1865, the furor surrounding Bacon's denunciation of the Maine Law had abated considerably, in part because he nearly ceased to defend his position in the press. Despite the intensity of Bacon's debate with his prohibitionist critics, it did not signal for him a long-term concentration on the temperance question. Much as he had subordinated the issue to the slavery question prior to the Civil War, he now devoted much of his attention to the reconstruction of the South and the place that African Americans would occupy in American society. In numerous articles that appeared in the *Congregationalist,* the *New Englander,* the *Independent,* and other publications, especially from 1865 to 1867, he influenced the thinking of large numbers of Protestants in the Northeast on these controversial matters.[8]

The audience that Bacon addressed was, like many other northerners, uncertain as to precisely what form Reconstruction should assume. No blueprint existed: the

6. *Independent,* August 17, 31, 1865; *Congregationalist,* July 28, 1865.

7. See *Independent,* July 27, August 10, 17, 31, September 7, 14, October 19, November 2, 9, 1865.

8. New Haven *Daily Palladium,* May 13, 1867; Linus Child to Bacon, February 7, 1867, Day Book for March 8, 1867, C. A. Richardson to Bacon, October 11, 1866, Henry C. Bowen to Bacon, August 1, September 21, 22, 1865, in Bacon Family Papers.

labor system that had emerged in the lower Mississippi River valley and the Sea Islands was largely a war measure, and no southern state government had been successfully reorganized. Although many northerners were uneasy about conditions in the South and desired protection for southerners who had remained loyal to the Union, they also favored some form of reconciliation with their former enemies.[9]

Bacon shared these ambivalent feelings. He was convinced that "all that kindness can do to conciliate those who were so lately our enemies must be done." Toward that end, he visited Richmond in July, 1865, under the auspices of the American Union Commission, which had been founded in 1864 to assist southern and border-state white loyalists who had been driven from their homes by Confederate sympathizers and to introduce northern ideas and institutions into southern society. While in Richmond he consulted with leading figures in the city on establishing a public school system throughout Virginia. A few months later he, along with Henry Ward Beecher and General George Meade, informed a public meeting held in New York City that numerous southern whites confronted a desperate situation.[10]

Yet Bacon's sympathy for southern whites who had been uprooted by the war did not extend to the former Confederate leaders. There were, he insisted, varying degrees of responsibility among southerners for "a crime unparalleled in the history of nations." The most culpable groups, which included the clergy, should, in his opinion, be severely punished. But he went even further. Unlike some Radicals, such as Gerrit Smith and Horace Greeley, he called for the execution of Jefferson Davis and other former leaders of the Confederacy, asserting that they were more deserving of hanging than John Brown had been. While Brown had acted to free the oppressed, he reasoned, Davis and his compatriots had consciously committed treason on behalf of the oppressors.[11]

Because he believed that the South must be punished for its treasonous act, Bacon was unwilling to accept its rapid return to the Union with minimal changes in its society. He pointedly reminded the president that the greatest danger in his desire to reestablish civil order in the South was that he "may proceed too rapidly,

9. Randall C. Jimerson, *The Private Civil War: Popular Thought During the Sectional Conflict* (Baton Rouge, 1988), 238–51 *passim,* studies the unformed attitudes of many northerners toward the South as they emerged from the Civil War.

10. *Independent,* December 28, 1865; C. T. Chase to Lyman Abbott, September 28, 1865, Lyman Abbott to Bacon, October 3, 12, November 10, 1865, in Bacon Family Papers; *The American Union Commission: Its Origins, Operations and Purposes* (New York, 1865), 1–8; *The American Union Commission. Speeches of Hon. W. Dennison, Postmaster-General, Reverend J. P. Thompson, D.D., President of the Commission, C. N. G. Taylor, of East Tennessee, Hon. J. R. Doolittle, U.S. Senate, Gen. J. A. Garfield, M.C., in the Hall of Representatives, Washington, February 12, 1865* (New York, 1865), 4–8, 17–22, 43; Ira V. Brown, *Lyman Abbott, Christian Evolutionist: A Study in Religious Liberalism* (Cambridge, Mass., 1953), 38–43.

11. *Independent,* January 18, February 1, 29, 1866; Alexander S. Sessions to Bacon, January 9, 1866, in Bacon Family Papers.

and peace may be proclaimed when there is no peace." Convinced that most white southerners were "*professedly* and obviously unchanged in temper and principle," he once more called for a fundamental and time-consuming transformation of southern society that would create a diverse economy, a free labor system, and a regenerated Christianity. In the meantime, a military presence would be required to guard against the revival of "old ideas."[12]

Like most other Republicans, whether moderate or Radical, Bacon insisted that the nation guarantee the basic rights of the former slaves. They must, he wrote, be free in all respects, with the full protection of the law and the ability, as free laborers, to rise and fall on their own merits. He was confident that, in the end, blacks probably would rise from "mere laborers for wages into the condition of petty landlords and petty capitalists," while many southern whites would be swept aside by emigrants from Europe and the North. Although Bacon realized that difficult times lay ahead for the South and the nation, he envisioned public education as a powerful instrument for diffusing knowledge and reshaping southern society in the image of the North. Likewise, he was confident that the demise of slavery would relieve the churches of a "terrible burthen" and pave the way for the advancement of the gospel.[13]

Bacon earnestly hoped that the president would uphold the honor and faith of the nation by meting out justice to traitors and by protecting the rights of those southerners who had been loyal to the Union. Indeed, despite concerns that Johnson had pardoned far too many former Confederates, he gave the president the benefit of the doubt until mid-1866—long after many Radical Republicans had turned against Presidential Reconstruction. He agreed with Johnson that it was the nation's "sacred engagement" to allow the southern states back into the Union. At the same time, he and other moderate Republicans became increasingly fearful that the Radicals had captured control of the party and would seek to concentrate power in Washington. These considerations help to explain his decision to speak at a public meeting in New Haven in early 1866, where he shared the dais with Senator James Doolittle of Wisconsin, a vocal Johnson supporter. Bacon told the crowd that, while he did not wish to endorse either Johnson or Congress, he believed that when the president determined that peace was restored Americans must allow the southern states to govern themselves. Moreover, he expressed concern that the mounting conflict between the executive and legislative branches was "fraught with harm and mischief; and it must be stopped."[14]

12. *Congregationalist,* October 6, 1865.

13. New Haven *Daily Palladium,* December 9, 1865; *Congregationalist,* December 29, 1865, January 12, March 12, 1866.

14. *Independent,* September 13, October 25, 1866; C. H. Bullard to Bacon, February 27, 1866, Union party meeting, 1866, in Bacon Family Papers; New York *Times,* February 27, March 2, 1866.

Some Radical Republicans immediately accused Bacon of abandoning the freedmen and the party. But this criticism was mild when compared with the firestorm of protest generated by Henry Ward Beecher's call for a speedy readmission of the southern states and limits to government assistance for the freedmen. Concerned that Radical editors and politicians were dangerous extremists, Bacon was one of the few friends of Beecher who expressed general approval of his views. Yet by September 1866, even Beecher had come to repudiate Johnson as "an uncultivated, untrained man, who never knew how to manage opposition except to fight it." Indeed, by directing vitriolic attacks at the Republican leadership; by refusing to denounce the draconian Black Codes, the election of numerous former Confederate leaders to the provisional governments, and the race riots that killed hundreds of African Americans; by vetoing both the Freedmen's Bureau Act and the Civil Rights Act; and by establishing the National Union movement as a direct challenge to the Republican party, the president had managed to alienate many moderate Republicans.[15]

Bacon was rather ambivalent toward the men who launched the National Union movement. Because he believed that all political organizations had an "inevitable proclivity to become a selfish faction," he concluded that it might be best if the Republican party were replaced by new parties. He also expressed the hope that James Dixon, Gideon Welles, and other National Unionists would address important questions that had arisen after the war. In addition, he worried that the Republican leadership sought to prolong Reconstruction largely for political gain. Nevertheless, he soon became thoroughly convinced that Dixon and his associates simply wished to divide the Republicans and were prepared to stand with the Democrats, who he believed did not have the welfare of the nation at heart. Equally important, Johnson's failure to commit himself to the "cause of freedom and eternal justice" deeply disappointed Bacon. Conditions in the South, he wrote, showed that the "old style of Southern civilization" had reemerged and that Johnson's "hasty and unguarded reconstruction" had left black and white southern Unionists entirely at the mercy of their enemies. "Our faith with the freedmen," he remarked solemnly,

---

15. C. H. Bullard to Bacon, March 14, 1866, S. Guiteau to Bacon, March 5, 1866, in Bacon Family Papers; Henry Ward Beecher to Bacon, September 21, 1866, in Beecher Family Papers; also William G. McLoughlin, *The Meaning of Henry Ward Beecher: An Essay on the Shifting Values of Mid-Victorian America, 1840–1870* (New York, 1970), 221–27. For treatments of the deteriorating relations between Johnson and congressional Republicans, see La Wanda Cox and John H. Cox, *Politics, Principle, and Prejudice, 1865–1866: Dilemma of Reconstruction America* (New York, 1963), 145–212; David Warren Bowen, *Andrew Johnson and the Negro* (Knoxville, 1989), 124–66, 227–29. On the ill-fated attempt to form the National Union party, see Albert Castel, *The Presidency of Andrew Johnson* (Lawrence, Kans., 1979), 78–88; Edward L. Gambill, *Conservative Ordeal: Northern Democrats and Reconstruction, 1865–1868* (Ames, Iowa, 1981), 56–74.

"will not be kept, if, for the sake of patching up a hasty and precarious peace, or for the sake of organizing a new party and carrying an election, or for the sake of commercial profits hoped for from speedy reconstruction, we leave them without adequate protection."[16]

Bacon's growing disenchantment with the president also appears to have been spurred by his developing sense that the Radical Republicans did not in fact control Congress. He gravitated naturally toward a cautious, moderate, yet generally progressive position on the Reconstruction issue, seeking to avoid the extremes represented by Johnson and the Radicals. While these implacable foes railed against each other, he informed his *Independent* readers, moderate Republicans had become "calmly resolute" in their attempts to avoid unnecessary obstruction of the president's policies while, at the same time, maintaining the rights of Congress as the duly constituted legislature of the nation, restoring the Union, and securing the rights of the southern loyalists. Bacon was particularly troubled by Johnson's refusal to consult with Congress in reestablishing state governments in the South. Congress, not the president, he insisted, had the power to determine whether and when a republican form of government existed in a state. But in the end, according to Bacon, the loyal people of a state must reconstruct "their own government in their own way, under the Constitution of the United States, without any dictation from the National Government."[17] Thus, once again, he struggled to find an acceptable balance between varied, and often contradictory, considerations. He agreed with the Radicals that the nation had a moral obligation to protect the former slaves and to grant them basic legal rights, but at the same time he remained convinced that they were too dogmatic and divisive and that their agenda posed the threat of centralized despotism.

Yet even after carefully weighing the relative merits of Congressional and Presidential Reconstruction, the Republican party and the National Union movement, the rights of the freedmen and states' rights, and more, Bacon was not prepared to articulate a clear-cut, consistent position on Reconstruction. Indeed, his vocal support for states' rights notwithstanding, he vigorously endorsed the Fourteenth Amendment, which was shaped by the moderate and Radical Republicans' conviction that federal action, short of granting suffrage, was needed to protect the rights of the freedmen. He feared that a mere act of Congress or a provision in a state constitution might be repealed, and he believed that states could not declare themselves to be republican in form. Thus, in his opinion, vigorous congressional action that effectively guaranteed to every state a republican form of government—with people protected in their basic rights and with no dominant race or caste as the

16. New York *Times,* March 2, 1866; *Independent,* August 23, September 6, 1866.
17. *Independent,* September 27, October 4, 18, 25, 1866; *Congregationalist,* November 23, 1866.

source of power—represented "the only hope for peace, liberty, progress and prosperity, throughout these recovered States."[18]

Indeed, in some respects Bacon thought that the proposed amendment did not place enough restrictions on the states. He would have preferred that it explicitly prohibit the states from abrogating the supreme law of the land or releasing any citizen from the obligation of allegiance to the United States. Above all, he was concerned that the amendment did not adequately "secure, directly, full protection for the freedmen against 'the mean whites' whose rivals they are, whom they will soon outstrip in knowledge and thrift if they have not already done so, and who are therefore their most malignant enemies." These reservations appear to have placed him close to the Radicals' views. But soon after seemingly declaring his unequivocal support for a strong constitutional guarantee of rights for the former slaves, he retreated to the position that this could not be accomplished without converting the national government into a "centralized despotism." In the end, as a number of postrevisionist historians have argued, Bacon, and many other moderate Republicans (and even some Radicals), gave a higher priority to defending states' rights than to protecting the rights of the freedmen.[19]

Likewise, though Bacon wished that the Fourteenth Amendment had stipulated that "no citizen shall in any state be excluded from the right of suffrage because of his race or his complexion" (language similar to that eventually incorporated in the Fifteenth Amendment), he concluded that few northern states would support this. For Republicans, black suffrage was a complex and difficult issue that deeply divided their ranks. On the one hand, most Radicals believed that suffrage was a natural right and that it should be universal, unrestricted, and under federal control. On the other hand, many moderates, including Bacon, considered the franchise a political privilege and favored qualified suffrage and the retention of state regulation.[20]

The first real test of Bacon's and the Republicans' commitment to black suffrage came in referenda held in Connecticut and two other northern states in 1865. Of all the northern states, only five New England states and, within limits, New York

18. *Congregationalist,* February 15, 1867. The debates on, and the characteristics of, the Fourteenth Amendment are discussed in William E. Nelson, *The Fourteenth Amendment: From Political Principle to Judicial Doctrine* (Cambridge, Mass., 1988), 40–63, 110–47; Robert J. Kaczorowski, "Searching for the Intent of the Framers of the Fourteenth Amendment," *Connecticut Law Review,* V (Winter, 1972–73), 368–98.

19. *Congregationalist,* February 15, 1867. See, for example, Michael Les Benedict, "Preserving the Constitution: The Conservative Basis of Radical Reconstruction," *Journal of American History,* LXI (1974), 65–90; Belz, *Emancipation and Equal Rights,* 77–78.

20. *Congregationalist,* February 5, 1867. The debate among Republicans on black suffrage is treated in William Gillette, *The Right to Vote: Politics and the Passage of the Fifteenth Amendment* (Baltimore, 1969), 21–22, 44–45, *et passim.*

permitted blacks to vote. Some historians have maintained that many Republican party officials did not enthusiastically endorse black suffrage because it was not a popular issue and that they ultimately came to support blacks' right to vote largely in order to make the North safely Republican. Bacon, however, does not fit this profile. In response to a request by Henry C. Bowen, he wrote a column for the editorial page of the *Independent* in which he vigorously urged the deletion of the word "white" from the Connecticut Constitution. The state, he wrote, must decide "whether her Christianity and Republicanism, being brought to the test, mean anything." A "deep and abiding obligation of justice," he insisted, was the crucial consideration on a matter that stood as "an essential condition of Reconstruction."[21]

Despite Bacon's ringing endorsement of the suffrage amendment, it was defeated by a wide margin; similar amendments in Minnesota and Wisconsin also went down to defeat. Likewise, in 1866 Congress overwhelmingly rejected a proposed constitutional amendment for black suffrage, and the subsequent provision in the Fourteenth Amendment for a reduction in representation proportionate to the number of blacks denied the franchise represented a quite modest step toward federally mandated black suffrage. These setbacks diminished the energy in the campaign for black suffrage. Nevertheless, Bacon remained convinced that there could be "no complete security for justice and permanent tranquillity" in the South until all political and civil disabilities based upon race or complexion were swept away. Only those males (he took it for granted that women should not have the right to vote) who were illiterate or had been convicted of a crime, he asserted, should be denied the franchise.[22]

Bacon's insistence upon a literacy test for suffrage set him apart from most Radical Republicans. His unequivocal demand that the right to vote be controlled by the states perhaps represents an even more striking difference between him and the Radicals. When Senator Henry Wilson of Massachusetts proposed legislation that would prohibit the denial of the franchise to any male on the grounds of race, color, or previous condition of servitude, Bacon emphatically rejected it as a direct threat to the rights of the loyal states, which had not lost their reserved powers. If Congress were allowed to do this, he warned, it could easily decree that women could vote or that one or another "obnoxious class" could be excluded from the franchise. His opposition to Wilson's franchise bill elicited stinging criticism from Radical Re-

21. Leslie H. Fishel, Jr., "Northern Prejudice and Negro Suffrage, 1865–1870," *Journal of Negro History,* XXXIX (1954), 12–15; Gillette, *The Right to Vote,* 37–40; Henry C. Bowen to Bacon, September 22, 1865, in Bacon Family Papers; *Independent,* September 28, 1865. Victor Howard errs in contending that Bacon remained silent on the issue. Howard, *Religion and the Radical Republican Movement,* 179.

22. Martin E. Mantell, *Johnson, Grant, and the Politics of Reconstruction* (New York, 1973), 52–53; Joanna Dunlop Cowden, "Civil War and Reconstruction Politics in Connecticut" (Ph.D. dissertation, University of Connecticut, 1974), 233–34; *Congregationalist,* April 5, May 3, 1867.

publicans. One writer accused Bacon of seeking to deny the franchise to blacks in Connecticut and of hypocritically asserting that the federal government could prevent violations of the Constitution in the South but not in Connecticut. Bacon responded to these charges by angrily accusing his critics of espousing *"doctrines and measures which threaten the entire loss of liberty"* and would have catastrophic results for the Republican party. Indeed, he was convinced that if Charles Sumner had not stated his intention of forcing black suffrage on the loyal states by an act of Congress, neither the 1867 suffrage referendum nor Joseph Hawley, the Republican candidate for governor, would have been defeated in Connecticut.[23]

Bacon's critic erred in accusing him of wishing to deny the vote to blacks. But his charge of hypocrisy (which has been reiterated by some historians) came close to the mark, for Bacon and many other moderate Republicans in fact sought to establish a very different standard for the South than the North on the black-suffrage issue. Beyond this, in the name of defending states' rights, he once more retreated from a position that he deemed just and right. While he considered Connecticut's constitutional ban on black suffrage "not only a disgrace, but a positive injury" and sincerely desired "to see our black citizens sharing equally with the whites in all political as well as civil rights," he was "not willing to give up that palladium of liberty, *the reserved rights of the states,* for the sake of gaining even so desirable an object." If those rights were surrendered, he warned in 1867, the nation "would not be fit for honest men to live in."[24] Thus, once more, when confronted with conflicting principles he chose the one that firmly ensconced him in the moderate wing of the Republican party.

In Connecticut and several other northern states, the Republicans had seriously misjudged public opinion on the black-suffrage issue, thus enabling the Democrats to sweep to power in the 1867 elections. Many Republicans, especially the moderates, responded to these setbacks with caution and evasion, including calling for federally mandated black suffrage in the South but not in the North. Ultimately, following extended debate, Congress passed the Fifteenth Amendment, and Connecticut and most other northern states ratified it in 1870. Although Bacon did not comment publicly on the amendment as it was being debated and ratified, it is quite likely that he supported it. His opposition to attempts by Wilson, Sumner, and other members of Congress to enact federal laws mandating black suffrage never precluded his support for a constitutional amendment that achieved the same objective. After all, state ratification was required to enact any such amendment. Moreover, the fact that the Fifteenth Amendment established a qualified suffrage cer-

23. *Congregationalist,* April 5, 19, May 3, 1867.

24. *Ibid.,* April 5, May 3, 1867. For the Republicans' hypocrisy on the suffrage issue, see Gillette, *The Right to Vote,* 37–43; Michael Perman, *Emancipation and Reconstruction, 1862–1879* (Arlington Heights, Ill., 1987), 113.

tainly appealed to Bacon. In the long run, of course, Congress's failure to guarantee black suffrage, with no conditions, enabled the southern states to employ literacy tests and poll taxes as means of disfranchising blacks.[25]

Bacon's silence during the debate surrounding the Fifteenth Amendment does not so much indicate a lack of interest in the Reconstruction issue as the fact that other responsibilities limited his contributions to newspapers and journals during the late 1860s. While he expressed the vague hope that the American people would find "a way of safety" regarding Reconstruction, he remained concerned that the process might well be undermined by groups seeking to push it in extreme directions. On this matter he stood, as he so often had, firmly between what he termed "idealists and political pedants" and "self-styled conservatives."[26]

Bacon was more hopeful that a system of public education would take deep root in the South. He was convinced that the diffusion of knowledge throughout the United States, especially in the South and among northern immigrants, was the means by which "we are to fulfill our destiny and lead the nations in their progress toward a perfect civilization," to maintain order and establish cultural conformity, and to enable people to develop their talents. His conviction that education could uplift and improve people goes far to explain why he strongly supported efforts to educate the former slaves. He heartily approved of his daughter Rebecca's decision to teach, and then serve as assistant principal, at Hampton Institute in Virginia from 1869 to 1871. Another daughter, Alice Mabel, also taught at Hampton in the 1870s. During these years, he urged Congress to support Hampton and advised Rebecca on issues relating to her employment by the American Missionary Association. Under the superintendence of Samuel Chapman Armstrong, the school emphasized a message of self-restraint, order, and Christian morality—values dear to Bacon's heart.[27]

25. Mantell, *Johnson, Grant, and the Politics of Reconstruction*, 63–64, 67, 98–99; Gillette, *The Right to Vote*, 37–43; *Congregationalist*, February 15, April 5, 1867. On the limits of the Fifteenth Amendment, see John Niven, "Connecticut: 'Poor Progress' in the Land of Steady Habits," in *Radical Republicans in the North: State Politics During Reconstruction*, ed. James C. Mohr (Baltimore, 1976), 40–45; Foner, *Reconstruction*, 446–47.

26. Bacon, "The Latest Work in the Schonberg-Cotta Series," *New Englander*, XXVII (January, 1868), 174.

27. New Haven *Daily Palladium*, December 9, 1865; Bacon, *Four Commemorative Discourses*, 31; Bacon to George Whipple, January 23, 1869, Rebecca to Leonard Bacon, February 5, November 22, 1869, January 4, March 1, 1870, June 13, 1871, Rebecca Bacon to E. P. Smith, August 23, 1869, February 24, 1870, Leonard to Rebecca Bacon, March 18, April 1, 1869, William Buckingham to Bacon, April 5, 1869, Leonard to Catherine Bacon, December 30, 1870, in Bacon Family Papers. Armstrong and the teachers at Hampton are studied in Robert C. Morris, *Reading, 'Riting, and Reconstruction: The Education of Freedmen in the South, 1861–1870* (Chicago, 1981), 148–61; Joe M. Richardson, *Christian Reconstruction: The American Missionary Association and Southern Blacks, 1861–1890* (Athens, Ga., 1986), 4–44.

The limited attention that Bacon gave to matters related to Reconstruction in the late 1860s was due largely to his career shift in late 1866. For a year and a half after he announced that he would retire from the ministry, he remained at Center Church while the congregation searched for a successor. In his retirement sermon he denied that he was leaving the ministry because of any diminution of his parishioners' affection for him. Rather, he felt that a younger minister would more effectively counteract the conservative tendencies of his congregation and would develop a stronger relationship with the young adults and children in the church.[28]

Catherine referred to her husband's retirement as "such a crisis in your life." Bacon, however, chose to present a brave front to his parishioners, telling them that he wished simply to be "a grateful pensioner" and "an elder brother" in the church. But his beloved congregation refused to relieve him of his position, and until his death he remained, at least technically, its pastor, without stated responsibilities. He was often asked to officiate at weddings and funerals, and he occasionally preached on Sundays and delivered lectures in the parish house. For a time following his retirement, he sat in the pews at church services, but his congregation persuaded him to sit in the pulpit, even though he had no important role in the service. Thus, he once more sat before them, dressed in a traditional black broadcloth suit, a swallowtail coat, and a necktie, which stood in stark contrast with his bushy white beard and white hair. His people also showed their deep affection for Bacon by continuing to pay him one thousand dollars a year until his death, and at times he received gifts from members of the congregation. This income was especially appreciated because five of his children still lived at home during the mid- and late 1860s and Catherine was an invalid who required special care.[29]

During the same year that he retired from the ministry, Bacon delivered the sermon at the funerals of Charles Cleaveland and S. W. S. Dutton, two Congregational ministers in New Haven with whom he had served for several decades. Their deaths reminded him that he was growing old. But despite his sense that his generation was rapidly passing from the scene, he remained deeply interested in the welfare of Center Church, seeking to influence the congregation's choice of a successor and, in 1868, helping to convince George L. Walker, a Hartford minister, to settle as pastor of the church. Bacon also continued to write articles for newspapers, though his contributions to the *Independent* virtually ceased until the early 1870s. Despite Bowen's pleas that he write for the paper, "with your sledge hammer strokes on any

28. *Leonard Bacon: Pastor of the First Church in New Haven,* 106–10; statement of May 21, 1867, in Bacon Family Papers.

29. Catherine to Leonard Bacon, September 12, 1866, G. B. Whittlesey to Bacon, December 31, 1867, Day Book for February 19, 1868, H. C. Kingsley to Bacon, December 19, 1870, in Bacon Family Papers; *Leonard Bacon: Pastor of the First Church in New Haven,* 41–43, 116; Theodore Dwight Bacon, *Leonard Bacon,* 508–509.

living theme you may elect," Bacon was furious with Theodore Tilton for moving the *Independent* away from its evangelical foundations, and he had little respect for Bowen, who he believed was controlled by Tilton.[30]

Bacon's teaching position at Yale Theological Seminary, however, proved far more time-consuming than his writing in the late 1860s. He was uncertain whether he wished to accept the professorship that had been offered in 1865. Convinced that a belief in the basic precepts of the Bible was a more important requisite for salvation than the doctrines interpreted by theological professors, he told his congregation: "There is no promotion in going from the pulpit to theological chair—as pulpits and professorships are to-day." In addition, because his only preparation for the position was forty years' experience as a pastor, he distrusted his ability to teach. Finally, the seminary's faculty, finances, and student body were at a low ebb in 1866. Some even suggested that the seminary be closed.[31]

In 1864 Bacon had appealed, without success, to Joseph Thompson to become professor of revealed theology; and in 1866 Samuel A. Harris, president of Bowdoin College, declined a similar offer from Yale. A few years later, Bacon explained to Harris that he ultimately had accepted the position because "I have all my life been a 'Jack-at-a-pinch,' put to do whatever nobody else would do." But this did not fully explain his decision. In fact, Bacon agreed to serve as acting professor of revealed theology largely out of a deep and abiding interest in the welfare of Yale. He had been reappointed to the Yale Corporation in 1864; as chairman of a committee that raised money for scholarships and established laws regulating the governance of the Theological Department, he gained insight into the seminary's difficulties. Determined to save the seminary, he accepted the corporation's appointment to its faculty.[32]

The fact that Bacon was much older and better known than his colleagues caused some apprehension among them. But as Timothy Dwight, a professor of sacred literature, later recalled, Bacon never placed himself above his younger associates, and his labors at the seminary were "very helpful and successful." For his part,

30. Leonard Bacon: *Pastor of the First Church in New Haven,* 114–17; funeral sermons of January 26, February 16, 1866, Bacon to Norman Seaver, May 21, 1867, Bacon to George Walker, September 26, 29, 1868, Leonard to Catherine Bacon, November 22, 1868, Henry C. Bowen to Bacon, February 19, 1867, Bacon to President Magoun, November 26, 1867, in Bacon Family Papers; also Housley, "The Independent," 184–85, 209–14.

31. *Leonard Bacon: Pastor of the First Church in New Haven,* 112; Bacon to Samuel A. Harris, March 28, 1871, in Bacon Family Papers; Dwight, *Memories of Yale Life and Men,* 253–56, 278–84; Kelley, *Yale,* 192–94, 199–200.

32. Bacon to Joseph P. Thompson, June 10, 1864, G. B. Philcox to Bacon, June 14, 1864, Bacon to Samuel A. Harris, March 28, 1871, in Bacon Family Papers; minutes of July 26, 1864, July 25, 1865, July 24, 1866, July 16, 1867, July 19, 1870, "Records of the Yale Corporation"; minutes of July 11, 1865, December 4, 1871, "Records of the Prudential Committee of the Yale Corporation."

though the salary was far lower than he had received at Center Church, Bacon was satisfied with the job. His teaching schedule gave him four months each year for work of his choice, including supplying vacant pulpits. And contrary to his concerns when he accepted the position, he came to view himself as an effective teacher, and did not find instruction "growing irksome by repetition."[33]

In his lectures Bacon gave greater emphasis to Biblicism, the life and work of Christ, and the relationship between religion and the natural sciences than to questions relating to moral ability and the divine permission of sin—preferences he shared with his associates in the theology department and at many other seminaries. He was especially concerned that the evangelical mission of the seminaries not be overshadowed by scholarship. In an article that appeared in the *Methodist* in 1867, he asserted that the primary objective of a seminary was not "to make great scholars, learned commentators, exact lexicographers, or profound theologians" but the more pragmatic one of training ministers who were "more effective in the advancement of Christ's kingdom by the salvation of men." This commitment to an evangelical theology that led to the conversion of all sinners through Christ and rested upon the belief that people were free and responsible agents was clearly manifested in his lectures to his students.[34]

Bacon remained an implacable foe of sectarianism. While he believed that Yale Theological Seminary should represent the evangelical theology of New England, he warned that it must not train Congregational ministers to exhibit a sectarian spirit. In his introductory remarks at the laying of the cornerstone of Divinity Hall in 1869, he told his audience that the seminary had "always valued Christian truth more than any form of ecclesiastical authority." Bacon's attack on denominational exclusiveness pointed toward the New Theology, which would spark heated debate among Congregationalists in the 1870s. As formulated and espoused by Theodore Munger, Newman Smyth, and others, the New Theology called for a return to the Scriptures and emphasized the right of private judgment, unrestricted by inferences deduced by the developers of theological systems. In a similar vein, Bacon warned his students against being either too literal in their reading of the language of the Scriptures or too eager to align themselves with one or another theologian's interpretation of the Bible. In this way, he assured them, they would avoid numerous *"theological stumbling blocks."*[35]

33. Dwight, *Memories of Yale Life and Men,* 301–302; Bacon to Joseph P. Thompson, November 30, 1867, Bacon to Samuel A. Harris, March 25, 28, 1871, in Bacon Family Papers.

34. *The Semi-Centennial Anniversary of the Divinity School of Yale College, May 15th and 16th, 1872* (New Haven, 1872), 24–25; article in *The Methodist,* December 21, 1867, lectures 12, 21, 37 on Dogmatic Theology, 1868, in Bacon Family Papers; *Addresses at the Laying of the Corner Stone of the Divinity Hall of the Theological Department of Yale College, September 22nd, 1869* (New Haven, 1869), 8.

35. Lectures 4, 6, 7, 32, on Dogmatic Theology, 1868, in Bacon Family Papers; also Rev. A. S.

Bacon also aligned himself with the progressive wing of evangelical Protestant-ism in insisting that the relationship between theology and science was both dy-namic and important. He believed that because theology was the science of final causes, the other sciences were to some extent tributary to it. But he also declared emphatically, as he frequently had done during the past two decades, that because both theology and the physical sciences had their own subject matter and sources of knowledge that must be analyzed and systematized, theology should not dictate to the other sciences what they should find in their proper fields. Not surprisingly, he opposed the mounting conservative assault on scientific discoveries that were deemed a repudiation of Christian revelation. The theologian who condemned any science and denied its right to discover what it could "by legitimate methods, in its legitimate field," he stated in a lecture delivered at Yale, "is a doubter rather than a believer."[36]

During his first few years on the seminary's faculty, Bacon devoted considerable energy not only to teaching but also to raising badly needed funds for the institu-tion. Convinced that "we must build or die," he made numerous trips to New York City and Brooklyn to solicit contributions for the seminary's endowment and its building fund and, despite his meager salary, donated several hundred dollars of his own money. Thanks in part to his efforts, during the years 1866–1871 the seminary was placed on a solid financial footing.[37]

Bacon also rose to the defense of Yale against those alumni who questioned its present leadership and mission. In doing so, he spoke as a conservative who, while willing to accept certain changes in the institution, was adamant in his opposition to any major deviation from Yale's traditional ways. When W. Walter Phelps, an alumnus who spoke for the Young Yale group, criticized President Woolsey, and especially the clergy who dominated the corporation, for refusing to adjust their policies to the needs of an increasingly modern, secular society, Bacon, in 1870, vigorously defended the clergy and accused Phelps of desiring to abolish all grades, recitations, and rules. A year later, in several *Independent* articles in which he posed as Timothy Pickering of Squashville, he combined sarcasm and anger in de-nouncing any attempt to lessen the role of religion in the affairs of Yale and in

---

Chessbrough, *Home Work: or, Parochial Christianization* (Boston, 1867), xiv–xv. The New Theology is discussed in Benjamin Wisner Bacon, *Theodore Thornton Munger: New England Minister* (New Haven, 1913), 256–60 *passim*.

36. Lecture at Yale Theological Seminary, September 18, 1868, in Bacon Family Papers. See also Barbara M. Cross, *Horace Bushnell: Minister to a Changing America* (Chicago, 1958), 120–24.

37. Circular of July 31, 1865, Leonard to Catherine Bacon, February 17, 1869, contribution for Divinity Hall, December 25, 1869, Bacon to John DeForest, November 29, 1871, in Bacon Family Papers; *Congregationalist*, June 18, 1868; Bacon to Oliver Henry Percy, March 19, 1869, in Oliver Henry Percy Papers; Dwight, *Memories of Yale Men and Life*, 285–86; Gerald Everett Knoff, "The Yale Divinity School, 1858–1899," (Ph.D. dissertation, Yale University, 1936), 77, 88, 95.

warning that the Young Yale group really wished to make the institution "a new-fangled university—something between a 'business college' and a lyceum with plenty of popular lecturers."[38]

Bacon's service to Yale, as a member of the corporation and a professor of theology, kept him extremely busy. Although he enjoyed a compressed teaching schedule and no longer had to prepare weekly sermons, during these years he maintained a frenetic pace. He frequently supplied churches in Connecticut and Massachusetts, partly to supplement his income and partly because it reassured him that he was "not considered past service." He also delivered numerous speeches before literary, benevolent, and religious organizations in New England and the Midwest, and in 1870 Harvard granted him the degree of doctor of laws. Moreover, he presented a series of lectures on Christianity at Phillips Academy in 1869 and on the history of the Congregational Church at Center Church in 1870. Perhaps most noteworthy were the courses of lectures that he presented to the middle and senior classes at Andover Theological Seminary in 1867, 1868, and 1869, in which he sought to strike a balance between "extreme independency" and a system of national or provincial church government that he believed denied the completeness of the local church. In the midst of these responsibilities, he found time to write a few articles for the *New Englander* and the *Congregationalist;* at the request of Henry Ward Beecher, editor of the *Christian Union,* beginning in 1870 he also wrote numerous pieces on religious and social issues for this New York newspaper.[39]

Although in his sixties, with several of his children grown and on their own, Bacon's family responsibilities continued to demand both time and energy. Several of his younger children still lived at home, and the ever-growing number of grandchildren often came to visit him and Catherine. Bacon visited his older children and their families whenever possible, and he continued to offer them advice and assistance. He especially counseled Leonard Woolsey, a minister in Brooklyn, and then Baltimore, during these years. He appears to have seen in his eldest son many of the personality traits and interests that he had exhibited, sometimes to his detriment, in his early years at Center Church. Thus, perhaps expressing second thoughts about his own determination to write for a broad audience and to be active in numerous benevolent and reform causes, he frequently urged his son to concentrate

38. Leonard Bacon, "A Voice from 'Squashville': A Letter to the New Englander from the Rev. Mr. Pickering," *New Englander,* XXIX (October, 1870), 678–91, 700–701; Bacon to W. Walter Phelps, November 11, 1870, in Bacon Family Papers; *Independent,* June 15, 29, July 13, August 3, 10, 24, 1871.

39. Leonard to Catherine Bacon, August 4, 1866, July 29, 1867, May 15, 22, 1869, April 25, 1870, Theron Baldwin to Bacon, October 28, 1868, Gorham D. Abbott to Bacon, October 28, 1869, Bacon to A. Blanchard, August 8, 1868, lectures 4, 5, Andover Course, Second Year, 1869, Henry Ward Beecher to Bacon, January 20, 1870, in Bacon Family Papers; Bacon to Theodore Dwight Woolsey, November 13, 1870, in Woolsey Family Papers; *Congregationalist,* June 4, 1868; Baldwin, *Bacon Genealogy,* 278; Lyman Abbott, *Reminiscences* (Boston, 1915), 328–34.

on preaching as "your one great business" and cautioned him against undertaking too much "impulsive activity." Such advice was not always appreciated by his sons, for it was seldom combined with words of praise and affection. Shortly after Bacon died, Leonard Woolsey noted, with obvious regret, that his father had been "shy, in fact, of direct expressions of affection, or of pride in any of their work" and "would never lift a finger to push one of his own boys forward." He admitted that, at times, he and his brothers had even thought that their father was ashamed of them. Bacon's reticence probably was in part the product of the Victorian culture, which encouraged self-control and the repression of feelings among males. Equally important, while he was growing up his parents do not appear to have served as strong role models for supportive and warm parenting. They cared deeply about him, and he was the privileged child in the family. But his father had often been absent from the home, and during Leonard's late teens and early twenties his mother had been so mired in poverty and depression and so envious of her son's privileged status that she found it difficult to offer him praise or encouragement. Yet as Bacon's own sons grew older, they became increasingly adept at deciphering certain of their father's words and actions and determining his inner feelings and thoughts regarding their lives. Leonard Woolsey in fact acknowledged that, over the years, they had developed ways of knowing that his "joy and pride" in all of his children and their families were responsible for "the happiest old age that was ever lived."[40]

The example that Bacon had long set for his children—of constantly seeking to juggle numerous responsibilities—was very much at odds with his advice to Leonard Woolsey. This pattern continued unabated even after his retirement from the ministry. Unable to complete a biography of Admiral A. H. Foote, a Union naval hero in the Civil War, he notified the publisher in 1871 that "the truth is, I am too busy a man—with too many sorts of work and too many calls to unexpected but urgent tasks—for such an undertaking." He was increasingly philosophical about his advancing age, and resolved to "lighten the load in some way." But this did not mean that he was prepared to slow down the pace of his life appreciably. As he wrote Catherine on his sixty-ninth birthday, "There is still I trust more work in me, and when the work is ended then let the rest come." Indeed, in 1871 his career took yet another turn when he accepted an offer to be lecturer on church polity and American church history at Yale Theological Seminary.[41]

40. See Leonard to Catherine Bacon, August 7, 14, September 12, 1867, December 17, 1868, May 12, 15, 22, 1869, December 27, 1870, Catherine to Leonard Bacon, June 25, 1869, Leonard Woolsey to Leonard Bacon, March 14, October 24, 1871, Leonard to Frank Bacon, May 28, 1868, Leonard to Leonard Woolsey Bacon, June 28, 1868, 1869, December 11, 1871, Susan to Leonard Bacon, September 29, 1869, Leonard Woolsey Bacon's reminiscences, December 31, 1881, in Bacon Family Papers.

41. Bacon to Clark and Maynard, April 1, 1871, Bacon to A. Blanchard, August 8, 1868, Leonard to Catherine Bacon, February 19, 1869, in Bacon Family Papers.

13

CONGREGATIONAL COUNCILS AND THE BEECHER-TILTON SCANDAL

WHEN Samuel A. Harris became Dwight Professor of Didactic Theology in early 1871, Bacon immediately resigned his position on the faculty. He had always viewed his professorship as temporary, and was pleased that he had played an important role in persuading Harris to come to Yale. Upon his resignation, the Yale Corporation expressed its gratitude for his services as an "able and successful instructor" and "a wise and diligent counselor for the general advancement" of the Theological Department; it then immediately created for him the position of lecturer on church polity and American church history, which he held until his death in 1881.[1]

Bacon's appointment made eminent sense, for he was perhaps the foremost American expert on Congregational history and polity. In his seminary lectures he traced the beginnings of church government in the New Testament and the reawakening of the Congregational idea late in the Reformation era in England. He also devoted considerable attention to the experience of the Separatists and the Puritans in Great Britain and America. Although he studied the history of church polity in other Protestant denominations, his interests, as well as the fact that most of his students planned to become Congregational ministers, led him to focus largely on the Congregational experience.[2]

At approximately the same time that he embarked upon his new teaching responsibilities at the age of sixty-nine, Bacon began to use his lectures in preparing *The Genesis of the New England Churches*. Ultimately completed in 1874, *Genesis* was

---

1. See Bacon to Samuel A. Harris, March 25, 1871, Samuel A. Harris to Bacon, April 19, 1871, in Bacon Family Papers; Dwight, *Memories of Yale Life and Men*, 294–95; minutes of April 12, 1871, in "Records of the Yale Corporation."

2. See Theodore Dwight Bacon, *Leonard Bacon*, 514; *Advance*, January 9, February 27, March 6, 13, 1873.

the first history of the origins of the Congregational Church to be published in the United States. In writing what he considered "almost the main work for the remainder of my life," Bacon admitted that because he had always been too busy to be a "great reader" or to spend much time in libraries, he limited his research primarily to secondary sources. Moreover, much as he had done in his *Thirteen Historical Discourses,* published in the 1830s, he was at least as interested in celebrating the Congregational Way and its struggles against persecution in England as in writing an objective historical account of the church. "The story which I tell," he noted in the book's preface, "is the story of an idea slowly making its way against prejudices, interests, and passions—a story of faith and martyrdom, of heroic endeavor and heroic constancy."[3]

Bacon devoted much of *Genesis* to a study of early Puritanism following the English Reformation. He was especially critical of the Anglicans and the Puritans for holding to the "fatal error" that the reformation of Christianity could only be effected within the framework of a national church. This assumption, he asserted, had led the Puritan leadership of the Massachusetts Bay Company to emphasize religious uniformity at the expense of religious liberty. His sympathy clearly lay with the separatists, whose commitment to the concept of voluntary churches he believed ushered in a new era of religious liberty. Yet in his relatively brief account of the Puritan experience in America he praised the Puritans for ultimately accepting a voluntary covenant of allegiance to God, which, he concluded, marked the beginning of a "distinctively American church history."[4]

Following the publication of *Genesis,* Bacon pointed out to the historian George Bancroft, who had favorably reviewed his book, that until the early nineteenth century there had been unrelenting conflict between the idea that people must be made religious by law and "that pure Voluntaryism which was the distinction of the Separatists, which dominates now in our country, and which is to dominate throughout Christendom." This issue of voluntarism and independency versus uniformity and nationalism, as well as that of catholicity versus denominationalism, was hotly debated by Bacon and other delegates to the National Council of Congregational Churches, held at Oberlin in November, 1871. He had presented the opening address at the Pilgrim Memorial Convention, held in Chicago in 1870, which called for a national Congregational convention every three years. Then, at a preliminary meeting that convened later that year in Boston, he and other state repre-

3. Leonard Bacon, *The Genesis of the New England Churches* (New York, 1874), v, vii, ix, xi; Leonard to Leonard Woolsey Bacon, October 5, 1872, in Bacon Family Papers; *Leonard Bacon: Pastor of the First Church in New Haven,* 129–30.

4. Bacon, *The Genesis of the New England Churches,* 72, 80–133, 477–78, *passim.*

sentatives appointed an executive committee that prepared a draft of a constitution which enunciated the self-government and fellowship of individual churches as the cardinal principles of Congregationalism and stated emphatically that the upcoming National Council would have no legislative or judicial power over either individuals or churches.[5]

Bacon played a major role at the Oberlin council, presenting the sermon and chairing the committee on unity of the Congregational Church. At the council, as well as in several articles that appeared in the *Christian Union* and the *Independent* during the months following the meeting, he acted as something of a mediator between the proponents of a pure Congregationalism and the proponents of a modified one. He reiterated his long-standing opposition to those within the Congregational Church who wished to move toward centralization and uniformity. Yet he also supported the concept of triennial national councils, assuring those who considered this a dangerous move toward a national church that such councils would constitute nothing more than "a perfectly free confederacy of churches for cooperation and mutual helpfulness." Likewise, he supported, as he had done at the Boston council in 1865, the formulation of a creed, arguing that Congregationalists should know the distinctive truths of religion that formed their special bond. But at the same time, he continued to warn that sectarianism would lead to a schism within the church and weaken the forces of Christianity. Convinced that Congregationalism was, in the final analysis, "nothing but Christianity," he heartily endorsed the council's explicit disavowal of any "pretension to be the only churches of Christ."[6]

Bacon's conviction that Congregationalists should adopt a doctrinal statement, not because they were Calvinists, Arminians, or Edwardsians but because they shared in common certain essential evangelical principles, led him in 1872 to call for the merger of Yale Theological Seminary and the conservative Theological Institute of Connecticut. The existence of two seminaries in Connecticut, he wrote in a paper that he sent to Congregational ministers throughout the state, was the product of theological controversies that were "already obsolete" and only vaguely remembered. Thus, he proposed that by 1880 each seminary would be funded independently but would share a common statement of belief and a board

5. Bacon to George Bancroft, February 26, 1876, in George Bancroft Papers, Massachusetts Historical Society, Boston, Mass.; "Triennial Conference of the Congregational Church," 1871, in Bacon Family Papers; *Minutes of the National Council of the Congregational Churches of the United States of America, at the First Session, Held in Oberlin, Ohio, November 15–21, 1871* (Boston, 1871), 9–10.

6. See Leonard Bacon, "Sectarian Symbols," *New Englander,* XXXI (October, 1872), 745–60; sermon at National Council, 1871, Center Church lecture, November 26, 1871, in Bacon Family Papers; *Christian Union,* January 10, 17, February 14, 1872; *Independent,* December 21, 1871, January 11, February 8, 1872; Benjamin Wisner Bacon, *Theodore Thornton Munger,* 195–96.

of nominations for the examination of candidates and the nomination of faculty. However, the trustees of the Theological Institute refused to move their seminary from Hartford, and the proposal came to naught.[7]

Bacon's responsibilities at the seminary, as well as his reputation as an authority on the Congregational Church's practices and polity, kept him busy during these years. He was acutely aware of his advancing age, telling Leonard Woolsey in 1872 that "I have only a fading remnant of my life before me." Despite his age, he labored diligently on his book and contributed numerous articles to the *Christian Union* and, following Bowen's firing of Tilton as editor in 1870, the *Independent*. He wrote for these newspapers in part because he needed the income to support Ruddy's and Alfred's education at Yale and three other children who still lived at home.[8]

One of the issues that Bacon addressed in the columns of these papers was Reconstruction. For nearly four years, he had devoted little attention to this complex and difficult matter. He was not alone in this regard. Even though the Fifteenth Amendment did not guarantee blacks' right to vote or hold office, many Republicans considered it Reconstruction's capstone. Indeed, the persistence of racial intolerance in both the North and South and the mounting popular reaction against an expanded federal role served to weaken the Radicals' position within the Republican party and to accelerate the moderates' retreat from the Reconstruction effort. In the early 1870s such Republicans as Carl Schurz and Charles Francis Adams, who had long supported rights for blacks, reacted to corruption in the Grant administration and in some of the Reconstruction governments in the South by forming the Liberal Republican movement. Espousing the concept of limited government, and increasingly skeptical of democratic principles and "class legislation," these men came to perceive the "southern question" as an annoying distraction that enabled party spoilsmen to remain in power.[9]

Bacon agreed with the Liberals on some key points. He concurred with their pronouncement that the central issues of the Civil War were "dead" and that civil service, tariff, and currency reforms were desperately needed. In 1870 he and a number of other New Haveners informed Secretary of the Interior Jacob D. Cox that civil service reform involved nothing less than the question of whether the people would be "served by competent and experienced men, or ruled by party

7. "Plan for Union of Hartford and Yale Seminaries," December 1872, in Bacon Family Papers; Knoff, "The Yale Divinity School," 207–209, 213–14.

8. Leonard and Catherine also derived income from two of Leonard Woolsey's sons, as well as two Japanese girls, who boarded with them in the early 1870s. Leonard to Leonard Woolsey Bacon, March 31, May 20, June 25, October 5, 1872, Bacon to Mr. Van Name, August 12, 1871, Bacon to Mr. More, October 31, 1872, in Bacon Family Papers.

9. For treatments of the Liberal Republicans, see James M. McPherson, *The Abolitionist Legacy: From Reconstruction to the NAACP* (Princeton, 1975), 24–34; Foner, *Reconstruction,* 488–511.

managers and political tricksters." Bacon remained contemptuous of the view that party loyalty should take precedence over principle. Consequently, he threw his support behind Orris Ferry, the Democratic candidate for the United States Senate from Connecticut in 1872—an act which elicited an angry rebuke from Republican loyalists. He also called upon both parties to pay off the national debt in specie as soon as possible and to move gradually toward the elimination of tariffs, which he termed "that quackiest and iniquitous method of taxing industry while pretending to protect it."[10]

Bacon also shared the Liberals' judgment that self-government was needed in the South. Because he remained especially adamant in his opposition to the consolidation of power in Washington, once again he was prepared to retreat from federal protection of blacks' rights and support for the Reconstruction governments in order to maintain the power and prerogatives of the states. In response to a lecture by Senator Oliver Morton of Indiana, who claimed that the states derived their authority from the United States Constitution, Bacon wrote in 1872: "Better ten years of terrorism in a few Southern districts than a hundred years of centralized government, crushing the states into mere municipalities, with no rights but such as, having been conceded by the sovereign nation, can be resumed at discretion." Likewise, he did not believe that the eradication of segregation laws directed against blacks—which he considered "absurd anachronisms" that the people would eventually grow tired of—was worth risking the usurpation of state authority by the federal government. Though Bacon did not question the motives of those who sought to expand central authority, he pointedly reminded them that "Hell is paved with good intentions." Thus, like many other moderate Republicans, his constitutional conservatism led him to draw back from his earlier endorsement of the Fourteenth Amendment, insofar as its effectiveness depended upon vigorous federal enforcement.[11]

In the summer of 1872, Schurz, William Cullen Bryant, and other leading Liberal Republicans invited Bacon to attend a meeting in New York City to devise a strategy for defeating President Grant. While he informed these men that his convictions regarding the need for important reforms were in "substantial agreement" with theirs, he, like many other moderate Republicans, refused to join the Liberals. He was pleased with Grant's attempts to lower the national debt and to move Reconstruction along "calmly and firmly," and he felt little but contempt for Horace Greeley, who became the candidate of both the Democrats and the Liberal

10. New Haven *Daily Palladium,* November 10, 1870; *Christian Union,* June 5, September 25, 1872; "The Warnerian Theory," 1872, Bacon to Carl Schurz and others, June 6, 1872, in Bacon Family Papers; *Independent,* June 26, August 12, 1872.

11. *Independent,* March 7, 21, April 18, 1872. On the moderate Republicans' constitutional conservatism, see Benedict, "Preserving the Constitution," 65–90.

Republicans. Because of Greeley's eccentricities, his lack of administrative ability and statesmanship, and his willingness to compromise on most issues, Bacon argued, no one could conceive of him as president "without laughing at the absurdity of it."[12]

Perhaps most important, Bacon was convinced that Greeley, as the Democratic standard-bearer, could not be trusted on the major issues. Although he was not satisfied with the Republicans' record on the civil service, tariff, and currency issues, he concluded that it was preferable to that of Greeley and the Democrats. The Democrats, he reasoned, had historically been linked to the spoils system; Greeley and his protectionist supporters had captured control of the Democratic convention; and many more Republicans than Democrats favored payment of the national debt in specie. Above all, he considered Reconstruction a "substantial fact." Whatever "grave mistakes" congressional Republicans had made in fashioning the Reconstruction program, he believed that it was not nearly as disastrous as would have been the plan proposed by Johnson and the Democrats. He was deeply concerned that an unregenerate Democratic party, now aligned with Greeley and the Liberal Republicans, would join with the "murdering banditti" in the South and usher in an "ancient regime of terror" designed to deny blacks their fundamental rights as citizens. Thus, he hoped that with a resounding triumph by Grant, the fundamental principles underlying Reconstruction would be preserved and "we shall be rid of three nuisances at once, Greeley, Sumner, and the Democratic party—for they are now all in one boat, and each is helping to sink the other." Much as he expected, Grant won the election handily, carrying every northern state.[13]

Between the elections of 1872 and 1876, Bacon devoted little attention to the issues surrounding Reconstruction. Although he generally supported the Republican party, he believed that many Americans, like himself, did so not out of respect or gratitude but out of fear of a Democratic party that, when in power, had proved itself "shamefully unworthy." Because Greeley's "serio-comico-ludicro-tragico" candidacy had made a mockery of the tariff, civil service, and currency questions and, most unfortunately, had sought to sabotage Reconstruction, he cautioned Americans who might contemplate establishing a new party that they should not do so until they had carefully developed a stand on important issues. One of the issues that he believed deserved close scrutiny and forthright action was the currency question, which had divided Americans since the end of the Civil War. Many Democrats, particularly in the Midwest, favored paying government bondholders

12. Bacon to Carl Schurz and others, June 6, 1872, in Bacon Family Papers; *Independent,* August 15, 29, September 5, 1872.

13. *Independent,* August 8, 15, 1872; *Christian Union,* September 25, 1872; Leonard to Leonard Woolsey Bacon, October 5, 1872, in Bacon Family Papers; Foner, *Reconstruction,* 499–511.

in greenbacks, whereas Republicans, with few exceptions, viewed bondholders as patriots and warned that the Democratic plan would be inflationary, destroy the nation's credit, and drive up interest rates.[14]

Although Bacon heartily concurred with the Republican position on the currency question, he was deeply distressed by the party's failure to pay off the national debt. In a number of articles that appeared in the *Christian Union* in the mid-1870s, he warned that this failure was "a commercial dishonor and a moral delinquency" that could conceivably destroy the party. Appealing to his readers as a person who had worked all of his life to provide the basic necessities for his family and had always felt legally and morally bound to pay his debts, he charged that both parties had failed to uphold the government's promise to pay its debts because they feared that to take a definite stand would divide their ranks. It was therefore incumbent upon Congress to enact legislation requiring the government, beginning in 1875, to redeem greenbacks with specie. Throughout the 1870s he steadfastly held to his hard-money position; late in the decade he came to oppose the remonetization of silver, maintaining that it would defraud the government's creditors, who had bought bonds during the war with the understanding that they would be paid in gold.[15]

Bacon's insistence that the federal government honor its promise to pay bondholders in gold, even though that might well earn them enormous profits, did not mean that he believed the government should act on behalf of the rich and well-born or that he sought to transform the traditional Protestant ethic into Horatio Alger's success myth or the Gospel of Wealth. Indeed, he hoped to sustain the concept of the free and responsible individual guided by a system of moral law. Following the Civil War, he echoed the concern expressed by a growing number of northerners that American society had failed to fulfill the promise of moral regeneration offered by the war. Convinced that a new balance must be struck between prosperity and civic duty and between self-interest and morality, he lashed out at "a luxuriously selfish extravagance of living" that he observed among the middle and upper classes.[16]

Even prior to the outbreak of labor violence in the mid- and late 1870s, Bacon

14. *Christian Union,* August 20, 1873. For treatments of the currency issue following the Civil War, see Robert P. Sharkey, *Money, Class, and Party: An Economic Study of Civil War and Reconstruction* (Baltimore, 1959), 56–94, 267–75; Irwin Unger, *The Greenback Era* (Princeton, 1964), 60–64.

15. See *Christian Union,* September 10, December 31, 1873, July 1, 1874, 1877, January 28, 1878; E. M. Noyes to Bacon, January 10, 1874, letter to Rep. Maynard in the Detroit *Free Press,* June 9, 1874, in Bacon Family Papers; Leonard Bacon, "The Political Outlook," *New Englander,* XXXVII (January, 1878), 89–91.

16. *Congregationalist,* November 7, December 5, 1867, January 2, 1868; "Address to the Oberlin Council," November, 1871, in Bacon Family Papers; *Independent,* November 14, 1872.

also expressed dismay at the growing distance between the wealthy and the poor. He, like Theodore Dwight Woolsey, Noah Porter, and other New Haven scholars, was ambivalent about the meaning of the Industrial Revolution for American society. He sought to hold on to an optimistic vision of the future, predicting in 1871 that technological innovation would eradicate "servile or reluctant toil," so that "all the human family shall have abundant means and leisure for intellectual enjoyments and pursuits." On another occasion, however, he warned that industrialism might well render laborers "a permanently inferior class in society," without dignity or freedom. Likewise, while he welcomed the expansion of the railroad system, he was increasingly troubled by the special privileges that state governments had granted the railroads and other corporations. By allowing the railroads to become monopolies, he wrote, the states had placed the railroads' customers at the mercy of "a consolidated tyranny." In his search for solutions to the deepening sense of alienation among the working class and the developing problem of monopoly, Bacon, as he so often had done, eschewed radical reform. Like most reformers of the time, including his fellow New Haven scholars, he unequivocally rejected socialism or any other form of state ownership of corporations, believing that they would destroy competition and individual enterprise. He in fact considered the corporation *"a public institution to be managed for the public, under a strict responsibility to the State."* Yet he was convinced that legislation intended to prevent economic consolidation was not only futile but also ran the risk of violating liberty. Thus, in the end, he opted for limited reforms, such as general rather than special legislation for the railroads and government encouragement of competing railroad lines, which offered little that would curb the growing abuses produced by economic consolidation.[17]

Bacon's concern that the railroads wielded undue influence with state governments, as well as his deep-seated distrust of political parties, were among the factors that led him to champion a fundamental revision of the Connecticut Constitution during the 1870s. Convinced that the rise of business corporations and large cities had dramatically changed the character of the state since 1818, the last time its constitution had been revised, he repeatedly called for a constitutional convention that would create a lower house which represented towns, an upper house, or senate, representative of the entire state, a more independent judiciary, and primary elections for state offices. His disgust with the rampant corruption in New York City and other urban centers even provoked him to suggest that urban governments be

---

17. *Congregationalist,* March 12, June 11, 1868; "Address to the Oberlin Council," November, 1871, in Bacon Family Papers; Leonard Bacon, "Railways and the State," *New Englander,* XXX (October, 1871), 713–23, 727–38; *Independent,* November 14, 1872. For a study of the New Haven scholars' views on the leading social questions of the time, see Stevenson, *Scholarly Means to Evangelical Ends,* 121–25.

placed in the hands of state officials. During the late 1870s, he, along with members of the Constitutional Reform Association and others, continued to urge the Connecticut legislature to call a constitutional convention. His recommendation that senate districts be equalized and that the governor, not the legislative caucus, appoint judges was praised by leading constitutional reformers. But he failed in his attempt to unite the reformers in support of a system in which every community would have at least two representatives in the lower house, with larger cities enjoying an ascending number based upon population. Despite their continued agitation for constitutional change, during the 1870s he and his fellow reformers were unable to convince the legislature to alter fundamentally the state constitution.[18]

During these years Bacon's interests extended beyond public policy issues. Although in his seventies, he remained extremely active in the affairs of the Congregational Church. Above all, as moderator of the Brooklyn councils of 1874 and 1876, spawned by the Beecher-Tilton scandal, he was thrust into the midst of a bitter controversy that received massive press coverage. His connections with both Henry Ward Beecher and Theodore Tilton had extended over many years, but were quite different. On the one hand, he had been a friend of Beecher's father and had worked closely with Henry Ward Beecher on the *Independent* and as a fellow antislavery moderate. In 1866 Beecher had asked him to join in founding a new paper, and four years later he had accepted Beecher's invitation to contribute to the *Christian Union*. On the other hand, he had long considered Tilton an irreligious, ill-mannered fanatic. It is not surprising, therefore, that throughout this complicated and sordid scandal Bacon, notwithstanding his protestations of neutrality, always seemed to give Beecher the benefit of the doubt. Unlike many of Beecher's partisans, who believed that for the sake of the Congregational Church and of society as a whole he must be considered innocent even if he were proven guilty, Bacon was prepared to see Beecher retire in disgrace if the charges against him were substantiated. Nevertheless, he shared with many other American Protestants an abiding concern that Beecher's reputation, and with it his influence for good, be preserved.

The facts of the scandal were as follows. While Tilton, a parishioner in Beecher's Plymouth Church in Brooklyn, was away lecturing in 1866, Beecher had suddenly begun visiting Tilton's wife, Elizabeth. Mrs. Tilton told her husband in 1870 that Beecher had seduced her; Tilton, in turn, told Henry C. Bowen, whose wife claimed that she too had been seduced by Beecher. To further complicate matters, Beecher dictated a retraction of Elizabeth Tilton's confession, which she accepted

18. "Outline of an address for the revision of the Connecticut State Constitution," 1871, "Notes on Constitutional Convention," 1871, "Municipal Government," n.d., Bacon to Simeon Baldwin, January 1877, Simeon Baldwin to Bacon, January 6, 1877, January 29, 1880, in Bacon Family Papers; Leonard Bacon, "Constitution-Making," *New Englander*, XXXIII (January, 1874), 17, 31, 34–37; *Independent*, May 8, 1873; *Cooley's Weekly*, February 3, 10, 17, 24, March 3, 31, 1877.

but later repudiated. Efforts to manage the scandal were dealt a severe blow when, in 1872, Victoria Woodhull, a radical feminist who espoused communism and free love, accused Beecher of adultery and of sharing Woodhull's opposition to marriage. Even an agreement by Beecher, Tilton, and Bowen to refrain from spreading rumors concerning the scandal could not suppress the controversy, for in 1873 Plymouth Church, citing Tilton's four-year absence from the church (though in fact acting on the conviction that he had slandered Beecher), dropped him from its rolls. This move aroused the ire of Richard S. Storrs, Bacon's old friend, and William I. Budington, pastors of two neighboring Congregational churches. These men had become increasingly disturbed by the scandal as well as by Beecher's emphasis on the independence of his church within the Congregational system and on a romantic Christianity that was at odds with the central tenets of evangelical Calvinism. When Beecher refused to subject himself to the judgment of a mutual council urged by Storrs and Budington, the Brooklyn council convened at Budington's Clinton Avenue Church in March, 1874.[19]

Bacon was deeply pained by this contentious dispute and was critical of all the parties involved: Beecher and his accusers for their pact of silence; Tilton for his slanderous charges while absenting himself from Plymouth Church; the neighboring churches for permitting scandal in their midst without taking swift action; and Plymouth Church for seeking to stifle the imputations against Beecher. But though he did not wish to be understood as taking sides in the Brooklyn controversy, from its inception he was convinced that "some unequivocal vindication of Mr. Beecher's good name—in which all the churches and the entire American people have so great an interest," was desirable.[20]

Bacon also protested against being "used as an authority" on questions of church polity generated by the controversy. Yet given his reputation as an expert on such matters, a number of Congregational ministers understandably looked to him "to mediate, to reconcile, to harmonize" elements within the church by staking out a middle ground on church government. Indeed, once he accepted an invitation to serve on the council and was elected its moderator, he was clearly in a position to exert a significant influence on its proceedings. The council, which consisted of Congregational ministers and laymen selected by Storrs's and Budington's churches, was asked to provide advice on seven questions that related to the dismissal of Tilton. Following several days of deliberation, the council, by a vote of 87–8, with 23 not voting, decided, as one observer noted, "to strike an average." Bacon and most

19. See Altina L. Waller, *Reverend Beecher and Mrs. Tilton: Sex and Class in Victorian America* (Amherst, Mass., 1982), 1–2, 4, 7–10, 67–73; McLoughlin, *The Meaning of Henry Ward Beecher*, 10, 63–70. For an excellent analysis of the differences between Storrs's and Beecher's congregations, see Waller, *Reverend Beecher and Mrs. Tilton*, 94–110.

20. Bacon to S. M. Pettengill, January 13, 1874, in Bacon Family Papers.

of his fellow delegates concluded that the principles enunciated by the complaining churches were sound. But, concerned that if they censured Plymouth Church for its actions it might drive the Congregationalists' largest church in America from the fold, they also criticized the tone of the neighboring churches' remonstrance and implored them to maintain fellowship with Beecher's church.[21]

Some members of the council praised Bacon for his decisive leadership and calming influence, but the press's reaction to the council's ruling was mixed. While some newspapers considered the decision forthright and generous, others criticized the council for being either too lenient or too harsh with Plymouth Church. Such criticism notwithstanding, the moderate tone of the council's report, crafted in part by Bacon, held out the promise of placating the warring parties. Yet in a curious move, immediately following the adjournment of the council Bacon helped to reignite the controversy by making unguarded and indiscreet comments during a lecture to the middle class at Yale Theological Seminary. After presenting a spirited defense of the Brooklyn council's decision, in which he argued that it did not have the authority either to arraign or to vindicate Beecher, he proceeded to castigate Woodhull and "other infamous women," whose testimony he believed was not "worth kicking a dog for," and to question Beecher's tendency "to let unprincipled men know too much of him." If he had ended his comments at this point, relatively few people would have found them controversial. But, as reported by a New York *Tribune* correspondent who was present, Bacon then made a thinly veiled, and quite derogatory, reference to Tilton: "Some one has said that Plymouth Church's dealing with offenders is like Dogberry's. The comparison was apt. 'If anyone will not stand, let him go and gather the guard and thank God that you are rid of such a knave.' So of Lance, who went into the stocks and pillory to save his dog from execution for stealing puddings and geese. I think he would have done better to have let the dog die. And I think Beecher would have done better to have let vengeance come on the heads of his slanderers."[22]

Few people doubted that Bacon's pejorative comments were directed toward Tilton. Nevertheless, Tilton, seemingly intent upon gaining Bacon's approval, chose to respond to his barbs with a "hearty laugh" and an earnest plea that Bacon forward a letter Tilton had written to Beecher. He also asked Bacon, rather defensively, whether his treatment of Beecher "in this sorrowful business has been marked by the magnanimity which you apparently intimate has characterized *his*

21. Albert J. Lyman to Bacon, March 18, 1874; in Bacon Family Papers; *Christian Union,* April 1, 1874; *Advance,* April 2, 9, 1874; *Independent,* April 2, 9, May 7, 1874.

22. See T. M. Post to Bacon, April 2, 1874, W. W. Patton to Bacon, April 9, 1874, in Bacon Family Papers; *Advance,* April 9, 1874; *Independent,* April 2, 1874; *Congregationalist,* April 3, 1874; *Christian Union,* April 2, 1874; Robert Shaplen, *Free Love and Heavenly Sinners: The Story of the Great Henry Ward Beecher Scandal* (New York, 1954), 182; New York *Tribune,* April 3, 1874.

toward *me.*" Bacon expressed his reluctance to confide in Beecher on a matter on which Beecher had chosen to be reticent, but he decided to forward Tilton's letter. At the same time, he informed Tilton that the question of whether Beecher was attempting to protect Tilton, Bowen, or another person was "more than I know, or would seem to know." Although Bacon probably knew more than he admitted to Tilton about Beecher's efforts to manage the scandal, he seems to have been genuinely mystified by the intrigue and deviousness that had characterized the scandal from its inception. But he left no doubt that he resented the many angry letters he received in response to the *Tribune's* account of his lecture. "There is," he commented in the *Independent,* "some annoyance in being spattered, even slightly, with the slops thrown at Mr. Beecher." Above all, he remained unmoved by the arguments of Tilton and his partisans, insisting that the scandals imputed to Beecher were slanders "originating either in a malicious heart or in a crazy brain."[23]

However much Bacon desired a "satisfactory" explanation by Beecher and Plymouth Church concerning their handling of the scandal, he proved incapable of objectively assessing Beecher and Tilton. Bacon's contempt for Tilton's behavior, religious views, and association with those who espoused principles "at war with the Christian doctrine of marriage" compelled him repeatedly to denigrate Tilton's character. At the same time, he confided to Beecher: "I have always assumed, as a primary fact in the case, your Christian integrity. I have not permitted myself to entertain any theory in which that assumption was not a corner-stone." Until a "responsible accuser" (presumably not Tilton or Woodhull) brought "competent and credible" charges against Beecher, he assured his beleaguered friend, he would continue to believe that Beecher was "a true man" and to hope that he could assist his friend in "this painful emergency."[24]

Beecher was deeply touched by these expressions of trust and sympathy. But although he informed Bacon that he was perhaps the first person in whom he should have confided when "the trouble" befell him, he rejected Bacon's offer to sit down and discuss the "whole affair." Some people close to Beecher, such as Lyman Abbott, the assistant minister at Plymouth Church, Harriet Beecher Stowe, and even Storrs lauded Bacon for his fairness and candor. However, a few of Beecher's partisans, who resented Bacon's mild criticism of the way in which he had handled the scandal, denounced him as a "dirty blackguard" and "the biggest fool of all" among "a parcel of jealous fools." Those who were convinced that Tilton had been terribly wronged by Beecher and Plymouth Church were, if anything, even more furious

23. Theodore Tilton to Bacon, April 3, 1874, Bacon to Theodore Tilton, April 10, 1874, Bacon to Henry Ward Beecher, April 10, 1874, in Bacon Family Papers; *Independent,* April 30, 1874.

24. *Independent,* April 30, May 7, 14, 28, June 4, 25, 1874; Bacon to Henry Ward Beecher, June 26, 1874, in Bacon Family Papers.

with Bacon. Numerous correspondents, most of them anonymous, accused him of being vain, cruel, dishonorable, and unethical. Yet Tilton, writing in the *Golden Age,* still seemed prepared to give Bacon the benefit of the doubt. Obviously angered by the tenor of Bacon's articles, he lashed out at his "numerous and extraordinary misrepresentations." Yet he immediately backpedaled, concluding, rather wistfully, that Bacon's misrepresentations must have been "wholly unintentional, for you are incapable of doing any man a wilful wrong."[25]

If Tilton hoped that he could persuade Bacon to turn against Beecher by flattering or shaming him, he was mistaken. Even though Bacon had expressed grave doubts that the Plymouth Church investigating committee, handpicked by Beecher to look into the accusations against him, would satisfy the public, he ultimately accepted its predictable conclusion that Beecher was innocent of all charges. Equally important, he told a Brooklyn *Eagle* reporter that Tilton and his associates had engaged in a "foul conspiracy" against Beecher. Finally, whether it was intended to placate Tilton or simply to counter accusations that he had treated him unfairly, Bacon's denial that his remarks at Yale Theological Seminary had provoked Tilton to bring suit against Beecher for adultery and perjury surely angered Tilton. Tilton, he informed the *Eagle* correspondent, "has, for the past three years been cackling to lay his egg, and used my lecture as a pretext." Indeed, he insisted that he had not referred to Tilton as a knave or a dog but, rather, had applied Dogberry's principle to Beecher's and Plymouth Church's "absurd lenity . . . that induced silence toward his accusers." Although not everyone was prepared to accept his rather strained explanation, even as Tilton filed criminal charges against Beecher Bacon continued to maintain the fiction that he had never spoken in the interest of either man but, rather, "only in the interest of truth and justice."[26]

During the six-month trial in 1875, which proved to be one of the greatest national spectacles of the 1870s, Bacon, like millions of other Americans, was little more than an interested spectator. At last, he could turn his attention to more pleasant matters. One of these was the celebration of his fiftieth anniversary as a minister. At the ceremony held at Center Church, he and Catherine were given nearly two thousand dollars in gifts from the congregation. He continued to perform various

25. Henry Ward Beecher to Bacon, June 28, 1874, in Beecher Family Papers; Lyman Abbott, *Henry Ward Beecher* (New York, 1887), 299; Harriet Beecher Stowe to Bacon, September 9, 1874, in Collections of American Literature; Richard S. Storrs, Jr., to Bacon, June 5, 1874, Charles B. Brook to Bacon, May 5, 1874, anonymous to Bacon, June 30, 1874, anonymous to Bacon, June 1, 1874, "Magnanimity" to Bacon, June 26, 1874, anonymous to Bacon, July 17, 1874, in Bacon Family Papers; *Golden Age,* June 27, 1874.

26. New York *Tribune,* August 1, 1874; *Independent,* September 3, 17, 1874; William Hayes Ward to Bacon, September 26, 1874, clipping in Susan B. Hodges to Bacon, September 25, 1874, in Bacon Family Papers.

functions in Center Church and, at times, represented it at ecclesiastical councils. In addition, he hosted the Congregational Church's second Triennial Council, held at Center Church in late 1874. As the meeting approached, some Congregational leaders, such as his friend Ray Palmer, expressed concern about the trend toward centralization of authority within the Congregational Church. Bacon shared this concern, cautioning the council, as he had in 1871, that it was merely a representative body, or "joint committee," of all the churches. While he was relieved when the council endorsed his view, he was sufficiently anxious about the future course of these councils to warn that the next triennial meeting should not consider denominational control of the benevolent organizations.[27]

Bacon, however, did not entirely avoid becoming enmeshed in the ongoing Beecher-Tilton controversy. His decision to preach at Plymouth Church shortly after Beecher's trial ended in a hung jury aroused the ire of some evangelical Christians, who feared that this indicated Yale Theological Seminary's endorsement of Beecher's contention that all people, especially sinners, would be saved. Bacon angrily denied this charge, noting that he had preached at the invitation of the parishioners, not Beecher, and that, given their displeasure with his opinion regarding the dismissal of Tilton, the invitation illustrated the church's willingness to reform its ways. He also denied that Beecher believed in universal salvation and, once more, took the opportunity to defend his old friend. The acquittal of Beecher in the civil trial, he wrote in the New York *Tribune,* showed that no one had the right to demand that he positively prove himself innocent.[28]

Bacon's decision to again inject himself into this seemingly endless controversy was merely a prelude to his role in the Brooklyn council of 1876. If he truly believed that Plymouth Church had mended its ways, he surely was disappointed by its dismissal of Emma Moulton and other members of the church who had testified against Beecher in the civil trial. When Andover Seminary Church responded to this action by requesting a mutual council to investigate the charges against Beecher, Plymouth Church and its pastor rejected it and called an advisory council. The removal of Mrs. Moulton further discredited Beecher and his church in the public eye, and the careful selection of numerous men to the advisory council who were known to be Beecher loyalists aroused even more suspicion.[29]

27. *Leonard Bacon: Pastor of the First Church in New Haven,* 10, 120; George Walker to Bacon, May 6, 1873, article in *Zion's Herald,* April 15, 1875, Ray Palmer to Bacon, October 12, 1874, in Bacon Family Papers; *Advance,* October 8, 1874; *Independent,* October 22, 29, November 5, 1874; *Christian Union,* October 7, 1874.

28. New York *Tribune,* July 28, 1875. For treatments of Beecher's trial, see Clark, *Henry Ward Beecher,* 209, 223–24; Paul A. Carter, *The Spiritual Crisis of the Gilded Age* (DeKalb, Ill., 1971), 116–23.

29. William I. Budington to Bacon, December 6, 21, 1875, Bacon to Egbert C. Smyth, February 5, 1876, Egbert C. Smyth to Bacon, February 5, 1876, in Bacon Family Papers; *The Result of the Brooklyn Advisory Council of 1876. Together with the Letters of Dr. Leonard Bacon, Prof. Timothy Dwight, D.D.,* etc.

When the council convened in February, 1876, Bacon, who had been asked to serve as a representative of Yale Theological Seminary, was unanimously elected moderator of the largest such church council held in the United States to that date. He, too, had questioned whether the council would accomplish "much good." But, once he agreed to serve, he labored diligently to persuade other Congregational leaders to attend and pledged that "if I live and am well enough, I will be there, and will do what I can in such a mob to have things proceed decently in order." Indeed, in his introductory remarks to the assembled delegates he cautioned that they were not there to whitewash Beecher and his church or "to amuse the public by drawing off their attention to any side issues, or to any questions merely incidental." Yet at the same time, he conceded that the council could not decide the question of Beecher's guilt or innocence, for it had no judicial function and was required to deal only with the questions contained in the letter-missive from Plymouth Church. Although these questions, which focused on whether Plymouth Church's order and discipline needed correcting, went to the core of Congregational Church polity—the proper authority of a church over its members, the liberty of the local church, and relations between neighboring churches—the council's inability to deal with the charges against Beecher was certain to disappoint most skeptics.[30]

Notwithstanding these acknowledged constraints on the council's authority and jurisdiction, Bacon, as its moderator and most influential member, sought to extend the boundaries of its deliberations as far as he could. Although he and other members of a special committee of the council declared Andover Seminary Church's call for a mutual council "untimely" and contrary to the rule that one church could not try another, he vigorously urged the council to hear testimony from Storrs, Budington, Bowen, and the representatives of Emma Moulton, not just the committee from Plymouth Church. Several delegates countered that it would be impractical to delve into the entire question of fact, but following extended debate, the council upheld Bacon's position.[31]

The council's report, which Bacon presented as part of his closing remarks, largely upheld Plymouth Church's position. Although it deemed the church's rule on terminating members deficient, the council, wishing to preserve "the good name" of Plymouth Church, expressed satisfaction that the rule had been changed. Moreover, it found no fault with the way in which the Plymouth Church Investigat-

(New York, 1876), 249–53; Waller, *Reverend Beecher and Mrs. Tilton,* 145; *Independent,* February 10, 1876; I. P. Warren to Bacon, February 4, 1876, in Bacon Family Papers.

30. Bacon to Egbert C. Smyth, February 5, 1876, in Bacon Family Papers; *Proceedings of the Advisory Council of Congregational Churches and Ministers Called by the Plymouth Church of Brooklyn, N.Y., and Held in Brooklyn from the 15th to the 24th of February, 1876* (New York, 1876), 5–6, 27; *The Result of the Brooklyn Advisory Council of 1876,* 342–43.

31. *Proceedings of the Advisory Council of Congregational Churches and Ministers,* 1–3, 6–7, 66–86, 142–43, 146–63, 175–200, 221–22, 242–46, 262–64, 321–24.

ing Committee had been constituted or had examined charges against Beecher. Finally, believing that Beecher truly desired to confront his accusers, it proposed that Plymouth Church empower a commission of five members, from a list of twenty eminent men, which would receive and investigate all charges against Beecher that it regarded as not having already been tried. Bacon succeeded in bringing the pro– and anti–Plymouth Church factions on the council together by suggesting that the "Scandal Bureau," as some termed it, would not be constituted unless formal charges were brought before Plymouth Church or its Examining Committee within sixty days of the council's adjournment by a party or parties "making themselves responsible for the truth and proof of the same."[32]

Hoping to bring peace to the Congregational Church in the wake of the second Brooklyn council, Bacon immediately sought to reconcile his old friends Beecher and Storrs. In an evenhanded manner, he pointed out to Beecher that both parties had legitimate grievances. Thus, he beseeched his friend to apologize to Storrs and Budington and to ask their forgiveness. Although deeply touched by Bacon's advice, Beecher concluded that he was too wounded to make the overture. Likewise, Storrs, believing that it was Beecher who had snubbed him, rejected any thought of a reconciliation.[33]

Undeterred by his failure to end the strife between Storrs and Beecher, Bacon embarked upon a wide-ranging commentary on the Brooklyn council that appeared in the *Advance,* a Chicago Congregational newspaper. Despite his protest that he had not been a partisan in the Beecher controversy, his bias against Tilton remained palpable. He repeatedly referred to Tilton as "malicious" and linked his dismissal from Plymouth Church to his "revolutionary" views on marriage, divorce, and sexual relations. Equally important, he insisted that only the filing of a definite complaint before the proposed commission would provide a fair hearing for Beecher.[34]

The commission was, in fact, the principal target of the council's critics. For example, although Storrs lauded Bacon as "the brave and eloquent veteran" who had lent real weight to the council's deliberations, he condemned the commission, which had no ecclesiastical standing or authority, as an "ecclesiastical Quaker-gun, which looks ready for service but through whose silent wooden mouth no shot can pass." Given the nebulous standing of the proposed commission, and especially the

32. *Ibid.*, 325–27, 329–32; *The Result of the Brooklyn Advisory Council of 1876*, 342–43; *Independent,* March 2, 1876; *Advance,* April 20, 1876.

33. Bacon to Henry Ward Beecher, February 27, 1876, in Beecher Family Papers; Henry Ward Beecher to Bacon, March 1, 1876, Richard S. Storrs, Jr., to Bacon, April 28, 1876, in Bacon Family Papers.

34. C. H. Howard to Bacon, February 24, 1876, in Bacon Family Papers; *Advance,* March 30, April 6, 20, 27, 1876.

fact that the list of prospective members included a number of men known to be favorable to Beecher, it is not surprising that no one dared or deigned to file charges. This situation angered Bacon. When Professor Egbert C. Smyth of Andover refused to lodge charges and to follow the steps laid out by the council, Bacon blamed him and other critics for the fact that the commission was never officially formed.[35]

Bacon could take some comfort in the praise that he received for his service on the council. Perhaps most touching was that offered by a member of Storrs's Church of the Pilgrims, who termed Bacon's defense of Congregational principles "one of the noblest and most lasting acts of your life." Yet Bacon, like many Americans who had closely followed the scandal from its inception, was clearly frustrated by the fact that truth and justice scarcely emerged from the Brooklyn councils of 1874 and 1876. As he noted gloomily to Egbert Smyth two months after the 1876 council adjourned, "It may be that when we all shall have passed away, the question of whether Henry Ward Beecher was an adulterer and a perjurer will remain, like the famous question about Mary Queen of Scots, a theme for debate among partisan antiquaries" (and, he might have added, historians).[36] What he could not bring himself to acknowledge was that his own abiding friendship with Beecher and intense dislike for Tilton, his fervent desire to keep Plymouth Church within the Congregational fold and to maintain peace among American Congregationalists, and his unshakable commitment to the traditional limits placed upon Congregational councils had, at times, served to impede the quest for truth and justice.

Although Beecher, Bowen, and the Tiltons were damaged by the scandal,[37] Bacon paid no discernible price for his role in the controversy. He retained the respect and trust of both Storrs and Beecher, and his harshest critics ceased to attack him a few months after the 1876 Brooklyn council ended. As the emotion surrounding the controversy subsided, his life returned to a slower pace. Although he continued to teach at Yale and to speak out on controversial issues, during his final years he would spend less time in the public spotlight than he had in any other period of his adult life.

35. Richard S. Storrs, Jr., to Bacon, April 28, May 3, 1876, Egbert C. Smyth to Bacon, May 2, 1876, in Bacon Family Papers; *Christian Union,* March 8, 1876; New York *Tribune,* April 18, 1876.

36. C. R. Palmer to Bacon, February 28, 1876, Charles Storrs to Bacon, April 18, 1876, in Bacon Family Papers; New York *Tribune,* April 18, 1876.

37. See Waller, *Reverend Beecher and Mrs. Tilton,* 11; Clark, *Henry Ward Beecher,* 223–25.

14

THE FINAL YEARS

I T is a marvel to me," Bacon confided to George Bancroft in 1876, "that I yet
live and am able to keep on working." But in the same breath he noted that if he
could continue to work "without failure of mind," he would attempt to write
another volume on New England church history. He was never able to write the
volume, but this was due largely to his numerous responsibilities during these years.
While he slowed the pace of his life in the late 1870s and early 1880s, he by no
means retired from public life. He continued to lecture on American church history
and polity at the seminary, to serve on the Yale Corporation, and to meet regularly
with other members of the Club to discuss a broad range of social, political, and
theological questions.[1]

Bacon also remained interested in the study of history, serving on the board of
directors of both the New Haven Colony Historical Society and the Connecticut
Historical Society and occasionally presenting papers before both organizations.
Moreover, he wrote a brief biography of his father, and the people of New Haven
accorded him the honor, as a revered community leader and historian of New
Haven, of presenting patriotic orations on the one hundredth anniversary of both
American independence and the British attack on the city.[2]

Yet Bacon's influence continued to extend far beyond New Haven and Connecticut. Although the volume of his writing diminished somewhat during these years,
he contributed numerous articles to the *Independent,* the *Christian Union,* the *New*

1. Bacon to George Bancroft, February 26, 1876, in George Bancroft Papers; Franklin B. Dexter to
Bacon, June 30, 1877, in Bacon Family Papers; *Independent,* December 29, 1881; Witherspoon, *The Club,*
57–70.

2. Bacon to R. A. Brock, November 20, 1880, Leonard to Catherine Bacon, July 5, 1879, in Bacon
Family Papers; Bacon, "David Bacon," 1–19, 260–82, 387–417, 562–91; *Papers of the New Haven Colony
Historical Society,* II, v; Theodore Dwight Bacon, *Leonard Bacon,* 521.

Englander, and other publications. He remained convinced that he could enlighten the public on contemporary questions, and editors still valued his contributions for their clarity and cogency.

One of the national concerns that Bacon addressed in his articles was the rising tide of labor-capital conflict during the postwar years. The violence in the Pennsylvania coalfields, along the nation's railroad system, and elsewhere deeply disturbed him and many other Americans. He had long expressed dismay at the worsening plight of the working class, which earned a precarious living and consumed all that they earned, and he now feared that class warfare was imminent. Much like Washington Gladden, Lyman Abbott, Phillips Brooks, and other moderate proponents of the social gospel, he generally accepted the existence of trade unions as a means of protecting the interests of workers. Rejecting the arguments of those who viewed unions as a threat to American individualism and industrial stability, he maintained that there was no harm in associations for the purpose of mutual assistance and improvement, or even for establishing prices for their labor. After all, he pointed out, professional men did just that. These social gospelers assumed that capitalism was not inherently evil. But, convinced that the golden rule was the true solution to the industrial ills of America, they sought to Christianize capitalism. One must not, they asserted, substitute Adam Smith for the Bible or consider economics apart from considerations of right and wrong. According to Bacon, it was necessary to transcend mere abstract economic theory and to take into account the human dimension. He subscribed to a social Christianity that emphasized the reciprocal duties and rights shared by members of society who were equal before the law and God. Because employers and workers were neighbors, he wrote in the *Christian Union,* "the higher law over them is the law of love." In some respects he looked to an earlier time when, he believed, master craftsmen paid their workers honest wages for honest work and concerned themselves with their employees' "surroundings, their amusements and home life, and their idleness and ambitions."[3]

Bacon's sympathy for the working class had its limits, however. He, like Gladden and many other liberal clergymen, believed that the wealth produced by workers was distributed among capital and labor under the operation of certain natural laws. Therefore, Bacon maintained, labor unions had no right to dictate to employers what they should be paid or who should be hired. His suspicion of labor unions was rooted in part in his feelings toward immigrant laborers, especially Irish Catholics, whom he blamed for much of the violence that increasingly characterized labor-

---

3. *Christian Union,* April 17, August 7, September 18, 1878. For treatments of the social gospel and the capitalist system, see Susan Curtis, *A Consuming Faith: The Social Gospel and Modern American Culture* (Baltimore, 1991), 15–46 *passim;* Arthur Mann, *Yankee Reformers in the Urban Age: Social Reform in Boston, 1880–1900* (New York, 1966), 73–80.

capital relations. These workers, he wrote, differed from "genuine Americans, born and trained under the influence of American institutions," who, no matter their circumstances, aspired to improve their condition. He was particularly contemptuous of the Molly Maguires in Pennsylvania, whom he considered "bonded assassins" engaged in a "conspiracy against liberty." At some level, he understood that those who eked out a precarious living and held out little hope for their future were deeply alienated from the capitalist system. But he found it difficult to identify with their grievances concerning wages, hours, and conditions; and, like most proponents of the social gospel, he never proposed a concrete program of reform.[4]

Bacon and his fellow moderate social gospelers clearly rejected the radical alternative set forth by Herbert Newton Casson, Jesse H. Jones, and others who wished to socialize Christianity. He inveighed against both communism and socialism, which he believed would destroy Christianity and "trample down and abolish the rights of individual men." Ever mindful of the Paris Commune of 1871, he also feared that, like their European counterparts, American workers who had come to hate capitalism "do not expect that, without some great revolution, their children will be anything else." Such an uprising, he asserted, would be disastrous for all concerned, for communism and socialism were tantamount to "slavery." In the final analysis, he insisted, the only way the spread of communism and socialism could be stemmed was for both capital and labor to recognize each other as mutually dependent allies. Likewise, Bacon and other moderate social gospelers condemned the sociology of Herbert Spencer for being devoid of the Christian principles of sympathy, cooperation, and responsibility and for denying the primacy of the moral individual. Spencer's *Study of Sociology,* he complained, ignored moral impulses as factors in society and concentrated solely upon material forces. Christian America, he stated defiantly, would never allow its sons to be taught to revile religion.[5]

Bacon and many other moderate social gospelers also embraced civil service reform as a meliorative measure that would establish honest government. He pointedly reminded President Hayes that many advocates of civil service reform had voted for him with the expectation that he would act forcefully on the issue. When Hayes's proposals generated opposition among a number of powerful congressional Republicans, he assured the president that "multitudes of thinking men" would stand by him in his struggle with "trading office-mongers." True to his word, in

4. *Christian Union,* April 17, August 7, September 4, 1878; Jacob Henry Dorn, *Washington Gladden: Prophet of the Social Gospel* (Columbus, 1966), 205–206; Mann, *Yankee Reformers in the Urban Age,* 78–81.

5. *Christian Union,* April 17, 1878; *Independent,* June 24, 1880; sermon of April 1, 1873, in Bacon Family Papers. On the radical social gospelers, see Mann, *Yankee Reformers in the Urban Age,* 86–97. Criticism of social Darwinism by Protestant clergymen is studied in R. J. Wilson, ed., *Darwinism and the American Intellectual: A Book of Readings* (Homewood, Ill., 1967), 93–97.

1880 he opposed James G. Blaine for the Republican nomination in part because of his stand on civil service reform.[6]

Bacon, however, considered the money question and the payment of the national debt more important issues than civil service reform. Concerned that the United States might swindle creditors by refusing to pay its debts, he condemned proposed legislation that would have demonetized gold by making ninety-three cents' worth of silver equal to a dollar in gold. He, like other fiscal conservatives, reiterated his longstanding conviction that the financial issue was a moral question that could well destroy the Republican party, much as the slavery issue had killed the Whig party. Nevertheless, his appeals had little effect, for in 1881 the national debt had not yet been paid off.[7]

The national issue that Bacon devoted most attention to during these years was Reconstruction. Following the election of 1872, he had written little on this subject, but as the presidential campaign of 1876 drew near, his interest in the "southern question" revived. Over the years, his faith in the integrity and competence of both major parties' leaders had declined. Thus, in early 1876 he joined Schurz, William Cullen Bryant, Charles Francis Adams, and other disgruntled critics in a Reform Conference held in New York City. In a forceful speech at the conference, he declared that "the parties rule the country. We must see who shall rule the parties." But although the conference indicated its preference for Adams as a presidential candidate, Bacon believed that Rutherford B. Hayes would reform the civil service, discharge the government's obligations to its creditors and redeem its notes in specie, and, above all, pacify the South.[8]

The Grant administration's Reconstruction policy regarding Louisiana, Arkansas, and Mississippi had proved inconsistent, and many Republican editors and politicians, guided by a spirit of conciliation, conservatism, and racism, had increasingly relegated the Reconstruction issue to a secondary place. These Republicans had come to emphasize the inability of African Americans either to govern the southern states or to play a role in government; in 1874 even the once-sympathetic American Missionary Association criticized black suffrage. Bacon joined the growing chorus of Republican voices that pronounced Reconstruction a failure. In a letter to the New York *Tribune* shortly following the election of 1876, he acknowledged that it had been necessary to protect the lives of the freedmen and that, had they

6. Bacon, "The Political Outlook," 87–89; *Independent,* April 22, 1880.

7. Bacon, "The Political Outlook," 89–91; *Christian Union,* January 1, 1879; *Independent,* March 10, 1881. For the tendency of monetary conservatives to discuss the currency question in moral terms, see Lawrence Goodwyn, *The Populist Moment: A Short History of the Agrarian Revolt in America* (New York, 1978), 9–11.

8. *Advance,* May 25, 1876; Bacon, "The Political Outlook," 81.

been in power, the Democrats would have rendered emancipation "little more than a word." Rather, in his estimation, the mistake made by the architects of the Reconstruction legislation had been "the more excusable blunder of universal suffrage without distinction of race or color—universal suffrage instead of intelligent suffrage."[9]

Bacon blamed party considerations for the enactment of universal manhood suffrage for African Americans. Had a few courageous Democrats in the late 1860s risen above the requirements of party and acknowledged the need for black rights, he reasoned, they would have weakened the "power of extreme and hot-headed men to lead or to drive the Republican party; and common sense would have asserted itself." But unfortunately, the Democrats had been intent upon embarrassing the Republicans rather than establishing the best possible system of government in the South. At the same time, he accused the Republicans of assuming that black suffrage would strengthen the party and that they could always manage the ignorant freedmen, much as the Democrats controlled the Irish immigrants in the northern cities. Bacon had long been alarmed by the growing election fraud in the northern urban centers, and he surely was aware of the corruption and violence often employed by the Redeemer forces to capture control of the southern state governments. Nevertheless, unable to transcend his racial bias, he chose to direct his criticism primarily toward the "Negro states," where blacks constituted either a majority or a large minority of the population. In these states, he concluded, the black population had "proved incompetent to govern the State or to protect itself" against hostile whites, and therefore was largely responsible for the fall of the Reconstruction governments. He also naïvely attributed the deep racial divide in the South to the absence of a literacy requirement. If Congress had enacted such a requirement in the 1860s, he stated, the line of demarcation in the South would have been questions of public policy, not race.[10]

Bacon and many other northern Republicans tended to be more charitable toward the carpetbag governors, such as Daniel Chamberlain of South Carolina, than the freedmen. Yet by the mid-1870s, they saw no future for the southern wing of the party. In letters to Chamberlain that appeared in the New York *Tribune* in 1877, Bacon defended Hayes's refusal to support Chamberlain's claim to the governorship of South Carolina, asserting that a republican form of government should not be equated with universal suffrage, or even an honest election or government. By insisting that federal authorities could only interfere in a state if that state's officials

9. William Gillette, *Retreat from Reconstruction, 1869–1879* (Baton Rouge, 1979), 60–72, 104–85; Foner, *Reconstruction*, 524–29; New York *Tribune*, December 16, 1876.

10. New York *Tribune*, December 16, 1876.

applied for assistance, and then only if domestic violence constituted "a riotous uprising against the established order," he essentially renounced federal efforts to protect blacks' fundamental rights, even though they were guaranteed by the Constitution. Even more disturbing to some Republicans, especially in the South, was his contention that because Chamberlain could be kept in power only by the United States Army, he was merely the *de facto* governor of South Carolina, whereas Wade Hampton, the Democratic challenger, held "real power"—no matter how he had achieved it—and therefore was the *de jure* governor whose claim to office Hayes had properly endorsed. This strained logic, which obviously ignored or, worse, condoned the Redeemers' widespread use of political violence to overthrow the Reconstruction forces in South Carolina and other southern states, led one irate Chamberlain supporter to accuse Bacon of being prepared to countenance the armed overthrow of the government of Massachusetts or any other state, without the possibility of federal intervention.[11]

With Reconstruction symbolically and technically at an end, Bacon engaged in a comprehensive assessment of the effort. His analysis indicates that, fifteen years after the Civil War, he still sought to juggle two quite different, and even contradictory, perspectives on the Reconstruction experiment. He conceded that Reconstruction had been "the most difficult problem ever presented to American statesmanship since the organization of the national government." He remained convinced that it had been necessary to secure political equality for blacks and that the proponents of Reconstruction had done what had been "perhaps the best thing that, in the extraordinary conditions of the problem, could be done." To have attempted to govern the southern states over many years as military prefects, he argued somewhat defensively, while justified by the law of nations, "would have made those States in their relation to the Union what Ireland has been to Great Britain, or Poland to the Russian power." Nonetheless, exhibiting his usual cautious moderation, he chastised the proponents of Reconstruction policy for failing to understand that years, perhaps generations, would be required to realize the beneficial results of the abolition of slavery.[12]

Bacon's acceptance of the end of Reconstruction did not mean that he was

11. New York *Tribune*, July 14, 21, 1877; Bacon, "The Political Outlook," 87; Moulton Emery to Bacon, July 21, 1877, in Bacon Family Papers. Northern Republicans' views on the Reconstruction governments in the South are studied in Richard H. Abbott, *The Republican Party and the South, 1855–1877: The First Southern Strategy* (Chapel Hill, 1986); McPherson, *The Abolitionist Legacy*, 40–46, 85–90. On Chamberlain, Hayes, and the South Carolina situation, see Ari Hoogenboom, *The Presidency of Rutherford B. Hayes* (Lawrence, Kans., 1988), 60–64; Foner, *Reconstruction*, 328–63 passim.

12. *Independent*, October 7, 1880; Bacon, "The Political Outlook," 82–83; sermon of November 27, 1879, in Bacon Family Papers.

devoid of sympathy for southern blacks. In 1879, for example, he was a member of a special committee of the Colored Refugee Relief Board, which sought to assist destitute blacks who had emigrated to Kansas. He also continued to believe that northerners should be indignant about "the compounded injustice and inhumanity" which characterized the treatment of African Americans in the South. In fact, however, he had given up on the Reconstruction governments as well as any meaningful federal efforts to protect the rights of the freedmen, and he continued to appear more committed to the defense of states' rights than human rights. To the very end, he held that the greatest danger to the political system since the Civil War had been "in the direction, not of disintegration, but of centralization." This concern, which was shared by many other northern Republicans, had the effect of seriously limiting the ability of the former slaves to withstand assaults on their newly acquired rights. Late in his life, he expressed the hope that a "Christian civilization of equal liberty" could be ensured in the South if each state conscientiously punished crimes committed within its jurisdiction. But he offered no clue as to how a federal government of very limited powers could compel racist state officials to uphold rights guaranteed under the Constitution. Likewise, while optimistic that American society was moving inexorably toward "the time when liberty shall be to the freedman more than a name," his assertion that the inability of African Americans to govern proved they were unworthy of suffrage rights helped to perpetuate racist stereotypes and to justify the widespread exclusion of blacks from public life. In the final analysis, the conditions that Bacon and other northern moderate Republicans attached to their support for the protection of fundamental legal rights for blacks rendered these rights virtually worthless.[13]

In contrast to his diminishing interest in the course of Reconstruction during the 1870s, Bacon remained extremely attentive to the welfare of the Congregational Church. As an elder statesman of the church, his views on a broad range of questions were, if anything, increasingly valued by other Congregationalists; therefore, the editors of the *Independent* and the *Christian Union,* who generally agreed with him on matters of doctrine and polity, frequently opened their columns to his articles.[14] He continued to stand forth as a progressive conservative, holding tenaciously to certain traditional Congregational principles while selectively adapting to changing realities and emphasizing the need for tolerance of diverse views within the church and among various Protestant groups.

13. Circular of the Colored Refugee Relief Board, April 22, 1879, Ebenezer D. Bassett to Gov. John P. St. John, May 15, 1879, sermon of November 27, 1889, in Bacon Family Papers; *Independent,* October 7, 1880; Bacon, "The Political Outlook," 83–85; *Independent,* October 7, 1880.

14. Lyman Abbott to Bacon, September 11, 1876, in Bacon Family Papers; Benjamin Wisner Bacon, *Theodore Thornton Munger,* 260.

Although Bacon continued to urge cooperation among Protestants and to believe that Christians must unite "across ages and faiths," he believed that the concept of "an organized unity" had never been considered by Christ and, when attempted during the past 1,500 years, had led to disunion, separation, and exclusion. He even expressed concern that Congregationalists had "fallen into a very broad and unguarded communion" with some evangelical denominations whose policies regarding ordination were highly suspect. Yet he strongly criticized Henry M. Dexter, editor of the *Congregationalist,* George Walker, and others who sought to fashion a cohesive denomination that would consciously compete with other Protestant groups and would adhere to uniform doctrines and practices. In concert with Noah Porter, Samuel Harris, Theodore Munger, and other progressives within the church, he spoke on behalf of toleration and religious liberty and attacked what he considered "excessive denominationalism" among Congregationalists. Speaking to the delegates at the 1876 meeting of the American Home Missionary Society, he exhorted them to "rise above the stifling narrowness of sectarian propagandism, into a serener, purer, freer air of the Christian idea." He was deeply disturbed that the church now seemed to speak more about the extension of the denomination than the church of Christ. This, he feared, would dishonor and weaken Christianity.[15]

As the New Theology controversy intensified, Bacon became increasingly outspoken in his defense of the progressive school of thought within the church. When some leading Congregationalists questioned whether the doctrines espoused by Theodore Munger should be tolerated, he sprang to Munger's defense. The true issue, he proclaimed in the *Congregationalist,* was not what the doctrines of the denomination were but what the truth was and what the Scriptures taught. In response to resolutions passed by the Vermont Congregational convention in 1879, which urged stronger denominational control over pastors' evangelical beliefs, he declared that if a minister departed from the truth, other churches should simply end communion with that church. He would prefer to deal with a presbytery rather than a Congregational association in a denominational church, he wrote caustically, because at least there were well-defined rules and appeals to a higher body in the Presbyterian Church.[16]

15. Bacon to Committee of the Church Unity Association, March 26, 1878, Bacon to T. C. Kernaken, April 1, 1880, in Bacon Family Papers; Leonard Bacon, *The Old Way: A Commemorative Discourse for the Fiftieth Anniversary of the American Home Missionary Society. Preached in the Broadway Tabernacle Church, New York, May 7, 1876* (New York, 1876), 24; *Independent,* January 20, May 8, 1879, February 26, 1881; *Christian Union,* January 3, 1877. For a treatment of this controversy, see Benjamin Wisner Bacon, *Theodore Thornton Munger,* 260–62.

16. *Congregationalist,* December 26, 1877, July 30, 1879; *Independent,* February 27, April 17, 24, 1879; Benjamin Wisner Bacon, *Theodore Thornton Munger,* 264, 266.

Bacon did not propose to initiate a war against "organized" denominations, for he was hopeful that they would be "silently dissolved in the growing warmth of love to God and love to man, and of Christ's promised presence." But as he labored to stem the tide of denominational sentiment within the Congregational ranks, his antisectarian and interdenominational bent became, if anything, more pronounced. He increasingly emphasized the close affinity between Congregationalists and Methodists, Presbyterians, Baptists, and other Protestants. Indeed, to the end of his life he maintained that it was "impossible to formulate a difference between Congregational evangelicalism and the common evangelicalism of all evangelical churches."[17]

Bacon was convinced that he stood with what he termed "the great central mass" of Congregationalists, who considered themselves Calvinists but rejoiced in the progress that theology had made since the Westminster Confession, were generous about differing religious theories, and were determined to resist efforts by extreme elements within the church that wished to impose a rigid confession of faith on members. To the very end, he insisted that any confession must be flexible, broadly evangelical, and subject to interpretation by each local church. Thus, when the 1880 National Council followed the example of the Boston council of 1865 by appointing a commission to devise an acceptable confession of faith, he and other progressives, confident that it would serve as a model for Congregationalists while having no binding force with local churches, applauded the move.[18]

Bacon's extensive writing for the *Independent,* the *Christian Union,* and other religious newspapers, as well as his teaching responsibilities at the seminary, constituted a large part, though by no means all, of his work related to religious matters during these years. When Center Church was without a settled pastor in the late 1870s, he occasionally preached and performed other functions. Moreover, he was active in the Connecticut Bible Society, serving as its president in 1878, and he periodically attended meetings of the American Board of Commissioners for Foreign Missions. In 1878 he also traveled to Pittsburgh for the Presbyterian General Assembly meeting as a representative of the Congregational Church. He combined this trip with a nostalgic journey to Hudson and Tallmadge, Ohio, with Edward, Frank, Leonard Woolsey, and Theodore. While in Tallmadge he visited a few elderly residents who had been his playmates seventy years earlier. Three years later, he made his final pilgrimage to Tallmadge, accompanied by Theodore, Leonard Woolsey, Ellen, and his granddaughter Alice. At this time, he placed a granite me-

17. *Christian Union,* September 3, 1879; *Independent,* May 2, 1877, January 2, July 3, August 7, 1879, January 22, 1881.

18. *Christian Union,* September 3, 1879; *Independent,* February 13, 1879, November 4, December 30, 1880, February 19, 26, 1881.

morial stone at the spot where his parents had built their cabin and recounted how his family had set out by wagon from Hudson in 1807.[19]

Bacon continued to devote considerable attention to family matters. He reveled in the news of the birth of each grandchild and regularly corresponded with, and occasionally visited, his children. But he also had to endure serious family difficulties and tragedies. For several years Catherine, who perhaps suffered from a chronic arthritic condition, had been "a helpless and suffering invalid," often bedridden, in pain, and increasingly depressed. By 1880, she required nursing care around the clock. In addition, he suffered the loss of two of his children during these years. George, a minister in New Jersey, died in 1876 at the age of forty. Bacon was deeply saddened by his death, informing Leonard Woolsey that "to us, his memory will always be fresh, and our sense of loss can never cease to be vivid." Rebecca's death in 1878 was perhaps even more painful for Bacon, for she had helped to raise her siblings for many years, and during the last years of her life had been the mainstay of the household. "Few lives are so full of self-sacrifice and self-forgetfulness as hers has been," Bacon wrote Edward, "so full of love and care and work for others. Thank God for her life!"[20]

By 1880, only Alice and Ellen lived with their parents, though Leonard and Catherine continued to board two of Leonard Woolsey's sons during part of each year. A heart condition that had bothered Bacon for several years steadily worsened, and his consciousness of old age intensified. "While I wonder to find myself among the living," he wrote Leonard Woolsey in 1880, "I look forward thankfully and hopefully to the great transition just before me." He gradually was forced to limit the number of meetings he attended, and he eventually ceased walking to the seminary. But once more, Bacon's prediction of his impending death was premature. Despite suffering several strokes in 1881, he was determined, as he wrote Leonard Woolsey, "not to give up while I am able to do anything." Indeed, during the last month of his life he attended a Yale Corporation meeting, preached a sermon at his old church, sought to persuade Edward B. Coe to fill the pulpit at Center Church, and worked on an essay on Utah and the Mormon question.[21]

19. See Leonard to Leonard Woolsey Bacon, February 19, 1880, Circular of Connecticut Bible Society, April 3, 1878, October 17, 1879, Leonard to Catherine Bacon, May 17, 18, 24, 1878, Day Book for June 1–2, 1881, articles in Akron *Daily Beacon,* May 28, June 4, 1881, in Bacon Family Papers; *Christian Union,* June 19, 1881.

20. Leonard to Catherine Bacon, September 1, 1877, September 9, 1878, September 4, 1881, Leonard to Leonard Woolsey Bacon, September 18, October 12, 1878, August 24, 1880, February 10, 1881, O. E. Dagget to Bacon, March 4, 1877, Rebecca to Leonard Woolsey Bacon, August 12, 1877, Bacon to Susan A. Whiting, January 14, 1881, Bacon to D. W. Hall, September 29, 1876, September 18, 1878, Leonard to Edward Bacon, October 20, 1878, in Bacon Family Papers.

21. Bacon to Susan A. Whiting, January 14, 1881, Leonard to Leonard Woolsey Bacon, February 19, June 1, 1880, February 10, December 15, 1881, Bacon to Henry M. Dexter, July 30, 1880, Bacon to

Bacon died of heart failure at his home on December 24, 1881, with Catherine and three of their children at his bedside. Many family members and old friends and associates attended a brief service at his home, which was conducted by Theodore Dwight Woolsey. At the public service held at Center Church, which was filled to capacity, his six sons served as pallbearers and Timothy Dwight presented the eulogy while the bells at City Hall tolled in the background; three weeks later George Walker eulogized Bacon at a memorial service. Numerous tributes poured in from former president Hayes and others whom Bacon had known and influenced over the previous six decades. Lyman Abbott, writing in the *Christian Union,* spoke for many of those whose lives Bacon had touched. In a tribute that Bacon certainly would have appreciated, he wrote: "America was his pulpit, and her people his congregation; and there was not a theme which concerned her prosperity which his incessantly active mind did not study; and upon which his ever vigorous voice and pen did not do some effective teaching."[22]

Bacon's influence indeed had extended far beyond his beloved Center Church congregation and New Haven. As a powerful force in the Congregational Church and a prominent activist in the temperance, missionary, anti-Catholic, and other causes, he helped to shape the thinking of large numbers of northern Protestants for nearly sixty years. He made his greatest mark as a spokesman for a broad centrist element in the North that hoped gradually to abolish slavery but also feared disorder and conflict in a society experiencing rapid social and economic change.

In some respects Bacon's approach to reform was flawed. For example, neither his expectation that colonization would elevate all African Americans nor his belief that "good" slaveholders would eventually abolish slavery squared with reality, and his relentless attacks on the abolitionists doomed his quest for a broad antislavery coalition. Likewise, in urging racial and religious toleration while articulating, in some measure, widely held prejudices, he scarcely was in a position either to challenge negative stereotypes of African Americans and Catholics or to break down barriers that deeply divided the American people.

In the final analysis, Bacon both reflected and spoke to the ambivalence that many northerners felt as they confronted a rapidly changing, diverse society that

---

Edward B. Coe, November 28, 30, December 21, 1881, Day Book for December 21–23, 1881, in Bacon Family Papers; Meeting of December 5, 1881, in "Records of the Prudential Committee of the Yale Corporation"; *Leonard Bacon: Pastor of the First Church in New Haven,* 138, 143, 158, 211, 215; Bacon to Justin Winton, February 22, 1879, June 22, 1880, in Leonard Bacon Correspondence, Houghton Library, Harvard University, Cambridge, Mass.

22. New Haven *Evening Register,* December 24, 26, 1881; *Advance,* February 5, 1882; *Leonard Bacon: Pastor of the First Church in New Haven,* 10–11, 149–58; *Christian Union,* December 28, 1881. See also, for example, Rutherford B. Hayes to Leonard Woolsey Bacon, December 30, 1881, in Bacon Family Papers; *Independent,* December 29, 1881.

held out the promise of social progress and individual liberty yet also generated deep-seated anxieties and social conflict. However flawed his vision of a reformed and redeemed America was, he endeavored, with some success, to convince nineteenth-century Americans of the wisdom of adapting to the changing needs and temper of the times while rejecting those who urged either a radical transformation of American institutions and values or a blind attachment to the ways of the past.

B I B L I O G R A P H Y

PRIMARY SOURCES
Manuscripts

American Antiquarian Society, Worcester, Mass.
   Edward Woolsey Bacon Papers.
   Cheever-Wheeler Papers.
Andover Newton Theological Seminary, Newton Center, Mass.
   "Constitution and Records of the Porter Rhetorical Society of the Theological
      Seminary."
   "Records of the Review Association and of the Bartlett Atheneum of the Theological
      Seminary."
   "Records of the Society of Inquiry Respecting Missions."
Boston Public Library, Boston, Mass.
   Milton Chamberlain Collection.
   William Lloyd Garrison Papers.
   Samuel May, Jr., Papers.
   Amos A. Phelps Papers.
   Weston Family Papers.
Congregational Library, Boston, Mass.
   C. A. Richardson Collection.
   Bennet Tyler Collection.
Connecticut Historical Society, Hartford, Conn.
   Oliver Henry Percy Papers.
   Isaac Toucey Papers.
   Gideon Welles Papers.
Harvard University (Houghton Library), Cambridge, Mass.
   Autograph File.
   Leonard Bacon Correspondence.
   Phillips Brooks Papers.
Library of Congress, Washington, D.C.
   American Colonization Society Papers.
   Breckinridge Family Papers.
   Thomas Hopkins Gallaudet Papers.

Lewis Tappan Papers.

Elizur Wright Papers.

Massachusetts Historical Society, Boston, Mass.

George Bancroft Papers.

New England Historic Genealogical Society, Boston, Mass.

"Records of the Boston Society for the Moral and Religious Instruction of the Poor," in William Jenks Papers.

New Haven Colony Historical Society, New Haven, Conn.

National and Local Historical Figures Collection.

Oberlin College, Oberlin, Ohio

Charles G. Finney Papers.

Syracuse University, Syracuse, N.Y.

Gerrit Smith Miller Collection.

Yale University (Beinecke Library), New Haven, Conn.

Amos Gerry Beman Papers.

Collections of American Literature.

Jeremiah Day Papers.

Yale University (Sterling Library), New Haven, Conn.

Bacon Family Papers.

Baldwin Family Papers.

Beecher Family Papers.

"Catalogue of the Brothers in Unity, 1768–1845."

"Constitution of the Brothers in Unity."

"Constitution of the Moral Society of Yale College."

"Journal of the Meetings, Proceedings and Transactions of the Moral Society of Yale College, 1797–1819."

"Records of the Prudential Committee of the Yale Corporation."

"Records of the Society of Brothers in Unity."

"Records of the Yale Corporation."

"The Talebearer."

Woolsey Family Papers.

Yale Lectures, 1874.

Bacon's Writings (in chronological order)

"Motives to Active Benevolence." *Christian Spectator,* IV (December, 1822), 617–22.

"The Reports of the American Society for Colonizing the Free People of Colour of the United States, 1818, 19, 20, 21, 22, 23." *Christian Spectator,* V (September–October, 1823), 458–94, 540–51.

The Social and Civil Influence of the Christian Ministry. A Sermon Preached at the Sixth Anniversary of the Auxiliary Education Society of the Young Men of Boston, Feb. 6, 1825. Boston, 1825.

A Plea for Africa; Delivered in New-Haven, July 4th, 1825. New Haven, 1825.

"Memoir of the Late Rev. Chester Isham." *Christian Spectator,* VII (December, 1825), 613–17.

"Brief View of the American Education Society." *Christian Spectator,* n.s., I (February, 1827), 92–98.

"Discourses on Intemperance." *Christian Spectator,* n.s., I (November and December, 1827), 587–604, 645–55.

"Memoir of Samuel Hooker Cowles." *Christian Spectator,* n.s., II (January, 1828), 1–9.

"Reports of Temperance Societies." *Christian Spectator,* n.s., II (May, 1828), 243–64.

"Duties of Young Christians." *National Preacher,* III (June, 1828), 1–8.

"The Example of Christ." *National Preacher,* III (June, 1828), 9–16.

"Reports of the Colonization Society." *Christian Spectator,* n.s., II (July, 1828), 358–70.

A Discourse Preached in the Center Church, in New Haven, August 27, 1828, at the Funeral of Jehudi Ashmun, Esq., Colonial Agent of the American Colony of Liberia. New Haven, 1828.

"Connecticut Colonization Society." *Christian Spectator,* n.s., II (September, 1828), 493–96.

"Hawes' Lectures to Young Men." *Christian Spectator,* n.s., II (September, 1828), 474–81.

"Review of the Remains of the Rev. Carlos Wilcox." *Quarterly Christian Spectator,* 3rd series, I (March, 1829), 52–78.

"Review of Works on Greece." *Quarterly Christian Spectator,* 3rd series, I (March, 1829), 178–200.

"Reviews of Works on Greece and the Mediterranean." *Quarterly Christian Spectator,* 3rd series, I (June, 1829), 312–39.

Total Abstinence from Ardent Spirits; An Address Delivered, By Request of the Young Men's Temperance Society of New Haven, in the North Church, June 24, 1829. New Haven, 1829.

"Review on the Economy of Methodism." *Quarterly Christian Spectator,* 3rd series, I (September, 1829), 509–26.

"Review of the Life of Summerfield." *Quarterly Christian Spectator,* 3rd series, II (March, 1830), 118–33.

"Review on African Colonization." *Quarterly Christian Spectator,* 3rd series, II (September, 1830), 459–82.

"Review of Speeches by Hayne and Webster." *Quarterly Christian Spectator,* 3rd series, II (September, 1830), 517–29.

"Review of Sprague's Lectures to Youth." *Quarterly Christian Spectator,* 3rd series, II (December, 1830), 647–60.

Select Practical Writings of Richard Baxter, With a Life of the Author. 2 vols. New Haven, 1831.

The Christian Doctrine of Stewardship in Respect to Property: A Sermon Preached at the Request of the Young Men's Benevolent Society of New Haven, Conn. New Haven, 1832.

"Voluntary Associations." *Quarterly Christian Spectator,* 3rd series, IV (March, 1832), 142–70.

"The Free People of Color." *Quarterly Christian Spectator,* 3rd series, IV (June, 1832), 311–34.

The Hopefulness of Efforts for the Promotion of Peace. A Discourse, Pronounced in the Center Church in Hartford, at the Celebration of the Hartford County Peace Society, on the Evening of the Lord's Day, June 10, 1832. Hartford, 1832.

A Manual for Young Church-Members. New Haven, 1833.

"Slavery and Colonization." *Quarterly Christian Spectator,* 3rd series, V (March, 1833), 145–68.

"Sketch of the Life and Character of Hon. James Hillhouse." *Quarterly Christian Spectator*, 3rd series, V (June, 1833), 238–47.

"Universalism." *Quarterly Christian Spectator*, 3rd series, VI (June, 1833), 266–90.

"On Efficacious Prayer." *Quarterly Christian Spectator*, 3rd series, VI (June, 1834), 250–59.

"Mrs. Child's Appeal in Favor of the Africans." *Quarterly Christian Spectator*, 3rd series, VI (September, 1834), 445–56.

Exposition of the Objects and Plans of the American Union for the Relief and Improvement of the Colored Race. Boston, 1835.

"Encouragements to Effort, for the Speedy Conversion of the World." *Quarterly Christian Spectator*, 3rd series, VII (March, 1835), 1–2.

"Gurley's Life of Ashmun." *Quarterly Christian Spectator*, 3rd series, VII (June, 1835), 330–52.

"Beecher's Plea for the West." *Quarterly Christian Spectator*, 3rd series, VII (September, 1835), 481–503.

"Christian Politics." *Quarterly Christian Spectator*, 3rd series, VII (December, 1835), 540–46.

"Beecher on Colleges." *Quarterly Christian Spectator*, 3rd series, VIII (September, 1836), 389–411.

"Maria Monk and Her Impostures." *Quarterly Christian Spectator*, 3rd series, IX (June, 1837), 263–82.

"The Present Commercial Distress." *Quarterly Christian Spectator*, 3rd series, IX (June, 1837), 327–40.

"The Revolution in the Presbyterian Church." *Quarterly Christian Spectator*, 3rd series, IX (December, 1837), 597–646.

A Discourse on the Traffic in Spiritous Liquors, Delivered in the Center Church, New Haven, February 6, 1838. New Haven, 1838.

"Memoir of Lovejoy." *Quarterly Christian Spectator*, 3rd series, X (June, 1838), 299–318.

"Emancipation in the West Indies." *Quarterly Christian Spectator*, 3rd series, X (September, 1838), 440–67.

"Valedictory Remarks." *Quarterly Christian Spectator*, 3rd series, X (December, 1838), 678–83.

Thirteen Historical Discourses, on the Completion of Two Hundred Years, From the Beginning of the First Church in New Haven. New Haven, 1839.

"The Proper Character and Functions of American Literature." *American Biblical Repository*, n.s., III (January, 1840), 1–23.

Views and Reviews. No. I. January, 1840. Seven Letters to Rev. G. A. Calhoun. New Haven, 1840.

Views and Reviews. No. II. May, 1840. An Appeal Against Division; With an Appendix of Notes on Mr. Calhoun's Letters. New Haven, 1840.

"What It Is to Become a Christian." *National Preacher*, XV (June, 1840), 141–48.

The Proper Character and Functions of American Literature. A Discourse Before the Society of Phi Beta Kappa, in Yale College, August 20, 1839. New York, 1840.

The Goodly Heritage of Connecticut. A Discourse in the First Church of New Haven, on Thanksgiving Day, November 19, 1840. New Haven, 1840.

"The Day Approaching." *National Preacher*, XVI (October, 1842), 217–28.

"The Post-Office System as an Element of Modern Civilization." *New Englander*, I (January, 1843), 9–27.

"Prospectus." *New Englander,* I (January, 1843), 1–3.

"Prolegomena." *New Englander,* I (January, 1843), 4–8.

"What Must Be Done to Provide an Educated Christian Ministry?" *New Englander,* I (January, 1843), 126–39.

"Two Hundred Years Ago in England." *New Englander,* I (April, 1843), 250–72.

"Public Affairs." *New Englander,* I (April, 1843), 299–304.

A Discourse on the Early Constitutional History of Connecticut, Delivered Before the Connecticut Historical Society, Hartford, May 17, 1843. Hartford, 1843.

"Public Libraries." *New Englander,* I (July, 1843), 306–11.

"Wittingham's Charge to His Clergy." *New Englander,* I (October, 1843), 545–55.

"Revivalism and the Church." *New Englander,* II (January, 1844), 175–80.

"Romanists and the Roman Catholic Controversy." *New Englander,* II (April, 1844), 233–55.

"The Martyrdom of Bishop Onderdonk." *New Englander,* III (April, 1845), 284–306.

Christian Unity. A Sermon Preached Before the Foreign Evangelical Society, in the Bleeker Street Church, New York, May 4, 1845. New Haven, 1845.

Oration, Before the Phi Beta Kappa Society of Dartmouth College, Delivered July 30, 1845. Hanover, N.H., 1845.

"The Relative Character and Merits of the Congregational and Presbyterian Systems." *New Englander,* III (July, 1845), 438–50.

"The New Post-Office Law." *New Englander,* III (October, 1845), 536–48.

Slavery Discussed in Occasional Essays, From 1833 to 1846. New York, 1846.

"Shall Punishment Be Abolished?" *New Englander,* IV (October, 1846), 563–88.

"Responsibility in the Management of Societies." *New Englander,* V (January, 1847), 28–40.

"The State of Political Parties." *New Englander,* V (April, 1847), 306–20.

"The War with Mexico." *New Englander,* V (October, 1847), 604–13.

"The Christian Basis of the Temperance Reformation." *American Temperance Preacher,* I (January, 1848), 1–14.

"Peace—And What Next?" *New Englander,* VI (April, 1848), 292–99.

Discourse, Before the Literary Societies of Hamilton College, Clinton, July 27, 1847. Utica, 1848.

"The Ethics of the Right of Suffrage." *New Englander,* VI (July, 1848), 441–53.

Christianity in History. A Discourse Addressed to the Alumni of Yale College, In Their Annual Meeting, August 16, 1848. New Haven, 1848.

An Address Delivered at the Annual Fair of the New Haven County Horticultural Society, September 27, 1848. New Haven, 1848.

Christianity and Learning. A Discourse Preached in the Second Presbyterian Church in Troy, October 26, 1847, Before the Annual Meeting of the Society for the Promotion of Collegiate and Theological Education at the West. New Haven, 1848.

"The New Earth." *New Englander,* VII (February, 1849), 1–16.

"The American Board and Slavery." *New Englander,* VII (May, 1849), 273–88.

"Review of Bushnell's 'God in Christ.'" *New Englander,* VII (May, 1849), 324–26.

"The Application of Political Economy." *New Englander,* VII (August, 1849), 419–42.

A Sermon to the First Church and Society in New Haven, 10th March, 1850, on Completing the Twenty-fifth Year of the Author's Service in the Pastoral Office. New Haven, 1850.

"The Question! Are You Ready for the Question?" *New Englander,* VIII (May, 1850), 292–312.

"Conscience and the Constitution." *New Englander,* VIII (August, 1850), 472–76.

"John Cotton." *New Englander,* VIII (August, 1850), 388–418.

"Moses Stuart." *New Englander,* X (February, 1852), 42–55.

The American Church. A Discourse in Behalf of the American Home Missionary Society, Preached in the Cities of New York and Brooklyn, May, 1852. New York, 1852.

"Evangelical Alliance." *New Englander,* X (May, 1852), 309–30.

"Prof. Park's Memoir of Hopkins." *New Englander,* X (August, 1852), 448–72.

"Literature of Slavery." *New Englander,* X (November, 1852), 581–613.

"The Editorial Profession." *New Englander,* XI (May, 1853), 210–22.

"Thornwell on Slavery." *New Englander,* XII (February, 1854), 93–124.

"Morality of the Nebraska Bill." *New Englander,* XII (May, 1854), 304–35.

"Prof. Schaff's Church History." *New Englander,* XII (May, 1854), 237–54.

"The New Post-Office Law." *New Englander,* XII (October, 1854), 530–44.

"The Southern Apostasy." *New Englander,* XII (November, 1854), 627–62.

"The Puritan Ritual." *New Englander,* XIII (August, 1855), 450–77.

"Hodge on Presbyterianism." *New Englander,* XIV (February, 1856), 1–32.

The Relation of Christianity to the Law and Government. A Discourse Before the Society of Phi Beta Kappa, in Harvard University, 17th July, 1856. New Haven, 1856.

"The President's Message." *New Englander,* XV (February, 1857), 1–38.

Two Sermons Preached to the First Church in New Haven, On a Day of Fasting, viz., Good Friday, the 10th of April, 1857. New Haven, 1857.

"Paul on Politics." *New Englander,* XV (August, 1857), 462–77.

"Buchanan on Kansas." *New Englander,* XV (November, 1857), 675–700.

A Commemorative Discourse, on the Completion of Fifty Years from the Founding of the Theological Seminary at Andover. Andover, Mass., 1858.

The Growth of the Kingdom of Heaven. A Discourse Before the Congregational Board of Education, in the Tremont Temple, Boston, on the 26th of May, 1858. Boston, 1858.

"A Burning and a Shining Light." *National Preacher and Village Pulpit,* n.s., II (January, 1859), 1–8.

"The Moral of Harper's Ferry." *New Englander,* XVII (November, 1859), 1066–78.

Established in Righteousness. A Discourse to the First Church and Society in New Haven, On a Day of Public Thanksgiving, November 24th, 1859. New Haven, 1859.

"The Minister's Wooing: From the Dr. Dryadust Point of View." *New Englander,* XVIII (February, 1860), 145–66.

"The Crime Against the Right of Suffrage." *New Englander,* XVIII (May, 1860), 453–72.

"A Half Century of Foreign Missions." *New Englander,* XVIII (August, 1860), 711–25.

"Palfrey's History of New England." *New Englander,* XVIII (November, 1860), 1020–48.

"The Pulpit and the Crisis." *New Englander,* XIX (January, 1861), 140–60.

"Puritan History." *New Englander,* XIX (January, 1861), 126–39.

"The Martyrs Under Queen Elizabeth." *New Englander,* XIX (April, 1861), 437–73.

The Jugglers Detected: A Discourse, Delivered by Request, in the Chapel Street Church, New Haven, December 30, 1860. New Haven, 1861.

[Pacificator, *pseud.*] *The Nail Hit on the Head; or, the Two Jonathans Agreeing to Settle the Slave Question With or Without More Fighting, As the South Pleases.* New Haven, 1862.

"The War of the Lord." *New Englander,* XXI (January, 1862), 115–34.

"Noah's Prophecy: 'Cursed Be Canaan.'" *New Englander,* XXI (April, 1862), 341–58.

Conciliation. A Discourse at a Sunday Evening Service, New Haven, July 20, 1862. New Haven, 1862.

"What Is the Cost of Tract Distribution?" *New Englander,* XXI (July, 1862), 587–613.

Christian Self-Culture; or Counsels for the Beginning and Progress of a Christian Life. New York, 1863.

"Reply to Professor Parker." *New Englander,* XXII (April, 1863), 191–258.

A Historical Discourse Delivered at Worcester, in the Old South Meeting House, September 22, 1863: The Hundredth Anniversary of Its Erection. Worcester, 1863.

Four Commemorative Discourses: Delivered on His Sixty-third Birth-day, February 19, 1865; On the Fortieth Anniversary of His Installation, March 12, 1865; and on His Retirement from Pastoral Duties. New Haven, 1865.

Two Sermons Preached on the Fortieth Anniversary of His Settlement. New Haven, 1865.

"A Roman Philosopher." *New Englander,* XXVI (January, 1867), 114–47.

"The 'Catholic World' More Catholic." *New Englander,* XXVI (July, 1867), 525–64.

"The Latest Work in the Schonberg-Cotta Series." *New Englander,* XXVII (January, 1868), 164–79.

An Adequate Ministry. A Sermon, Delivered Before the American Education Society, at the Anniversary Meeting in Boston, May 25, 1869. Boston, 1869.

"Father Hyacinthe." *New Englander,* XXIX (January, 1870), 37–72.

"How the Rev. Dr. Stone Bettered His Situation." *New Englander,* XXIX (July, 1870), 471–95.

"A Voice from 'Squashville': A Letter to the New Englander from the Rev. Mr. Pickering." *New Englander,* XXIX (October, 1870), 678–704.

"Railways and the State." *New Englander,* XXX (October, 1871), 713–38.

"Missionary Work in Hawaii." *New Englander,* XXXI (July, 1872), 494–541.

"Sectarian Symbols." *New Englander,* XXXI (October, 1872), 745–60.

The Genesis of the New England Churches. New York, 1874.

"Constitution-Making." *New Englander,* XXXIII (January, 1874), 16–37.

Half-Century Sermon: A Commemorative Discourse, March 9, 1875, on the Completion of Fifty Years, From the Beginning of the Author's Ministry as Pastor to the First Church of Christ in New Haven. New Haven, 1875.

New Haven One Hundred Years Ago: A Centennial Address Delivered in Center Church, July Fourth, 1876. New Haven, 1876.

"David Bacon." *Congregational Quarterly,* XVIII (January, April, July, and October, 1876), 1–19, 260–82, 387–417, 562–91.

The Old Way: A Commemorative Discourse for the Fiftieth Anniversary of the American Home

Missionary Society, Preached in the Broadway Tabernacle Church, New York, May 7, 1876. New York, 1876.

"The Political Outlook." *New Englander,* XXXVII (January, 1878), 80–91.

"Reaction of New England on English Puritanism in the Seventeenth Century." *New Englander,* XXXVII (July, September, and November, 1878), 441–62, 628–41, 790–810.

Three Civic Orations for New Haven. New Haven, 1879.

"Concerning a Recent Chapter of Ecclesiastical History." *New Englander,* XXXVIII (September, 1879), 701–12.

The Providential Selection and Training of the Pilgrim Pioneers of New England. A Paper Read to the Connecticut Congregational Club, December 21, 1880. Hartford, 1880.

Newspapers and Journals

Advance, 1874–1882.

African Repository and Colonial Journal, 1826–1834.

American Spectator and Washington City Chronicle, 1830–1832.

Boston *Post,* 1862.

Boston *Recorder and Religious Herald,* 1829–1835.

Christian Spectator (also *Quarterly Christian Spectator*), 1821–1838.

Christian Union, 1870–1880.

Colonizationist and Journal of Freedom, May, December, 1833; March, 1834.

Congregationalist, 1862–1879.

Congregational Quarterly, July, 1875; January, July, October, 1876.

Connecticut Evangelical Magazine, November, 1800.

Connecticut Journal, October 4, 1831.

Cooley's Weekly, February–March, 1877.

Emancipator, October 24, 1845.

Freedom's Journal, April 27, August 10, 1827.

Golden Age, June 27, 1874.

Hartford *Courant,* January 18, June 7, 1862.

Independent, 1848–1881.

Journal of Commerce, 1851–1874.

Journal of Freedom, 1834–1835.

Liberator, 1831–1837.

National Preacher, 1828–1859.

New Englander, 1843–1881.

New Haven *Chronicle,* May 22, 1827; July 2, 1830.

New Haven *Daily Herald,* 1839.

New Haven *Daily Palladium,* December 9, 1865; November 10, 1870.

New Haven *Daily Register,* February 18, 1854.

New Haven *Evening Register,* December 24, 26, 1881.

New Haven *Journal,* 1837.

New Haven *Morning Journal and Courier*, October 31, 1856.

New Haven *Palladium*, January 31, February 28, 1854.

New Haven *Record*, 1839–1840.

New York *Evangelist*, 1845–1848.

New York *Observer*, 1828–1860.

New York *Times*, February 27, March 2, 1866.

New York *Tribune*, 1874–1877.

Religious Intelligencer, 1829–1837.

Other Published Primary Sources

Abbott, Lyman. *Reminiscences*. Boston, 1915.

Addresses at the Laying of the Corner Stone of the Divinity Hall of the Theological Department of Yale College, September 22nd, 1869. New Haven, 1869.

Address of Joseph R. Ingersoll at the Annual Meeting of the Pennsylvania Colonization Society, October 25, 1838. Philadelphia, 1838.

Address of Rev. Drs. Edwards Amasa Park, Truman Marcellus Post, and Leonard Bacon, at the Anniversary of the American Congregational Union, May, 1854. New York, 1854.

Address of the Rev. L. Bacon, D.D., and Rev. E. N. Kirk, at the Annual Meeting of the Christian Alliance, Held in New York, May 8, 1845, With the Address of the Society and the Bull of the Pope Against It. New York, 1846.

An Address to the Public, on the Subject of the African School, Lately Established Under the Care of the Synod of New-York and New-Jersey. New York, 1816.

An Address to the Public by the Managers of the Colonization Society of Connecticut. New Haven, 1828.

Alexander, Archibald. *A History of Colonization on the Western Coast of Africa*. Philadelphia, 1846.

The American Board and American Slavery: Speech of Theodore Tilton, in Plymouth Church, Brooklyn, January 28, 1860. N.p., 1860.

American Board of Commissioners for Foreign Missions. *Report of the Committee on Anti-Slavery Memorials, September, 1845*. Boston, 1845.

American Colonization Society. *A Few Facts Respecting the American Colonization Society, and the Colony at Liberia*. Washington, D.C., 1830.

The American Union Commission: Its Origins, Operations and Purposes. New York, 1865.

The American Union Commission. Speeches of Hon. W. Dennison, Postmaster-General, Rev. J. P. Thompson, D.D., President of the Commission, C. N. G. Taylor, of East Tennessee, Hon. J. R. Doolittle, U.S. Senate, Gen. J. A. Garfield, M.C., in the Hall of Representatives, Washington, February 12, 1865. New York, 1865.

Andrews, E. A. *Slavery and the Domestic Slave-Trade in the United States. In a Series of Letters Addressed to the Executive Committee of the American Union for the Relief and Improvement of the Colored Race*. Boston, 1836.

Annual Report of the African Improvement Society of New Haven. New Haven, 1829.

Annual Report of the American and Foreign Christian Union. New York, 1852.

Annual Report of the Executive Committee of the American Union for the Relief and Improvement of the Colored Race. Boston, 1836.

Annual Report of the Vermont Colonization Society. Montpelier, Vt., 1834.

Annual Reports of the American Board of Commissioners for Foreign Missions. Boston, 1845, 1851.

Annual Reports of the American Society for Colonizing the Free People of Colour of the United States. Washington, D.C., 1823–1834.

Annual Reports of the Executive Committee of the Connecticut Temperance Society. Hartford, 1832–1834.

Annual Reports of the Ladies Home Missionary Society, of the Center Church—New Haven. New Haven, 1856–1859.

Annual Reports of the Managers of the Colonization Society of the State of Connecticut. New Haven, 1829–1844.

Annual Reports of the Society for the Promotion of Collegiate and Theological Education at the West. New York, 1844–1845.

Autobiography of Andrew Dickson White. Vol. I of 2 vols. New York, 1905.

"Autobiography of Rev. Joseph Badger," *American Quarterly Register,* XIII (February, 1841), 317–28.

Bacon, Leonard Woolsey. *A Discourse Delivered in the Memorial Presbyterian Church, Detroit, Michigan; On the Occasion of the Unveiling of a Tablet, in Memory of the Late Leonard Bacon, D.D., December 24, 1882.* N.p., 1882.

————. *The Mistakes and Failures of the Temperance Reformation.* New York, 1864.

Baldwin, Ebenezer. *Observations on the Physical, Intellectual, and Moral Qualities of Our Colored Population: With Remarks on the Subject of Emancipation and Colonization.* New Haven, 1834.

Barnes, Albert. *An Inquiry into the Scriptural Views of Slavery.* Philadelphia, 1846.

Beecher, Catharine E. *An Essay on Slavery and Abolitionism, With Reference to the Duty of American Females.* Philadelphia, 1837.

————. *Truth Stranger Than Fiction: A Narrative of Recent Transactions, Involving Inquiries in Regard to the Principles of Honor, Truth, and Justice, Which Obtain in a Distinguished American University.* Boston, 1850.

Benham's New Haven City Directory, for 1846–7. No. 7. New Haven, 1846.

Benham's New Haven Directory and Annual Advertiser: 1851–52. Number Twelve. New Haven, 1851.

Benham's New Haven Directory and Annual Advertiser. Number Seventeen. 1856–7. New Haven, 1856.

Benham's New Haven Directory and Annual Advertiser. Number Twenty-two. 1861–62. New Haven, 1861.

Benham's New Haven Directory and Annual Advertiser, for 1865–6. Number Twenty-six. New Haven, 1865.

Blagden, George W. *Remarks, and a Discourse on Slavery.* Boston, 1854.

Bradley, Franklin S. *Recollections of Dr. Leonard Bacon.* N.p., n.d.

Calhoun, Rev. George A. *Letters to the Rev. Leonard Bacon, In Reply to His Attacks on the Pastoral Union and Theological Institute of Connecticut.* Hartford, 1840.

Carroll, J. Halsted. *A Letter to Rev. Leonard Bacon, D.D.* New Haven, 1866.

Catalogue of the Professors and Students of the Theological Seminary, Andover, Massachusetts, December, 1823. Andover, Mass., 1823.

Catalogue of the Professors and Students of the Theological Seminary, Andover, Massachusetts, February, 1822. Andover, Mass., 1822.

Cheever, George B. *God Against Slavery: and the Freedom and Duty of the Pulpit to Rebuke It, as a Sin Against God.* New York, 1857.

Chessbrough, Rev. A. S. *Home Work: or, Parochial Christianization.* Boston, 1867.

The Christian Alliance: Its Constitution, List of Officers, and Addresses. New York, 1843.

Church Anti-Slavery Society. *Proceedings of the Convention Which Met at Worcester, Massachusetts, March 1, 1859.* New York, 1859.

Circular of the American Protestant Society. New York, 1847.

Circular of the Temperance Society of the Medical Institution of Yale College. New Haven, 1835.

The Congregational Year-Book, 1882. Boston, 1882.

"Connecticut Education Society." *Christian Spectator,* III (September, 1821), 495.

Contributions to the Ecclesiastical History of Connecticut. . . . New Haven, 1861.

Cross, Barbara M., ed. *The Autobiography of Lyman Beecher.* Vol. I of 2 vols. Cambridge, Mass., 1961.

Dana, Daniel. *A Discourse Addressed to the New-Hampshire Auxiliary Colonization Society, At Their First Annual Meeting, Concord, June 2, 1825.* Concord, N.H., 1825.

Debates and Proceedings of the National Council of Congregational Churches, Held at Boston, Massachusetts, June 14–24, 1865. Boston, 1866.

Discourses and Addresses at the Ordination of the Rev. Theodore Dwight Woolsey, LL.D., to the Ministers of the Gospel, and His Inauguration as President of Yale College, October 21, 1846. New Haven, 1846.

"Doctrine of the Higher Law." *New Englander,* XI (May, 1853), 161–71.

"The Doings of the Last Connecticut Legislature on Temperance and Liberty." *New Englander,* XII (August, 1854), 449–56.

Dutton, Rev. S. W. S. "Address Commemorative of the Life and Services of Hon. Roger Sherman Baldwin." *New Englander,* XXII (April, 1863), 259–82.

Dwight, Timothy, Jr. *Memories of Yale Life and Men, 1845–1899.* New York, 1903.

Edwards, E. A. *Slavery and the Domestic Slave-Trade in the United States. In a Series of Letters Addressed to the Executive Committee of the American Union for the Relief and Improvement of the Colored Race.* Boston, 1836.

Evarts, Jeremiah. "The Missouri Question." *Panoplist and Missionary Herald,* XVI (February, 1820), 59–72.

———. "On the Condition of the Blacks in This Country." *Panoplist and Missionary Herald,* XVI (June and November, 1820), 241–45, 481–94.

Fay, Warren. *A Sermon Delivered at the Funeral of Rev. Benjamin B. Wisner, D.D.* Boston, 1835.

Freeman, F. *A Plea for Africa, Being Familiar Conversations on the Subject of Slavery and Colonization.* 2nd ed. Philadelphia, 1837.

Garrison, William Lloyd. *Thoughts on Colonization.* Boston, 1832.

Goodenow, Rev. S. B. "The Oberlin Council and its Doctrinal Statement." *New Englander,* XXXI (October, 1872), 726–44.

Griffin, Edward. *A Plea for Africa; A Sermon Preached on October 26, 1817, in the City of New York Before the Synod of New York and New Jersey at the Request of the Board of Directors of the African School.* New York, 1818.

Hawes, Joel. *To Commend Truth to the Conscience the Object of a Faithful Minister. A Sermon Delivered March 9th, 1825, at the Installation of the Rev. Leonard Bacon, as Pastor of the First Congregational Church and Society in New Haven.* New Haven, 1825.

Hay, Philip C. *Our Duty to Our Coloured Population. A Sermon for the Benefit of the American Colonization Society, Delivered in the Second Presbyterian Church, Newark, July 23, 1826.* Newark, 1826.

Hosmer, William. *Slavery and the Church.* Auburn, N.Y., 1853.

Jay, William. *Inquiry into the Character and Tendency of the American Colonization and American Anti-Slavery Societies.* 6th ed. New York, 1838.

Jocelyn, Simeon S. *College for Colored Youth. An Account of the New-Haven City Meetings and Resolutions, With Recommendations of the College, and Strictures on the Doings of New-Haven.* New York, 1831.

Kitchell, H. D. "The Congregational Convention." *New Englander,* XI (February, 1853), 72–92.

Laws of the Theological Institution of Andover. Andover, Mass., 1817.

Leonard Bacon: Pastor of the First Church in New Haven. New Haven, 1882.

Letter to the Rev. Leonard Bacon, D.D. of New Haven, Connecticut, from John Marsh, D.D. New York, 1865.

Manual of the First Church in New Haven, 1860. New Haven, 1860.

Manual of the First Church in New Haven, For the Year 1882. New Haven, 1882.

Memoirs of American Missionaries, Formerly Connected with the Society of Inquiry Respecting Missions, In the Andover Theological Seminary: Embracing a History of the Society, etc. Boston, 1833.

Milnor, Rev. James. *Plea for the American Colonization Society: A Sermon, Preached in St. George's Church, New-York, on Sunday, July 9, 1826.* New York, 1826.

Minority Report of a Committee of the General Association of Connecticut, on the Sin of Slavery. Presented, June, 1849, at the Meeting of the Association, at Salisbury, Connecticut. N.p., 1849.

Minutes of the General Association of Connecticut. Hartford and New Haven, 1838–1863

Minutes of the National Council of the Congregational Churches of the United States of America, at the First Session, Held in Oberlin, Ohio, November 15–21, 1871. Boston, 1871.

Minutes and Proceedings of the First Annual Convention of the People of Colour. Philadelphia, 1831.

Mitchell, John. *Reminiscences of Scenes and Characters in College.* New Haven, 1847.

Morse, Sidney E. *Premium Questions on Slavery, Each Admitting of a Yes or No Answer; Addressed to the Editors of the New York Independent and the New York Evangelist.* New York, 1860.

Moseley, Laura Hadley, ed. *Diary (1843–1852) of James Hadley: Tutor and Professor of Greek in Yale College, 1845–1872.* New Haven, 1951.

"On the Peculiar Characteristics of the Benevolent Efforts of Our Age." *Christian Spectator,* IV (March, 1822), 113–20.

Papers of the New Haven Colony Historical Society. 2 vols. New Haven, 1865, 1877.

Patten's New Haven Directory, For the Years 1841–2. Number 2. New Haven, 1841.

Patton, William W. *The American Board and Slaveholding.* Hartford, 1846.

Phelps, Amos A. *Letters to Professor Stowe and Dr. Bacon on God's Real Method with Great Social Wrongs in Which the Bible Is Vindicated from Grossly Erroneous Interpretations.* New York, 1848.

A Plain and Candid Statement of Facts of the Difficulties Existing Between Mr. B. L. Hamlen and Mrs. S. Dean; Being an Appeal to the Moral and Religious Community, From a Defenseless and Injured Widow for Justice and Protection. New Haven, 1843.

Porter, Ebenezer. *Signs of the Times. A Sermon Preached in the Chapel of the Theological Seminary, Andover, on the Public Fast, April 3, 1823.* Andover, Mass., 1823.

Proceedings in Commemoration of the Fiftieth Anniversary of the Settlement of Tallmadge; With the Historical Discourse of Hon. E. N. Sill, and Rev. L. Bacon. . . . Akron, 1857.

Proceedings of the Advisory Council of Congregational Churches and Ministers Called by the Plymouth Church of Brooklyn, New York, and Held in Brooklyn from the 15th to the 24th of February, 1876. New York, 1876.

Proceedings of the General Association of Connecticut. Hartford, 1825–1838.

Proceedings of the General Convention of Congregational Ministers and Delegates in the United States, Held at Albany, New York, on the 5th, 6th, 7th, and 8th of October, 1852, Together with the Sermon Preached on the Occasion, by Rev. Joel Hawes, D.D. New York, 1852.

Questions Answered in Regard to the American and Foreign Christian Union. New York, 1849.

Rebecca Taylor Hatch, 1818–1904: Personal Reminiscences and Memorials. New York, 1905.

Reese, David M. *Letters to the Honorable William Jay, Being a Reply to His Inquiries into the American Colonization and American Anti-Slavery Societies.* New York, 1835.

Report of the New-York General Association on the Relation of the American Board of Commissioners for Foreign Missions, the American Home Missionary Society, the American Tract Society, the American Missionary Association, and the American Sunday School Union, to the Subject of Slavery. New York, 1855.

Report of the Proceedings at the Formation of the African Education Society: Instituted at Washington, December 28, 1829. With an Address to the Public, by the Board of Managers. Washington, D.C., 1830.

Report on the Relations of the American Home Missionary Society to Slavery. Adopted by the General Association of Michigan, June, 1853. N.p., 1853.

The Result of the Brooklyn Advisory Council of 1876. Together with the Letters of Dr. Leonard Bacon, Prof. Timothy Dwight, D.D., etc. New York, 1876.

The Semi-Centennial Anniversary of the Divinity School of Yale College, May 15th and 16th, 1872. New Haven, 1872.

Sigma [pseud.]. "Pulpit Portraits; Or, Sketches of Eminent Living American Divines: Rev. Leonard Bacon, D.D." *Holden's Dollar Magazine,* V (January, 1850), 48–54.

Society of Brothers in Unity. *Constitution and Laws of the Society of Brothers in Unity.* New Haven, 1861.

Sparks, Jared. *A Historical Outline of the American Colonization Society, and Remarks on the Advantages and Practicability of Colonizing in Africa the Free People of Color from the United States.* Boston, 1824.

Speeches and Other Proceedings at the Anti-Nebraska Meetings, Held in New Haven, Connecticut, March 8th and 10th, 1854. New Haven, 1854.

"The Supremacy of God's Law—Mr. Seward's Speech." *New Englander,* VIII (August, 1850), 378–88.

Tappan, Lewis. *The Life of Arthur Tappan.* New York, 1970 reprint.

Thompson, Joseph P. "Christian Unity." *New Englander,* IV (January, 1846), 132–39.

———. "Dr. Taylor and His System." *New Englander,* XVI (May, 1858), 373–406.

———. "The Fugitive Slave Law." *New Englander,* VIII (November, 1850), 615–45.

Tracy, Joseph. *Natural Equality. A Sermon Before the Vermont Colonization Society, at Montpelier, October 17, 1833.* Montpelier, Vt., 1833.

Wainwright, J. M. *A Discourse on the Occasion of Forming the African Mission School Society, Delivered in Christ Church, Hartford, Connecticut, on Sunday Evening, August 10, 1828.* Hartford, 1828.

Whipple, Charles K. *Relations of Anti-Slavery to Religion.* New York, 1860.

Wright, Robert W. [Quevedo Redivivus, Jr., pseud.]. *The Vision of Judgment, or the South Church: Ecclesiastical Councils Viewed from Celestial and Satanic Standpoints.* New York, 1867.

SECONDARY SOURCES

Books

Abbott, Lyman. *Henry Ward Beecher.* New York, 1887.

Abbott, Richard H. *The Republican Party and the South, 1855–1877: The First Southern Strategy.* Chapel Hill, 1986.

Ahlstrom, Sidney E. *A Religious History of the American People.* New Haven, 1972.

Allmendinger, David F., Jr. *Paupers and Scholars: The Transformation of Student Life in Nineteenth-Century New England.* New York, 1975.

Anbinder, Tyler. *Nativism and Slavery: The Northern Know Nothings and the Politics of the 1850s.* New York, 1992.

Anderson, Eric, and Alfred A. Moss, Jr. *The Facts of Reconstruction: Essays in Honor of John Hope Franklin.* Baton Rouge, 1991.

Andrew, John A., III. *Rebuilding the Christian Commonwealth: New England Congregationalists and Foreign Missions, 1800–1830.* Lexington, Ky., 1976.

Andrews, Charles C. *History of the New York African Free Schools.* New York, 1830.

Armstrong, M. F., and Helen W. Ludlow. *Hampton and Its Students.* New York, 1874.

Atkins, Gaius Glenn, and Frederick L. Fagley. *History of American Congregationalism.* Boston, 1942.

Bacon, Benjamin Wisner. *Theodore Thornton Munger: New England Minister.* New Haven, 1913.

Bacon, Leonard Woolsey. *Anti-Slavery Before Garrison: An Address Before the Connecticut Society of the Order of the Founders and Patriots of America, New Haven, September 19, 1902.* New Haven, 1903.

———. *The Congregationalists.* New York, 1904.

———. *A History of American Christianity.* New York, 1923.

Bacon, Theodore. *Delia Bacon: A Biographical Sketch.* Boston, 1888.

Bacon, Theodore Dwight. *Leonard Bacon: A Statesman in the Church.* Edited by Benjamin W. Bacon. New Haven, 1931.

Bainton, Roland. *Yale and the Ministry: A History of Education for the Christian Ministry at Yale from the Founding in 1701.* New York, 1957.

Baldwin, Thomas W. *Bacon Genealogy: Michael Bacon of Dedham, 1640, and His Descendants.* Cambridge, Mass., 1915.

Belz, Herman. *Emancipation and Equal Rights: Politics and Constitutionalism in the Civil War Era.* New York, 1980.

———. *A New Birth of Freedom: The Republican Party and Freedmen's Rights.* Westport, Conn., 1976.

———. *Reconstructing the Union: Theory and Policy During the Civil War.* Ithaca, 1969.

Berk, Stephen E. *Calvinism Versus Democracy: Timothy Dwight and the Origins of American Evangelical Orthodoxy.* Hamden, Conn., 1974.

Billington, Ray Allen. *The Protestant Crusade, 1800–1860: A Study of the Origins of American Nativism.* Chicago, 1964.

Bingham, Harold J. *History of Connecticut.* Vol. II of 5 vols. New York, 1962.

Blue, Frederick J. *Charles Sumner and the Conscience of the North.* Arlington Heights, Ill., 1994.

———. *The Free Soilers: Third Party Politics, 1848–1854.* Urbana, 1973.

———. *Salmon P. Chase: A Life in Politics.* Kent, Ohio, 1987.

Bodo, John R. *The Protestant Clergy and Public Issues, 1812–1848.* Princeton, 1954.

Bogue, Allan G. *The Congressman's Civil War.* Cambridge, Mass., 1989.

———. *The Earnest Men: Republicans of the Civil War Senate.* Ithaca, 1982.

Bolt, Christine, and Seymour Drescher, eds. *Antislavery, Religion, and Reform: Essays in Memory of Roger Anstey.* Folkestone, Eng., 1980.

Boritt, Gabor S., ed. *Lincoln, the War President: The Gettysburg Lectures.* New York, 1992.

Bowen, David Warren. *Andrew Johnson and the Negro.* Knoxville, 1989.

Bremner, Robert. *The Public Good: Philanthropy and Welfare in the Civil War Era.* New York, 1980.

Brown, Ira V. *Lyman Abbot, Christian Evolutionist: A Study in Religious Liberalism.* Cambridge, Mass., 1953.

Brown, Jerry Wayne. *The Rise of Biblical Criticism in America, 1800–1870.* Middletown, Conn., 1969.

Buckham, John Wright. *Progressive Religious Thought in America.* Boston, 1919.

Calhoun, Daniel. *The Intelligence of a People.* Princeton, 1973.

Callow, James T. *Kindred Spirits: Knickerbocker Writers and American Artists, 1807–1855.* Chapel Hill, 1967.

Campbell, Stanley W. *The Slave Catchers: Enforcement of the Fugitive Slave Law, 1850–1860.* Chapel Hill, 1968.

Carter, Paul A. *The Spiritual Crisis of the Gilded Age.* DeKalb, Ill., 1971.

Caskey, Marie. *Chariot of Fire: Religion and the Beecher Family.* New Haven, 1978.

Castel, Albert. *The Presidency of Andrew Johnson.* Lawrence, Kans., 1979.

Cheney, Mary Bushnell. *Life and Letters of Horace Bushnell.* New York, 1880.

Chesebrough, David B., ed. *"God Ordained This War": Sermons on the Sectional Crisis, 1830–1865.* Columbia, S.C., 1991.

Clark, Calvin Montague. *American Slavery and Maine Congregationalists: A Chapter in the History of the Development of Anti-Slavery Sentiment in the Protestant Churches of the North.* Bangor, 1940.

Clark, Clifford E. *Henry Ward Beecher: Spokesman for a Middle-Class America.* Urbana, 1978.

Clark, Norman H. *Deliver Us from Evil: An Interpretation of American Prohibition.* New York, 1976.

Clebsch, William A. *American Religious Thought: A History.* Chicago, 1973.

Cole, Charles C., Jr. *The Social Ideas of the Northern Evangelists, 1826–1860.* New York, 1954.

Conkin, Paul K. *The Uneasy Center: Reformed Christianity in Antebellum America.* Chapel Hill, 1995.

Cox, La Wanda. *Lincoln and Black Freedom: A Study in Presidential Leadership.* Columbia, S.C., 1981.

Cox, La Wanda, and John H. Cox. *Politics, Principle, and Prejudice, 1865–1866: Dilemma of Reconstruction America.* New York, 1963.

Croffut, W. A., and John M. Morris. *The Military and Civil History of Connecticut During the War of 1861–1865. . . .* New York, 1866.

Cross, Barbara M. *Horace Bushnell: Minister to a Changing America.* Chicago, 1958.

Crouthamel, James L. *James Watson Webb: A Biography.* Middletown, Conn., 1969.

Current, Richard Nelson. *Those Terrible Carpetbaggers: A Reinterpretation.* New York, 1988.

Curry, Leonard P. *The Free Black in Urban America, 1800–1850: The Shadow of the Dream.* Chicago, 1981.

Curtis, Susan. *A Consuming Faith: The Social Gospel and Modern American Culture.* Baltimore, 1991.

Davis, David Brion. *The Problem of Slavery in the Age of Revolution, 1770–1823.* Ithaca, 1975.

Davis, Hugh. *Joshua Leavitt, Evangelical Abolitionist.* Baton Rouge, 1990.

Degler, Carl. *At Odds: Women and the Family in America from the Revolution to the Present.* New York, 1980.

Deming, Clarence. *Yale Yesterdays.* New Haven, 1915.

Dexter, Franklin Bowditch, comp. *Historical Catalogue of the Members of the First Church of Christ in New Haven, Connecticut (Center Church), A.D., 1639–1914.* New Haven, 1914.

Dillon, Merton L. *The Abolitionists: The Growth of a Dissenting Minority.* DeKalb, Ill., 1974.

———. *Benjamin Lundy and the Struggle for Negro Freedom.* Urbana, 1966.

Donald, David. *The Politics of Reconstruction, 1863–1867.* Baton Rouge, 1965.

Dorn, Jacob Henry. *Washington Gladden: Prophet of the Social Gospel.* Columbus, 1966.

Dunham, Chester Forrester. *The Attitude of the Northern Clergy Toward the South, 1860–1865.* Toledo, 1942.

Dunlap, Leslie W. *American Historical Societies, 1790–1860.* Madison, 1944.

Dunning, Albert E. *Congregationalists in America: A Popular History of Their Origin, Belief, Polity, Growth and Work.* Boston, 1894.

Eells, Robert J. *Forgotten Saint: The Life of Theodore Frelinghuysen. A Case Study of Christian Leadership.* Lanham, Md., 1987.

Fehrenbacher, Don E. *Slavery, Law, and Politics: The Dred Scott Case in Historical Perspective.* New York, 1981.

Finkelman, Paul, ed. *His Soul Goes Marching On: Responses to John Brown and the Harpers Ferry Raid.* Charlottesville, 1995.

Fisher, George P. *Life of Benjamin Silliman.* Vol. II of 2 vols. London, 1866.

Fladeland, Betty. *James Gillespie Birney: Slaveholder to Abolitionist.* Ithaca, 1955.

Foner, Eric. *Free Soil, Free Labor, Free Men: The Ideology of the Republican Party Before the Civil War.* New York, 1970.

————. *Reconstruction: America's Unfinished Revolution, 1863–1877.* New York, 1988.

Foner, Philip S. *Business and Slavery: The New York Merchants and the Irrepressible Conflict.* Chapel Hill, 1941.

Foote, Henry Wilder. *Three Centuries of American Hymnody.* Cambridge, Mass., 1940.

Foster, Charles I. *An Errand of Mercy: The Evangelical United Front, 1790–1837.* Chapel Hill, 1960.

Foster, Frank Hugh. *The Life of Edwards Amasa Park (S.T.D., LL.D.): Abbott Professor, Andover Theological Seminary.* New York, 1936.

Franchot, Jenny. *Roads to Rome: The Antebellum Protestant Encounter with Catholicism.* Berkeley, 1994.

Franklin, John Hope. *The Emancipation Proclamation.* Wheeling, Ill., 1995 reprint.

Fraser, James W. *Pedagogue for God's Kingdom: Lyman Beecher and the Second Great Awakening.* Lanham, Md., 1985.

Fredrickson, George M. *The Black Image in the White Mind: The Debate on Afro-American Character and Destiny, 1817–1914.* New York, 1971.

————. *The Inner Civil War: Northern Intellectuals and the Crisis of the Union.* New York, 1965.

Freehling, William W. *The Reintegration of American History: Slavery and the Civil War.* New York, 1994.

————. *The Road to Disunion.* Vol. I, *Secessionists at Bay, 1776–1854.* New York, 1990.

Friedman, Lawrence J. *Gregarious Saints: Self and Community in American Abolitionism, 1830–1870.* Cambridge, Eng., 1982.

Fulton, John F., and Elizabeth H. Thomas. *Benjamin Silliman, 1779–1864: Pathfinder in American Science.* New York, 1947.

Gabriel, Ralph Henry. *Religion and Learning at Yale: The Church of Christ in the College and University, 1757–1957.* New Haven, 1958.

Gambill, Edward L. *Conservative Ordeal: Northern Democrats and Reconstruction, 1865–1868.* Ames, Iowa, 1981.

Garrison, Wendell Phillips, and Francis Jackson Garrison. *William Lloyd Garrison, 1805–1879: The Story of His Life Told by His Children.* Vols. I and II of 4 vols. New York, 1885–1889.

Geer, Curtis Manning. *The Hartford Theological Seminary, 1834–1934.* Hartford, 1934.

Gerteis, Louis S. *From Contraband to Freedom: Federal Policy Toward Southern Blacks, 1861–1865.* Westport, Conn., 1973.

————. *Morality and Utility in American Antislavery Reform.* Chapel Hill, 1987.

Gienapp, William E. *The Origins of the Republican Party, 1852–1856.* New York, 1987.

Gillette, William. *Retreat from Reconstruction, 1869–1879.* Baton Rouge, 1979.

————. *The Right to Vote: Politics and the Passage of the Fifteenth Amendment.* Baltimore, 1969.

Gilman, Daniel C. *The Life of James Dwight Dana: Scientific Explorer, Mineralogist, Geologist, Zoologist, Professor in Yale College.* New York, 1899.

Goen, C. C. *Broken Churches, Broken Nation: Denominational Schisms and the Coming of the American Civil War.* Macon, Ga., 1985.

Goodheart, Lawrence B. *Abolitionist, Actuary, Atheist: Elizur Wright and the Reform Impulse.* Kent, Ohio, 1990.

Goodwyn, Lawrence. *The Populist Moment: A Short History of the Agrarian Revolt in America.* New York, 1978.

Goodykoontz, Colin Brummitt. *Home Missions on the American Frontier.* New York, 1971.

Griffin, Clifford S. *Their Brothers' Keepers: Moral Stewardship in the United States, 1800–1865.* New Brunswick, N.J., 1960.

Gusfield, Joseph R. *Symbolic Crusade: Status Politics and the American Temperance Movement.* Urbana, 1976.

Hall, Peter Dobkin. *The Organization of American Culture, 1700–1900: Private Institutions, Elites, and the Origins of American Nationality.* New York, 1982.

Hallock, William H. *Life of Gerard Hallock, Thirty-three Years Editor of the New York "Journal of Commerce."* New York, 1869.

Hamilton, Holman. *Prologue to Conflict: The Crisis and the Compromise of 1850.* Lexington, Ky., 1964.

Hanley, Mark Y. *Beyond a Christian Commonwealth: The Protestant Quarrel with the American Republic, 1830–1860.* Chapel Hill, 1994.

Harding, Thomas S. *College Literary Societies: Their Contribution to Higher Education in the United States, 1815–1876.* New York, 1971.

Harding, Vincent. *A Certain Magnificence: Lyman Beecher and the Transformation of American Protestantism, 1775–1863.* Brooklyn, 1991.

Hardman, Keith J. *Charles Grandison Finney, 1792–1875: Revivalist and Reformer.* Syracuse, 1987.

Harlow, Ralph Volney. *Gerrit Smith: Philanthropist and Reformer.* New York, 1939.

Hatcher, Harlan. *The Western Reserve: The Story of New Connecticut in Ohio.* Cleveland, 1949.

Hedrick, Joan D. *Harriet Beecher Stowe: A Life.* New York, 1994.

Hegel, Richard. *Nineteenth-Century Historians of New Haven.* Hamden, Conn., 1972.

Henry, Stuart C. *Unvanquished Puritan: A Portrait of Lyman Beecher.* Grand Rapids, 1973.

Hess, Earl J. *Liberty, Virtue, and Progress: Northerners and Their War for the Union.* New York, 1988.

Hewitt, Glenn A. *Regeneration and Morality: A Study of Charles Finney, Charles Hodge, John W. Nevin, and Horace Bushnell.* Brooklyn, 1991.

Hill, Samuel S., Jr. *The South and the North in American Religion.* Athens, Ga., 1980.

A History of Plymouth Congregational Church in New Haven, Connecticut, 1831–1842. New Haven, 1942.

Hofstadter, Richard. *Social Darwinism in American Thought.* 2nd ed. revised. Boston, 1955.

Holt, Michael F. *The Political Crisis of the 1850s.* New York, 1978.

————. *Political Parties and American Political Development from the Age of Jackson to the Age of Lincoln*. Baton Rouge, 1992.

Hoogenboom, Ari. *The Presidency of Rutherford B. Hayes*. Lawrence, Kans., 1989.

Hopkins, Charles Howard. *The Rise of the Social Gospel in American Protestantism, 1865–1915*. New Haven, 1940.

Hopkins, Vivian C. *Prodigal Puritan: A Life of Delia Bacon*. Cambridge, Mass., 1959.

Howard, Victor B. *Conscience and Slavery: The Evangelistic Calvinist Domestic Missions, 1837–1861*. Kent, Ohio, 1990.

————. *Religion and the Radical Republican Movement, 1860–1870*. Lexington, Ky., 1990.

Hutchison, William R. *Errand to the World: American Protestant Thought and Foreign Missions*. Chicago, 1987.

Hyman, Harold M. *A More Perfect Union: The Impact of the Civil War and Reconstruction on the Constitution*. New York, 1973.

Hyman, Harold M., and William M. Wiecek. *Equal Justice Under Law: Constitutional Development, 1835–1875*. New York, 1982.

Isely, Jeter Allen. *Horace Greeley and the Republican Party, 1853–1861: A Study of the New York Tribune*. New York, 1965.

James, Joseph B. *The Framing of the Fourteenth Amendment*. Urbana, 1965.

Jimerson, Randall C. *The Private Civil War: Popular Thought During the Sectional Conflict*. Baton Rouge, 1988.

Johannsen, Robert W. *Lincoln, the South, and Slavery: The Political Dimension*. Baton Rouge, 1991.

————. *Stephen A. Douglas*. New York, 1973.

————. *To the Halls of Montezuma: The Mexican War in the American Imagination*. New York, 1985.

Johnson, Curtis D. *Redeeming America: Evangelicals and the Road to Civil War*. Chicago, 1993.

Johnson, Paul E. *A Shopkeepers' Millennium: Society and Revivals in Rochester, New York, 1815–1837*. New York, 1978.

Johnson, William A. *Nature and the Supernatural in the Theology of Horace Bushnell*. Lund, Neth., 1963.

Jones, Donald G. *The Sectional Crisis and Northern Methodism: A Study of Piety, Political Ethics and Civil Religion*. Metuchen, N.J., 1979.

Jones, Howard. *Mutiny on the Amistad: The Saga of a Slave Revolt and Its Impact on American Abolition, Law, and Diplomacy*. New York, 1987.

Jordan, Winthrop D. *White over Black: American Attitudes Toward the Negro, 1550–1812*. Chapel Hill, 1968.

Kelley, Brooks Mather. *Yale: A History*. New Haven, 1974.

Kilby, Clyde S. *Minority of One: The Biography of Jonathan Blanchard*. Grand Rapids, 1959.

King, George A. *Theodore Dwight Woolsey: His Political and Social Ideas*. Chicago, 1956.

Kinshasa, Kwando M. *Emigration v. Assimilation: The Debate in the African American Press, 1827–1861*. Jefferson, N.C., 1988.

Kraus, Michael. *A History of American History*. New York, 1937.

Krout, John Allen. *The Origins of Prohibition*. New York, 1925.

Kuhns, Frederick Irving. *The American Home Missionary Society in Relation to the Anti-Slavery Controversy in the Old Northwest.* Billings, Mont., 1959.

Kuklick, Bruce. *Churchmen and Philosophers: From Jonathan Edwards to John Dewey.* New Haven, 1985.

Lane, J. Robert. *A Political History of Connecticut During the Civil War.* Washington, D.C., 1941.

Lender, Mark Edward. *Dictionary of American Temperance Biography: From Temperance Reform to Alcohol Research, the 1600s to the 1980s.* Westport, Conn., 1984.

Levine, Bruce. *Half Slave and Half Free.* New York, 1992.

Litwack, Leon. *North of Slavery: The Negro in the Free States, 1790–1860.* Chicago, 1961.

Mabee, Carleton. *Black Education in New York State: From Colonial to Modern Times.* Syracuse, 1979.

McKitrick, Eric L. *Andrew Johnson and Reconstruction.* Chicago, 1960.

McKivigan, John R. *The War Against Proslavery Religion: Abolitionism and the Northern Churches, 1830–1865.* Ithaca, 1984.

McLoughlin, William G. *The Meaning of Henry Ward Beecher: An Essay on the Shifting Values of Mid-Victorian America, 1840–1870.* New York, 1970.

———. *Modern Revivalism: Charles Grandison Finney to Billy Graham.* New York, 1959.

———, ed. *The American Evangelicals: An Anthology.* New York, 1968.

McPherson, James M. *The Abolitionist Legacy: From Reconstruction to the NAACP.* Princeton, 1975.

———. *Abraham Lincoln and the Second American Revolution.* New York, 1990.

———. *Drawn with the Sword: Reflections on the American Civil War.* New York, 1996.

———. *The Struggle for Equality: Abolitionists and the Negro in the Civil War and Reconstruction.* Princeton, 1964.

———. *"We Cannot Escape History": Lincoln and the Last Best Hope of Earth.* Urbana, 1995.

Magdol, Edward. *The Antislavery Rank and File: A Social Profile of the Abolitionists' Constituency.* Westport, Conn., 1986.

Mandel, Bernard. *Labor: Free and Slave; Working-men and the Anti-Slavery Movement in the United States.* New York, 1955.

Mann, Arthur. *Yankee Reformers in the Urban Age: Social Reform in Boston, 1880–1900.* New York, 1966.

Mantell, Martin E. *Johnson, Grant, and the Politics of Reconstruction.* New York, 1973.

Marsden, George M. *The Evangelical Mind and the New School Presbyterian Experience: A Case Study of Thought and Theology in Nineteenth-Century America.* New Haven, 1970.

Marty, Martin E. *Righteous Empire: The Protestant Experience in America.* New York, 1970.

Mathews, Donald G. *Slavery and Methodism: A Chapter in American Morality, 1780–1845.* Princeton, 1965.

Maurer, Oscar Edward. *A Puritan Church and Its Relation to Community, State, and Nation: Addresses Delivered in Preparation for the Three Hundredth Anniversary of the Settlement of New Haven.* New Haven, 1938.

Mead, Sidney E. *The Lively Experiment: The Shaping of Christianity in America.* New York, 1963.

———. *Nathaniel William Taylor, 1786–1858: A Connecticut Liberal.* Hamden, Conn., 1967.

Mears, David Q. *Life of Edward Norris Kirk, D.D.* Boston, 1877.

Meredith, Robert. *The Politics of the Universe: Edward Beecher, Abolition, and Orthodoxy.* Nashville, 1963.

Messerli, Jonathan. *Horace Mann: A Biography.* New York, 1972.

Miller, Floyd. *The Search for a Black Nationality: Black Emigration and Colonization, 1787–1863.* Urbana, 1975.

Miller, Randall M., and John R. McKivigan, eds. *The Moment of Decision: Biographical Essays on American Character and Regional Identity.* Westport, Conn., 1994.

Miller, William Lee. *Arguing About Slavery: The Great Battle in the United States Congress.* New York, 1996.

Mohr, James C., ed. *Radical Republicans in the North: State Politics During Reconstruction.* Baltimore, 1976.

Moorhead, James H. *American Apocalypse: Yankee Protestants and the Civil War, 1860–1869.* New Haven, 1978.

Morison, Samuel Eliot, Frederick Merk, and Frank Friedel. *Dissent in Three American Wars.* Cambridge, Mass., 1970.

Morris, Robert C. *Reading, 'Riting, and Reconstruction: The Education of Freedmen in the South, 1861–1870.* Chicago, 1981.

Morris, Thomas D. *Free Men All: The Personal Liberty Laws of the North, 1780–1861.* Baltimore, 1974.

Morrison, Chaplain W. *Democratic Politics and Sectionalism: The Wilmot Proviso Controversy.* Chapel Hill, 1967.

Morse, Jarvis Means. *A Neglected Period of Connecticut's History, 1818–1850.* New Haven, 1933.

Mott, Frank Luther. *A History of American Magazines, 1741–1850.* Vol. II of 5 vols. New York, 1930.

———. *A History of American Magazines, 1850–1865.* Vol. III of 5 vols. New York, 1938.

Muelder, Hermann R. *Fighters for Freedom: The History of Anti-Slavery Activities of Men and Women Associated with Knox College.* New York, 1959.

Munger, Theodore Thornton. *Horace Bushnell: Preacher and Theologian.* Boston, 1899.

Nash, Gary B. *Forging Freedom: The Formation of Philadelphia's Black Community, 1720–1840.* Cambridge, Mass., 1988.

Neely, Mark E., Jr. *The Fate of Liberty: Abraham Lincoln and Civil Liberties.* New York, 1991.

Nelson, William E. *The Fourteenth Amendment: From Political Principle to Judicial Doctrine.* Cambridge, Mass., 1988.

Niven, John. *The Coming of the Civil War, 1837–1861.* Arlington Heights, Ill., 1990.

———. *Connecticut for the Union: The Role of the State in the Civil War.* New Haven, 1965.

Nugent, Walter T. K. *Money and American Society, 1865–1880.* New York, 1968.

Nye, Russell B. *Fettered Freedom: Civil Liberties and the Slavery Controversy, 1830–1860.* East Lansing, 1949.

Oates, Stephen B. *To Purge This Land with Blood: A Biography of John Brown.* New York, 1970.

Osterweis, Rollin G. *Three Centuries of New Haven, 1638–1938.* New Haven, 1953.

Paludan, Phillip Shaw. *"A People's Contest": The Union and Civil War, 1861–1865.* New York, 1988.

————. *The Presidency of Abraham Lincoln.* Lawrence, Kans., 1994.

Pease, Jane H., and William H. Pease. *They Who Would Be Free: Blacks' Search for Freedom, 1830–1861.* New York, 1974.

Perman, Michael. *Emancipation and Reconstruction, 1862–1879.* Arlington Heights, Ill. 1987.

Perry, Lewis. *Boats Against the Current: American Culture Between Revolution and Modernity, 1820–1860.* New York, 1993.

————. *Childhood, Marriage, and Reform: Henry Clarke Wright, 1797–1870.* Chicago, 1980.

Phillips, Clifton Jackson. *Protestant America and the Pagan World: The First Half-Century of the American Board of Commissioners for Foreign Missions, 1810–1860.* Cambridge, Mass., 1968.

Phillips, Joseph W. *Jedidiah Morse and New England Congregationalism.* New Brunswick, N.J., 1983.

Rabinowitz, Richard. *The Spiritual Self in Everyday Life: The Transformation of Personal Religious Experience in Nineteenth-Century New England.* Boston, 1989.

Ratner, Lorman. *Powder Keg: Northern Opposition to the Antislavery Movement, 1831–1840.* New York, 1968.

Rawley, James A. *Race and Politics: "Bleeding Kansas" and the Coming of the Civil War.* Philadelphia, 1969.

Richards, Leonard L. *"Gentlemen of Property and Standing": Anti-Abolition Mobs in Jacksonian America.* New York, 1970.

Richardson, Joe M. *Christian Reconstruction: The American Missionary Association and Southern Blacks, 1861–1890.* Athens, Ga., 1980.

Ripley, C. Peter, ed. *The Black Abolitionist Papers.* Vol. III, *The United States, 1830–1846.* Chapel Hill, 1991.

Ritter, Gretchen. *Goldbugs and Greenbacks: The Antimonopoly Tradition and the Politics of Finance in America, 1865–1896.* New York, 1997.

Roediger, David R. *The Wages of Whiteness: Race and the Making of the American Working Class.* London, 1991.

Roper, Daniel C. *The United States Post Office: Its Past Record, Present Condition, and Potential Relation to the New World Order.* New York, 1917.

Rorabaugh, W. J. *The Alcoholic Republic: An American Tradition.* New York, 1979.

Roth, David M. *Connecticut: A Bicentennial History.* New York, 1979.

Rowe, Henry K. *History of Andover Theological Seminary.* Newton, Mass., 1843.

Rugoff, Milton. *The Beechers: An American Family in the Nineteenth Century.* New York, 1981.

Russell, Gurden W. *"Up Neck" in 1825.* Hartford, 1890.

Schmidt, Jean Miller. *Souls or the Social Order: The Two-Party System in American Protestantism.* Brooklyn, 1991.

Schriver, Edward O. *Go Free: The Antislavery Impulse in Maine, 1833–1855.* Orono, 1970.

Schroeder, John H. *Mr. Polk's War: American Opposition and Dissent, 1846–1848.* Madison, 1973.

Scott, Donald M. *From Office to Profession: The New England Ministry, 1750–1850.* Philadelphia, 1978.

Sewell, Richard H. *Ballots for Freedom: Antislavery Politics in the United States, 1837–1860.* New York, 1976.

Seymour, George Dudley. *New Haven.* New Haven, 1942.

Shaplen, Robert. *Free Love and Heavenly Sinners: The Story of the Great Henry Ward Beecher Scandal.* New York, 1954.

Sharkey, Robert P. *Money, Class, and Party: An Economic Study of Civil War and Reconstruction.* Baltimore, 1959.

Sklar, Kathryn Kish. *Catharine Beecher: A Study in American Domesticity.* New Haven, 1973.

Slaughter, Thomas P. *Bloody Dawn: The Christiana Riot and Racial Violence in the Antebellum North.* New York, 1991.

Smith, H. Shelton. *Changing Conceptions of Original Sin.* New York, 1955.

Smith, Timothy L. *Revivalism and Social Reform in Mid-Nineteenth-Century America.* New York, 1957.

Spivey, Donald. *Schooling for the New Slavery: Black Industrial Education, 1868–1915.* Westport, Conn., 1978.

Sproat, John G. *"The Best Men": Liberal Reformers in the Gilded Age.* New York, 1968.

Stampp, Kenneth M. *America in 1857: A Nation on the Brink.* New York, 1990.

———. *And the War Came: The North and the Secession Crisis, 1860–1861.* Baton Rouge, 1950.

———. *The Era of Reconstruction, 1865–1877.* New York, 1965.

Staudenraus, Philip J. *The African Colonization Movement, 1816–1865.* New York, 1961.

Stevenson, Louise L. *Scholarly Means to Evangelical Ends: The New Haven Scholars and the Transformation of Higher Learning in America, 1830–1890.* Baltimore, 1986.

Stewart, James Brewer. *Holy Warriors: The Abolitionists and American Slavery.* New York, 1976.

———. *Joshua R. Giddings and the Tactics of Radical Politics.* Cleveland, 1970.

Strane, Susan. *A Whole-Souled Woman: Prudence Crandall and the Education of Black Women.* New York, 1990.

Sweet, Leonard I. *Black Images of America, 1784–1870.* New York, 1976.

———. *The Evangelical Tradition in America.* Macon, Ga., 1984.

———. *The Minister's Wife: Her Role in Nineteenth-Century American Evangelicalism.* Philadelphia, 1983.

Sweet, William Warren. *Religion on the American Frontier, 1783–1850.* Vol. III, *The Congregationalists.* Chicago, 1939.

Swift, David E. *Black Prophets of Justice: Activist Clergy Before the Civil War.* Baton Rouge, 1989.

Taylor, John M. *William Henry Seward: Lincoln's Right Hand.* New York, 1991.

Thayer, Eli. *A History of the Kansas Crusade: Its Friends and Its Foes.* New York, 1889.

Thomas, John L. *The Liberator: William Lloyd Garrison.* Boston, 1963.

Thornbury, John F. *God Sent Revival: The Story of Asahel Nettleton and the Second Great Awakening.* Grand Rapids, 1977.

Tise, Larry E. *Proslavery: A History of the Defense of Slavery in America, 1701–1840.* Athens, Ga., 1987.

Todd, John E., ed. *John Todd: The Story of His Life.* New York, 1876.

Trecker, Janice Law. *Preachers, Rebels, and Traders: Connecticut, 1818–1865.* Chester, Conn., 1975.

Trefousse, Hans L. *Impeachment of a President: Andrew Johnson, the Blacks, and Reconstruction.* Knoxville, 1975.

————. *The Radical Republicans: Lincoln's Vanguard for Racial Justice.* New York, 1969.

Tyler, Bennet. *Memoir of the Life and Character of Rev. Asahel Nettleton, D.D.* Boston, 1850.

Tyrrell, Ian R. *Sobering Up: From Temperance to Prohibition in Antebellum America, 1800–1860.* Westport, Conn., 1979.

Unger, Irwin. *The Greenback Era.* Princeton, 1964.

Van Deusen, Glyndon. *William Henry Seward.* New York, 1967.

Van Tassel, David D. *Recording America's Past: An Interpretation of the Development of Historical Studies in America, 1607–1884.* Chicago, 1960.

Walker, Williston. *A History of the Congregational Churches in the United States.* New York, 1894.

————. *Ten New England Leaders.* New York, 1901.

Waller, Altina L. *Reverend Beecher and Mrs. Tilton: Sex and Class in Victorian America.* Amherst, Mass., 1982.

Warner, Robert Austin. *New Haven Negroes: A Social History.* New Haven, 1940; rpr., New York, 1969.

Welch, Claude. *Protestant Thought in the Nineteenth Century.* Vol. I, *1799–1870.* New Haven, 1972.

Whitehall, Walter Muir. *Independent Historical Societies: An Enquiry into Their Research and Publication Functions and Their Financial Future.* Boston, 1962.

Whittaker, Frederick William. *Samuel Harris, American Theologian.* New York, 1982.

Williams, Daniel Day. *The Andover Liberals: A Study in American Theology.* New York, 1941.

Wilson, R. J., ed. *Darwinism and the American Intellectual.* Homewood, Ill., 1967.

Wishy, Bernard. *The Child and the Republic: The Dawn of Modern Child Nurture.* Philadelphia, 1968.

Witherspoon, Alexander M. *The Club: The Story of Its First One Hundred and Twenty-five Years, 1838–1963.* New Haven, 1964.

Woods, Rev. Leonard. *History of the Andover Theological Seminary.* Boston, 1885.

Woodson, Carter G. *The Education of the Negro Prior to 1861.* New York, 1915.

Wyatt-Brown, Bertram. *Lewis Tappan and the Evangelical War Against Slavery.* Cleveland, 1969.

Yacovone, Donald. *Samuel Joseph May and the Dilemmas of the Liberal Persuasion, 1797–1871.* Philadelphia, 1991.

York, Robert M. *George B. Cheever, Religious and Social Reformer, 1807–1890.* Orono, 1955.

Articles

Ahlstrom, Sidney E. "The Scottish Philosophy and American Theology." *Church History,* XXIV (1955), 257–72.

Bacon, Leonard Woolsey. "The Services of Leonard Bacon to African Colonization," *Liberia,* I (November, 1899), 1–21.

————. "The Services of Leonard Bacon to African Colonization." *Liberia,* II (February, 1900), 40–55.

Banner, Lois. "Religion and Reform in the Early Republic: The Role of Youth." *American Quarterly,* XXIII (1971), 677–95.

Barnard, Henry, ed. "Hartford Grammar School." *American Journal of Education,* XXVIII (1878), 187–224.

Barton, W. E. "Early Ecclesiastical History of the Western Reserve." *Papers of the Ohio Church History Society.* Vol. I., edited by Frank Hugh Foster. Oberlin, 1890, pp. 29–31.

Baym, Nina. "Delia Bacon, History's Odd Woman Out." *New England Quarterly,* LXIX (1996), 223–49.

Benedict, Michael Les. "Preserving the Constitution: The Conservative Basis of Radical Reconstruction." *Journal of American History,* LXI (1974), 65–90.

Bennett, Stephen Earl. "'Know-Nothings' Revisited Again." *Political Behavior,* XVIII (September, 1996), 219–34.

Berwanger, Eugene H. "Negrophobia in Northern Proslavery and Antislavery Thought." *Phylon,* XXX (1972), 266–75.

Blackburn, George M. "Radical Republican Motivation: A Case History." *Journal of Negro History,* LIV (1969), 109–26.

Bogue, Allan G. "The Radical Voting Dimension in the United States Senate During the Civil War." *Journal of Interdisciplinary History,* III (Winter, 1973), 449–73.

Boylan, Ann M. "Sunday Schools and Changing Evangelical Views of Children in the 1820s." *Church History,* XLVIII (1979), 320–33.

Cole, Charles C., Jr. "Horace Bushnell and the Slavery Question." *New England Quarterly,* XXIII (1950), 19–30.

Cooper, Frederick. "Elevating the Race: The Social Thought of Black Leaders, 1827–50." *American Quarterly,* XXIV (1972), 604–25.

Curry, Richard O., and Lawrence B. Goodheart. "'Knives in Their Heads': Passionate Self-Analysis and the Search for Identity in American Abolitionism." *Canadian Review of American Studies,* XIV (Winter, 1983), 401–14.

Davis, David Brion. "The Emergence of Immediatism in British and American Antislavery Thought." *Mississippi Valley Historical Review,* XLIX (September, 1962), 209–30.

———. "Reconsidering the Colonization Movement: Leonard Bacon and the Problem of Evil." *Intellectual History Newsletter,* XIV (1992), 3–16.

———. "Some Themes of Counter-Subversion: An Analysis of Anti-Masonic, Anti-Catholic, and Anti-Mormon Literature." *Mississippi Valley Historical Review,* XLVII (September, 1960), 205–24.

Davis, Hugh. "The New York *Evangelist,* New School Presbyterians, and Slavery, 1837–1857." *American Presbyterians,* LXVIII (Spring, 1990), 14–23.

———. "Northern Colonizationists and Free Blacks, 1823–1837: A Case Study of Leonard Bacon." *Journal of the Early Republic,* XVII (Winter, 1997), 651–75.

Egerton, Douglas R. "'Its Origin Is Not a Little Curious': A New Look at the American Colonization Society." *Journal of the Early Republic,* V (1985), 463–80.

Ellsworth, Clayton S. "American Churches and the Mexican War." *American Historical Review,* XLV (1940), 301–26.

Elsbree, Oliver Wendell. "Samuel Hopkins and His Doctrine of Benevolence." *New England Quarterly,* VIII (1935), 534–50.

Fellman, Michael. "Rehearsal for the Civil War: Antislavery and Proslavery at the Fighting

Point in Kansas, 1854–1856." In *Antislavery Reconsidered: New Perspectives on the Abolitionists,* edited by Lewis Perry and Michael Fellman. Baton Rouge, 1979.

Filler, Louis. "Liberalism, Anti-Slavery, and the Founders of the *Independent*." *New England Quarterly,* XXXV (1954), 291–306.

Findlay, James. "Agency, Denominations and the Western Colleges, 1830–1860: Some Connections Between Evangelicalism and American Higher Education." *Church History,* L (1981), 64–80.

Fishel, Leslie H., Jr. "Northern Prejudice and Negro Suffrage, 1865–1870." *Journal of Negro History,* XXXIX (1954), 8–26.

———. "Repercussions of Reconstruction: The Northern Negro, 1870–1883." *Civil War History,* XIV (1968), 325–45.

Foner, Eric. "The Wilmot Proviso Revisited." *Journal of American History,* LVI (1969), 262–79.

Foner, Philip S. "Prudence Crandall." In *Three Who Dared: Prudence Crandall, Margaret Douglass, Myrtilla Miner—Champions of Antebellum Black Education,* edited by Philip S. Foner and Josephine F. Pacheo. Westport, Conn., 1984.

Foster, Charles I. "The Colonization of Free Negroes in Liberia, 1816–1835." *Journal of Negro History,* XXXVIII (1953), 41–66.

Franklin, Vincent P. "Education for Colonization: Attempts to Educate Free Blacks in the United States for Emigration to Africa, 1823–1833." *Journal of Negro Education,* XLIII (1974), 91–103.

Fredrickson, George M. "A Man but Not a Brother: Abraham Lincoln and Racial Equality." *Journal of Southern History,* XLI (1975), 39–58.

Friedman, Lawrence J. "Purifying the White Man's Country: The American Colonization Society Reconsidered, 1816–1840." *Societas,* VI (1976), 1–24.

Gara, Larry. "Slavery and the Slave Power: A Crucial Distinction." *Civil War History,* XV (1969), 5–18.

Gerteis, Louis S. "Salmon P. Chase, Radicalism, and the Politics of Emancipation, 1861–1864." *Journal of American History,* LX (1973), 42–62.

Gienapp, William E. "The Crime Against Sumner: The Caning of Charles Sumner and the Rise of the Republican Party." *Civil War History,* XXV (1979), 218–245.

———. "Nativism and the Creation of the Republican Majority in the North Before the Civil War." *Journal of American History,* LXXII (1985), 529–59.

Griffin, Clifford S. "The Abolitionists and the Benevolent Societies, 1831–1861." *Journal of Negro History,* XLIV (1959), 195–216.

Gross, Bella. "Freedom's Journal and the Rights of All." *Journal of Negro History,* XVII (1932), 241–86.

Guelzo, Allen C. "Abraham Lincoln and the Doctrine of Necessity." *Journal of the Abraham Lincoln Association,* XVIII (Winter, 1997), 57–81.

Harlow, Ralph V. "The Rise and Fall of the Kansas Aid Movement." *American Historical Review,* XLI (1935), 1–25.

Heisey, D. Ray. "On Entering the Kingdom: New Birth or Nurture." In *Preaching in American*

History: Selected Issues in the American Pulpit, 1630–1967, edited by DeWitte Holland. Nashville, 1969.

Hood, Fred J. "The American Reformed Tradition in African Colonization and Missions." *Journal of Church and State,* XIX (1977), 539–55.

Johnson, James E. "Charles G. Finney and a Theology of Revivalism." *Church History,* XXXVIII (1969), 338–58.

Kaczorowski, Robert J. "Searching for the Intent of the Framers of the Fourteenth Amendment." *Connecticut Law Review,* V (Winter, 1972–73), 368–69.

Keller, Ralph A. "Methodist Newspapers and the Fugitive Slave Law: A New Perspective for the Slavery Crisis in the North." *Church History,* XLIII (1974), 319–39.

Klebanow, Benjamin J. "Poverty and Its Relief in American Thought, 1815–61." *Social Service Review,* XXXVIII (1964), 382–99.

Krug, Mark. "The Republican Party and the Emancipation Proclamation." *Journal of Negro History,* XLVIII (1963), 98–114.

Kull, Irving S. "Presbyterian Attitudes Toward Slavery." *Church History,* VII (1938), 101–14.

Lacy, Edmund Emmett. "Protestant Newspaper Reaction to the Kansas-Nebraska Bill of 1854." *Rocky Mountain Social Science Journal,* VII (October, 1970), 61–72.

Lewit, Robert T. "Indian Missions and Anti-Slavery Sentiment: A Conflict of Evangelical Humanitarian Ideals." *Mississippi Valley Historical Review,* L (1963), 39–55.

Linden, Glenn M. "The Radicals and Economic Policies: The Senate, 1861–1873." *Journal of Southern History,* XXXII (1966), 188–99.

Litwack, Leon. "The Abolitionist Dilemma: The Antislavery Movement and the Negro." *New England Quarterly,* XXXIV (1961), 50–73.

Loveland, Anne C. "Evangelicalism and 'Immediate Emancipation' in American Antislavery Thought." *Journal of Southern History,* XXXII (1966), 172–88.

Luker, Ralph E. "Bushnell in Black and White: Evidence of the 'Racism' of Horace Bushnell." *New England Quarterly,* XLV (1972), 408–16.

McLachlan, James. "*The Choice of Hercules:* American Student Societies in the Early Nineteenth Century." In *The University in Society,* edited by Lawrence Stone, vol. II, *Europe, Scotland, and the United States from the Sixteenth to the Twentieth Century.* Princeton, 1974.

Maclear, J. F. "The Evangelical Alliance and the Antislavery Crusade." *Huntington Library Quarterly,* XLII (Spring, 1979), 141–64.

McLoughlin, William G. "Evangelical Childrearing in the Age of Jackson: Francis Wayland's Views on When and How to Subdue the Willfulness of Children." *Journal of Social History,* IX (1975), 21–34.

McPherson, James M. "Who Freed the Slaves?" *Reconstruction,* II (no. 3, 1994) 35–40.

Mead, Sidney Earl. "Denominationalism: The Shape of Protestantism in America." *Church History,* XXIII (1954), 291–320.

———. "The Rise of the Evangelical Conception of the Ministry in America, 1607–1850." In *The Ministry in Historical Perspective,* edited by H. Richard Niebuhr and Daniel D. Williams. New York, 1956.

Mendenhall, T. C. "The Town of Tallmadge—the Bacons and Shakespeare." *Ohio State Archaeological and Historical Quarterly,* XXXII (1923), 590–612.

Mohl, Raymond A. "Humanitarianism in the Preindustrial City: The New York Society for the Prevention of Pauperism, 1817–1823." *Journal of American History*, LVIII (1970), 576–99.

Moorhead, James H. "Social Reform and the Divided Conscience of Antebellum Protestantism." *Church History*, XLVIII (1979), 416–30.

Nichols, Roy F. "The Kansas-Nebraska Act: A Century of Historiography." *Mississippi Valley Historical Review*, XLIII (1956), 187–212.

Pearson, Samuel C., Jr. "From Church to Denomination: American Congregationalism in the Nineteenth Century." *Church History*, XXXVIII (1969), 67–87.

Pease, Jane H., and William H. Pease. "Antislavery Ambivalence: Immediatism, Expediency, Race." *American Quarterly*, XVII (1965), 682–95.

————. "Confrontation and Abolition in the 1850s." *Journal of American History*, LVIII (1972), 923–37.

Perry, Lewis. "Psychology and the Abolitionists: Reflections on Martin Duberman and the Neoabolitionism of the 1960s." *Reviews in American History*, II (1974), 309–22.

Rollins, William S. "The Northeastern Religious Press and John Brown." *Ohio State Archaeological and Historical Quarterly*, LXI (April, 1952), 128–45.

Rosen, Bruce. "Abolition and Colonization, the Years of Conflict: 1829–1834." *Phylon*, XXXIII (1972), 177–92.

Sandeen, Ernest R. "The Distinctiveness of American Denominationalism: A Case Study of the 1846 Evangelical Alliance." *Church History*, XLV (1976), 222–34.

Scott, Donald M. "Abolition as a Sacred Vocation." In *Antislavery Reconsidered: New Perspectives on the Abolitionists*, edited by Lewis Perry and Michael Fellman. Baton Rouge, 1979.

Sehr, Timothy J. "Leonard Bacon and the Myth of the Good Slaveholder." *New England Quarterly*, XLIX (1976), 194–213.

Shiels, Richard D. "The Second Great Awakening in Connecticut: Critique of the Traditional Interpretation." *Church History*, XLIX (1980), 401–15.

Small, Sandra E. "The Yankee Schoolmarm in Freedmen's Schools: An Analysis of Attitudes." *Journal of Southern History*, XLV (1979), 381–402.

Stewart, Charles. "Civil War Preaching." In *Preaching in American History: Selected Issues in the American Pulpit, 1630–1967*, edited by DeWitte Holland. Nashville, 1969.

Stirn, James R. "Urgent Gradualism: The Case of the American Union for the Relief and Improvement of the Colored Race." *Civil War History*, XXV (1979), 309–28.

Streifford, David M. "The American Colonization Society: An Application of Republican Ideology to Early Antebellum Reform." *Journal of Southern History*, XLV (1979), 201–20.

Sturtevant, J. M. "Theron Baldwin." *Congregational Quarterly*, XVII (July, 1875), 395–419.

Sweet, Leonard I. "The View of Man Inherent in New Measures Revivalism." *Church History*, XLV (1976), 206–21.

Sweet, William Warren. "Rise of Theological Schools in America." *Church History*, VI (1937), 260–73.

Swift, David Everett. "Conservative Versus Progressive Orthodoxy in Latter Nineteenth Century Congregationalism." *Church History*, XLI (1947), 22–36.

Thomas, John L. "Romantic Reform in America, 1815–1865." *American Quarterly,* XVII (1965), 656–81.

Thompson, J. Earl, Jr. "Abolitionism and Theological Education at Andover." *New England Quarterly,* XLVII (1974), 238–61.

———. "Lyman Beecher's Long Road to Conservative Abolitionism." *Church History,* XLII (1973), 89–109.

Twaddel, Elizabeth. "The American Tract Society, 1814–1860." *Church History,* XV (1946), 116–32.

Tyrrell, Ian R. "Temperance and Economic Change in the Antebellum North." In *Alcohol, Reform, and Society: The Liquor Issue in Social Context,* edited by Jack S. Blocker. Westport, Conn., 1979.

Volpe, Vernon L. "The Liberty Party and Polk's Election." *Historian,* LIII (1991), 691–710.

Warner, Robert A. "Amos Gerry Beman—1812–1874, A Memoir on a Forgotten Leader." *Journal of Negro History,* XXII (1937), 200–21.

Welter, Barbara. "The Cult of True Womanhood, 1820–1860." *American Quarterly,* XVIII (1966), 131–75.

Woolsey, Theodore S. "Theodore Dwight Woolsey." *Yale Review,* n.s., I (January, 1912), 239–60.

Dissertations

Bruser, Lawrence. "Political Antislavery in Connecticut, 1844–1858." Columbia University, 1974.

Cowden, Joanna Dunlap. "Civil War and Reconstruction Politics in Connecticut." University of Connecticut, 1974.

Evans, Linda Jeanne. "Abolitionism in the Illinois Churches, 1830–1865." Northwestern University, 1981.

Gossard, John Harvey. "The New York City Congregational Cluster, 1848–1871: Congregationalism and Antislavery in the Careers of Henry Ward Beecher, George B. Cheever, Richard S. Storrs, and Joseph P. Thompson." Bowling Green State University, 1986.

Housley, Donald David. "The *Independent:* A Study in Religious and Social Opinion, 1848–1870." Pennsylvania State University, 1971.

Johnson, Clifton Herman. "The American Missionary Association, 1846–1861: A Study of Christian Abolitionism." University of North Carolina, 1958.

Knoff, Gerald Everett. "The Yale Divinity School, 1858–1899." Yale University, 1936.

Noonan, Carroll John. "Nativism in Connecticut, 1829–1860." Catholic University of America, 1938.

Senior, Robert Cholerton. "New England Congregationalists and the Anti-Slavery Movement, 1830–1860." Yale University, 1954.

Wayland, John Terrill. "The Theological Department in Yale College, 1822–1858." Yale University, 1933.